Nicole Cooke's glittering sporting career includes the rare trifecta of Olympic, Commonwealth and World gold medals as well as being a ten-time victor of the British national road race, the first of which made her the youngest-ever champion at the age of 16. She won more than 70 professional titles in Europe, North America and Australia, highlighted by twice winning the UCI Road World Cup (2003, 2006) as well as triumphing in the 2004 Giro d'Italia and being a two-time victor of the women's Tour de France, in 2006 and 2007. She was appointed Member of the Order of the British Empire (MBE) in 2009 for services to cycling and retired in January 2013.

Acclaim for *The Breakaway*:

'Battling against sexism, drug-taking and blind obedience to authority ... Cooke became Olympic and world champion ... Typically, she has written her own book, a fine one, and she takes no prisoners,' Nick Pitt, *Sunday Times* Sport Book of the Year

'A ferocious, furious book by the multi-medal-winning British cyclist, whose road to the top was impeded by useless coaches and petty officials who thought men's cycling was all that mattered ... But Cooke also writes with surprising grace about her many achievements, her rivals and, particularly, her family, whose support was unstinting. The most substantial and impassioned of this year's sporting memoirs,' Marcus Berkmann, *Daily Mail*

'Standing out from the flood of books exploiting Britain's cycling boom, Nicole Cooke's The Breakaway is the bracing, often abrasive story of an outsider who found her own route to an Olympic gold medal and the world championship in the summer of 2008, fighting the system all the way,' Richard Williams, *Guardian*

'A sharp reminder of just how tough life on two wheels can be. In 2008, the Welsh rider became the only cyclist to win world and Olympic road-race titles in the same year, but felt her successes came despite, rather than because of, British Cycling's administrators at the time, as chapters entitled: "The GB Plan: Stop That Girl!" and "The Laurel and Har   nevertheless did

more than practically anyone else to champion the rights of female cyclists, and spoke out loudly and often against the drug-taking she says was endemic on the women's circuit as well as the men's,' Simon Redfern, *Independent*

'So who was the first British cyclist to win the Tour de France? If you answered Bradley Wiggins, you must reproach yourself. Six years before Wiggo did his stuff, Nicole Cooke showed him how. She was the one who showed the world that British riders could take on the world's best in the great stage races and beat the stuffing out of them ...

'Sport is not about money. Sure, it's a nice bonus for those that can get it, but pure sport – the thing that has us enthralled, the thing that sends you and me back for more – is about the pursuit of excellence. And excellence knows no gender. If you appreciate sport in any kind of depth, you are a feminist. Such a stance is logically inescapable. Cooke spells out the inevitability of such a stance in her book, and still more eloquently, she did so with every turning of the wheels of her bike,' Simon Barnes, espn.co.uk

'*The Breakaway* is hugely motivating and inspiring in its message that even in the face of seemingly insurmountable odds, it's possible to get to the top if you have the work ethic, courage, drive and determination to do so ... The descriptions of riding in races ... are beautifully captured, as exciting as any I've read in any cycling autobiography, and motivating enough to make any young, aspiring rider want to experience similar thrills. The accounts of team and individual tactics, decisions made on the fly at 60kph when surrounded by a tightly packed peloton of riders bearing down on a finish line are edge-of-the-seat thrilling,' Huw Williams, onthedrops

'An absorbing and eye-opening account of the trials faced by Nicole Cooke, one of Britain's greatest ever athletes... But what truly sets this book apart from numerous other sporting biographies is seeing from behind the scenes, the sharp differences that exist in sport in the treatment of men and women and a very different perspective on the highly successful British Cycling World Class Performance Plan that has produced so many Olympic champions over recent years. The contents will unsettle even the most partisan of male cycling fans,' Guy Elliott, tourofbritain.co.uk

THE BREAKAWAY

My Story

Nicole Cooke

SIMON &
SCHUSTER

London · New York · Sydney · Toronto · New Delhi

A CBS COMPANY

First published in Great Britain by Simon & Schuster UK Ltd, 2014
This paperback edition published by Simon & Schuster UK Ltd, 2015
A CBS COMPANY

copy1
inadve

or omissions brought to their attention.

A CIP catalogue record for this book
is available from the British Library

ISBN: 978-1-47113-035-9
Ebook ISBN: 978-1-47113-036-6

Typeset in the UK by M Rules
Printed in the UK by CPI Group (UK) Ltd, Croydon, CR0 4YY

CONTENTS

Foreword
by Graeme Obree

Cycling is a tough sport. To succeed in disciplines like the hour and road racing requires years of total dedication. Racing itself takes up little time but training, bike maintenance, sponsor duties and living the athletic life, with its diet and sleep requirements, leave little time for anything else. For male riders on professional teams, the training can be social and a rider can go out with a group of similar ability where there will be conversation to break the monotony of hours of graft. For male pros, there will be mechanics to clean and ready the bike for the next day of graft.

Nicole carved out her own path as a female British professional rider where the financial reward was little compared with her male counterparts and the graft would generally be done on her own. Each day required her to reach into herself to do her gruelling and monotonous training alone, driven only by her ambition and vision. Not only that, but a professional road cyclist faces the unavoidable and inevitable crash and injury scenario which only adds to the harshness of the sport. For a rider conducting the majority of their training alone, on the road, the risk of crashes and injury is multiplied. Nicole was no stranger to this and displayed amazing tenacity in coming back from injuries.

Today there is a fully Lottery-funded, military-style system. Not so in the days when Nicole first came to the fore. I remember meeting her briefly when she had her first successes in the early years. None of us could have foreseen the changes that would be made in both funding and approach. Unfortunately for Nicole, she probably started with one foot on the wrong side of change. Her articulate intelligence and lack of subservience would also single her out as dangerous to the emerging regime.

Then there was the gender issue. If Nicole had been born 'Nicholas' and had achieved the exact same results in the male world, she would have been not just equal to, but elevated above both Mark Cavendish and Sir Bradley Wiggins. She was the youngest-ever winner of the Giro d'Italia, in the fastest-ever time. She won the Tour de France. She won one-day classics such as the Amstel Gold Race, Flèche Wallonne and Tour of Flanders. She won the World Cup. She won sprints, mountain-top finishes and broke away to win alone. She won green jerseys, polka dot jerseys and time-trials. In 2004, she didn't win the only women's road races that appeared on UK television, the Olympics and World Championships, because there was no British team worthy of that name to support her against other nations. Nevertheless, a string of silver and bronze medal positions bore witness to her talent and she was (and still is) the only British road rider to be ranked World No.1. Then in 2008, Nicole became the first-ever rider to win the Olympic and World road races in the same year. Unsurprisingly, she achieved this at the same time as the UK developed talent to provide some support for her.

The general attitudes that portray women in sport as second best, which in itself can lead to injustice and discrimination, were even on show when I was interviewed by Alastair

Campbell for a series he was doing for *The Times* on the greatest sports figures of all time. When he asked me for my choice, and I named Jeannie Longo, he was clearly taken aback that I had chosen a woman, and a woman cyclist at that, given the fame and aura that surrounded male cyclists. Bear in mind that at the time Jeannie had not been implicated in drugs and Nicole would go on to achieve so much more. My argument that peer-group dominance made her pre-eminent did not convince him. I told him he was sexist, said he should also include Ellen MacArthur in his list of greats, and we moved on. This was not new, as I had witnessed both subtle and blatant sexism in the heart of the sport itself and in the media for a long time. In fairness, Alastair perhaps took my outburst to heart and later went on to write a good article in support of Nicole. Sadly, this issue is not merely historical and there is current debate about why there is no longer a women's Tour de France on the calendar. Road cycling remains hugely male-dominated, and achievements in women's sport in general go largely under-reported. When you add to that the huge disparity in sponsorship, funding and support, then you can begin to understand and sympathise with Nicole's story.

She was a trailblazer who forged a path that was clearly defined for the male riders, but equally she struggled to get women's cycling treated seriously in the UK, and there were many barriers placed in her way. Perhaps the most eloquent witness to those bruising encounters with a British establishment not willing to embrace the individual can be seen at the Manchester velodrome, which houses the headquarters of British Cycling. As you walk in from the entrance, there is a corridor packed with full-size portraits of GB stars – Sir Chris Hoy, Victoria Pendleton CBE, Chris Newton, Rob Hayles and the rest. Visiting some years ago, I noticed that the achievements of both Nicole and myself were not worthy enough to elevate us to such company.

Nicole was the first female to join a continental team. She left home for Italy, aged 18, with a minimal grasp of the language, and was on her way. Like my own experiences, it was not long before she was exposed to the dark world of drug abuse that pervaded road cycling. Her accounts of dealing with this are engrossing. Despite this, she was still able to produce the results that she did. One such performance touched me and even changed my own perspective. I was watching live on TV when in a wet, uphill finish, coming from behind, all hope momentarily lost, she powered to win the Olympic road race. I had that instant 'wow' feeling and a tear in my eye for the first time ever after a sporting performance. Knowing Nicole personally, and knowing the honourable and genuinely nice person she is, made this possible. People told me over the years how I had that same effect on them when I was racing but only now, 15 years later, and thanks to Nicole, could I feel it for myself. Here is a remarkable story: one young girl doing it her own way and getting to heights never dreamed of by British Cycling. Afterwards came the British men on the road. This is the story of the events that preceded those exploits and were necessary for those later successes. I can only hope that a spark of change can happen around gender inequality in the sport, as a consequence of Nicole's amazing contribution to enlightenment.

CHAPTER ONE
A Very Welsh Childhood

I am blessed with being both Welsh and British. I have represented both with pride and have sung the Welsh national anthem 'Mae Hen Wlad Fy Nhadau' ('The Land of My Fathers') and 'God Save the Queen' on winners' podiums with equal gusto. I was born at Morriston Hospital in Swansea on 13 April 1983. Our family home was in the small village of Wick in the Vale of Glamorgan, 'near Cowbridge' as noted when addressing mail which would otherwise end up in the Highlands of Scotland.

Growing up was idyllic. We lived a mile or so from the sea, surrounded by a web of high-hedged, narrow country lanes, twisting and turning to reveal around every corner the sorts of things children find exciting. Streams, bridges, little sandy coves, long, broad tide-washed beaches, and cliffs with steel ladders set in them to escape the incoming tide. Overgrown paths into woods, stepping stones across rivers that flood when the tide comes in, giant sand dunes, disused quarries, and wild common with even wilder sheep. There were medieval castles, ruined, and, in the case of St Donats Castle, restored, by the American newspaper magnate William Randolph Hearst before it became Atlantic College. We lived in an adventure playground – it was like child 'heaven' – and testing yourself in one way or another became second nature. The village also had a green, on which every Sunday during the summer formal cricket was played, but during the rest of the week an impromptu game of football would take place most days after school. Often the group was split into two teams of all ages. The participants would change as children left for their tea and then returned. New arrivals joined the losing team until they got ahead; the little ones played with the eldest, all learning to be mindful of the abilities that come with growth. All the children in the village had a fantastic time. We wanted for nothing.

One day my brother Craig and I took our bikes to the ford at the bottom of a nearby hill. I was probably eight at the time. The weather had been awful and the river was flooding across the road. When we hadn't returned by teatime, my mum, Denise, got on her own bike to come down to check on us. We met her halfway up the hill, dripping wet and laughing, having spent the afternoon daring each other to ride our bikes into the middle of the flooded roadway and then do a sort of track stand to see who could stay upright longest without falling off. We had also helped out a young motorist whose car had spluttered to a halt in the middle of the road. He'd opened his car door, not expecting the river to flow into his car and his credit cards to float out. Craig and I chased his cards, wading down the river and retrieving them for him, then helped him push his car out of the water. Whatever the weather, there were never anywhere near enough hours in the day to do the things you could do. It was a great time and certainly set me up for a life where exploration and adventure into the unknown were a significant element.

Later, as we got older, jumping on a bike to ride to the next town to go to the music shop or pet shop was quicker and more fun than waiting around for the bus. This was the time before mobile phones. You left home and you were gone. Mum and Dad were great. Sometimes they came with us and other times they let us go off alone, always striking the right balance. With only 20 months between us, Craig and I were very close, and we learned to be self-reliant and enjoy the freedom that came with a country upbringing and an outdoor life.

Mum and Dad had taken us cycling around the lanes on the back of their bikes from a very early age. As I grew too big for the child seat, we needed to upgrade. I spotted an old tandem bike frame in the loft of our house. I was five at the time and not sure what the object was, sitting big and dark in the corner. Dad had ridden it with his older brother, Chris, when they were youngsters. Somehow, sentimentality meant that the frame was never thrown away. Dad hauled it out of the loft, had it re-enamelled then rebuilt the wheels and re-equipped it. Because I could not yet reach the pedals, he made up a separate crank system with an extra set of pedals connected to the crankset below. So we were mobile again, with Craig having the choice of a child seat behind either Mum, on her bike, or Dad and I on the tandem. Stopping us on one of our excursions, a neighbour told us about another tandem in a local antique shop. We bought it, and Dad created a second set of cranks and specially set-back handlebars for Craig. Now we could all ride as a family, usually Dad and Craig on one bike and Mum and I on the other.

In the summer of 1990, when I was seven, we went on our first cycling holiday, loading the tandems onto the roof rack and driving down to Lymington to catch the ferry to the Isle of Wight. Now that might not seem such a big deal to a world-weary adult, but to two children aged seven and five, spending a week touring the island when the sun seemed to shine constantly was fantastic. We explored the scenery and wildlife, and we had two buckets and shovels on the top of the bags at the back, so that we could play in the sand on the beaches and in rock pools. We had our transport and could just go wherever we wanted. Craig and I loved every minute of it, and so bikes became the focal point of being together as a family.

The next three years we had similar holidays, with Mum and Dad organising everything. One summer, we just rode from the house, through the Vale of Glamorgan to the seaside town of Penarth. There we had a big ice cream each while we waited at the pier for the steamer *Balmoral* to arrive and take us to Ilfracombe, from where we went exploring Dartmoor. Every night, after Mum and Dad had cooked our meal in the youth hostel, they would read out the options for the next day with possible routes and activities, factoring in the weather and how tired we might feel. Although each day was a new adventure, nothing was happening by accident, as Mum and Dad would research everything for months before. Ever since those early days, that is how I have approached life, weighing up everyone's views before coming to a communal decision that's best for everybody.

My first school was Wick and Marcross Church in Wales Primary School, opposite the church and the memorial hall and a short walk from the village green and pub. The teachers were excellent, and the school encouraged us in all types of sport. In addition to the traditional netball and rounders, local schools were allowed by Atlantic College to use their facilities, so there was swimming in the indoor pool, canoeing in the outdoor pool, rock climbing and abseiling, even archery. At Wick and Marcross, sport and outdoor activities were a part of school life every bit as much as learning maths and discovering science, and I can see now how lucky I was in that respect.

Sports day was a red-letter day at the school where pupils were divided into three houses named after the local castles Ogmore, St Donats and Dunraven. We did the usual 'egg and spoon', 'going through hoops' and 'wheelbarrow' races, as well as running. Like the Olympics, we finished with the 4 × 400m relay on our undersized school track – with the older children running more lengths to make up the distance. Each team had one person from each year running a leg. A teacher and a couple of mums would keep the score. I remember one sports day when Sophie Moore (née James) was Year 6 representative and team captain of St Donats. After the boys' relay, St Donats had to win the final event to come first overall, and I saw Sophie talking to her team before the girls' relay. She took over in last place, ran as if her life depended on it and won.

She wasn't big-headed or brash, she was just lovely Sophie who walked further down the road from our house to her mum and dad's farm with her brother and sister. Her family worked really hard to make a living, just like my mum and dad. We all celebrated and took pleasure from her achievement, regardless of which house we were in. Everybody crowded around the track that sunny afternoon was captivated by Sophie's heroism in inspiring her team and then finishing off the job herself.

In that glorious sporting summer of 2012, the whole nation took to heart its sporting heroes, just as that crowd of teachers and parents did at that school sports day. Exactly like that little group, the nation didn't care if they were male or female, the colour of their skin, whether they were disabled or able-bodied. Our nation – a nation of mums and dads, teachers and children – proved in that summer, that those pundits and

NICOLE COOKE

journalists and marketing managers who had perpetuated the myth that 'only men's sports are interesting, we are only interested in sponsoring men's events, the prizes can only be for the men' were wrong. Our nation showed that they were far more fair and bigger than those feeble people, with their own personal prejudices, gave them credit for.

Cycling was a means of transport, a freedom, a method of getting to somewhere where exciting things could happen more quickly than walking. At primary school, many sporting options were open to us and this inspired me. Mum and Dad played tennis and we would cycle to Llantwit Major to play on the municipal courts in the summer. Craig and I became sufficiently competent at tennis to play to modest success. I was also captain of the netball team. Mum often came to sports days and other events to watch us, whereas Dad, due to work, was a very rare attender. Our Year 5 netball team were great, and I'm sure my competitive streak was shining through by then. I was goal defence. The other team had to get past me if they were going to score. Dad had an afternoon off and we were playing at home. 'Please come and see me.' He turned up at the due time, but there was no sign of the opposing team. It looked like it was a no-show, so Dad went back home and said he would walk up later and see if anything was going on. He came back and caught the last ten minutes. We won, and our opponents failed to score. Dad was obviously proud, but in a quick word to me before I went back to join the final lesson of the afternoon, he offered his advice. I didn't seem to be following the match quite as much as I should have been when the action was down the other end. I needed to concentrate 100% on the ball and the movement of the players off the ball, for the whole match.

During tea, Mum and Dad noticed that I was not using my left hand to hold the fork. When Mum asked me, I told her I couldn't hold the fork because it hurt my hand too much. Mum and Dad inspected my hand and everything seemed okay – until they tried to roll up my jumper sleeve. My arm was very clearly broken. Mum asked when the pain had started. 'Oh, in one of the first attacks by the other team in the game. The ball came awkwardly and I had to dive to get it and crashed onto the floor. After that it hurt a lot trying to use my left arm to stop their attacks, so I used my right hand and only used my left when I had to. Nobody got past me, so it finished fine and I didn't need to tell anybody about it.'

As Dad drove me to hospital, he said he was sorry that he had criticised my performance and that a broken arm was more than adequate reason to be distracted when the action went up the other end. We finished the season unbeaten and Mum and Dad have the classic photo of the primary school netball team with me at the centre, as captain, holding the ball. It goes alongside the matching photo of Craig at the centre of the cricket team. Mum and Dad wrote a nice letter to the school telling them not to worry that nobody spotted my broken arm – Nicole was trying to keep it a secret!

The local hospital casualty ward was familiar territory to our family. I was given a lovely girl's pink bike with dropped handlebar for my birthday; asked what I might like to go with it, I selected a speedometer. One Sunday morning, I was out riding my bike when I made a mistake and fell, cracking my head hard on the road. Back home, when I got to the kitchen Mum, who was obviously shocked by my appearance, screamed for Dad. Dad came in and asked calmly, 'You say you can't see clearly ... tell me how many fingers am I holding up on my hand?'

'Dad, I can't see your hand, just a sort of shape.'

I was more concerned about my bike, which I had deserted in the road. The accident had happened about 300m from the house. I had slowly made my way back home by feeling the garden walls of the houses on the street until I came to ours, which I could recognise by the feel of the gate. I had a cracked skull. Apparently I was slipping in and out of consciousness as Dad drove me to the hospital. Mum stayed with Craig, and most importantly they retrieved my bike. I had a helmet in the shed, but I was not wearing it. Mum and Dad made me promise that I would wear one every time I rode a bike after that incident. I have kept my word ever since.

I was into every sport. One summer holiday, a couple of years later, we stayed at a youth hostel in Ely which happened to be a school that was being put to other use for part of the summer. We slept in a classroom. The school came with a fully marked out athletics track and all the facilities. Early one evening, after a day exploring Ely Cathedral and Oliver Cromwell's house, Mum, Dad, Craig and I held our own athletics festival. We had a long jump and triple jump competition, three attempts at each, with the best one counting. We had the 100m, 200m and 400m, all with some bizarre handicap system, so Mum and Dad had to chase hard to catch us in the dash to the line. I'm not sure what stood in to be hurled as the discus, but something was thrown. The weather was glorious.

As we lay on the grass that summer evening, with that slacking pair Mum and Dad feigning that they were tired and needed a rest before the final of the 800m, we read a report in the *Cycling Weekly* magazine that we had picked up earlier in the day at a newsagents, about a series of ESCA (English Schools Cycling Association) races for youngsters. There and then, I wrung out of Dad a commitment that on our return from holiday, he would find out about cycle races near to us. Then it was back to our athletics festival.

Something about cycling was starting to grab me, but it was still just one of many sports I loved and in which I could unleash my competitive instincts. With a child's intuition, I soon realised that apart from rugby, Wales, with limited numbers and resources, was generally going to struggle in team sports. To cite a contemporary example, Gareth Bale might be one of the top footballers in the world, but the fact remains he is unlikely to ever play in a winning team in a European Championships or World Cup. If I was going to achieve sporting victories, I needed something in which my success was not too dependent on those around me. Win or lose, it needed to be down to me alone. I could not aim for success if it relied upon people who were not willing to show the same dedication and professionalism in preparation that I was.

My interest in cycle races did not come out of the blue. Mum had been a swimmer in her youth and Dad a cyclist, though my uncle Chris was far more serious about cycle racing than Dad ever was.

Every July, Dad would watch the Tour de France highlights on Channel 4 and Craig and I would sit with him, often wearing team jerseys brought by Uncle Chris, who at that time was working for a company which organised sporting events, including the Kellogg's Tour of Britain cycle race. Mine was the blue, yellow and pink jersey of the Z-Peugeot team, and I quickly became a fan of their British rider, Robert Millar. Until Bradley Wiggins's and Chris Froome's victories in the Tour de France, Robert had been Britain's most successful male competitor in the Tour, finishing fourth in 1984 when he also won the King of the Mountains.

It was the 1993 Tour coverage in particular that sticks in my mind. Millar had attacked the leaders on the Col d'Izoard, to escape with Pedro Delgado. As he ascended the long and difficult Col de la Bonette, the highest road in Europe, he dropped Delgado, climbing alone to the summit. These were mountains several times higher than Snowdon, the biggest mountain I had encountered. I could only marvel at the thought of cycling at those heights. Millar was riding to glorious victory, but behind him all was not right. Delgado had been caught by a small group and they were now ganging up to pull in the lone British rider. On the long chase off the mountain and along the valley floor to the final climb, Delgado pushed himself to his limits to get the group within tactical distance of Millar. It was an epic struggle, one against many. On the final climb to Isola 2000, the small chasing group caught Millar and the race seemed over; they were fresher and he was exhausted from his lone efforts.

Millar would not match them in the dash to the line; he was a spent force. Then, in a show of absolute defiance, to prove to everyone watching who the moral victor was, he attacked the group again. The pain was obvious. His arrogant rivals were shocked as he sprinted off up the road. The commentator described the move as heroic; I felt the same way. That he would be caught and passed was obvious, but Millar's bravery was inspiring.

When the programme was over, I ran outside, jumped on my bike and headed for the hills behind Wick where I rode up and down the steepest climb I knew, five times. I did it as fast as I could, inspired by the deeds of Robert Millar. I still don't know what possessed me, given that I had not even started competing, but there was something about the event and the notion of being King of the Mountains, dressed in the polka dot jersey. At the first opportunity a few years later, I asked Millar for his autograph and in the late '90s I struck up a friendship with him. I wanted to know as much as possible about how to live the life of a successful elite cyclist. There were so few British road cyclists, men or women, who'd had prominent international careers at that point, and I wanted to learn as much as I could. He had been there and got the T-shirt. I wanted a few T-shirts as well.

When the family returned from our summer holiday, our first move was to make contact with the Cardiff Ajax cycling club and we were invited to their club evening at Maindy Stadium in Cardiff the following Wednesday. I'd never seen a cycle track before in real life, let alone ridden on one, so Dad spent the trip in the car warning me about the need to stay on the inside, hold my line and not use my brakes. The track itself, which didn't hold any fears for me, even as an 11-year-old, was a large cement track built for the 1958 Empire Games, with a gentle 25-degree embankment.

I followed Dad's instructions and rode a couple of laps while he went off and spoke to some of the club officials and members. Riding against other riders on the track was out of the question, as I didn't have the appropriate bike, but the official and Dad came back and asked if I wanted to do a time-trial that Friday night. My eyes lit up: from everything I had seen of the Tour on TV, the time-trial was the boring bit, with no tactics, but it had to be done before you could ride over the Alps in a polka dot jersey, and the sooner a start was made, the better. So it was a resounding 'Yes'.

A time-trial takes place on the open road among the traffic, so questions about riding on the road and road safety followed. I had ridden to Bridgend and other places on my own, many times, so I was well versed in the etiquette of the road. I also told the club official other things I thought important, like the fact I had watched the Tour de France on TV, and had even been to watch the Tour of Britain. All went well until I was asked how old I was. I was 11. Too young! What? My career was on the launch pad; mentally the countdown to Friday night had commenced. I rode loads more than anyone else my age. I could think of some who couldn't even ride a bike. No sane person would release them out into the traffic. What has age got to do with it? Who came up with that as an idea of how good a cyclist you are? I wasn't speaking, but I'm sure Dad recognised the look in my eyes was the same as Mum's in the moments before she would let rip with a torrent of common sense. A solution was needed – and quickly. 'Well, how about if she was on the back of a tandem behind me?' asked Dad. Agreed. The countdown started again.

No concession or preparation was made to the tandem prior to the event. For the record, this 1930s tandem featured massive steel drum brakes, front and rear, and had a totally removable tube so that the back could be quaintly converted to 'ladies' style and ridden with a full skirt. It had an 86-inch top gear of only five in total, which was tiny for going down the massive hill on the course, and meant we would have to freewheel. The plan would be that Dad would shout 'free-wheel in five' and we both would sprint while he counted down and then we would stop pedalling and sit in the most aerodynamic tuck position we could until the bike slowed enough for us to start pedalling again. There were carriers, a dynamo and large lights front and rear, the tyres were low-pressure 26 × 1 3/8 inch and we had to ride 15 miles from home to get to the start point. Dad was telling me that if we got near 'evens', or 30 minutes for the 10 miles, we would have done very well. We arrived and I was raring to go.

Years later, the timekeeper wrote an account for the club history: 'The timekeeper looked at the duo's tandem which looked like a relic from the industrial revolution against the sleek carbon and aluminium of other riders' machines, and expected nothing special from dad on the front and the slim, youthful figure on the back. At the finish, everyone was startled to find that Tony and Nicole had returned a time of 26 minutes 30 seconds, among the fastest of the evening on a hard, hilly course. Clearly, Tony must be fitter than he looks was the consensus among the onlookers and we didn't realise then how much of a power pack Nicole must have been pedalling behind him, even at the age of 11.'

Roger Pratt, the club timekeeper, had ridden the Alps in the '60s in a prelude to the Isle of Man cycling festival, where he competed against a youthful Eddy Merckx. There's a fantastic picture of Roger and a couple of other riders, in the break with Eddy on the mountain. The Ajax club is like a family, with Christmas parties for the youngsters and all sorts of social events. Club members celebrate success together and support each other through difficulties. I am a life member and couldn't be prouder about that. There was one member, Jill Pring, who was always given the first starting time in the time-trial because she brought along a canteen of tea and boxes of home-made cakes. After finishing, she would set up the food and drink on a bench outside the church, ready for the others. That evening, as we all tucked into Welsh Cakes and shared our tales before Dad and I got back on our tandem and rode home, I was so excited. It was the real beginning of my love for the sport.

CHAPTER TWO
Nobody Said It Was Going to Be Easy

Secondary school life was jam-packed with lots of interesting and worthwhile activities. Brynteg School is a large comprehensive on the south side of Bridgend with over 1,700 students. Its alumni include the current First Minister of Wales, Carwyn Jones, distinguished scientists such as Professor Keith Burnett, who became Oxford University Professor of Physics, and a host of sportsmen and women. Well, to be fair, mainly sportsmen such as rugby stars JPR Williams, Gavin Henson, Rob Howley, Mike Hall and many others. Lynn Davies, yes that Lynn who won the Olympic gold medal in the long jump at the 1964 Tokyo Olympics, was a past pupil and teacher. At Brynteg, my childhood heaven continued into the teenage years, with everything any youngster could want.

In my first year, in the summer of '95, the school PE department put forward a few boys and girls to the county borough 'Champion Coaching' scheme. This after-school event was another athletic festival, like those with Mum and Dad, but on this occasion we had everything – hurdles, high jump, javelin, even a real discus. I was riding my bike the six miles to school, so after lessons my friend Rhianne Biddescome and I would walk my bike down to Newbridge fields, in a beautiful setting alongside a river with a bridge across it.

There were three coaches. Senior coach was Roy Anthony, who had coached Tanni Grey-Thompson. Roy was assisted by Ridley Griffith and Rob Howley, who was playing for Bridgend at the time and would later captain the Wales rugby team. Roy told us that the sport of pole vaulting developed from people having to cross rivers. With Roy standing in the middle and Rob and Ridley on either bank, the masterplan was that we boys and girls would run at the river, pole firmly and confidently grasped, time the entry of the pole into the centre of the river with great precision, and hold the pole as we sailed serenely from one bank to the other. Rob and Ridley gave a demonstration and then it was over to us, with predictable results. We all got soaked. Roy was superb, most times grabbing the pole and helping us on our way to make up for lack of speed and timing. We sprinted, jumped upwards and lengthways, threw javelins and the discus, and we had water fights with Rob and Ridley. What a delightful way to learn together: sport for the sheer innocent enjoyment of it.

Sport was only one of the many fun and worthwhile things with which I was filling my life. Whatever the task put in front of me, it got done to the very best of my ability, whether that was poor, satisfactory or excellent. In the main hall in Brynteg is the Roll of Honour. Pride of place goes to the list of those pupils who receive the award of Rankin Scholar. This is given, each year, to a boy and a girl in Year 13 (the upper sixth) who has attained the highest level of academic achievement in the school. Straight 'A's and marks of 100% at A-level are *de rigueur*. This is a very big school, with a lot of clever pupils who leave to go to the best universities in the world. Each assembly, I would look at the Roll of Honour on the board by the stage and see one boy and one girl for each year. I am extremely proud that my name is on that list, in that hall. 'Rankin Scholar' is something I put on my CV, alongside World and Olympic champion. It wasn't all about cycling and nothing else, but also about becoming a rounded and balanced person. Qualifications are just as important as any gold medal, as a sporting career can be cut cruelly short.

I loved my teachers and I loved school. Being Welsh, we have our own language and own cultural festival. At school, we had the Eisteddfod – a festival of singing, dancing, acting, and playing musical instruments on stage together with competitions. Craig won the boys' contest for the 'off stage' competitions once, and I did likewise for the girls'. Music was not my strong suit and I apologise now for all the hard work my music teachers put in with me over the years, for such modest results. We got that exam grade but it was very hard work and the violin is somewhere in Mum and Dad's loft. They always wanted to go out when I practised.

Brynteg encouraged you to be independent and resource-ful. At first, together with my friends we competed in all sports. Gradually it narrowed down to just cycling and athlet-ics. Some experiences speeded up that process. Hockey was wild and crazed. That very hard ball hurts, but not quite as much as one of your own team-mates who swings, misses the ball, but scores a direct hit on your skull. That big bump on my forehead took ages to go down.

Rhianne and I went to all sorts of athletics events together. I am proud of my distance/age group records in the district, and I hope those who break them have as much fun as Rhianne and I did. At one South Wales Championships she battled her way into the 100m final. Unfortunately, the bus taking us back to school had to leave early. The PE staff trusted us, so I stayed after my 1500m event to support her and then we cadged a lift in another bus to somewhere in the Bridgend vicinity. It had been a long, tiring day, but we just walked back to school and then I rode home six miles on my bike. I wouldn't have missed Rhianne's 100m for anything.

Later in my school life, in 1999, I represented Wales in cross-country. We were in Ireland for the Home Countries International and Mo Farah was running for England in the same age category as me. The Welsh team oozed inferiority; we were there as pack fill. In the girls' race, I think England had seven runners in the top ten, maybe even better. I was competing as one of the best in Wales, but it was not a sporting highlight of my life. Mo might remember four feisty Welsh girls coming up to him and engaging in the typical things young boys and girls do when going abroad. We certainly weren't going to stick in anybody's mind because of our athletic performances. I could see that at a higher level, an athletics career was never on the cards, as I was always going to be beaten by athletes taller and skinnier than me.

I was proud of my school, teachers and schoolmates, and I remained on call for duty at all times. In the summer of 2000, as I pressed for a place in the Olympic team, it was my final sports day and I was going to sign off from 13 years of school sports in style. It was my final sports day. I wanted 'N Cooke' to be engraved on the Senior Victrix Ludorum trophy. It's there now, a few lines below 'S James', after Sophie had also won the prize.

So how did I get to be good at cycling?

Firstly, I rode to school every day, even though the bus to school stopped just 50m from our house. Dad had changed careers and was now a teacher at a school on the other side of

Bridgend. He was used to riding in to work every day, he did it before I joined him and he still does it today. Rain, snow, wind, hail and shine, we rode in. Initially, it was just a steady ride and the shortest way to school; then as I got stronger and my interest in racing developed, the pace got harder and we added hills to the route, including riding down to Southerndown Beach, and doing a U-turn in the car park so we could ride back up and add another hill to our route. Craig was two years my junior at school and when he joined us we now had a little pack. Every day, we finished with a sprint on a wide deserted road. It was full bore, we gave it everything.

Later, as we became more serious about race preparation, Craig and Dad were more often a leadout train, occasionally joined by the odd renegade sheep that had strayed onto the road. Craig would cover 1.3km to 600m, Dad 600m to 200m, myself the last 200m. The sign of the Volvo garage in Ewenny marked the finish line. Every day. While in the glorious days of summer riding down to the beach was entrancing, in winter, with a force 10 gale, it had its own charm. As the trees were bent alarmingly by the onshore south-westerly wind, so we would be 'echeloned' and leaning at nearly 30 degrees to stay on our bikes, each gust trying to blow us across the road.

An echelon is when a rider does not ride behind the leading rider, but because the wind is from the side, they ride half behind and half to the side, in order to gain maximum shelter. The idea is that after a period on the front, the lead rider swings off, to move to the back of the echelon and so another rider is on the front. The slope of the echelon depends on relative road speed and wind speed and direction. Some mornings, behind Dad, the echelon was nearly 90 degrees when he was on the front. However, the most important aspect of that daily ride was exactly that: it was daily. The physicality of the ride is one thing. The resilience it taught you was another altogether.

Punctures were a regular occurrence. This was the countryside, hedges needed cutting and the fragments easily pierced bicycle tyres. Chains broke, cables broke, axle spindles broke. A lunchtime walk to the bike shop in town was a common event, so Hayden and Stuart at the shop became great friends. If I didn't have the money on me, I could come in a couple of days later and pay then. Going to school, we were with Dad, but on the way back, we were on our own. Eleven years old, stuck at the side of the road, in the wind and rain, trying to put a new inner-tube in, heightens the senses. Sometimes there were long walks home, but mostly it was a lot of fun.

Even though we were riding practically the same roads every day, there was always something different to notice: the sheep on the common, seeing them with their newborn lambs, then the lambs growing up; the trees blossoming in spring, then in full leaf followed by their vivid autumn colours; riding along by the coast watching out for the massive waves crashing over the rocks, whipped up by gale-force winds. The seasons and life cycle went by each day in front of Craig and me, as we rode to school and back. The sun shone on us and we rode in short sleeves. It rained, it was icy, we crashed. We slid in the snow on our bikes. When the snowfall was very heavy we would walk through the deep drifts, perhaps with our bikes on our backs, only to find the school closed. Great news! We could go back and slide some more on our bikes on the big hill, then go sledging. We added more hills, more miles, and the sprints became ever fiercer. We did our homework, we got our grades. We rode home quickly to share with Mum and Dad our latest news. We marvelled at the world around us.

*

During that first summer of races back in 1994 at the Ajax cycling club, we did a couple more time-trials on the tandem before the end of the season. After chatting to club members, we found out that there would be a series of winter cyclo-cross races in South Wales every Sunday morning, which meant I could continue my competitive activities during the winter.

It was around this time that I started keeping my scrapbooks. These record detailed accounts of those races as if I was my own cycling correspondent. There were also hand-drawn maps of the courses and notes on my main rivals, things I must do to prepare for the next event and how to improve – the skills I should practise in one of the disused quarries nearby and so on. Some of British Cycling's 'world-class' coaching staff of the time could have learnt quite a bit from studying the level of detail recorded in preparation for the next event in the U12 South Wales calendar.

The Welsh U12 Championships were held in December, and in my scrapbook I describe it as 'my first serious event'. I'm not sure too many people would agree with that description, but I defy anyone to tell an 11-year-old that the Welsh Championship they are engaged in is not serious. In the life of that 11-year-old, it was a turning point. I beat the boys, who were undoubtedly stronger than me, and beat them with technique and wits. I felt on top of the world, even though I was wet and muddy with a jersey down to my knees, standing on a podium in front of a stadium. Over the years, I have kept in contact with both lads with whom I shared the podium. When I won Beijing gold in 2008, Jason Price even put the photo of our U12 medal ceremony on his Facebook page. They are both smashing lads.

For each race, I had to remove the carrier and mudguards from my bike and then, on returning on the Sunday afternoon, put them back on, ready for my school bags the following morning. Again I learned to be independent and self-reliant. Mum and Dad regaled me with tales of the comic book character Alf Tupper, the 'Tough of the Track' from *The Victor*. Alf was an independent amateur athlete who competed despite the system, a welder who was always mending and fixing things. That was us. One time, after Dad had watched me struggle up the muddy slopes in a race, he cut out two steel plates, welded two short bolts to them and attached them to my trainers to provide some grip at the front. Dad did lots of things like this, all the time.

Normally both Mum and Dad took us to races, but sometimes it was just Mum. She drove, while I pretended that I could map read, and then when we got somewhere near the venue, we asked lots of people for directions. Craig learnt to keep quiet in the back if the tension got too high. One Sunday, Dad took me to Abergavenny, I remember it well because I forgot my helmet and the organiser loaned me one for the race. It was the day my lists went into overdrive. Thereafter, I always had a list, checked for content days before, and then packed my kit well before departure time, with every item ticked off. Strangely, it worked every time.

On that occasion, Phil Jones the Welsh coach was there. I won the U12 race and afterwards Phil spoke with Dad, who was expressing his personal concerns about cycling. Dad was aware of his brother Chris's experiences and was not at all sure about the sport. Chris Boardman had won the Olympic track pursuit in Barcelona '92 and now was in the middle of his rivalry with Graeme Obree. These were two very different characters, with two very different ways of approaching the same event, but there was only one corner the Cooke family were backing. We had listened as the Union Cycliste

International (UCI), cycling's world governing body, came up with rule changes overnight to ban Graeme and his hand-made bike at the World Championships. We heard the radio report that stated UCI president Hein Verbruggen had stood in the track to try to stop Graeme, and Graeme had ridden at him. Verbruggen's colleague, UCI vice-president Ian Emmerson, who was also president of the British Cycling Federation (BCF), was implicated in the betrayal of Graeme and years later was ousted in a coup at the BCF amid a whole range of allegations from both sides.

Apart from Robert Millar, now coming to the end of his career, and Chris and Graeme, British prospects looked quite slim at this time. Colin Sturgess had seemed a great prospect but why hadn't he gone further in the sport? Something was wrong. If Britain was any good at coaching and supporting cyclists, there would not just be Robert Millar on TV, there would be other British riders. The odd maverick, with talent, ability and a stubborn refusal to bend to the will of others, appeared to be the only Brits who made it in cycling. Products of a system, they definitely were not. Were the British riders no good or was the system broken?

Dad was pouring cold water on the whole show. However, Phil was eloquent and assured. 'I know how you feel and agree with you that it was like that, but the sport has changed quite a bit. Nicole has talent and I think you should let her try.'

Phil pointed out the changes that had occurred in cycling. The first women's Olympic cycling event, the road race, had been introduced in 1984, and events were gradually being intro-duced at the Olympics, World Championships and Common-wealth Games. While there was still a huge way to go, changes were happening each year. By comparison with when Dad and Uncle Chris were racing, women's road events were now moving towards reasonable distances, rather than token races which were not long enough to allow the classic tactics of road racing to unfold. Phil was also able to point to the fact that his wife, Louise Jones, had won the first women's sprint event when it was introduced at the Commonwealth Games in Auckland in 1990. There was now a Tour de France and Giro d'Italia, and although the format was continually evolving it was clear that compared with just over a decade before, when there had been no women's cycling events at the Olympics and the sport was really a no-go area for any aspiring female, it now offered opportunities. Dad was still not wholly convinced, but gradually introduced me to the things I would need to do to succeed.

The first thing I needed, clearly, was a proper bike to race on, as I was riding the heaviest and cheapest bike among my U12 rivals. Dad scoured the small ads in *Cycling Weekly* as clearance bargains and sales became our lot. Still at home are the remains of a job lot of top-quality 18mm racing tyres Dad bought for £2 each at the time. The retail was something around £45 each. We purchased a second-hand Brian Rourke frame in superb condition. It needed a group set to kit it out. My birthday was coming up and I had a brand new, not quite bottom-of-the-range, Campagnolo group set for my present. The spirit of Obree and the 'Tough of the Track' was everywhere. A little later in my career, we made contact with Brian Rourke, and I would later win world titles on his hand-built bikes. Together, we would take a leaf out of Graeme Obree's book and, being of a smaller build than a 12-stone man, we designed frames with narrow bottom brackets and other features suited to me.

Anyway, I now had a bike, I had become a member of ESCA – which was a great organisation run by fantastic people – and at the age of 12, I could now ride time-trials on my own. I rode a season of club time-trials. It was 15 miles there with Dad on a Friday night, ride the 10-mile TT and then 15 miles home. On Saturday mornings, there was a track session at Maindy in Cardiff and about once a month there were mountain bike races where I could use my school bike. There was a lot to try and sample.

Things were looking good, but there was still so much to learn about road racing. I was fascinated watching the Tour on TV. Road racing was the king of sports, it had everything. I now view it as having three equally weighted contributing factors: the physical capability of the rider, the technical efficiency of the bicycle and equipment, and the tactical moves and counter moves at both individual and team levels. Failure in any one of the three can render any amount of supreme talent in the other two irrelevant. I was riding to school, and so developing physically as best I could, but I needed to develop tactically.

Laws in the UK stipulate that cyclists who have not attained the age of 16 are not allowed to ride on the road in massed start events – i.e. road races. There was, at this time, only one closed road circuit in the UK built for cycle racing, at Eastway in London, and very few other closed road racing events put on throughout the year. Those that existed would attract tiny fields of sometimes fewer than ten riders. As a result, no British youngster under 16 was any good at road racing. There might be somebody who was British champion, but that person would be totally outclassed on the world stage. Nobody was going to be any good because there was absolutely no chance of developing any sense of tactical awareness until you were 17, and by then all the continental youngsters were so far advanced that no British rider could catch up. British road cyclists were pack fill. It wasn't complicated to work out why.

We weren't the only people to recognise this. The senior

coaches at ESCA understood, and each year they took groups
to events in Holland. These weren't just races for equipment
nerds to compare crank lengths and discuss tyre pressures or
tread patterns. They were exactly what youngsters needed and
exactly what I wanted. They were holidays with games and
fun, with some cycle races in the day – and did they know
how to put on a cycle race! This was a world of cycling completely different from how the sport had developed in the UK.

The Helmond Youth Tour was a five-day event, extremely
well organised and catered for youngsters of all ages, in just the
same way our games evolved on the green at Wick. Children
were split up by year of birth. The youngest, Category 1, were
going to be aged eight that year. The oldest would be 15 for
the girls and 14 for the boys in Category 7. We were in teams,
but not grouped by year. A team was one child from each
category, so the little ones were integrated with the big ones.
We had an adult team leader and all eight of us, seven riders
and our team leader, slept in a very basic but entirely satisfactory dormitory together. There were games, treasure hunts
and discos. It was everything under the sun for a week, at a giant
hostel set in lovely grounds. For the cycle races, the rules were
superb – simple, yet entirely effective.

This was not like the adult sporting world, this was more
like that primary school sports day, where boys weren't 'better'
and therefore girls 'worse'; here, both were treated equally and,
as a consequence, there were nearly as many girls as boys. To
even up the racing, girls would ride with the boys of the year
category below. Every competitor had to ride a single-speed
bike, no gears were allowed and the ratio was limited to something small, so that the strong boys could not simply use brute
force to get away from the rest of the field, they had to use
tactics. The idea was to work with others, form breaks. The

fields stayed together, not scattered in a collection of individual time-trials as I'd witnessed in my first races in the UK. The finish was always a group sprint; you needed to think about where to be on the road, who to follow and when to start to sprint.

There was more. The bikes had to be low-tech. No carbon fibre, no fancy frames, no deep section. Wheels had to be conventional flat aluminium rims with a minimum of 32 round spokes. Back home, you might turn up and race against some boy with a £3,000 replica 1992 Lotus, the bike Chris Boardman rode at the Olympics, but the environment was entirely different at Helmond. Parents who sought to use their wealth to buy advantage for their offspring were trumped, and being those type of parents, they went and found another sport where money could buy success. Cycling in the UK was encouraging the 'arms race' and so killing the sport, with many leaving, not having funds to access superweapons. In Helmond the exact opposite was taking place.

We certainly raced to win, but winning just meant points and the difference between a win and second at the top age group only had the same effect for the team as the rider coming 23rd or 24th in the eight-year-old category. With only one category competing at any one time, all the rest of the team would be rounded up by the team leader and encourage their representative to do their best, wherever they were finishing. Games and other fun things sometimes had competitions with points that were of identical importance as well. Each day there was organised relaxation and time for unorganised relaxation, with everybody trying their best to communicate in Dutch, Belgian, French or English. There were treasure hunts in the woods when it got dark. This was as far removed from my first experiences going away with the GB team as it could possibly be. This was *fun*.

This was an activity holiday for children centred on cycling. It was run with stages, so there had to be a yellow jersey. And if there was a yellow jersey, there was also a polka dot jersey. In fact, it was all like a mini Tour de France. Each day, three jerseys were given out to the leader of each competition in each age group, plus jerseys for the leading team in the combined 'cycling plus games' competition. On the final day, the suburbs of Helmond were converted to the Champs Élysées. There were motorbike marshals to create a proper race convoy, a giant 'jury wagon', a large lorry with offices on the back, to park up, do the photo finish and provide a centre for commentary and music throughout the day. Hearing my name over the loudspeaker in Dutch and my exploits explained to the crowd and the very good-natured crowd cheering, whatever it was that I was meant to have done – this was child heaven! Everything they could do to make this like the Tour de France for youngsters, they did. We watched as each category raced its final stage, with its own sprint. I did my race. I had not won the hill climb, but came second. The winner was in yellow, so as the next rider in the 'mountains' category, I was able to wear the polka dot jersey, the jersey I dreamed about. I even got to take it home – what more could anyone want?

Each year I went back and each year I developed. It wasn't a place for many British riders. The winners in the UK tended to be those well involved in the 'arms race', and with that degree of parental investment came parental control and direction. One British champion went to Helmond to win. He was under strict instructions not to participate in any of those energy-sapping things like games, water fights or, heaven forbid, the disco. While all the rest of us ran around, screamed and rolled in the grass and danced, he lay on his bed alone. He only went once. He did not win.

Similarly, just as it was not the place for a certain type of rider, neither was it the place for certain types of coach. The ESCA coaches who took us were highly experienced and were also technically accomplished in the sport of cycling. However, they also joined in the whole theme of making it fun for the children. These were not the type imbued with an extravagant view of their own self-worth; these were kind, considerate and trustworthy individuals. I went to Helmond year after year. Mum and Dad never came and one phone call home in the whole week was all that they requested, just to say I had arrived safely. Beyond that, they waited to learn all the news of the racing when I returned. Walter Rixon, Geoff Greenfield and Ron Dowling were our ESCA coaches – absolute stars, every one of them.

The sport was littered with coaches at the other end of the extreme. I'll recall another episode, well ahead in chronological order from our story now, just to illustrate the difference. It was an ESCA residential training weekend. I was towards the older age range, and there were the younger ones with us, aged 10 and 11. There were a couple of the ESCA stalwarts, Geoff and Ron. There was also this guy (I will save his blushes) who repeatedly told us he had worked at the British Cycling Federation's Manchester track. He worked with the 'important track men' and one day, if we listened carefully to everything he told us and did everything the way he told us to, we might just get to join that elite group. Unlike Geoff and Ron, he wore his tracksuit top and fancy outfit and posed in it, puffing his chest out as he continually berated virtually everyone. He repeatedly blew his whistle and demanded we come off the track and gather round him, straightaway, to hear him share his latest valuable gem that was going to turn us into the next star.

The little ones started it that night, 'bobby knocking' on his door and running off. We bigger ones were summoned out of our rooms and told not to do it. Our protests of innocence fell on deaf ears. It continued. We were called out again: could we please stop it. Well, that was the last thing he needed to say. I'm not sure how much sleep he got that night. Adorable Walter, Geoff and Ron were never troubled with such tricks, and we never saw that coach again. If only, later on in life, we could have rid ourselves of totally useless coaches and staff so easily. A night of 'bobby-knocking' – well worth the investment! A few door numbers would have been on my list. The 10- and 11-year-olds, all on their own, could spot what was wrong with this guy. They didn't need anyone telling them.

Over the years, ESCA had taken the very best British youth cyclists across to Helmond. Most were, of course, boys, and the odd girl tagged along. A couple of surprise stage wins taken against the grain was not much to show for ten years of trying. My experience at Helmond inspired me. Despite the handicap of living in the UK, I came back determined to give my utmost, applying myself through preparation, hard work and smart tactics to show that Britain could produce winners to match those who I had met there.

CHAPTER THREE
'Team Cooke' Go to Work

Cycling had become my main passion. After home-work, I would find out all about the latest techniques for training and research the history of the sport. Sadly, beyond the Tour de France there was no other cycling on TV. Together with Craig, Mum and Dad we did our best to create a full and interesting racing programme. With a dearth of local road races, it became cyclo-cross in the winter and everything else in the summer, so naturally I became an all-rounder, competing with equal determination at mountain biking, road races, time-trials or on the track. I became fitter, stronger, more accomplished and more committed as the months passed. We travelled to events and sometimes observed the senior women perform. At cyclo-cross races, Dad would put a stopwatch on my laps in the youth race and then record times in the senior race that followed on the same course. The results did not need great analysis.

Riding cyclo-cross races became a family affair. Rather than simply watching Craig and me race, we all took part – Craig rode the U12s, I rode the youth race and Mum and Dad the senior race. The courses were naturally in the countryside, sometimes in woods, sometimes out on the heath and always interesting. The great British weather played its part in greasing the paths, providing many a challenge where a mistake could give you an unexpected mud bath. After the race, we would clean the excess mud off ourselves and our bikes and then pile in the car to go home, where a military-style machine would swing into action.

Mum would go to the shower first, others followed in rotation – Craig, me and then Dad. Outside, first it was take the bikes off the rack then pack the rack away. Then power washer out and clean bikes. Check bikes for damage and make a note of needed repairs. Shoes were scraped. Shoes power washed. Mud rinsed off kit. Kit put in washing machine. Bikes oiled as necessary. Power washer packed up. Bikes put into storage for the following Sunday. Mum cooked up a lovely roast dinner. When we had completed our allotted tasks – which was generally within five minutes of the last bike being put away – we all sat down and ate together, regaled each other with how our races had gone and showed each other our cuts and bruises. Dad was always falling off and wrecking equipment, even if most of the time he seemed to 'bounce' quite well.

Money wasn't plentiful and economy had always been important in our house. Nothing, absolutely nothing, would get wasted. Plates were always totally clear before we left the table and nothing was cooked that wasn't eaten. We all divided up the chores and Friday night was when Craig and I presented our job charts to Mum and Dad for approval prior to receiving pocket money. Mum and Dad were keen to support Craig and me, but extravagance in unnecessary luxuries was not on the chart at this stage of their lives. There was a dog, cat and fish to look after and two children to get to adulthood. Having a bit of competitive fun with some second-hand equipment, bought cheap, was acceptable for the time being.

Apart from the races there was also a residential coaching

event, 'Youth Week', left over from when the sport had been far more popular in the UK, run by the ABCC (Association of British Cycling Coaches). A generation before, Uncle Chris had attended the same event at Alexandra Palace; now it was held at Easton College in Norfolk. It was very pleasant, a series of talks and lectures about cycle racing, diet, training and preparation, and each day there were several short races for us to practise what we had been taught. It was virtually all boys, with just three girls so we tended to stick together. It's here that I met and made friends for life with Helen and her brother Greg, who would be at my side in France in 2008.

Twice more I would return to Easton for the Scholar's 3-Day Race. Here, Helen was my great rival in a three-way tussle for victory with another Welsh girl, Anneliese Heard, who was one year older than me. Anneliese was undoubtedly a great athlete. She would go on to win the World Junior Triathlon title in 1999 and 2000. A glittering career on that stage should have become a reality. I can't help but compare the media treatment of her and me, and the reaction of her governing body at the time. It was almost as if her undoubted success was not embraced by her governing body but used by them to galvanise their efforts to work with and promote other athletes to outshine her. On the BBC TV coverage of the London triathlon from the converted docks, Anneliese would barely be mentioned, while other athletes were hailed as stars of the future. I had much empathy with Anneliese's position.

For the Scholar's event, we attended as representative teams from the regions. At that time, Wales had a part-time youth coach, but with his sexist attitude, questionable driving antics and the fact that pornographic magazines were on view in his car, Dad took an instant dislike to him. Happily, Walter Rixon, one of the ESCA staff, shared the same opinion of the coach and found a place for me in his Wessex team instead. While the Welsh team were Lottery funded, the Wessex team wasn't, which meant Mum and Dad had to pay my way, but they viewed it as money well invested. I won the girls' section after a terrific tussle with Helen, and Wessex won the team event. Dad made himself unpopular in Welsh circles by insisting on change, but I'm glad that now other youngsters don't have to put up with offensive behaviour that was presented to me as 'take it or leave it', particularly when funded out of the public purse.

By the end of 1995, I had won the ESCA national age-group titles in the road race, time-trial and grass track. The following year, I made a clean sweep of the ESCA national titles in the road race, time-trial, mountain bike, grass track, hill climb, cyclo-cross, track sprint and track pursuit. I won the U16 British Mountain Bike Championships and above all of these, where the competition was strongest, at Helmond, I went on to achieve third overall. I also won a series of Welsh age-group championships, but often there were only two or three other riders so these were of little relevance.

By now I was dreaming of a career as a professional cyclist, and I would be turning senior the year I left school. Vital to gaining a professional senior contract would be performing well at the Junior World Championships in 2000.

Dad was doing two part-time jobs, alongside his very demanding full-time employment, to fund it all. He was managing, but only just. While the enlightened souls at Helmond put a barrier on the 'arms race' and limited entry to virtually the cheapest bike possible, elsewhere the race to endless wind tunnel testing and special materials on different parts of your outfit, that became the 'marginal gains' for the track riders at Beijing, continued. I was riding a patchwork quilt of equipment. Some bikes featured hand-painted frames we could not afford to get enamelled, and a couple of bikes were of frame sizes which I never did grow into. Therefore, I needed to somehow start moving my equipment up-market.

During 1996 we had become aware that grant money was available in Wales from the Elite Cymru fund, monies from the National Lottery to high-performing and emerging Welsh sporting talent. One older boy had received enough to purchase the latest carbon fibre bikes, one for the road time-trial and another for the track pursuit. At £3,000, a bike like this was quite some support (and quite some sale for the bike shop!). No one would begrudge him funding, but the extent of the financial aid seemed to be at the expense of others. When I put in an application and got nothing, I inquired why not. The system was that applications were made and then given to the Welsh Cycling Union (WCU) to endorse, and the individual within the WCU entrusted with making recommendations to approve or reject was the newly appointed national coach, Shane Sutton.

Shane will now be with us every step of the way through the rest of this book and my whole career. Shane has achieved recent fame for his work alongside Sir Bradley Wiggins. He is highly experienced and very knowledgeable about the sport of cycling and road racing in particular. He rode the Tour with the ill-fated British ANC team in 1987. The exploits of this team are documented in *Wide-Eyed and Legless* by Jeff Connor, a read I heartily recommend. With team-mates such as Malcolm Elliott and support staff like *soigneur* Angus Fraser, the account is action-packed all the way. Some aspects are unrelated in so many ways to how the men's Tour functions now. However, in terms of unpaid wages and weird events, personally there is much I can empathise with. He later won the British Milk Race in 1990. After retiring and becoming a coach, he then became Welsh Sport Coach of the Year in 1998, and in 2008 was UK Sport Coach of the Year. When Shane is supporting you, he is a fantastic ally to have; but when he is not, the reverse can be true. I have first-hand experience of both.

Shane advised the funding gatekeepers that I didn't have any results to justify a grant. It seemed an astonishing thing to say, given that by this time I had won Welsh and British Championships across the several disciplines available and a host of ESCA titles, in addition to racing well in Holland. My application was rejected because I hadn't won a BCF track or road championship, even though the BCF provided no such titles for girls. How could I get the results if the competitions didn't exist? The Welsh boys had won some of these titles and so were eligible. They received the support, but I got nothing. Our pleas fell on deaf ears and the process left us disillusioned. We doubted that the British public, paying for their Lottery tickets, wanted it to be 'boys only'. So we tried to get some BCF track and road championships for girls, but were told by the BCF there was 'no demand, not enough interest'. Where would I hear that again?

And so it went on. One of the fun events of the cycling year is the Mildenhall festival. We went there often, joining others camping around the track. The Mildenhall event, although run on grass rather than cement or wood, is a track meeting and therefore held under BCF rules. In 1997, it included the British Women's Open 800-metre Championship. We had attended the event the year before and Dad contacted the organiser, enquiring about the possibility of me riding, aged 14. The organiser suggested confirming entry with the BCF at their Manchester headquarters. Dad wrote, informing the BCF that, since there was no U16 championship for girls, I would like to enter their 800m championship event. Rather than embrace my enthusiasm, the BCF sent us a three-page letter expressly forbidding me from riding the event because I was not aged 16, that I was not as fast as the adult women, it was not 'safe' to ride against them; and, anyway, I did not stand a chance in the race, as if that was somehow a valid reason for not competing.

We contacted the organiser. He was aware of the decision of the BCF, but it was entirely possible for me to ride the accompanying women's omnium that ran on the same day, which would feature an 800m handicap. Helen MacGregor, a smashing person for whom I have absolutely nothing other than the greatest respect, both as a rival competitor and as a person, duly won the British Senior Women's Grass Track title. She was presented with the cup and the national champion's jersey with the red and blue bands on, indicating that at that discipline, she was the No.1 rider in the country and could wear it for the next 12 months.

Later that day, we lined up for the 800m handicap in the women's omnium. The idea of handicapping is to create an exciting event in which it is possible for every single rider to win, regardless of their ability. Always on scratch is the British champion. The handicapper had also been aware of my exclusion from the 800m championship and, having seen me race the previous year and followed my progress, placed me on the same starting point as Helen, in last place. Helen and I moved through the field together, watching one another as we overtook the slower riders. We had to keep the pace up, because the riders who had started furthest ahead were going flat out trying to get the win. I took the lead as we came around the final bend to win by a bike length. I remember punching the air with my fist to the cheers of the crowd as I crossed the line. The crowd at Mildenhall is generally very knowledgeable, very sociable and not unfamiliar with controversy. They knew exactly what was going on and appreciated the point I was making and applauded wholeheartedly.

The BCF may have been embarrassed at that moment, but they literally rolled the red carpet out at the first-ever set of British Youth Track Championships for girls the following year, 1998. I took a clean sweep of the four titles on offer: pursuit, sprint, 500m and points race. The medal ceremony was conducted with all the pomp and circumstance of the men. The presentations were not tucked away in some corner or done in silence when something else 'important' was going on elsewhere. All the presentations were made only when there was a break in the racing, so that the attention of the whole crowd was on the three medallists, and always the commentator introduced the occasion and personalities with dignity. Looking back, I'm proud of the 14-year-old me performing as I did at Mildenhall. Together with Dad and the BCF official, we made a change so that now British Cycling holds championship titles equally for boys and girls, on both track and road, for all youth and junior age-groups.

Meanwhile, some were asking how I could ride like that when I was just 14. Victoria Pendleton was in that race and she was older than me, and of course there was the Senior British Women's 800m champion. What had I done to enable me to beat them? It wasn't all the water fights, was it? The truth is I just rode my bike, a lot, because I liked it and wanted to become good. I have a work ethic that tells me, the more you do the better you are likely to become. Admittedly, that doesn't always work, and later I failed miserably with overtraining. But at this stage of my life, where I had to sit down in school lessons for a huge chunk of time each day, there was enforced rest. The rides to school with Craig and Dad continued to be the backbone of my training programme, but we also developed a series of rides up through the hills behind Bridgend to be completed on the weekend. The longest of the rides I did regularly at this time took just under three hours, cycling up over the Bwlch, a notoriously long and hard hill, passing through the village of Nant-y-Moel, birthplace of Lynn Davies, before looping back through Maesteg and Bridgend to Wick. We were always the only cyclists on the road, just us and the sheep.

We started our stopwatches at the clock-tower in Nant-y-Moel and stopped them at the top of the Bwlch. Flat out, every time. It always hurt a lot. Each ride, you knew your form. The mid-range ride, which took just under two hours, was dubbed the Windmill because it took us past windmills on the ridges of the hills between Blackmill and Pencoed. The Coast Road ride was the shortest, which gave us the suite of distances to mix and match depending on our targets. The rides have remained unchanged over the years and our reference points for improvements marked by times collected at the same points. We raced the Ajax club time-trial on Friday nights, the track league at Maindy on Wednesday nights and some evenings we went sprint training around the deserted roads of Llandow airfield. Occasionally, I did longer rides with Craig or Dad. We would do the Ajax club 100-mile reliability trial. I was very fortunate to have such a pleasant variety of training rides available from home.

A heart-rate monitor added a new dimension. My scrapbooks were replaced with digital records with heart-rate profiles and I kept meticulous details of training rides, route, distance, wind speed and direction, and times recorded up our standard hills. I never made an excuse for myself, saying the weather was too bad, or if I had a puncture came home early, or used a short cut. I was convinced that through enough work I would eventually be able to achieve my dream of becoming the Tour de France winner, and World and Olympic champion.

In 1997, I became the first-ever British winner at Helmond. The joy of the accompanying staff and the other boys and girls with me, was exactly like that day on the sports field in Wick. My sex was irrelevant. ESCA had by now changed their name to BSCA (British Schools Cycling Association – I'm very proud of how they told us they wanted to change the name to make sure we felt included) and as Craig and I attended all their events, we engaged with other children, as did Mum and Dad with other parents, all who had an affinity for how we went about things. When the flag dropped and the race started, we gave everything. Other mums and dads saw Craig and me achieving, and following my success at Helmond I became a totem to others and the whole feel of the British group changed. The coaches became more confident and parents had more confidence in them. Others joined us around this time and followed on sharing in this new atmosphere. I was delighted that one year we mustered five from the Ajax club and a very young Ben Swift and Adam Blythe who have now moved to successful professional careers. Dad has a wonderful sweet tale of Ben coming up to him and asking what he might do to help, at the BSCA Cyclo-Cross Championships in 1999, and Ben insisting on cleaning my muddy bikes during a long epic battle. Apparently, Ben was as excited as I was that I eventually won.

By 1998, I had also picked up some sponsorship, riding for Mick Ives Cycles, in mountain bike races. Road races for girls in the UK were in very short supply, with no races available anywhere most weekends, so for the previous three years I had competed in mountain bike races. Locally, at Margam Park we have a great venue which hosts rounds of the British series. That year, Mick wanted me to ride the whole series, which was fine. There was no petrol money, and the sponsorship was limited to equipment: bike, clothes, shoes and helmet. Looking ahead, I needed commercial support, and a 'toe in the water' with Mick was a great place to start. I was really thrilled; this was my first 'team' and Mick is a genuine enthusiast. If anyone thinks I love riding my bike, this is the man who can put me to shame. You name it, if it has a bicycle involved with it, he can tell you about it. A great guy, he is still competing right now. He got together as many sponsors as he could – bottles, drinks, shoes, puncture repair outfits, bicycle locks – and all these sponsors had their names on the jersey and the team took its title from his car sponsor, Peugeot 406.

As I was to find out for myself so many times, sponsors come in two types. There are the good sponsors who sign an agreement and do what they say they will and the equipment or money arrives exactly as it should. There are not too many of those around. Thank you – all of you. Then there is the other type. They are quite keen to tell you all the things they will do, and getting the artwork for the name on the jersey is often the easy bit with them, but then something is always 'lost in the post'. Mick's team had both sorts, so Mum needed to keep right up to date with Mick. After the first few weeks, we were told a certain sponsor had not paid. Mick's answer: to cover over the name or logo on the jersey. 'Can you sew this new badge on over that name there?' It seemed that I never raced in the same jersey twice. Names were added, covered over and taken away. It was an endurance challenge in itself. I did the odd one, but Mum was kept really busy. We have lots of great memories of those times.

*

Like sponsors, officials and organisers also came in different types.

In 1998, we encountered the British system and their ideas of keeping to the rule book. At this time, there were still four totally independent governing bodies for the sport of competitive cycling with jurisdiction for their own particular discipline across the UK. A single individual organiser might put on events under the rules of these differing governing bodies throughout the year, in line with the seasonal nature of the varying disciplines.

On one occasion, an organiser fell out with Dad over the rules in a cyclo-cross race. Dad pointed out what the rules actually were, but that didn't seem to matter to this guy, who believed that *his* version of the rules was what counted, but then he subsequently took it out on Mum. Craig, Dad and I were away at the British Cyclo-Cross Association (BCCA) Championships and Mum, who was fitting her cyclo-cross racing around working alternate weekends, was riding the last round of the Welsh Cyclo-Cross series in order to get her minimum number of qualifying rides in the season-long league. This was run under BCCA rules, a totally independent body from the BCF. He refused to allow her to ride, quoting a BCF rule for road races that extraordinarily empowered an event organiser to refuse entry to any rider they didn't want to ride the race.

So, after catching the train and riding from the station to the event, Mum was left standing at the side watching, before making the long journey home. She therefore didn't qualify for the series. We were all very upset when we got back home and found out. This organiser was the secretary of the BCCA in South Wales, but when we appealed in writing to BCCA headquarters, nobody wanted to take him on. After that, we didn't ride any more cyclo-cross events in South Wales until he was no longer secretary.

Meanwhile, I was riding the British Mountain Bike series for Mick and that was put on under the rules of the BCF. One of the rounds was at Margam Park. The BCF organised things differently from the BCCA. In their case, you made a central entry to Manchester for all those events in the series you wanted to ride. I think there were only four rounds that year and you had to ride all four to be able to qualify. We didn't gatecrash the show. Weeks in advance, Dad wrote to the BCF at Manchester and asked if I would be allowed to ride at Margam, where our favourite 'organiser' was the site manager. Was he gifted the power to prevent me riding? The answer came that, as the entries were central, he was 'not the organiser' and so could not stop me riding. That was the good bit, but they didn't want to upset him, so could we please keep it quiet? We did.

Next thing we knew was that 'our friend', who was not the organiser, had found out that I was riding and had declared, to all who would listen, that he was going to stop me, and so I would not be able to qualify. Dad rang Mick and the BCF, but nobody wanted to upset our friend – presumably because if they did he would pack up his toys and there would not be any Margam round. Happily, Dave Mellor, a BCF official who we will encounter many more times in this book, came up with the most cunning of plans. I was to be driven onto site, hidden in the back of Mick's Peugeot van, and I was to do my warm-up on rollers in it. Then, just when they were calling starters to the line, the doors of the van were to burst open and I was to spring forth and chase after the rest just after they got going. It would all happen so quickly that our friend would not have time to pull me off my bike and he would not be able to dissemble the course before I was finished and gone from the site. Genius! Problem solved!

The Cooke family were having none of that. We told them that we would be as discreet as possible, but being smuggled into a race in the back of a van was not something I would have any part in.

There was a further problem. I needed to recce the course to find out where it went and obstacles and descents I might encounter. Although familiar with the park, different courses were used for different events. One time, a year or two earlier, we were doing our recce of the course on a Friday night. The course was not marked out and we took a wrong turn and ended up in somebody's garden so we apologised to the house-keeper. 'Oh don't worry, I had the whole field in here one year, hundreds of them, the ones at the front couldn't get back because of the ones that kept on coming up the hill!' For this event, we suggested I just turn up, complete the recce and then leave without showering.

At the BCF, Colin Clews, who we will again meet later, was now the point of contact, once Dave Mellor's cunning plan had been discarded. Colin was fine, and agreed this was the minimum interaction we could have. He was very good about it. We agreed timings of these visits and Colin kindly stated that he would be on hand to deal with anything, should our friend seek to do something else out of the ordinary.

So I did my recce lap on the Saturday and was back at the car changing shoes when our friend showed up, shouting and being outrageous. Dad and I left without responding in kind. Apparently he was taken home after being prevented by BCF staff from single-handedly pulling out every marker post around the whole course there and then. I'm not too sure if I ever saw him again, but I do remember that I won the race and series.

Events like this seem incredible now, but this type of thing was not a one-off. Let me finish the theme with one more example, a year forward but this time in cyclo-cross. For females, cyclo-cross had two British Championship races. The senior event was for anyone over 16, while the youth event, run with the boys' event – with everyone starting and finishing together over an identical course in the same race – was for all males and females, aged 12 to 16. January 1999 was my last year as a youth and my last chance to directly measure up against the best British boys. Within this single race there were trophies awarded to the first finisher aged 14 and another to the first finisher aged 15. The fields were generally very good for these championships, with 40 to 50 competing. The adrenaline at the start was something to behold. That charge across the open section before the first narrowing of the course was critical. If you weren't in the top positions, you weren't going to figure in the results.

Two years earlier, I had won the trophy for top-finishing 14-year-old. I had beaten the boys. A year later, I was the second 15-year-old, beaten by a single boy of my age. This time was my last chance to compete with the other sex in a title event and to sign off in style. Now at 16, boys' hormones had seriously kicked in and while I was a small girl, the best British boys were very big. In any other discipline, I could no longer be competitive, but cyclo-cross shifted the balance from brute strength to technique in terms of the mounts and dismounts, as well as the ability to control and manage the bike. I was never going to win, but to stand on the podium in third was a very real possibility. Whereas my achievement in being the best 14-year-old had been ignored, because there was no podium presentation, this would now be with the whole crowd around and they would have to see the little girl standing alongside the big boys. I was fired up, I had practised and practised across that muddy common all winter. Now I would have my moment.

It was a freezing cold January day. The trick was to keep warm by gently riding around the start area with lots of layers on and leave it until the last possible moment to line up and remove the layers. We had a nominal start time and the starter would call us to the line with a couple of minutes to go. But there was all that adrenaline running high, and some boys were stripped down to their race kit and waiting on the start line with ten minutes to go.

Dad was at the car, locking it up before coming across to collect my over-tops and leggings. I had ridden across from the car after the last lubricating of my chain. He heard the starter's pistol fire and ran across to the starting area. He got there to see the last few riders arguing with their parents about whether it was worth starting, now that they were so far behind after missing the start. He followed the trail of my kit that I had discarded as I rode out of the field and around the course. Another dad we knew well ran across and told him what happened. Nobody had been called to the start. The gun went off and some lads on the start got going, others chased. Some had kit to take off, others just went how they were. I was quite quick to start, but then, as I was taking off a top as I was riding across the field, it caught in my rear wheel and chain and jammed. I had to get off and fight with it to pull it out of the chain and gears. There was no use shouting or screaming, I just got on with the race.

With so much single track on the course, there were only certain places I could get past the slower riders. People clapped as I finished first girl, just out of the top ten boys, but inside the fire raged. The senior official explained what had happened: he had brought a good friend to the race and the friend had asked if he could start the race. Unfortunately, while he was looking over the pistol he had been given, he happened to pull the trigger by accident and it just went off in his hand! The boys on the line decided this was their chance and off they went. There was no way of calling them all back for a proper start.

The BCCA Championships were *the* British Championships, they featured in the single British cycling magazine of the time *Cycling Weekly*. The BSCA also ran a championship event, but it garnered no external kudos or magazine coverage. Most of the youth riders from the BCCA event also rode in that one, too, which took place three weeks later. Importantly for me, the boy who took the third podium place earlier rode again. We spent the whole race within ten metres of each other; we both knew what this was about. With a lap to go, I thought I had cracked him, but for the whole of that last lap he kept chasing really hard and finished right behind me at the line. I shook his hand afterwards; it was one of the toughest cyclo-cross races I ever did. That was January 1999. Perhaps if I had been on the podium at the BCCA National Championships, which would have been reported, my 'emergence' later that year might not have come as the unacceptable shock it was to so many in authority.

Cycling in the UK now is nothing like it was then. At the time, the bungling, petty, political and indiscreet nature of the incompetence of so many, was personified in those two incidents. The original concept of a solution for Margam was a farce – jumping out of the van like a scene from a comedy show. Why not deal with the issue properly at the very first instance? It's easiest in the long run.

*

Around this time, there were huge changes taking place in British sport generally. At the 1996 Olympic Games in Atlanta, Great Britain won only one gold medal, in rowing, and finished below Algeria and Ethiopia in the medal table. The description 'team of shame', as one athlete described it on return, was a bit over the top, but the performance was a major embarrassment and probably the catalyst that helped create the magnificent success of the Beijing and London Olympics that followed.

The government decided to step in, to what until then had been very much an amateur affair in most sports. It gave teeth to a body formed in the wake of Atlanta called UK Sport, with a remit to oversee all the different sports' governing bodies, both in terms of governance and in respect of elite performance. The National Lottery had started in 1994 and public funds were available for distribution. It was recognised that supporting emerging talent and sustaining elite talent was something the public wanted Lottery funds spent on. The images in the newspapers of British athletes coming out of the closing ceremony at Atlanta and auctioning their uniforms to the crowds were yet more embarrassment. The public did not want the country's finest to have to exist as paupers in order to take on the rest of the world. It was obvious what happened when you did that: you won nothing. However, it was clear that if public money from the Lottery was going to be made available to the governing bodies, then most needed significant overhaul.

Senior competitive cycling in the UK was at this time run by three separate governing bodies, each with their own unrelated rule books and systems of governance. For younger categories, there were four bodies, with the BSCA having national and regional championships across all disciplines and age categories based on the school year.

UK Sport made it quite clear that going forward there could be only one organising body – British Cycling – and that future funding would depend on success; they were not going to throw money at a sport which didn't come back with results, and in particular results were seen as Olympic medals. This created a dilemma for British Cycling. The great champions of cycling, such as those that I wanted to emulate, raced the Tour de France and the classics, which are for professional riders. The Olympics was traditionally for amateur riders. Therefore the Olympics historically catered for track riders, with a significant number of medals available there and, prior to 1996, just a single medal available to the road disciplines.

A very early decision in the formation of the British Cycling World Class Performance Programme (BC WCPP) was that it would be more focused towards delivering track cycling medals and, reflecting the sport's imbalance of events, supporting the men far more than the women. The 'Plan' was born. The idea was to provide senior riders on the Plan with equipment, access to facilities and coaching but also a 'salary' or their own personal subsistence funding, which allowed them to become full-time cyclists. This was necessary in track cycling as there was no viable full-time scene on the world stage. The glory days of track cycling in the post-war era, when packed stadiums of paying fans created large prize pots, were long gone.

This change was to have a fundamental impact on the rest of my career. Even if I could find ways to fund myself through individual sponsorship, I could only compete for Great Britain if I was selected by British Cycling. The management team of the Plan managed the coaching education, structure, facilities and athletes. It also wrote the selection criteria, whether there was any logic or fairness in those criteria or not.

Quickly, with funding freely available, the support structure, coaches, mechanics, equipment programmes and of course the management of all of these elements, increased in size such that the public funds needed to run it became many times that granted to the individual athletes. This created a new reality that had not existed before. The management of this new support structure would find it almost impossible to countenance the selection of a rider *not* on the Plan over those it supported, coached and managed, who *were* on the Plan. Therefore the key to being selected for a GB team was to be on the Plan rather than performance in races. It didn't fill anybody who understood what was happening with much confidence that many of those coaches and administrators who moved into the key positions on the Plan, as it started to evolve, seemed to be those who had been responsible for Great Britain's chronic underperformance in the years leading up to Lottery funding coming on tap.

At the beginning of 1998, I was totally unaware of where all this would lead. My main concern was that my results had finally been recognised and that I had been given an Elite Cymru Lottery grant, which was a breakthrough. It covered only a small portion of what Mum and Dad spent supporting me. They and I were very grateful that the Lottery-playing public indulged me in this manner.

The summer of 1998 was busy. I went to Holland twice to ride at Helmond and then another 'Tour' for older riders at Achterveld. I was starting to get a nice little collection of T-shirts. There were the inaugural British Track Championships at Manchester, which had to be fitted in around the British Mountain Bike Championships at Builth Wells taking place at the same time. It was a lot of fun being part of Mick's set-up and after gaining the series win, I wanted to win the British title. Mum and Craig set up on the campsite at Builth and Dad and I based ourselves at Manchester. Dad did the driving back and forth during the small hours of the night with me asleep in the back of the car.

The track championships were a joy to take part in. Aside from my own races, there were times when Dad and I could just sit in the stands and watch. People would come up to us and chat about the sport. If there was a women's race on the track, Dad got the stopwatch out and made a video, just as he did of my races for later analysis.

Next up was our new summer holiday; we were going abroad to find the Alps. We based ourselves at a lakeside campsite in an Alpine valley in south-east France. When we arrived, there was evidence that the women's Tour de France had passed through a few days before. We were frustrated to miss it, but there had been nothing about it in *L'Équipe* before we left. I'm not sure how many households in Wales took daily delivery of *L'Équipe*, but in the summer the paper boy delivered one to us. The reason we had selected this spot was that there were a number of major mountain climbs surrounding it, including the Col de la Bonette on which Robert Millar had made his amazing ride in the 1993 Tour. I wanted to ride the same climb to know what it was like.

Each morning Mum, Dad and I (Craig was at an air cadet's camp) would tackle one of the peaks, each at our own pace. After reaching the top, we would pause to have a drink before the spectacular ride back down the mountains to our campsite and tent.

On the day of the Bonette, Dad and I didn't actually intend to do that climb. Dad was suffering in the heat and wanted to do a climb before the heat of mid-day. We set off to tackle the

Col de Vars together. About halfway up, we got to a road block which said it was closed due to roadworks, so we had to go somewhere else. Dad wasn't entirely at his happiest, as the aborted half-climb up the Vars now placed us on the Bonette during the hottest part of the day.

Dad wanted to pace himself over the 26km of climb, and I soon left him doing his human snail impersonation. I was riding nicely at my own pace when some better competition than Dad turned up. A tanned, slim Frenchman, looking the genuine article, perfect bike and outfit, rode up from behind me and passed the 15-year-old girl with barely a sideways glance. At first, as I latched on behind him, he wasn't concerned. The gradient changed a couple of times – steeper, shallower, all fine. I continued to follow, locked in behind him. A steep section came up and now he was determined to drop me. I wasn't going to let that wheel get away! He tried on the hard bits and the less steep bits. He tried for the next 18km, right up to that last steep section on the Cime. By the time I got to the top, I had found a whole new spectrum of suffering in training, but here I was at 2,802m, on the highest road in Europe and the highest point ever taken by the Tour. I had ridden the same road that Robert Millar had, five years earlier, when he was alone at the head of the Tour.

There was no prize that day and no crowds cheering for me, but I had overcome a significant psychological test. I realised I could really push myself and ride well in the toughest of the high mountains. As I sat at the top, I knew the women's Tour de France was still some years away for me, but I could go home to Wick even more convinced that I would win it one day.

Dad showed up at the top over 30 minutes later, pretending to be exhausted and with swollen eyes bulging out of his head,

and puffing so much that people stared. It was so embarrassing when he sat near me. Our ride back to the campsite
included another 1,300m climb en route, where again I kept
on having to wait for Dad. I thought he was overdoing the
'I'm too tired' act when he later refused to walk down to the
lake for a swim with Mum and me, saying his legs hurt.

I came back down to earth with a bump a few days after
getting home. The British Criterium Championships were
held on a closed road circuit at the end of August. I applied for
dispensation to race with the seniors, which was granted by
the BCF, and I lined up, aged 15, confident that based on my
track performances a few weeks earlier, I should be in with a
good chance. For the first lap, it all looked good as I blasted
away from the start line. When I pulled off the front and took
a quick look behind, gaps were opening up everywhere. Then
it all went seriously wrong. I moved over, hoping to slot in
behind the riders chasing me, but when they came past I could
not stick with them and ended up riding by myself. I couldn't
pull the skin off a rice pudding. Towards the end of the race,
I was passed by the leader Sara Symington. Lapped! Looking
back, it is easy to see what went wrong. We only had seven
days in the Alps and were determined to do a major alpine
climb or two, every single day. I had done more riding in that
time than I had ever packed into a week before, and by some
long margin. I was completely exhausted.

CHAPTER FOUR
Fluke Win

According to legend, August 1999 was all about me beating the WCPP girls in the British Road Race Championships. If that was the case, I went a pretty odd way about it! The reality was very different. I was 16, this was GCSE year and I had two more years in school to look forward to. I was making progress in cycling and I just wanted some markers. Ahead in 2000 were the World Junior Championships and I was looking forward to those. August was all about proving to the system that we were just fine. I didn't even want what I deserved, which was to be treated like the boys. I just wanted a little bit of support and to be left alone. Bradley Wiggins had won the World Junior Pursuit title the year before with his little team and I wanted to replicate that operation.

But things were changing very fast. By 2000, the support structure building around the WCPP had sucked into Lottery-funded, full-time employment a whole collection of individuals with a wide spectrum of abilities. In the preceding years, significant Lottery funding had already been entering the sport and many a job had come and gone. The transient and unstructured nature of British Cycling and the recent history of these short-term appointments were such that in the past

not many seriously minded individuals with a professional attitude to a career had joined.

Now some able people were taking up various posts. In the
main, the most able would be directed to the most attractive
roles, working with the senior men. At the bottom of the
priority list, in this male-dominated sport, was the support for
junior women. Some had talent but most had an ability set inappropriate for their roles, and these were the people who would
be gathered around me. Mostly, these individuals had the wrong
attitude and skills, and too often they were ex-cyclists who
had failed. They were lucky to find themselves in these jobs.
That they were universally male may not have been a problem,
but these were 'lads' who hadn't sacrificed a steady career for
their calling and who, regardless of their age, enjoyed the
pranks that lads get up to. A clash of cultures was inevitable.

Late August 1999 was the catalyst for events that would have
a huge negative impact on the rest of my career. I just wanted to
win races. So far, I had been racing for five years and it had been
against youth and junior girls and boys. How good was I really?
I was confident in my own abilities, but I was hugely frustrated
by the condescending way I was treated most of the time.

Winning the 800m event at Mildenhall against Helen
MacGregor in 1998 was a pointer, but she was not on the
WCPP. For two years I had been at the National Track
Championships and sat in the stands with Dad as the senior
women rode their races. Watching a race with Dad was an
education; he would give a running commentary on the
tactics predicting moves that were about to happen or moves
not made that caused the loss of the race. Not that we were
the only ones drawing comparisons between the relative
performances of the women on the WCPP and myself. After
I won the scratch race the previous year, an informed observer

told me that I had raced more aggressively than anyone he had seen the night before at the senior women's event over the same distance and I had finished my race several minutes faster than them. Even if the WCPP management were about to get a shock, here was one observer who could predict the outcome. As yet, I was still too young to join the WCPP, which was restricted to those in the Senior and Junior categories.

It might sound incredibly arrogant, but, such is youth and my confidence, I genuinely wasn't focused on the Women's National Road Race as a target in itself. I wanted to be racing to win in the international races; how I rode against the WCPP girls would be an indicator on my progress towards that goal.

When I turned 16 in April, I could convert my BCF road licence to 'Junior Woman'. It was a bit crazy, because there were no junior women's road races in the UK that year, but there were many races categorised '3VJW' – featuring the least able of the amateur men (Category 3, out of 1, 2 and 3), juniors, veteran men and all women above U16. These races can be some of the hardest to win and most frustrating due to a majority of riders who are desperate for points to move up to the next category, yet who don't know the tactics of how to race. A good wheel to follow is an elite rider returning to the sport after a long break. He will be Category 3 and has to pick up points before he can get back to Category 1 status. And then there are a lot of worthy clubmen enjoying their sport and contributing effectively. These are also good wheels. Now, with my new licence, I could enjoy this quality of racing.

In my first outing in this category in '99, I tried to form a break with various men but none of the attacks stayed away, and it came down to a 40-rider bunch sprint. I had selected the right rider who, as I expected, took the lead into the last bend and then chose my moment to come off his wheel and sprint for the line to win the race. I'm not too sure how many senior women win such races; certainly I had never seen a result in *Cycling Weekly* where a woman had the win. A junior man winning his first-ever 3VJW race happens sometimes. A junior woman – in fact not a junior woman but a youth woman racing up as a junior – winning her first race against a full field of senior men, I think, remains unique. I rode back from the race with Dad having put down another marker, and it was back to school the next day.

The previous year when racing the Achterveld Tour in Holland, where foreign riders stay with host families, I had stayed with the Boterman family and became good friends with their daughter, Andrea, who was racing in the junior category in the Tour. After finishing my GCSEs, I took up their offer to return to stay with them again, this time for three weeks. I trained at Andrea's club on their closed circuit, which even had a cobbled straight, and I took part in a number of local races and the Achterveld Tour. Each race was an important experience learning to cope in the large bunches that did not exist in the UK. After that we returned to the Alps in August, camping, and the grand cols around Barcelonette. Before we got there we took in the total eclipse of the sun in Alsace – a wonderful day which I will never forget.

Although the British Championship would be a key indicator of my progress, I wasn't going to be obsessed by it and rest up. I wanted to enjoy my riding that summer. Craig and I fought every centimetre up every mountain – Vars 2,109m, St Jean 1,333m, Larche 1,948m, Allos 2,247m, Cayolle 2,326m and Bonette 2,802m – wheel to wheel past every kilometre post to the summit and then started the stopwatch to see how far behind Dad was.

Having once missed seeing the women's Tour, this year, with the help of the new-fangled internet we planned where we could watch it. There was to be a mountain-top finish at Vaujany, where I would have the opportunity to see at first hand those I might be joining in three years' time. On the day we saw the women's Tour, we first rode the Alpe d'Huez and then went to Vaujany. There was all the usual excitement of a pre-race publicity caravan with sponsors tossing out freebies. At the top, the crowds were huge, encroaching onto the road to a point where the competitors would have to force a route through them. The expectation was building as the first motor-bikes appeared and then, finally, the riders, already strung out in groups, led by a breakaway of three. It was the first time I had seen such a mass of elite women riders and the noise, colour and sense of excitement were overwhelming. I couldn't wait until I got in there, racing with them.

We finished the holiday a bit tired but very happy to have crammed in so much activity. Within a week of our return, I received my GCSE results, lots of 'A*'s and 'A's, and even a 'B' in Music; I had confirmed my A-level choices with my teachers and was looking forward to starting those. Then it was Mildenhall time again. We caught up with our friends, sat around the track in the sun, I met Helen and Greg Saunders, and with Sean and Kathryn McClelland we prepared for the quiz night on the Sunday, when our combined parents were to be in one team and we were in another. Everyone knew I was riding the National Road Race the next day. Many of the younger riders who had come to Holland with us – as our BSCA contingent changed from also-rans to contenders – were there and wished me luck. On the Saturday, the signs weren't good. There was not much zip in my legs at all, and I was being beaten by boys I normally beat. Craig, who was following the wheel of a boy who beat me in the lunge to the line, had the good sense to think better of it and slowed down to come third. The next morning, Mum was up early, cooked a pasta meal and kissed me good luck. I was off to meet the Plan.

There was no British Junior Women's Road Race Championships, although such an event existed for the men. I had to use a BCF rule which said that if there was no British Championships event in a given discipline for a junior woman, she could compete in the senior event. Months before, we had got in touch with the organiser, Jon Miles, to check if he was in agreement. He was great. I didn't need to recce the course as he had given me an incredibly detailed description of it. The black wooden barn was exactly where I expected to find it on the left. The sharp junction was at the foot of the descent as he described.

Peter Keen, director of the WCPP, was the personal coach to Chris Boardman for a great deal of his career and personally coached two of the female cyclists on the Plan, Caroline Alexander and Yvonne McGregor. A popular shot of Peter and Yvonne together after Sydney is readily available on the internet. Undoubtedly, beyond any friendship, Peter had a great professional pride in Yvonne's achievements. He was, after all, responsible for specifying every training ride and every gym session she undertook. She was the standard bearer for the women's programme.

Yvonne was head and shoulders ahead of the rest of the WCPP road riders in terms of endurance. There were other riders in the WCPP group who could sprint, but they were way below Yvonne's level in terms of sustained speed. The circuit included two climbs each lap, and the finish itself would be a long uphill sprint, the sort on which I feared no one. Dad and I had discussed tactics in the week before the race. Since taking the world hour record in 1995, Yvonne's form had varied a little but she had been in good shape when we watched her at the National Track Championships a few weeks earlier. Yvonne was not a strong sprinter and would want to break away. The course would provide a suitable anvil for her. My strategy was simple – 'never let Yvonne go up the road without me'. If she had a 20m lead, I would be racing for second place. Anything else I would have to deal with on the road. We arrived at the course and drove around it. Everything was as we expected; the race was going to split up.

My bike, courtesy of my sponsorship from Mick Ives, was a nice little Peugeot machine. In *Cycling Weekly*, one of the traders was offering it new for £200 including delivery. The wheels were replaced, not with fancy, expensive aero or deep sectioned wheels, but just slightly up from 'entry level' so as not to be embarrassed by the £200 price tag. The WCPP spend of the public's money would run at around £3,000 per top bike per rider. However, the biggest drag factor is the human on the machine.

For several years, I had taken to Helmond two elasticated straps which Mum made for me. The jerseys, polka dot or more lately yellow, were a one-size-fits-all affair. I could prob-ably get two of me in each one, maybe more. Instead of riding with a sail attached to me, I would slide the straps over the top of the swathes of yellow and fold the material neatly, so that I presented the most flush little me into the wind. Of course, quite a bit of the top had to be tucked down my shorts as well, which was not quite so svelte, bulging in the lycra in all sorts of weird ways. Mick Ives was an enthusiast and he needed no persuasion from Dad to get a skin suit with pockets made for me for this race. I was small and all the jerseys were big. With a well-fitted skin suit, I now had an advantage that more than offset any advantage of my competitors' exclusive bicycles.

Mick had one made perfectly – even if its reduced size meant that quite a few of the sponsors' names were missing or only had the first two letters! I rode to the start. I might have gone very slowly at Mildenhall the day before, but I was quite happy. After France, I had done the Windmill circuit back home and recorded my fastest-ever time for the whole thing, by some margin. So bring it on; 110km with these girls was not going to be as hard as some of the rides we had just done in the Alps. Things to remember? Don't let Yvonne get 20m of daylight between her back wheel and my front wheel.

During the first two laps, there were several attacks but each time they were negated as other riders chased them down. On the third lap, one attack resulted in a group of 12 of us getting away. With 50km still remaining, Yvonne put in an attack, just at the moment I was boxed in by other riders and not able to respond immediately. In a flash, the gap was bigger than that magic 20m figure. How did that happen? This was now a tricky situation. Yvonne had caught everyone by surprise, but now the bunch would be alert and waiting to see who would respond. If I just simply accelerated, the other riders would be able to sit on my wheel, benefiting from the slipstream. I needed to manoeuvre myself into a position where I could put in an attack where there would not be an immediate response. This meant finding a place as far away as possible from the strongest remaining riders and making sure that when I attacked, I would be so fast that I would deter anyone from following. However, the longer I waited to create the right situation, the further away Yvonne went, which would make the job of catching her more difficult.

I attacked hard, created a gap and then settled down to catching Yvonne. When I'd done that, I looked around and could see that the bunch was still together, so no one else had got away. My heart-rate trace would record this period as my biggest effort in the race, well beyond what I needed to make in the final sprint. It was a sustained period of 198-200 beats per minute. I caught Yvonne and we worked together – the seasoned champion and the 16-year-old upstart – taking turns on the front. With two laps to go, we were told that there was one rider, Ceris Gilfillan, chasing on her own but rather than allowing a third rider to join us, I continued working with Yvonne.

We would pass Dad twice a lap as he rode round on his bike, complete with a saddlebag of supplies. He would be waiting at the side of the road on the climb, ready to run alongside me offering me bottles, or a selection of energy bars. Yvonne had a support car with Ken Matheson, the WCPP women's road manager and another member of the WCPP coaching staff in it. They followed us. After seeing Dad's offerings, it obviously caused them to think they should be doing the same, so they drove alongside and asked Yvonne if she needed them to get her anything. Were they going to pop off and get her a take-away if she asked them? 'One cod and chips please, and go easy on the salt!' She retained her composure far better than I could have done in her place, and politely told them she did not need them to go and get her anything.

Ken told Yvonne the time gaps. We had gained two min-utes on the bunch, so I knew it was going to be just the two of us at the finish. We had been riding strongly for quite some distance. Towards the end, Yvonne was still going well, and I was starting to weaken. Yvonne sensed this and tried to get away from me a few times. I then sat behind her. The men in the car seemed agitated by this action, certainly more agitated than Yvonne ever was. She was in the classic impossible posi-tion. She was stronger than me and over ten, or even five minutes she would be able to go faster. If she could create enough of a gap between us, she would be able to ride away from me. However, she didn't have enough acceleration to create that initial gap. I was always going to be faster in a short burst, even if I was more tired than her.

For the modest distance that remained to the finish, I sat behind Yvonne. I was tired, still a bit overcooked from France and I could have done without all the races I did the day before at Mildenhall. I chose the moment to start my sprint – and won comfortably. Yvonne was a great rider who had broken the hour record and would win a bronze in the pursuit at Sydney the following year as well as the world title. However, this was a road race. We could re-run this 50 times with the same contestants, and given their relative conditions, there would always be the same result. Yvonne had come to cycling late in life, and eventual third-placed rider Ceris Gilfillan was a convert from triathlons. Both were tactical ingénues. Even if Ceris had caught us and we got to a finish together, I would win the sprint. They would need the help of a number of other riders to wear me down before they could ever hope to get away from me.

Later in 1999, Philip Ingham, the BCF communications manager, would describe my win as a fluke to the nation's press. This was not an idea of his own construction but the accepted wisdom of staff at Manchester. That is why he said it. Only a complete fool could have observed the race and come to that conclusion. Dad and I cycled back to headquarters, with Dad appearing to have eaten most of the energy bars himself. Jon Miles had arranged a nice prize, a white watch with 'British Champion 1999' in tiny gold writing inside it. Putting on the Senior British Road Race champion jersey, white with a single band each of red and blue, was a privilege.

Phil Jones, the Welsh coach was there as well. He said he was confident of my victory 40km from home.

As we drove back to Mildenhall, we saw BSCA chairman Jo Tym and her husband John going the other way and they waved crazily at me. Obviously, the news had got there first. I waved back. This was a victory for the BSCA and their way of doing things, we all understood that. Everyone I knew ran up to me and congratulated me, and I was asked to do a lap of honour. In the late afternoon, we watched Craig finish his omnium. Freed from the need not to beat his big sister, he was riding much better than the previous day. Mum cooked us a special meal in our tent and we enjoyed relaxing with our friends camped around us. The next day, when I was a marshal for the cyclo-cross race, Craig ripped round to win.

While I went back to school, in Manchester the WCPP undertook a forensic and highly detailed analysis of the race. How on earth did a 16-year-old girl from outside the programme win with such ease? They came to a very different conclusion from the one that Phil, Dad and I did; one that would reverberate through every day of my career that followed.

CHAPTER FIVE
'Too Young' for Sydney

At the end of 1998, I had applied to the BCF to request permission to ride any of the Junior World Championships in 1999. Other nations were sending girls who were younger than the official age range. Could the BCF do so and allow me to gain valuable experience competing at this level? Unsurprisingly, the answer was 'No'. So 2000 would be very important for me, as I would be 17 and officially eligible to compete in the Junior World Championships – track, mountain bike, and of course the road events. Here was my opportunity to prove myself at a world level. It was also the year of the Sydney Olympics, and as reigning British Road Race champion surely I would have a chance to compete for selection and show how good I was there?

The one race that I definitely knew I would be able to ride was the World Junior Road Race Championships, due to be held in October 2000 in Plouay, Brittany, so we thought we should go and have a look at the course. We went in the October 1999 half-term school holidays; after all, there is nothing like planning well ahead. Elite Cymru eventually agreed to fund our recce, contributing to the petrol and modest accommodation, but insisted that we find a race in which to compete while we were there to justify the expense. So we loaded two road bikes and a cyclo-cross bike on the back of the car and drove to Plymouth to catch the ferry and then made our way to Plouay. We rode the world road race course, looking at the various points of the 14km circuit, especially the three climbs, to work out where I might attack. We also rode the world time-trial course as well, and then looked out for suitable accommodation that would be handy for getting to and from the circuits during times when the course would be open the following year.

To find out if there was a local race I could enter, we visited the bike shops in town. There was a 'duathalon' being held in Clegeur on the Saturday afternoon, which seemed suitable. I was a reasonable cross-country runner, so I expected to do quite well. On the Saturday morning, Dad and I rode and completed our recce; we did an easy lap, then a fast lap together and finally I did one lap on my own with Dad chasing behind. Following this, we drove to Clegeur. Dad was getting my bike ready as I went to pay my entry and sign on. I came back to Dad a few minutes later with the news that it was a team race, which meant I needed to find a runner to be able to compete – and that he was going to be that runner! It took Dad a full five minutes to walk from the car to the restaurant that night – he was pretending to do his malingerer act again – but we had won our category. We finished first in the combined category of senior/junior male or female. We had done our race as requested by Elite Cymru, and we had a winner's trophy to prove it.

Elsewhere it wasn't going so smoothly. In September 1999, I heard the news that the WCPP, had decided to remove the junior WCPP programme for 1999–2000. The year before I had met the performance criteria but couldn't join because

I was too young; now, when I was old enough, the programme suddenly disappeared. This meant that instead of moving into the WCPP, I would have to stay with the Elite Cymru programme.

On 23 September, British Cycling issued the Olympic selection criteria. The selection races were almost exclusively World Cup races that clearly I could not attend because I was still at school. However, there was discretionary selection available to the director of the WCPP. Then on 16 December, Shane Sutton rang Dad to tell him that he had been informed that the UCI had put out a new rule that precluded me from going to Sydney. Dad rang up the BCF the next day and asked for a copy of the UCI rule and they replied by return of post. There it was. UCI information Bulletin 29 November 1999: Part 11.1.003 – 'To take part in the Olympics each rider shall be 19 years old for the road race and mountain bike events.'

When the press spoke to BCF communications manager Philip Ingham, he gave the following quote: 'Rules are rules and as a National Federation we have to abide by them. The UCI rules are there to protect juveniles in what is a very demanding sport. I would say that a BCF Appeal on her behalf is unlikely. Some would say that Nicole was very fortunate to win the British Championship. She hung on the wheel of the favourite and outsprinted her. It's different at world level as it is a lot more tactical. I don't think anyone can say that Nicole is a medal hope.'

Shane Sutton was quoted: 'We will fight this all the way because Nicole is clearly good enough to go to the Olympics. We have not given up hope that this ruling can be overturned. I can't see the difference, Nicole can compete at the Cyclo-Cross World Championships yet she is told she can't do the road racing at the Olympics. It doesn't make sense.'

The Olympic Charter actually has a very clear section which states that age shall not be a barrier to participation. However, the IOC (International Olympic Committee) can approve exceptions presented to it by world governing bodies. So we had a rule that suddenly appeared from the UCI, with the BCF happily pouring cold water on any possible challenge. There was also the contradiction that the same UCI were holding a Cyclo-Cross World Championships in January at which there was no junior event for women, so now I was going to represent Britain at senior level in that event. If the UCI felt so passionately about this rule change, why just introduce it at the Olympics and not in their own forthcoming events? Where did this new rule come from? Believe me, I asked, Dad asked, my solicitors asked. The IOC stated it was a request from the UCI, not their choice. My route to the UCI was via my home federation, the BCF. We asked many times in writing, with many follow-ups asking why there were no responses. All we were met with was prevarication and nonsense.

You will recall that at the end of the previous year I had written to the BCF, asking if I could ride a Junior World Championships event in 1999, and was told that I could not. Now having reached the standard age, all I had to do was meet the selection criteria, and that surely was written with the aim of making sure the best British rider represented the country. Peter Keen wrote the selection criteria and invested himself with the power of selection.

Peter stated that despite three years of not being beaten by a single other British female rider in any discipline in any age group event, he was not going to pre-select me for any Junior World Championships. I would have to prove I was worth selection by performances during 2000; nothing I had done before counted. An extensive programme of selection events was proposed. If I didn't show or didn't perform, I wouldn't be able to go.

The situation at that time was that opinion was split two ways regarding the British Road Race Championships and my worthiness in the British Olympic team – those who thought I had a flukey win and others who thought that the girls and the support staff on the WCPP had been travelling around the world for three years at the public's expense and didn't know how to race. I was burning for a re-match, but an extensive programme of junior qualification rides meant I was UK based, while the Plan went training and racing overseas. I couldn't go and meet them.

In order to qualify for the World Junior Mountain Bike Championships in June, I had to ride rounds one and two of the British Mountain Bike series. I also had to liaise with the national mountain bike coach so he could see me perform. The first round was at Thetford in Norfolk, well known for being the flattest part of the UK. I had to ride the junior women category race that set off behind a load of 'Fun' men, who fell off a lot and could go even slower than Dad. So my lap times were not a reflection of my ability, merely a measure of the traffic ahead on the single-track sections where I could not get past. Any comparison of my lap times with later elite women would be irrelevant because they would not have traffic problems.

To cap it all, when I had finished my race by mid-morning – we had started driving from South Wales at 2.30am – I met the national coach who asked me when I was riding. When I told him I had already showered and changed, he said, 'Oops!' *Ooops?* I was incredulous and very angry. Just 20 minutes from my house, I had a real mountain bike course and I wanted to train on that, but Peter Keen had insisted I go to Thetford, dodge in and out of a bunch of guys riding off their hangovers and then the national coach couldn't get there in time to see me. Ten hours' driving, a round trip of just under 600 miles. This was sheer lunacy. I won, but I proved nothing. So I was better at overtaking slow men than the other junior women. What does that count for? Why were they setting such selection conditions?

The second round was on 23 April at Margam. That was fine, and so close to home that I rode to the course and back. Then on 27 April, it was track, riding at Manchester to do some qualification testing for the Junior Track World Championships – to check what, I have little idea. Hundreds more miles of travel in the car. The Cheshire classic road race was on 7 May, a selection event for the Junior Road World Championships. More miles on the car. It also doubled as a round in the Women's Road Race series. I certainly did not know the WCPP girls were going to be there and would have done a taper and reduced my training leading into the event to freshen up, had I known.

I now look at my training diary for the five days before the event: an arduous mountain bike session at Margam; a pursuit on a turbo fitted with a contraption straight out of Alf Tupper's workshop, in this case fabricated by Dad, to replicate the starting load; and a flat-out ride around the Windmill circuit. My preparation was far from that which I would have undertaken for a grudge revenge match, with Olympic selection on the line.

Shane Sutton was there. He greeted us as we prepared the bike in the car park and asked if we knew the WCPP girls were there. We had no idea, we thought they were on the continent at this time. Shane wandered off and then came back and told me that Ken Matheson was boasting, saying that the WCPP girls were going to fill the top six places, and there was nobody here who could touch them. I have no idea if that was true, but all I needed to know was they were here. I joined them on the start line wearing the jersey that showed I was the champion of Great Britain and Northern Ireland. I looked across at my challengers and thought, 'You are full-time athletes and have been for years. All paid for by the Lottery. You have full-time coaches and mechanics and a whole bunch of the best equipment money can buy. Well, let me tell you . . . I'm a full-time schoolgirl and on Tuesday I have a Biology test and that chap over there, who I pretend is nothing to do with me, has a saddlebag of energy bars and hopefully he won't have eaten them all by the end of the race. Starter, bring it on!'

The race was very boring, and if anyone tried to do anything the WCPP girls chased them down. This was fine. 'Let's have a bunch sprint. The finish is at the top of a hill, there's none of you here that is going to worry me,' I thought quietly to myself. You could see the same thought starting to go through a few of their minds as they were looking at me. 'Maybe this cunning plan is not quite so cunning as we first thought.'

Then Yvonne McGregor attacked. Very kindly, she chose to do so on a section of dual carriageway, so I had a nice wide road to move out into and chase after her. Again, her plan to get away from me failed, I had the speed to catch her. We worked together again and built up a nice lead. Then Ken must have found out. He was in a WCPP car in the convoy. Yvonne and I were on one side of the dual carriageway and Ken was overtaking the bunch on the other side, leaning out of the open window and shouting at Yvonne, 'Ceris is coming up to you, sit on her!' pointing at me. Dad was on my side of the road just ahead and saw this, and I could see he was laughing his head off as we rode by. We did not have far to go and I was in much better form than the previous August, despite not doing a taper. This time, Yvonne sat on my back wheel as I towed her to the finish. I beat Yvonne in the sprint. Ceris didn't join up with us and finished alone in third.

So, according to the records, that made it an identical 1-2-3 finish to the British Championships of the previous summer. I have no idea what they thought in the WCPP – could lightning have made some random strike in exactly the same place? It had been a long journey to Cheshire, but we barely noticed the drive home.

Five days later, in a letter dated 12 May, Brian Cookson, BCF president, wrote saying that he intended to bring up the issue of age limits in Olympic events, informally, at the next UCI conference in October. Thanks for that Brian, it was a tremendous help and comfort, as you can imagine. Dad and my solicitor wrote back, putting into more formal prose the idea that after careful scrutiny, this new, very cunning plan had one minor flaw in it: the Sydney Olympics would be held the month before, in September.

We kept trying to force the issue but with heavy hearts, as we knew there would be no will to find a resolution in my favour. My solicitor Gareth Williams, who was kind enough to do everything for free, was sending chasers on the 20 June to Peter King, CEO at the BCF, asking why he had not responded to letters concerning the BCF challenging the UCI on the reasons for the age-limit rule change.

It really didn't matter how many times I beat the WCPP riders. They were on the WCPP, coached by the WCPP coaches and managed by the WCPP management. I was a schoolgirl. If they sent me to Sydney, they would be telling the rest of the world they were wasting the Lottery-playing public's money. They *were* wasting it, but did not want to admit it. I wasn't going to Sydney and that was that. I watched the Olympics on TV, with Mum and Dad sat either side cuddling me.

CHAPTER SIX

The GB Plan:
Stop That Girl!

I have been in racing situations alone, without team-mates for support. However, at least most of the time, I had to accept the situation as being within the rules. I treasure the photo of the podium at the Commonwealth Games held in Melbourne, in 2006, where the Welsh Cycling Union decided it was in my best interests to face a full team of six Aussies alone. The road race podium should feature just the first three finishers. The shot shows one podium and seven riders, six of them all delighted that they have overcome the World No.1. The six were fined for non-compliance with podium proto-col – but I was very glad my competitors chose to make the compliment.

Another occasion was the British Road Race Championships of 2000 and the process was definitely not within the rules. With two identical, fluke top three finishes in succession, the great minds at Manchester had worked out they needed to change something, otherwise lightning might hit the same spot three times. They added in all the resources at their command. Two girls from the mountain bike WCPP were drafted in to join those on the road WCPP as they sought to rid themselves of 'this turbulent priest'. Our new additions were Caroline Alexander, who was personally coached by Peter Keen, and Tracey Brunger. Many mountain bike specialists do ride road races and Caroline took part in World Cup road events through her career. The counter claim is that they just happened to show up, so presumably it was just coincidence that they queued up on my back wheel and Caroline just happened to attack only me, while neither chased any of the other WCPP girls when they attacked me one at a time. Once again, Peter Keen did not attend to see how his protégés performed.

I have no idea who 'Jan of Skipton' is, but in *Cycling Weekly* the week after the championships, the following letter appeared:

> Congratulations to Ceris Gilfillan on her win in the Women's National Road Race, although I thought it a hollow victory – it was totally unnecessary to resort to the practice employed by the World Class Performance Plan (WCPP) riders, as Gilfillan had the talent to win anyway. Surely it must be against the rules to employ team tactics? If it's not, then it's certainly against the spirit of the sport. I was at the race and challenged one of the WCPP riders, and was told that the tactics were planned by the WCPP coaching staff and the team was riding to instructions. The obvious target for all this brainstorming was a 17-year-old rider, who came out of the race with dignity and proved herself to be the best on the day. Well done, Nicole Cooke.

Team tactics were strictly against the regulations of a race being held under UCI rules which stated that a national championship was an individual race. The following year, the chief commissaire (official referee) read out the rules verbatim to all the riders before the race began.

For the record, Rachel Heal and Lucy Jude did help me close down attacks of the WCPP girls. Rachel and Lucy, thank you, while Tracey Brunger did not join in the attacks on me. As to the attacks, reading my heart traces from the race now, I can see that the race was 3 hours 10 minutes long and that the first attack came after 15 minutes. Six more attacks occurred during the next 25 minutes. There was then a period without attacks, and my notes indicate that I formed a break with Yvonne McGregor and Ruth Ellway but then state 'drift back to bunch', so presumably Yvonne had recalled the mantra 'do not go in a break with Nicole'. By the time we get to mid-race, 1 hour 30 minutes to 2 hours 30 minutes, I was trying to fend off attacks like midges on a sunny day. I responded 34 times during this period and had an average heart rate for that hour of 185. Eventually, they overwhelmed me. Caroline Alexander made an attack and I no longer had the strength to respond. There was then a lull until Ceris – who had been sitting behind in the group not doing anything, while the rest of the Plan attacked me – now made her first attack and got away, quickly catching Caroline. Together they finished first and second. Towards the end, Yvonne also got away and the rest of us finished as a bunch. I was an exhausted seventh.

They were paying me the highest possible compliment that day. The WCPP left no stone unturned. On the course was a single designated feed zone (where riders would be handed drinks by their support staff) and before and after this race, in 18 years of racing, myself and Dad only ever missed just one other handover. At this championship, we missed at least three that very hot day. As we entered the feed zone, a WCPP rider attacked. On such occasions, I had the choice of ignoring the attack and going slowly to pick up a bottle, or I could sprint after the attacking rider and chase before the gap became too great, trying to grab a bottle as I shot past Dad. For a team it was easy: one rider going slowly at the back of the bunch picks up the bottles and hands them over to team-mates later, when the bunch is back together. I was getting a proper working over. Not that such behaviour was unique. Two years earlier a rider had been allowed to ride on ahead to victory while the rest just dawdled behind. The chief commissaire stopped the race and threatened to cancel it because of this, so madness was not new in 2000.

I had brought the Championship Cup with me and had given it to the organisers to give to Ceris. We made sure we stayed for the prize presentation, and Dad and I clapped as loudly as any when the trophy was presented to Ceris. I was no sore loser. I would prefer a contest that was within the rules of the event. The following year, somehow, the trophy was forgotten.

Just to complete the story, I offer a few quotes from Ken Matheson, the WCPP manager, and Ceris, that appeared in Cyclingnews.com, the biggest cycling website. 'I'm very pleased with the result. It was a very powerful display of team riding,' enthused Ken, while Ceris also confirmed the overall game plan: 'We were committed to working together ... The most important thing was that one of us won.'

The report ends with a poignant eulogy to Ceris, who was coached by Ken. 'Gilfillan, from Malvern in Worcestershire has had a wonderful 12 months ... talented in both the mountains and against the clock, she appears to have a very bright future.' Just over 12 months later, Ceris had left the sport, disillusioned. I would have loved to work with Ceris, we would have made a great team. She is three years older than me and we could have achieved much. Certainly the Athens Olympics would have worked out differently had she been there. Sadly, poor-quality managers, who demanded via a signed Team Agreement that the riders had to obey every instruction they gave, created the conditions which ultimately resulted in her leaving the sport. All that investment was totally wasted.

I went back to school and tried to concentrate on my A-levels. I had my dignity, had ridden a fair race myself and been overwhelmed only by sheer numbers. The overt nature of what went on and the comments in Cyclingnews.com enraged many. I would go to events and the unfairness of it all was the only thing many people wanted to talk to me about. The ill feeling towards the WCPP from so many club cyclists and mums and dads of other youngsters, many of whom were following me, was staggering. As custodians of GB selection and funding, the WCPP management just 'bunkered down' in their offices below the track at Manchester. They did not have to answer to the club cyclist, nor to the Lottery-playing public who were expecting to see some results from all this invest-ment. It should have been the moment for the most senior elements of British Cycling management to step forward and to defuse the rapidly polarising situation. Instead, they appeared to ignore the issues my solicitor and I raised, and appeared to have joined the management of the WCPP in their 'bunker'.

In each age-group following me, there were plenty of girls filled with enthusiasm and talent and who loved competing in cycling. However, no British girl competed in the Junior World Championships for several years after me. Why did these girls leave? I know what they were telling me at the time, and most of it is not printable.

*

My first Junior World Championship would be the Mountain Bike Championships in Spain in early June. For UCI championships, riders are selected by their national federations and race for their country, as opposed to the rest of the year when riders race for their trade teams. This meant that unlike my trips to Holland, where I was simply able to enter the race by myself, I would need to be selected by my national federation. I had driven around the country to meet the selection criteria laid down by BC; however there was still one further hurdle. British Cycling required me to sign a Team Agreement.

Riding to represent your country is the ultimate privilege for a sportsman. It's not you on display, it's everyone at home via yourself and I understand that fully. Whenever I was about to put on my national jersey, I took a deep breath and made a pledge to myself. I hoped I would never let anyone down. Sadly, some time earlier, a few of the British track sprint men decided to re-arrange and discard some of the letters of the sponsor's name on their aero helmets. They peeled off the stick-on letters and thought they were being very funny using them to make up other words. Another time and another place, it could have been funny. Phil Griffiths, the sponsor, was entirely right to remind BC management of their responsibilities to manage the team. So now, with this and other inappropriate antics generating the need to achieve control, there was a Team Agreement.

It was a poorly worded document. I was required to wear every item of team clothing – hats, gloves, jerseys, etc – until I had gained express permission to take them off. So each day, I was to come to breakfast like the Michelin man, with six jerseys on and two pairs of gloves, and ask permission to take some off? I don't think so. I could point out other trivial things, but at its heart was a serious issue. I had to obey every decision of the coach or manager and I did not have any right of appeal.

I didn't object to BC officials making decisions, as long as they were 'reasonable' – that was their prerogative – but the denial of appeal rights was over the top and I refused to sign. I negotiated with Peter Keen and we agreed an amendment. I inserted the word 'reasonable' and had a means of appeal. So now I would abide by all 'reasonable' decisions. I actually think we resolved it all quite well.

GB had an appalling record in the World Mountain Bike Championships: no gold medals in any category, and many years since their last medal in cross-country. The Sierra Nevada circuit was tricky, particularly one steep and rocky descent which presented a dilemma: do I ride and risk falling, or dismount and clamber down? There was only one way to find out, so in training I rode off the edge, realising almost immediately that it was the wrong decision. Halfway down I lost control and went over the handlebars. Imagine a 'black' ski slope with rocks. I did a complete flip and landed on my back, cutting the ends of three fingers on one hand.

Not that falls and rocks were my biggest problem. The support staff decided that they would modify my bike for me. At the time, the equipment was such that you either rode with a 'long' chain or a 'short' chain. With a 'long' chain, you would be able to get the big front ring and biggest sprocket at the rear, and this enabled you to put it in any gear during the race. The disadvantage was that in the middle ring and smallest sprocket, the chain was loose and could jump off very easily and you would normally have to dismount to put the chain back on. With a 'short' chain, there was little danger of unshipping the chain during a race, but it required that you remember not to select the biggest sprocket and large chain-ring, otherwise you would wreck the shifter mechanism. I never found remembering that too taxing and always rode with a 'short' chain. Also, if you were dull enough to ride in big ring, big sprocket, the chain was most out of line and most inefficient. I was rather keen on winning, so did not have lots of spare power to waste in this manner. I always made sure the alignment was good.

This was my first time away with GB. I did my recce of the course the day before my race, decided on my strategy and left my bike with the mechanic, alongside all of the state-of-the-art machines bought with Lottery funds for the WCPP riders. When I collected my bike on the morning of the race, the gear mechanism had been changed and the chain was now 'long'. My bike had been changed without me being asked or consulted in any way. It was my bike, my equipment, so I got the mechanic and the team manager, Simon Burney, together and asked them to change it back. I was very polite and explained that I was not used to riding with my chain long. Simon was having none of it; he told me the mechanic was not changing it, and I had to ride it like it was. I insisted I wanted it changed, but they seemed annoyed that I was questioning their decision. Simon is very tall and even if he doesn't intimidate some people, he intimidated me then. Nowadays I would just tell him he was an overbearing fool and if the mechanic wouldn't do it, I would find someone else who would, but at that stage I didn't feel I could do this.

The race was two laps. During the last lap, I was in the lead and just ahead of Sonja Traxel of Switzerland as we both elected to run down the tricky descent. At the bottom, we both leapt on our bikes. The long chain had become unshipped during the run, just as I feared it would, and I was left at the side of the track putting a long chain on, as Sonja rode past and away from me to win.

As I crossed the line, the GB staff all came and congratulated me on getting a bronze medal. I cried; I was in the lead and could have won. As I chased after Sonja I made mistakes, becoming more upset after each one, so I was even passed for silver. Simon never apologised, nor did British Cycling. Even after Dad wrote to the CEO, Peter King, the only concession we got was the assurance that as the bike I rode was my property, not a WCPP machine, the mechanics could do only what I specifically asked. No longer could they modify my bike against my wishes. Was this an unreasonable request? Given the reluctance with which the agreement was given, this seemed to be the case.

There is one more necessary twist to recount from Sierra Nevada. At the end of 1998, I had asked BC to send me, as other nations chose to do for their riders, to the Junior World Championships despite being one year younger than the UCI age range. BC informed me that they would not do this. Had they done so, then during 1999 they would have seen a number of performances which may have prevented the 'shock' that occurred in August of that year. I had been British Youth U16 champion for four years and not lost a single race in that time. In the GB team at Sierra Nevada was a girl the same age as me. We were talking about attending the event and I was telling her that it was the first World Championships for me. 'Oh, BC sent me to the World Championships last year,' was her response. I was speechless. It took all my self-control not to run down the corridor and storm into the manager's room.

That summer was a tough time. I was trapped in a surreal vortex: age restrictions coming out of nowhere, Olympic selection issues, travelling to the flattest place in the country to ride behind the 'Fun' riders to qualify for the Mountain Bike World Championships. There was the pack hunting me at the National Road Race and then the fiasco with the chain. It was all crazy. My form was beginning to disappear under the stress of it all.

I was still keen, however, and there was still plenty to look forward to with the Junior World Track Championships ahead in Italy. Craig and Dad would drive down to the Alps, drop Mum off and then head over to Fiorenzuola d'Arda to watch me race. Ahead of them, I would be going to Italy with Shane Sutton and Marshall Thomas. Marshall was the British junior track team manager and although an employee of the WCPP, he never gave the impression of wanting to be involved in the politics, which was a blessed relief. He just did his job, very well. He rang up twice on the night of 13 June just before the ill-fated National Championships, trying to get me to miss the race and concentrate on the World Track Championships instead. Why did he ring up twice? Had he got wind of what was afoot? Certainly he was not ringing up to try and be difficult, Marshall was always totally supportive.

My first race was the individual pursuit where I felt I was a medal contender. I had completed my warm-up routine and was moving across ready to race, when one of the support staff announced that one of my wheels had a puncture. There was now a general panic as a replacement wheel had to be found. During this time, I was losing the timing effect of my warm-up routine, as well as being made nervous by the general pandemonium of the helpers. This was in complete contrast to when Craig and I rode track meetings, where Dad always had a spare wheel ready for instant replacement and everything like this was handled calmly and quietly. Spooked out, I finished in seventh place, which was disappointing and well below my expectations.

I was really down and needed my family with me. All those miles, Thetford and back, Manchester and back, Cheshire and back – the stress was building and it was then I got a phone call. The car had broken down and my family were marooned a hundred miles away. I made a tactical mess of my other world title bid, the points race, and missed out on the bronze medal by just one point. I was distraught. My attempts at World Champion-ship level that summer had produced a third, fourth and seventh, which was a long way short of what I knew I could do. I didn't fear the riders I was competing against. I had beaten the girl who took gold several times when riding against her in Achterveld. There was a different and bigger threat to me.

Straight after the track championships, I joined the family at our regular campsite in the Alps. We went out for a gentle ride and had a swim in the mountain lake. After supper, Dad said it would make a relaxing job to repair the punctured tubular on the track wheel. He pumped it up to find out where the air was leaking from. There was no hissing. We left it and checked it the next day. It was fully inflated – in fact, on our return to the UK, Craig used the wheel for the rest of the season without replacing the tube – and as we sat around that evening I realised very clearly where the main threat was coming from. It was a real low point, but from that nadir I started to feel strong and confident. I rode the mountains with Craig, Mum and Dad and had a great few days with them.

My mood lifted again when I got home and received an 'A' grade in my A-level Maths and would have one less A-level to do in the Upper Sixth, which meant one thing – more time for training.

*

The debacle at the National Road Race had certainly rever-
berated around a lot of places. The British Olympic team were
due to ride a stage race in Canada in late August, as preparation for the Sydney Olympics. Other nations were adopting
the same strategy, so there was going to be a strong field there.
Louise and Phil Jones were sympathetic to my situation: they
arranged Elite Cymru funding and they planned a trip for a
Welsh team to compete in the Canadian race, which would be
ideal preparation for the World Junior Road Race. With Phil
heading up the support crew, I wouldn't have to inspect my
bike every time I picked it up. I could relax and enjoy the
racing which consisted of 470km in six stages over five days.
It was the longest race I had ever attempted, and I needed to
conserve energy to make sure I was competitive to the end.
Apart from Louise, our Welsh team was relatively inexperi-
enced, but nevertheless we were highly motivated to do our
best. The GB team, managed by Ken Matheson, included
Sara Symington and Ceris Gilfillan who had been selected
for Sydney. Yvonne, the third selected rider, had opted to
complete her Olympic preparations back in Manchester, with
Peter Keen. One out of every six riders in the field was off
to Sydney for their respective nations; this was going to be
a good race.

The first day over 97km was about settling into the race for
me and I finished a respectable 14th in a bunch sprint. I also
played it carefully on the second day, which at almost 130km
was the longest. I was not unhappy to miss a breakaway of two
riders, but at the end of the stage, and now feeling confident,
I put everything into winning the bunch sprint for third place.
My first senior international podium was a great boost.

Stage 3 was 100km that climbed into mountains compara-
ble with the Alps. With 15km to go, I broke away with three

other riders, Ceris, Lyne Bessette (the Commonwealth Road Race champion from Canada) and reigning Olympic champion Jeannie Longo of France. We were still together at the end. It was an unusual and exciting finish. Lyne was racing into her home town and judged it perfectly to win; I nearly got up to her, with Ceris and Jeannie behind. I was content to have just beaten the defending Olympic champion and almost pipped the Commonwealth champion, not to mention the recent winner of the British Championships.

I often found I had quite a few GB jerseys around me for the rest of the race. I felt that if I had turned off the course and gone into a Wal-Mart car park, I would have been trailed in there by my new 'fans', so keen were they to follow in a little queue behind my rear wheel.

For the time-trial the next day, Ceris, Jeannie and all the Olympians were on their state-of-the-art, low-pro carbon fibre bikes with aero helmets doing a run-out for a couple of weeks later at Sydney. Nicola Bedwell's husband and I were at my machine where we took off a bottle cage and struggled to get the special 'clearance offer' tri-bars, of which Dad had invested in four sets, onto my road bike. The Welsh team was run on a shoestring but we loved it. I was so grateful of the opportunity to race there and the financial backing from Elite Cymru that made our little adventure possible. Each rider had one jersey for the week and we washed them every night and hung them in our rooms hoping they would be dry for the next morning.

In the time-trial I was okay, but without all the equipment I was never going to be competing for the win. However, in the afternoon came another chance. The Sydney Olympic course was so flat it was more than likely going to come to a bunch sprint, and the selected GB Olympic sprinter was Sara Symington. In the short 40km criterium, a break of five riders went away early in the race, which left Sara and myself available for the bunch sprint. We both knew that it was not about sixth place. Sara and the GB team had been shaken that I had won the bunch sprint for third place on the second day. Sara couldn't go on the climb on the next day; that was Ceris's forte and I had beaten her there. My GB 'fan club' deserted my rear wheel and were now setting up Sara. I saw her looking at me. We both knew what this meant. One sprinter was going to the Olympics and another wasn't. It was a fair and square sprint and Ken didn't look very happy after I had beaten Sara.

Five continuous days' racing was four more than I had done at this level before, and blowing up on the final hill of the final day was nothing for me to get worried about. Ceris won the General Classification (GC), narrowly beating Jeannie Longo, with me in fifth, about two minutes behind. I was fully satisfied to have shown to myself that I could hold my own with some of the world's best riders. Did I deserve to go to the Olympics? Well, the facts were that I certainly beat quite a few who were going. I had made my point.

I returned to the UK while the British team went on to Sydney. As they prepared for the Olympics, British Cycling had requested that I attend yet another qualifying event, this time for the World Junior Time-Trial Championships. I had to win to guarantee to be selected; any other places were entirely discretionary. I knew exactly how to translate 'discretionary' when it related to me. What I had done in Canada was irrelevant. Instead, I had to do my best on a dodgy course which we had to share with quite an assortment of local traffic. At one stage, a tractor created a mobile roadblock and then I punctured.

A possible – *probable* – scenario played out in my mind. I might have beaten the GB Olympic team and a whole pile of other Olympians in Canada, but I felt sure that a DNF (did not finish) would absolutely guarantee my non-selection for a junior event, as I felt there was one set of rules for me and, as the Mountain Bike World Championships showed, rules could be applied differently to other riders. I knew what I had to do. Dad was riding round the course watching and he came across a man with a puzzled look on his face, holding my bike. Dad stopped and spoke to him. He had a tale of a little girl pulling up and asking, very politely, if she could borrow his bike for a short time. I jumped on his bike and sped off, leaving mine with him. I won and I was on my way.

A few nights later, I was up in the early hours of the morning with Mum, Dad and Craig watching the Women's Olympic Road Race. Yvonne and Ceris did an excellent job as the leadout train. Sadly, they had not worked out that they needed to have Sara Symington, rather than the Dutch riders, behind them. Leontien van Moorsel, the winner, should forever be in their debt. If we were disappointed by the result, at least Ken Matheson sent us back to bed with some great memories. I don't know where doing live TV interviews during the race sits in the team manager's job description, but Hugh Porter, the BBC commentator, was speaking to Ken during the race. At one stage, Hugh asked him what he thought about the current position of the race, and Ken said he didn't know because he had just been out for a coffee.

Just been out for a coffee! It's the biggest race in four years for the GB WCPP and he doesn't know what's going on.

I knew I would have to be patient and wait another four years for my turn at Olympic glory. In the meantime, there were plenty of races to look forward to, starting the following month with the World Junior Road Race Championships title in Plouay.

CHAPTER SEVEN
The Laurel and Hardy Support Team

I was away with the British team again. You cannot look at it with the perspective of the current well-oiled BC machine. Although Mandy Jones had won the senior Women's World Road title in 1982, that was our last world road race medal. Year after year, GB had simply entered riders who mostly didn't even finish let alone ride with any thought of victory. While I have had many issues with British Cycling over the years, I must admit that now we are light years ahead of where we were. Plouay, however, was possibly the all-time low.

Where to start? There was the GB coach who arrived without a map of the area. Unsurprisingly, the local shops had sold out when the World Championships came to call. The year before, Dad and I had bought three, so I had mine and a spare one. I did the decent thing and gave him one and then we went out on our bikes. At one stage, he insisted that we should go down a road that I was certain was only a farm drive. I refused and waited for his return. The look on his face was priceless.

On another occasion we were driving to the course in two of the brand new BC WCPP team cars. No expense spared, custom roof racks, interconnecting radios, colourful decals and all sorts of gadgets – some of which they knew how to use and others maybe not. We had already got lost once on the way to the course, so now we were in a bit of a hurry trying to make up time. Suddenly, there was the wail of an emergency vehicle siren. This, I kid you not, is what transpired:

Front vehicle to back vehicle: 'You need to pull over and let him past.'
Back vehicle: 'There is nothing behind us. It's you, you have turned on the siren.'
Front vehicle: 'No, it's not me, it's you. You must have turned it on.'
Back vehicle: 'No it's you, I've done nothing.'
Front vehicle: 'Let's pull over and see who it is.'

So the cars pull over and the drivers leap out. They inspect each other's car and decide that one of them is making the noise. They decide it was the back vehicle.

Front vehicle: 'There has to be a switch here somewhere – what were you fiddling with?
Back vehicle: 'I wasn't fiddling with anything – it just went off.'

It was like watching two naughty kids. After some time searching, without any luck, they then got on their knees and were looking underneath the dashboard. All the time, the wailing continued. Eventually, they rang British Cycling at Manchester to find out where the switch was. Peace at last. I was trying to win a world title and somehow I had stumbled on to the set of a Laurel and Hardy film! What next? Somebody showing up with a ladder and a pot of paint?

The day before the time-trial we set off in the cars at 9.30 when the sun was shining and all was briefly well with the world. After way too many detours and disappearing up blind alleys, we eventually got to the wrong point on the course at about 3pm – just when it was beginning to chuck down with rain, exactly as the weather forecast stated it would. We were racing the World Championship the next morning and here we were, soaking wet, freezing cold and hadn't eaten since early in the morning, with yet another hour's drive back to the hotel to contemplate our misery. Still we hadn't seen the entire course. What a shambles. Dad had rung that morning and offered to pick both of us girls up and take us to and from the course to do the ride. 'No thank you, Mr Cooke, we are more than capable of doing that.'

Mum and Dad had hired a cottage that was a short walk from the course. British Cycling were based 30 miles from the course and the staff clearly had only a hazy idea on how to get there. Weeks before, aware of the potential disasters, Dad had asked Peter King if I could stay with Mum and Dad. 'Certainly not.' Dad had then offered to move our family out of the cottage and give the booking completely free to the British team. 'It's a walk from the course, please take it.' 'No thank you, Mr Cooke, we are quite content the best arrangements are being made.' I could go on and on.

The time-trial, not unexpectedly, was a complete mess. I was not rested or in anywhere near the right place mentally and I came tenth. Not that I was the only victim of their incompetence. At the start area, I had completed my warm-up and was making my way to the start ramp when I saw Claire Dixon already waiting, standing there shivering in the rain. She was scheduled to start 12 minutes after me, so what was she doing there? Apparently, Laurel and Hardy didn't want her to miss the start, so they had cut her warm-up short, without any discussion, and made her stand in the freezing cold rain close to the start, while they went and got in the warm car. You couldn't make it up.

I was fed up and angry after the time-trial. This should have been the year of my emergence on to the world cycling scene. Instead, all I had to show was a bronze in the mountain bike championships, nothing from the track and time-trial and I had been blocked from going to the Olympics. Mum likes her poetry and is a big fan of Rudyard Kipling's 'If', particularly the second verse and the part that goes:

> If you can dream and not make dreams your master
> If you can think and not make thoughts your aim
> If you can meet with Triumph and Disaster
> And treat those two impostors just the same.

I could never go along with that. I have never wanted to be consoled about a failure, I am just plain angry. I want to live with that anger, not to feel consoled about losing. To say that I was pumped up for the road race would be an understatement. If anyone else had ideas about winning, then they would have to deal with me first.

My race started at 9.15am and three full days before, I was advising that I would need an early breakfast. British Cycling had taken their own chef, especially for the event. Cyclists need to be eating about three hours before a road race, so digestion is complete. Even though I asked very nicely, apparently it was entirely impossible for the chef to do anything whatsoever until 7.30am, so I got up early and cooked my own breakfast and enjoyed every second of doing so. I hope the chef was snoring. This was my day, my show.

I got to the front quickly, knowing the danger of crashes early on in junior races. After about 3km the road narrowed and I heard the sound of a crash behind; unfortunately all my team-mates were caught up in it, so any tactics we may have had were now gone. I was now on my own against the other teams. But this wasn't a race where I was going to let anyone else dictate the tactics. I was going to ride this race from the front. I attacked on a climb and established a break of four with Clare Hall-Patch of Canada, Russia's Natalia Boyarskaya and Magdalena Sadlecka of Poland. Like me, none of my fellow breakaway companions had been in the medals in the time-trial, so we were all well motivated for the break to stay away. On the other hand, it meant that the bunch still contained good strong riders, the medallists from the time-trial including winner Juliette Vandekerckhove of France aiming to do the double in front of her home crowd.

We built up a lead of 30 seconds, so most of the time we were out of sight of the bunch in the winding hilly lanes, but the last long climb was on a straight wide road and every lap the bunch were able to see us and become incentivised to chase. It was clear that we had to continue working hard to maintain our slender lead, but as the laps went by it seemed more likely that we were going to be able to stay away and my thoughts started turning to how I might win.

Being four was good in that we could share the work, but it also meant that someone was going to miss out on a medal. I was confident if it came down to a sprint finish; I had prac-tised enough on the course with Craig and Dad. However, the grand way to win any race is alone. The question was when to attack. Too far from the finish, with more than one lap to go, and they would probably combine forces to bring me back and I would be weakened, so I opted for an attack on the last lap using a climb. I attacked but they all came back to me; however I was not too concerned as there was still the final long climb to come and my attack had provided me with some useful intelligence about the relative strengths of my breakaway companions.

All four of us were still riding well together, sharing the pace-making. There was always an extra effort to be made during your spell on the front, and then as you went to the back of the group you were able to recover in the slipstream of the other riders, ready for your next turn on the front. I wanted to shuffle our order, so that by the next time I attacked, I had set up a situation with Clare and Magdalena in line still recovering after their efforts and Natalia on the front. Natalia was showing some signs of tiring, she would be the least effective chasing and would momentarily block the other two. I got my rivals into the order I wanted, with a couple of discreet moves on corners.

Approaching the final climb, I started to feel the tension build as I waited for the right moment to attack. We were about a third of the way up when I made my move. I succeeded in dropping Natalia and Clare, but Magdalena was able to respond and clawed her way back to me. I still had a significant portion of the climb left. I attacked again towards the top, and this time gained the gap I needed to prevent Magdalena taking advantage of my slipstream.

I still had over 2km to the finish line. I rode like a demon, my style shot to pieces. I was just so desperate to get to that finishing line, my body bobbing up and down as I used every muscle I possessed to make that bike go as fast as it could. I let out a huge roar of triumph as I crossed the line. I had done it. I had finally won the right to wear a World champion's jersey. I had fought the whole year through a system in which very few seemed to want to help me, and many more appeared to want to block me. I even managed a smile the next morning when the chef found himself cooking breakfast for the junior boys at 6.00am.

At the conclusion of Plouay, there was time for reflection. Together with Mum and Dad and a few other people, we constructed a 29-page report for British Cycling. I have printed it off again as I write this. There are pages of recommendations: lists of emergency contact numbers, travel plans, accommodation addresses, daily bulletin board, communication of travel arrangements, eating times, arranging that chefs are available to do early meals, etc. I look at that document now and see how complete it was and am proud of its professionalism. We sent it off to British Cycling.

Up until the early '90s, even as late as Bradley Wiggins's junior track campaign of 1998, little groups could be fairly self-contained within the BC structure, but Lottery funding had changed all that. In 2000, there was a large machine. It comprised lots of people, many of whom were competent – they weren't all Laurel and Hardy figures – but from where I was looking there wasn't enough high-quality talent to spread around.

Prior to Plouay, Dad stood accused by Peter King of not letting his staff get on with 'looking after' his daughter when away with the British team. Why couldn't he just let go? Dad ripped into him. Had Peter actually looked closely at some of his staff? Had he watched the way some of them behaved? (At that time, we did not have Graeme Obree's autobiography, where Graeme states that during a track World Cup in Milan, some members of the British cycling team urinated in his bed. But tales of these antics and worse were rife at the time. Professionals they were not.) Plouay provided more than enough evidence that change was needed in British Cycling. This was in contrast to other areas of cycling such as the BSCA, where my parents had been happy to let me go away between the ages of 12 and 16 to Holland, because they could trust the people I was going with.

In more philosophical moments, I tell myself I just happened to crash into the wrong people at the wrong time. It was only one gold medal, and a junior one at that, but nearly 20 years without any road race medals of any form was a very long time. At least some people at British Cycling were now paying attention. Peter King, the CEO, received the report and assured us that many lessons had been learnt and things would change.

And they did. They needed a new women's endurance coach. Recognising that they had no one who was capable, they made their search global and recruited an experienced Canadian with a successful record, and, unique among BC coaching staff, she was female. Peg Hill was going to be different. By the time of the 2001 World Championships in Lisbon, most of the Laurel and Hardy support staff were out. British Cycling was moving towards being the professional organisation that it is today.

The World Road Championships are always a time for meeting people, and although it is a gathering of national teams, the managers of professional teams are always there to keep an eye out for potential riders from the U23 and junior races. Giancarlo Ghillioni, a Swiss, introduced himself as a representative of the Italian team Acca Due O. He'd been on the phone to the team president after watching the race and wanted to know if I'd be available to be a *stagiaire* (a temporary, unpaid position) with the team the next season.

Wow! Acca Due O was the No.1 women's road team at the time. There was also a feeling of relief that I was finally talking to someone who knew what the sport was all about.

I was still only 17 and had my A-levels to complete the next summer, which meant I couldn't join the team for another year. Education came first, but in the meantime Giancarlo said it was important to learn Italian, or at least make a start. When I returned to Brynteg, I approached my French teacher, Mrs Walsh, asking if there was someone who could help. She suggested Mrs Hodges, who taught German but was Italian, from Bolzano. She was excited by the idea and recommended some *Teach Yourself* books from which I could start learning, and then she took me for revision one lunchtime a week. The decision to do some of my exams early had paid dividends, because now I could take this extra study burden without worrying about time at school. My future beckoned and 2001 promised to be an exciting year on all fronts.

CHAPTER EIGHT
First Taste of Italy

U ncle Chris had been at Plouay with us and he too met some interesting people. Travelling home to Moscow, where he worked as a finance director for an international company, he bumped into Natalia Boyarskaya and the rest of the Russian junior team. He congratulated her on her ride and introduced himself to their coach, Anatoly Voronin. Somehow the conversation turned into an invitation for me to go to Russia and join the team the following year at their pre-season training camp at Sochi.

To me, Sochi sounded even colder than Wick in February, but this was an unusual opportunity not to be missed. I'd watched the footage of the various races in Plouay many times and seen how well the Russian team rode together, and there were a good number of Russian riders in the women's professional teams. Natalia was likely to end up at the sharp end in Lisbon later in the year when I aimed to defend my title, and having a friendly face in the race would be useful – for all the sincerity and enthusiasm of the British girls my age, the performance gap was just too large.

I joined the Russians in my half-term school holiday. It was surreal from the moment Uncle Chris met me at Moscow airport and took me on a tour driven by his chauffeur Igor. We

101

saw the Kremlin and Red Square, its colours and turrets bright against the snow all around. Early the next morning I was back at the airport bound for Sochi.

Anatoly met me at the airport in his very old Mercedes and drove me to an old Soviet-period 'house of rest' that had been closed down for the winter and made available to Anatoly's squad of 20 or so promising boys and girls. They had organised themselves rather traditionally, with the boys taking care of the maintenance and cleaning of the bikes, while the girls did all the cooking in the kitchen, preparing food bought from the local market each morning by Anatoly. The facilities were very basic, adequate for our needs, but the place was freezing cold. I had a sitting room and bedroom upstairs, each with a small portable radiator. I needed both of them in my bedroom at night. To do this, I had to stretch the cable of the one connected to the wall in the sitting room so I could have it in my bedroom and jam the door shut over the cable to keep the heat in. Clothes were hand-washed in the bathtub.

I loved it. The team did not have much in the way of good equipment and clothes, but they all really enjoyed what they were doing, and that made a difference. Many of the riders, like Natalia who was from Siberia, had travelled thousands of miles by train, taking several days, in order to be there. Training was based on the classic formula of gradually building stamina by long, steady, relatively slow rides each day.

The harsh surrounds matched their attitude to team tactics. One night after a ride into the mountains, Anatoly showed me the video he had taken that day of the girls behind us, who were practising team tactics while riding on the snow-covered roads. The idea was for two riders, acting as team-mates, to try to prevent a single rider behind them from getting ahead, by slowing down and even using pincer movements to block and harry, while the rider changed angles to counter the blocking moves and somehow get in front. Finally, after being frustrated for a while, the rider tried to find a gap on the left – only to be cut off and knocked sideways into the snow piled up at the side of the road! Barging each other off into the snow was all part of the 'toughening up'. These were girls who were younger than Natalia and me, and good on them. After a memorable week of adventures on the roads around Sochi, I bid farewell to my new friends and looked forward to meeting them at races later that year.

The dates of my half-term had also coincided with the big presentation of Acca Due O in Italy. Giancarlo had kept in touch and I'd been invited to be there to join the team. If that went well, I could have a trial placement in the summer when my exams were finished.

I arrived in Treviso directly from Sochi and felt honoured to be on the same training ride as the best riders in cycling. I tried my basic Italian on the girls; they were very welcoming and I enjoyed the camaraderie. I met Maurizio Fabretto, the team president, who was inspired to create the team four years before when he came across a group of Lithuanian riders living out of the back of a van as they competed around Europe. He was a flamboyant character.

On the night of the team's official presentation Maurizio was in his element, hosting a spectacular launch party in Castelfranco Veneto. It seemed like there were millions of journalists, we had a fancy meal and then every guest went home with 'Team Edition' bottles of Astoria Prosecco labelled with a photo of Diana Ziliute and her Olympic medal. I couldn't wait to be part of something like this.

Cycling is a fantastic sport; only one rider can win races, but the collaborative element is really important and can often be the reason why certain riders win and others don't, and it's fabulous to see what a good team can collectively achieve. It was not something I had experienced in any meaningful way in my life so far, and I couldn't wait for this next phase of my career to begin.

Meanwhile, back in Manchester the BC WCPP had read our 29-page document and taken on board our comments. Things were going to change for 2001. Ken Matheson and the member of staff who had been responsible for the junior women's team at Plouay were heading for pastures new. The WCPP was evolving and I felt very optimistic about the season ahead, where my goals were world junior titles in track, mountain bike, time-trial and road race. It was agreed that I would be able to take a trusted neutral mentor with me to both the track and road championships, and for mountain biking the British coach Gary Foord would work individually with me. I was highly motivated. My winter training had gone well, it was now just Craig and me on the school ride as Dad had changed jobs to teach at another school. Craig was becoming stronger and the rides were becoming very competitive, with the sprint to the Volvo garage reaching new heights of intensity. With maths out of the way, I had more free time due to less school work and could add in an extra ride like the Windmill circuit, to increase the volume of training when I didn't have lessons.

We continued to ride cyclo-cross races through the winter, although I knew it was likely to be my last season. My heart lay in road racing and I wanted to concentrate on that. The cyclo-cross scene in Britain was fairly small, the big races were all in Holland and Belgium and if I wanted to ride international World Cups the whole season, it would be really hard to do with such little support. So it was time for a final blast.

The British Cyclo-Cross Championships were held in Sutton Park, near Birmingham. With both Craig and me racing, we arranged that we would pack all the equipment on the Saturday morning and then travel up, hoping to do some easy practice laps in the afternoon. We were halfway through the journey when the car broke down. What to do? Should we wait for the recovery vehicle to pick us up – which would probably mean we would get back to Bridgend when everything was closed – and how were we going to get to Birmingham for our races first thing on Sunday?

Dad had a plan. Instead of calling the recovery service and being taken home, he called Mum at home and asked her to ride down to the local van hire centre in Bridgend and rent a vehicle big enough to take the three of us, the four bikes, spare wheels, a generator, power washer and our bags, then drive up to where we were stranded, an hour and a half away. He waited before calling the recovery company and they came out to us, arriving shortly after Mum reached us with the hired van. As soon as Mum had arrived, we loaded the bikes and everything into the back of the hire van and set off to Birmingham, leaving Mum with the broken car with her bike in the back, going home on the back of the recovery truck. We arrived just over two hours later than scheduled but did everything we needed to do. We rang Mum at home to make sure she had arrived safely.

I won the senior cyclo-cross title, beating Louise Robinson by four seconds. Louise was silver medallist in the inaugural World Championships the previous year and so this was quite a scalp. Craig's race was due to start as soon as mine finished. Journalists wanted to take photos and ask lots of questions, as Louise was a very accomplished and decorated cyclo-cross rider, so the result obviously generated a lot of interest, but I needed to be there for Craig's start. After the medal ceremony on the podium, I paused for the barest number of pictures and I was off. I ran from the podium, telling the journalists I would be back later, I popped my big silver trophy into the plastic box where we kept the bits and pieces like gloves and brushes and rags to clean the bikes, zipped up my tracksuit top over my British champion's jersey and then leapt back on my bike and zoomed over to Craig who was on the start line, so I could take his top and gloves from him just before he started. Dad was busy in the pits adjusting the spare bikes from my seating position to Craig's and making sure all was ready for him. I arrived just in time. Later, I went back to the journalists and then helped Dad out. Craig was third, which was pleasing as a first-year junior. We went back home, showed the medals to Mum and then put them in boxes under our bed in our rooms – ostentatious displays of awards were not allowed. After listening to our account, Mum just asked Dad to confirm that we had both given everything in our races and behaved properly.

We often had people come up to us at races. Many of the compliments were very touching. Sometime after this, at another race where just Craig and Dad were present, a lady came up to them. She had been attending cycling events for many years, she said, and had often noticed our family with Craig, me and Mum competing, while Dad ran around and organised everything. The lady just wanted to tell Dad that she liked the way we supported each other, which she said had been epitomised by me not dwelling on my race result at the British Championships and instead putting my trophy in a plastic box so that I could sprint off and help my brother. I didn't find out about that conversation for some years, but it just reiterated how bonded we have been as a family and how important that was to my career.

With all my enthusiasm and the extra time on my hands, I added in more training to get really fit for the Cyclo-Cross World Championships in Tabor, Czech Republic, at the end of January. Well, that was the idea anyway. Preparation was going well through November and into December, and I was training harder than I had ever done in my life. I rode in the senior World Championships, as there was no women's junior category. Craig was selected for the junior male category. Martin Eadon of BCCA was manager of the British team for Tabor and it was a real pleasure going away with him and the team. We had a few days to test the snowy course and get the hang of sliding round the corners on the snow and ice. I liked the circuit, it was fast and had short run-ups along a slope, and even had one section where it went through the main beer tent – the crowds were really loud in there! In the race, I didn't do as well as I'd hoped, finishing seventh and just behind Louise Robinson, who was sixth.

As the cyclo-cross season finished, there was a terrible out-break of foot-and-mouth disease forcing the slaughter of millions of sheep and cattle. It caused the closure of numerous community and festival events and also meant no mountain bike races or training, which made preparing for the World Championships in September very challenging. I was now working closely with BC mountain bike coach Gary Foord, who was very supportive and entirely professional in his atti-tude. It was another good working relationship and epitomised how things were changing during 2001. In the meantime, it gave me more freedom to concentrate on road and track, as my first big target would be the World Track Championships, in Los Angeles in July. At that time, Manchester was the only indoor track in Britain, meaning that each track session involved a 400-mile round trip.

In May, I went to Lisbon to check out the course for the road championships, which would be held in October, with Claire Dixon, her coach Peter Vernon and Dad. We were met by a representative of the Portuguese Cycling Federation who couldn't do enough for this World champion, making me feel very special – an unusual experience. He showed us all the details of the course, including the dual carriageway that would host the start–finish area. This was newly constructed and not quite finished, so that although it was surfaced, no traffic was allowed on it. Claire, Dad and I did a leadout train and sprints along it. If the race was to finish as a sprint, I would be looking forward to it.

In June, I competed in a round of the Junior Nations Track competition in Orleans, France. I took part in an omnium, with four events held over one day. I felt awful and performed badly. The poor results made it clear I was doing too much of everything.

I needed to rest. I had to stop and consider the fine balance between not enough training and not enough rest. If I rested now, it meant my track preparation would be pushed back to July, giving me only a few weeks of specialist training before the World Track Championships, but so be it. I gave it a couple of weeks. Shane Sutton was rightly adamant that I needed a lot of rest. I had tests and these confirmed exactly what my own training traces were showing – that the decline had started in late December – as I belatedly looked at them with a critical eye. I had a simple philosophy – more is better – and had been overdoing it, seeing every opportunity without lessons and homework as a time to train as hard as I could.

For 2001, British Cycling was very good about the selection criteria. As opposed to the situation 12 months before, I was now pre-selected for all Junior World Championships. No one felt the irony more than me when I now deselected myself from the World Track Championships. I was just not recovering fast enough during those first four weeks after Orleans. Those around me were concerned that I might not even be recovered by the end of the year.

While I rested, I thought hard about my future. Although I had wanted to ride all disciplines for as long as possible, it was clear that too much could go wrong if I tried to do everything. The risk was that the other events – mountain bike, time-trial and road races – could also suffer and I would end up with nothing. I wondered for a while if I was just taking the easy way out, but I had reached a crossroads and had to make some tough decisions. It was time to start specialising.

In the UK, many cyclo-cross venues did not have washing facilities. Although Dad had a portable generator and could always manage to boil up enough water for us to have a good wash and get clean, either Craig or myself, or more often both of us, had a stinking cold at some time during the season. Cyclo-cross was not an Olympic sport and therefore was the poor relation in terms of the funding – they had virtually nothing. Whether this was the reason why the support staff and selectors were such a good bunch of people, who did it for love, not reward, I don't know, but certainly I was going to miss working with them.

Riding the track meant going to the only full-sized indoor velodrome in the country at Manchester. Logistically, it was difficult and expensive. Giving up aspirations for 2001 freed up a lot of time and made my programme far more flexible as I recovered. I thought that maybe I would keep my options open to come back to track racing in 2002.

CHAPTER NINE
Triple Junior World Champion

Maurizio and Giancarlo had been happy with my first visit to Acca Due O and offered me a *stagiaire* place with the team. About a week after my last A-level exam, the signs were that I was now recovering and I needed some good workouts, but not too many. I packed my road and mountain bike, my team jersey and shorts that I'd kept safely since February, and travelled to Treviso. Mum and Dad were at work, so I took all my bikes and kit on my own. As I settled into my seat on the airplane, I thought this was it. I had spent my last day in school and now I was off to the centre of the professional cycling world. I was Junior World champion and was about to go and stay with the world's No.1 team. I was only 18 and this was going to be the start of a terrific adventure.

It had been warm in the UK when I left. When I walked out of the air-conditioned luxury of Venice's newly opened Marco Polo airport, the heat of the Italian summer hit me. I arrived on a Friday and was informed that we would be leaving at 7am the next morning for a race. I was going to ride in their team! Brilliant.

Now that I was in the mad and occasionally bad world of professional racing, I was fully aware that I might encounter a doping culture. Mum, Dad and I had a conversation about drugs towards the end of 2000. It was short but stays in my memory. I promised them that I would not do drugs in any way; and I have always kept that promise.

Dad made it his business to be aware of the possible pitfalls of the sporting arena his daughter was now entering. BBC radio's *Inside Edge* programme broadcast a report on the Tour de France and the use of Performance Enhancing Drugs (PEDs). At one stage, the reporter claimed the sport was doing everything it could, they were trying hard but no test was yet developed, and that after the Festina 1998 Tour scandal all the riders were now clean. Dad was livid and rang up the BBC and spoke to them about the shallowness of the report.

Drugs had moved on from stimulants and muscle enhancements, and endurance athletes were now using the drug erythropoietin (EPO) which artificially increased the number of red cells in the blood. Dad had researched a Canadian laboratory that was developing a test for EPO and forwarded the details to the BBC, including the name of the professor leading the project. The BBC followed up and did another radio interview, this time with Hein Verbruggen, president of the UCI. For this programme, they now had some decent background facts to counter the platitude the doper is so fond of, that 'we're doing as much as we can, move along, nothing to see here.' The journalists did a great job as they really gave Verbruggen a tough time, asking him why the UCI was not introducing EPO testing. 'Don't tell us the excuses about not having a test,' they put to him, confident in their knowledge after having spoken with the Canadian professor. Hein was taken aback by the journalists' understanding of the subject.

We were realists about what I might find in Italy. I understood that the introduction to the drugs culture in cycling was probably not going to be obvious but more by gradual exposure, and the first 'little' steps would be presented as not really doing anything bad. And then we came back to 'IF'. Mum and Dad could not have made it clearer: doing my best was all that mattered. If my best got me 24th place, that was exactly as good as third or first. If I got beaten and beaten by cheats, then as long as I'd done my best, walking away with my integrity was going to be a lot better for my life than living it out as a perpetual lie. Imagine shaking the hands of people that came up to you, when you were old, and them telling you what a great winner you were, when you knew inside you were a rotten fraud. Fortunately, I was in a team that did not urge its riders to take that path. While I was at school attaining my qualifications, this adventure into cycling and becoming a professional cyclist was there alongside a very distinct possibility that it might well be a short-lived enterprise. That I might just end up applying for university one year later than my peers was a very realistic probability.

At the Plouay worlds, we had watched the women's senior road race together. Over the winter, Dad and I spoke about it many times. In a 130km nine-lap race, the Belorussian winner Zinaida Stahurskaya had broken away from the field in lap 5 and ridden alone to the finish, holding off a peloton that was really quite active. Dad made sure the realities of that unbelievable performance were not lost on me before I went to Sochi to train with Natalia and her Russian team-mates. What I had found there was fine, with no mention ever being made of PEDs. Of course, my command of the language was close to zero and we were only youngsters after all, but at their 'warm weather' camp it looked like everyone there had enough challenges riding in the snow and ice, self-catering, daily bike maintenance sessions and keeping warm.

In Italy, my first race was the Carnevale di Cento, a UCI Category 2 race. I was near the front at the start line. Then I saw World champion Zinaida Stahurskaya, in her rainbow jersey, move onto the front row. She was tall and imposing, certainly, but her physique was quite startling. She had so very little body fat, it was definitely not a natural look. I remembered what Dad had told me.

My biggest worry in this first race was the heat, and during the morning I had learnt the Italian words for 'bottle', 'drink', 'water' and 'very hot' off by heart. The peloton was huge, well over 130 starters, and among the buzz of conversation it sounded like the peloton spoke either Italian or Russian. The starter waved the flag and we were off. But, just 10km into the 110km race, my chain snapped. My race was over. I was so frustrated at such an anti-climax after everything.

Back in Treviso I settled in quickly, staying in a team house with Valeria Pintos from Argentina, who was also having a trial with the team. We became good friends and our Italian language skills picked up no-end. Valeria spoke no English and I spoke no Spanish, so we both tried out our new words on each other. We normally trained as a pair, but on some days we met the other riders on the team and sometimes Maurizio followed us with the team car to see how we were getting on.

One evening, Maurizio organised a 14km time-trial test for me along the Montello Road, while he drove the team car behind, leaning out of the car window, shouting, sounding the car horn and cheering me on. I loved it! I also asked if Maurizio could find someone to take me mountain biking, and I did a couple of off-road rides each week so I could get ready for the Mountain Bike World Championships. There were not many road races on at the time, so my only other race was a semi-classic, the Giro del Veneto Femminile. On a hilly course, I finished in the top 20 but I had been on my limit for the last 20km, hanging on to the wheels and barely aware of what was happening tactically in the race. There was clearly a long way to go.

Maurizio ran his business and his team in the same way, full of energy and emotion. His office was adorned with huge photos of his riders winning World Championships and the Tour de France. Signed jerseys were everywhere and there was even a giant photo of Mussolini behind his desk. He was interested to hear my opinion about the Lisbon course for the World Championship and assured me that I would win it. Next year, I would join the team and we would set a programme that would not be too demanding yet give me the opportunity to develop and test myself against the best riders. Maurizio oozed confidence and charm.

I came back to the UK for the event that brings down the curtain on school life: A-level students' results day. Before this, I spent some time with my school friends; we even went on a road trip to Devon for Menna Hamel's 18th birthday. On the day of the results, we set off really early in the morning from Devon and drove to Brynteg to find out how we had got on. Menna had stayed on with her family, so one of us had to open her envelope and phone her with the results. The support and advice of a handful of close friends – Helen, Menna, Hayley, Kate, Claire and Tara – has been something I have always cherished over the years and it is wonderful to see them and touch base with normality, after long periods of time away in the circus that is racing. That evening, I went out to dinner with my grandfather George to celebrate my extra two 'A's. He was at home, looking after our pets while Mum and Dad were on holiday cycling in the Alps.

Next, it was the British Women's Road Race

Championship in Oakley, Buckinghamshire. After the race the previous year, although too late to appeal, one gentleman wrote to tell us that the conduct of the National Championships was not the subject of the BCF rules but rather UCI ones. Just for the record, the rules stated:

> 1.2.027 National Championships: National Championships shall be run under UCI regulations.
>
> Conduct of participants in cycling races 1.2.079 to 1.2.083:
>
> 1.2.081: Riders shall sportingly defend their own chances. Any collusion or behaviour likely to falsify or go against the interests of the competition shall be forbidden.
>
> 1.2.080: All licence holders shall, in whatever capacity, participate in cycling races in a sporting and fair manner. They shall look to contributing fairly to the sporting success of the race.

These were not regulations relating to normal races but specifically referred to National Championships, and we pointed them out to Peter King at BC, well in advance of the 2001 event, and suggesting that the organiser and commissaire also be made aware so we could have a fair race in 2001. Peter politely declined to do this and assured us that the race would be ridden according to the rules. Dad then contacted the organiser directly and identified our concerns and asked if the organiser could communicate with the commissaire. The organiser was most helpful and suggested we contact the commissaire direct. This we did and the commissaire confirmed our understanding of the UCI regulations.

Before the race, after we had signed on, the commissaire held a riders' briefing and at that meeting she read out the rules and her expectation of them. There was no team competition in this event and riders 'defending their own chances' and not 'colluding' both related to a personal level. The commissaire's absolute professionalism only contrasted with the way the race had been conducted the year before.

I was especially excited as I would be able to ride wearing the very special rainbow colours of the World champion. Those awarded for time-trials, track events, mountain biking or any other discipline feature a motif within them to designate that fact. In effect, the track sprint is a discipline taken from the finale of a road race; the pursuit, a formation of the chase of a break. It is a bit like having a championship for place-kicking in rugby. Place-kicking is a very important feature of the game but it is only a part of it. The road race jersey is pure with no logo, since to win the road race you need to combine the ability to be good in all aspects of cycling, and therefore it is recognised as the ultimate challenge in the sport.

It would also be my first meeting with the new British women's road coach, Canadian Peg Hill, who had raced internationally through the '90s and was highly knowledgeable in respect of road racing and what standards elite women can achieve. It was very heartening that the WCPP were taking on board so many of the recommendations from our document and putting excellent people in place to work with the women's squad. Certainly all contacts relating to British Cycling were entirely different from how they had been 12 months before.

In the race, the WCPP riders were rather quiet. There were various attacks and towards the end we became a group of four: three WCPP girls in their new black outfits and me in my new white World champion skin suit. I have some lovely photos of that contrast. I attacked and only Ceris could stay with me. We worked together and I won the sprint. Regretfully this would be the last time I would see Ceris. I never felt any anger towards her over the way the previous year's event was run. Undoubtedly, the girls were riding to the instructions of the coaches, who were so unsuited to their roles. They were the problem; massive egos without the ability to match and supported by a Team Agreement that gave them absolute power. The girls should have had the sense to stand up to them, but perhaps they just weren't as 'difficult' as me to work with.

Here is what Peg had to say about my win:

Before the 2001 National Road Championships, the Women's Endurance Squad Manager (Ken Matheson) filled me in on all the 'trouble' Nicole Cooke and her family caused the WCPP. Nicole wanted to compete with the elite women while still a junior. I knew this had been done elsewhere (in the US) and couldn't understand why they resisted. She was already a World champion. What was she going to do, waltz around the other juniors? If a young ambitious rider wanted to upgrade, why wouldn't she be encouraged? I was being prepared to witness a combative prima donna. I was also informed that it would be considered an 'embarrassment' to the programme should she win, as she was not a product of the system. He told me it had been practically mandated that the Squad beat Nicole at the previous Nationals. At the National Championships each athlete races for themselves, not the National Team. Therefore as National Coach my role was one of an observer. I followed in the lead commissaire's car. I watched as Nicole broke away with Ceris Gilfillan. It was no surprise when Nicole sprinted to the win. What was a surprise was how happy Nicole was. Her father and brother surrounded and congratulated her at the finish. She did not look like some bratty, spoiled kid to me. She was genuinely pleased.

The result in the race was not a surprise, more of a confirmation. My heart-rate traces showed that while I was not fully recovered and back to my best form, I was now making good progress. What I was most happy about was the new WCPP attitude and the meeting going so well with Peg. It looked like the treble of World Championships was on, so we went home happy. I showed Mum my medal. Craig had 'blown up' in the last stages of his race after being involved in a big crash and lone chase earlier on. Mum asked the usual questions and Dad gave the usual reply. Craig got an extra big hug and I put the medal in the box under the bed.

Things continued to get better in terms of relationships with British Cycling. Peg Hill together with Shane Sutton arranged that I would ride with the British team at the Grand Prix du Quebec. The previous year, our happy band had given an excellent account of ourselves, while most of the British team spent the time trying to read the lettering on the back of my saddle. Now we were to be together, which was not a problem for me, as I felt no animosity towards any of the riders. It was a little odd that Peg Hill did not accompany us. The race began with a disaster for me. A break had gone up the road and the bunch was chasing hard when a couple of riders both went for the same gap and suddenly about ten of us were sliding along the tarmac. It took some time for us to become untangled, my shoe had even come off in the pile of bodies and bikes, and I was one of the last to get going. I chased with Rachel Heal working hard alongside me, but we couldn't catch the speeding bunch and we finished ten minutes down.

I looked a bit like an Egyptian mummy with my bandages on my arms and knees at the start line of the 123km Stage 2, but I was determined to race hard and got in a break of five. The strongest rider was Saturn sprinter Ina Teutenberg, a former Junior World champion with a string of wins and World Cup podiums. At the finish, I positioned myself on her wheel for the sprint, but when she kicked I couldn't match her and had to settle for second place. Saturn ran both a men's and women's squad and had developed under René Wenzel, who earlier had worked with Angus Fraser, into a team that achieved a significant number of victories.

Saturn was the strongest team in the race and indeed would finish the season as the world's No.1 ranked team. Their main riders for this very mountainous Stage 3 were Commonwealth Games champion Lyne Bessette, and South African Anke Erlank, who had been present in the breakaway that stayed away on Stage 1 and was Saturn's best-placed rider for GC. The other rider to watch would be the Canadian 'phenomenon' Genevieve Jeanson of RONA.

Genevieve is two years older than me and had achieved the Junior World Time-Trial and Road Race double in 1999. She had blasted into the senior ranks, winning her first stage race, the six-day, nine-stage Tour de Snowy in Australia in early 2000, and backed that up by winning the Flèche Wallonne World Cup a few weeks later. Already in 2001 she had won the Redlands Classic tour in March by nine minutes, then the Tour of Gila, beating Saturn's best two climbers by a massive 15 and 24 minutes respectively. At the Montreal World Cup in May, Genevieve had attacked on the third of 12 laps, and ridden alone to win by seven and a half minutes. These were unbelievable performances, by any measure. Genevieve attacked on the first ascent of Jay Peak and I went into serious limpet mode, clinging to her back wheel while others were dropped. Eventually, I could do no more and at least had the honour, as reported, of 'Cooke being last to give up'. I formed part of a group of four riders chasing Genevieve with Saturn duo Lyne Bessette and Anke Erlank, and Finn Pia Sundstedt who had recently left the GAS Sport Team in Italy and was now racing for American team Intersports.

All four of us worked together and eventually caught Genevieve – after a 60km chase! There were more attacks over the Echo Mountain peaks but as we approached the finish the five of us were all together. I remembered the fast downhill finish from last year and got on Lyne's wheel. I gave it everything in the sprint but could not pass Lyne and was actually beaten by Genevieve who finished in second place. I knew that of the five, I was the only rider to have been in the 80km break the previous day while they would have been taking it easy in the bunch. But I was a bit surprised to be beaten in a sprint by Genevieve, who had also made a big break of her own today.

The next day, we had the time-trial stage and while I was warming up, I could see a lot of a fuss over at the RONA team parked alongside us. There was a big crowd around Genevieve. I had to take my start and thought nothing more of it. After blasting around the time-trial course, I was told Genevieve had developed a knee strain and pulled out. It seemed an unusual turn of events. After my two days in breakaways, I had reclaimed some of my time deficit and moved up the GC into the top ten. With Genevieve's withdrawal, I was now the leading U23 rider and King of the Mountains.

That evening I was back in attacking mode and got in a breakaway in the criterium with three riders including Saturn's Petra Rossner, resplendent in her German national champion's jersey and widely accepted as the No.1 sprinter in the world with five World Cup victories to her name. Coming down the finishing straight, I gave it everything and at least Petra had to keep going all the way to the line to claim her victory. Second behind the best sprinter in the business was very pleasing, along with my third podium in three days.

On the final stage, Rachel Heal rode really well to get in a breakaway with Amber Neben of Autotrader and Melissa Holt of RONA. Melissa was dropped and although Rachel could not stay with Amber, she showed that she had great potential as she finished in second place behind Amber. I ran out of energy, fading on the climb to the finish. Overall I was seventh, best U23 and King of the Mountains – more T-shirts to take home – and was really pleased that the British team had finished the stage race so strongly. It looked like the WCPP changes and Peg's good work were now starting to shine through. With the riders in Canada, plus Ceris who did not race here, it was exciting to think that we could be one of the strongest teams at the Athens Olympics in three years' time. The atmosphere in the team was good, even if no one spoke about the recent past.

I expect those of you familiar with the current men's road racing scene are becoming a little confused as I talk about national teams and commercial teams in the same breath. Women's cycling does not have the same depth of sponsors as the men's. Therefore major races are open both to commercial trade teams – Saturn, RONA, Acca Due O, etc – as well as national teams. The Australians in particular used the national format probably because being based in the southern hemisphere they needed to come as a national team to ride the northern hemisphere season.

After the race, I stayed with some family friends near

Montreal to recharge the batteries for a couple of days. Then it was off to Colorado to join the British mountain bike team to acclimatise to the high altitude of Vail at 2,484m, in preparation for the Mountain Bike World Championships. My Brian Rourke mountain bike was waiting for me when I arrived, and over the next two and a half weeks Gary Foord helped me sharpen up my technical skills.

Vail is a ski resort in winter and so we were accommodated in chalets. One morning, a member of staff came in and told us to turn on the TV. What we saw was horrifying. We watched live as the second plane went into the South Tower during the New York terrorist attacks of 11 September. The whole community in Vail was deeply shocked and I really felt for the riders and staff on the American team. There was much debate in the aftermath about whether to carry on with the championships. Immediately, the junior programme was stopped for a memorial service which I made sure I attended.

There was talk of cancelling the championships but eventually all the cross-country races were moved to the Sunday. My race began at 07.35am, five minutes after the junior men. Then it would be U23 men at 10.00, senior women 13.00 and finally senior men starting at 16.00. Gary and I had talked through the race strategy. Rather than going out hard in the first lap and building up a lead, I chose a race plan of holding back on the first lap, assessing my rivals' strengths and weaknesses and then choosing my tactics for the last lap to try to attack at the best moment. Technically, I had advanced this year. I felt comfortable that none of my rivals would be able to spring any surprises on me over any section that was difficult to ride, and my form was good.

Soon there were just two of us in the lead, me and Maja Wloszczowska of Poland, who had finished second ahead of me the year before, after my long chain came off. The press reported that they were surprised that both Maja and I decided to 'ride the heart-stopping Jetta Jump drop-off down a huge rock'. Cyclingnews.com showed a picture of the elite men at this feature, almost all of whom elected not to ride this particular section. Maja and I were both very motivated and both coveted that top step on the podium.

As we started the second lap, there was a section where the trail changed from gravel to a steep grass climb, before narrowing into a single track. It was important to lead into this section. I had done the tricky bit and was leading as we reached the bottom of the climb, and then I fell on the corner. The bike slid out from beneath me and I went sprawling as Maja swept past me up the climb toward the forest trail. I knew that if she got to the trail before me then the race was almost certainly over, because she would be able to keep the pace high and I would struggle to recover and get back on terms with her. If I could pass her before the single track, I could go slowly there and she would not be able to get past me. I could recover ready for the finish. I leapt back on and sprinted as hard as I could up the grassy climb. In the space of 200m I had gone from lying on the ground to back into the lead just before we disappeared into the trail. My lungs were bursting and my legs were badly cut, but it didn't matter now that I had the lead. I could afford to take a breather as there was no way for Maja to pass me.

Once I had regained my composure, I prepared for the rest of the lap. Maja put in a big attack, which I matched, then another on the last climb. I just managed to claw my way back to her over the top, but I was at the edge of my technical ability as we sped down a treacherous descent, before approaching the finish. Then it would be down to a sprint. Maja would be giving everything not to get another silver medal. This was no formality. I chose my moment and kicked past her. I drove for the finish line, not looking round. I won, elated and exhausted and barely able to raise one arm. All I could do was gasp for air as officials tried to help me to some nearby chairs, and then the emotions came out, tears of joy and relief that I had achieved what I set out to do. Maja went on to have an illustrious career in mountain biking, winning the Senior World Mountain Bike Championships and many silver and bronze medals at this level. She also came second in the mountain bike race at Beijing.

My original travel schedule was based around a race that should have taken place two days earlier. I now needed to get back to Europe to complete my preparations for Lisbon. Air transport across and out of the USA had been thrown into chaos after 9/11 and was certainly a long way from normal right now. Security at the airports was immense. I didn't have time to celebrate, rushing back to the accommodation so I could shower, change and grab my bags. On the way out Caroline Alexander, who was due to race later in the day, stopped me. She and other team members had watched my race from their balcony, which overlooked the spot where I had crashed; they couldn't believe my response and the effort I made to make sure I got back in front before that single track. I certainly was not gracious and should have shown a better attitude. With greater maturity, I could have chosen the moment to build some bridges with the riders. Perhaps memories of a year ago were still too vivid and in the absence of any apology, I wasn't going out of my way to ingratiate myself with anyone in the squad. I was on a mission; impervious to discomfort and absolutely focused on one thing – winning – and that should be a normal attitude for anyone wanting to win a race, right? I went back to the course to be presented with the gold medal and rainbow jersey with a mountain on it and then it was a mad dash for the airport and a series of unconfirmed and constantly changing connections that I hoped might get me to Milan in time for the race in Tuscany on the Tuesday night.

A beaming Maurizio was waiting at the airport to greet me off my early-morning flight. It was almost embarrassing as he started shouting out 'Campionessa del Mondo!' as I came out of arrivals, but it made me laugh. Finally, I could relax. We drove to the race and found the hotel; it was lunch time when I walked in and all the riders and staff were together in the restaurant. They started clapping. A couple of months before, I was at school. Now, still a junior, I was walking into a restaurant with stars of the international road scene all clapping me. I'll never forget that moment.

Our race was the hotly contested Giro della Toscana. I got straight into the racing that night with the prologue and during the race had two top ten places. Maurizio was relaxed enough to insist that I did not race the final day because it was raining, and there was no sense in catching a cold or risking a crash with the World Road Championships in a few weeks. He wanted to ensure that I was in the best condition to defend my junior title. I had done enough to book a place on the team for the next season, he told me before I left. All that was needed was to negotiate a salary, and that could wait until after the World Championships.

The Lisbon course was great with several places to make it hard and force a selection. The lap had a 2km climb, a steep descent, then a 3km climb, before a long downhill stretch of 4km, finishing in a flat section to the line. With the benefit of my recce a few months before, I had designed a route around

Cowbridge near my home, which resembled the Lisbon course. I had trained on this course during the year, particularly practising the downhill section to the finish, where I had to make sure I could drive the restricted junior gear, pedalling really quickly and then tucking into an aerodynamic position when the cadence became impossible, just as I had done with Dad on the tandem so many years before. In the last few weeks before departing, Shane helped replicate the warm-up and then would follow me in the WCU car around the route, offering encouragement and advising me afterwards. These tactics of devising a local route on which to practise before a race were ones I adopted throughout my career.

As in the previous year, the time-trial would be held early in the week, a few days before the road race. Those test rides with Shane around Cowbridge had helped a lot, but I was nervous about the time-trial. I had been seeded as the last rider to start. I knew that the pressure was on me to perform.

Given the course with its two climbs, it was no good going flat out on the last climb as you needed energy to keep a high cadence on the fast 4km descent. Peg Hill was there and was a calming and supportive presence and agreed with the tactical plan. I could only marvel at how different the experience was 12 months after the Laurel and Hardy show.

At the time check at the top of the second hill, I was fourth, 13 seconds behind my friend Natalia Boyarskaya. I span that gear for all I was worth on the descent, with Shane supporting me from the car behind. I really wanted this win to make up for last year. I crossed the line not knowing the result, the support staff ran over and caught me just as I was about to collapse and they shouted out that I had won. Tears welled up as I tried to take it all in. Shane passed me the phone; he had already got through to Dad.

Winning the time-trial was fantastic, but now there was even more pressure on me to win the road race. If I could win, it would be only the second time a junior had won and defended the road race, and so far across all categories, male and female, only four riders had ever won the time-trial and road race double in the same year. Unfortunately, I was likely to be riding this without a strong team. Claire, who had joined me on the recce, was ill and that left Lorna Webb as my only team-mate. Lorna is a smashing girl and always gave her best but she finished 50th at nearly 18 minutes, so was not in the position to assist my efforts to retain the title. The other nations would know my situation and I was likely to be attacked every kilometre of the way. Unlike the infamous National Championships of 2000, here working as teams against the lone favourite was exactly what they were meant to do. The rules of engagement were entirely different.

Looking back, I never felt as much pressure in my career as I did for this race. The other teams knew me from the previous year, they knew my style and they could base their strategies on me. Every time I turned up on the course, the other coaches and riders motioned and pointed. I couldn't hear but I knew what they were saying. I would only ever get this one chance to do my 'Double Double'. Fortunately, Peg Hill really understood racing and the pressures that riders were under. She was great in helping me prepare myself mentally for the race. The other big difference between this race and the British Championships was the distance; being a junior race this was a relatively short 73km while the British Championships were 115km.

Halfway through the first lap, there was a crash behind and Lorna went down, so I was well and truly on my own in this six-lap race. I attacked on the second lap, wanting to create a breakaway of strong riders. Five riders came with me, including Maja Wloszczowska, my mountain bike competitor, Natalia Boyarskaya (again), Pleuni Möhlmann and Lithuanians Modesta Vzesniauskaite and Indre Januleviciute. Natalia, Maja, Pleuni and I worked hard but the gap never got above one minute as the four Italians, in particular, together with the Germans chased behind. We were caught at a critical point, on the first climb of the final lap.

We were then joined by riders who had been protected by their team-mates and were fresh compared with those of us in the break. I was careful in selecting the moment but decided to attack again. It worked and Maja, Natalia and Pleuni, all from our previous breakaway group, joined me as we rode away from the surprised riders who expected us to be absorbed into the bunch. Clearly they also felt that having committed so much to this break, they didn't want to be caught either.

On the second climb, I launched more attacks but Pleuni stuck with me. I had one last place to attack, just before the crest of the hill. I gave it everything. I got a gap and sprinted along the top of the hill and into the descent. As I came into the finishing straight, I knew I'd opened up a big enough gap, so I raised my hands in the air with about 200m to go and saluted the crowds as I enjoyed the ride to the line. I felt the relief; I'd done it.

The cycling journalists were generous in their conclusions. The *Guardian* wrote: 'The 18-year-old Welshwoman pulled off her 12-month hat-trick of world junior titles – mountain bike, time-trial and now successful defence of the road championship she won last year in Brittany – with a stunning display of sheer strength and sang-froid, of mental maturity as much as pedalling muscle. It was clear from the off that the other medal contenders were going to base their race on what

Cooke did, and that they would shadow her every move. The knowledge that she would be followed wherever she went, and that she would be expected to dictate the race pattern, could have broken a lesser competitor's nerve but Cooke was simply too strong.'

I look at those results sheets now and see names of riders with whom I would become so familiar over the years. Maja had a bronze to go with her two silvers but would go onto senior gold. Giorgia Bronzini was set up that day to win the bunch sprint by her Italian team. They would work very effectively with her many times throughout her career and she would take two world road titles. At senior level, she would have five and not three team-mates. Vera Koedooder, who had thrashed me so easily at Orleans, was also in the top ten. She was for some time touted as the replacement for Leontien van Moorsel. Vera is still a full-time rider. Natalia and Emma Johansson were in that race in 2001 and both would have major roles at Beijing.

I revelled in the atmosphere for the next few days with Uncle Chris and Craig, as Mum and Dad were at work. We watched the senior races and then celebrated with Maurizio who was on top of the world. His Lithuanian rider, Rasa Polikeviciute, had won the elite women's road race. He already counted me as one of the team so had two World champions and threw a massive party that we all enjoyed. I started dreaming about winning the Senior World Championship road race and what it might be like for me.

When I got home, the Cardiff Ajax had gone crazy; I think the whole club was at Cardiff airport with banners and balloons. When I came out of arrivals, it was a huge surprise to see them all together, along with Mum and Dad. Then it was back to Wick and a celebration at the Star Inn, where Ajax friends joined us and most of the village in a celebration for the whole community. My friends were there and as the party quietened down towards the end of the night, we talked about our futures. They had all just started university a couple of weeks previously and our adult lives were beginning. I was now on a new path, unsure of where it led, while at the same time thrilled that I was entering the professional ranks of cycling: I had my three golds for 2001; the WCPP were being helpful at World Championships; and Peg Hill, the new coach, was great. The issues that had so blighted the year before looked to be a thing of the past. I'd had a big wake-up call with my overtraining episode in the first half of the year and realised I had to keep better track of my training and recovery.

I didn't have to go to school the next morning but I still got up early and did the school ride with Craig. I raced off down the road toward Bridgend, with a bag full of my old textbooks strapped to my carrier to make sure we kept our loads fair. We rode over all the hills and we finished, like always, with the full throttle sprint to the Volvo garage. Craig went on to Brynteg and I rode home, thinking about my training ride that afternoon, a steady four-hour endurance ride.

I flew to Treviso in November, full of excitement and ready to sign a contract with Maurizio's Acca Due O team, buoyed by how well our telephone calls had gone and the enthusiasm the team was showing for me. Maurizio arrived, bounding in with his arms waving everywhere, and seemed to be trying to get as many 'campionessa's' as possible into each sentence. We quickly got into the details of his favourite subject: dominating the world of women's cycling. Despite my rough Italian, we were now speaking the same language.

For no apparent reason, Maurizio stood up, grabbed his

papers, put on his coat, said he'd send me a contract in the next few days and then left. I was amazed; there seemed to be no reason for what just happened or why. Maurizio was a man capable of actions that were not readily explained, but this was unusual even for him. Instead of signing a contract and planning next year's racing calendar, I was left alone and empty handed and there was nothing much I could do but go back to Wick and wait.

Giancarlo telephoned me a week later. My bright 'Hello' was met with pleasant greetings but quickly the tone changed as we got on to the news that Giancarlo was delivering as Maurizio's messenger: 'You're not on the team for next year.'

My heart pounded. What did he mean *not on the team for next year*? Until then everything had been so positive. After winning three world titles in a year, I thought it was just a matter of negotiating a contract. Giancarlo tried to explain: Rasa Polikeviciute's victory in the elite race had thrown a proverbial spanner in the works. Maurizio had been expecting to release her from her contract at the end of the year. Her best year had been in 1997, when she had been overall winner of the prestigious Hewlett Packard Challenge, but since then Rasa's results had declined and it was thought she was about to retire. A further complication was that Rasa had an identical twin sister Jolanta, and they only rode as a pair. Now Rasa was World champion, and the sponsors wanted her in the team. So instead of two planned vacancies, there were none. Giancarlo tried to put a positive spin on it. Even if I had been accepted, there were some very senior riders already in place, including Diana Ziliute and Swiss Nicole Brandli who had won the Giro d'Italia, so I would be bottom of the pecking order, which would offer limited opportunities in my first year. It would be much better for me to look elsewhere. We said goodbye and

I was left shattered. I went back to the kitchen where we were eating dinner and told Mum, Dad and Craig the news. No one knew what to say. How could this happen?

So what were those talks with Maurizio in his office back in the summer all about? I remembered Maurizio's joy at the World Championships in Lisbon and the party we'd had to celebrate. Perhaps he didn't know what complications were ahead on the night, but he should have been fully aware of the problem a month later when I was encouraged to fly to Treviso to negotiate a contract. Why would he do that? And now he didn't even have the decency to tell me himself! Giancarlo was the messenger, a good foil for Maurizio whom he advised as a friend rather than a paid scout. He was organised, known to lose his temper for something he felt passionately about, and clever enough to make things happen regardless of the circumstances. I valued his friendship and saw him as a long-term mentor to value in the years ahead.

I pulled myself together and contacted a couple of other teams – Équipe Nürnberger in Germany and Farm Frites in Holland – but this was the wrong time of year to be attempting to find a contract. Most teams had completed their rosters months before and their budgets were spent. They were offering me a pittance that I wouldn't be able to survive on, even if board and lodging were provided.

As I reflected on my predicament, I knew that the only thing I could do was put my head down and get back into training, taking my frustration out on the hills of South Wales, thinking about how I could make a mark on the peloton in 2002 that no one would be able to dismiss. I couldn't immediately solve the team problem, but there was one race that I could prepare for in the full knowledge that I would be able to ride it. The 2002 Commonwealth Games were to be held in Manchester and I was desperate to perform for Wales. So I drove to Riverton at the beginning of December to look at the course, testing myself on the hills and taking photos to help remind me of the important features of the course. The field would include current World No.1, Australian Anna Millward, backed up by a powerhouse of five other Australians. The Canadian duo of defending champion Lyne Bessette and the unbelievable Genevieve Jeanson would also be backed up by a full squad of strong riders, just like the New Zealanders. In the case of Genevieve, I was hoping those EPO tests in Canada were being tried to the full. And then Team England would also field six riders, all of whom would be delighted to make a pact and work with anyone to make sure one of their number finished ahead of me.

Looking back, it seems astonishing that I was planning for the win. I was 18, the only female in Wales competitive at an international level and there was no way we would be able to develop one or two more riders, let alone five, by July. Shane was making some modest efforts in this regard but Julian Winn was starting to get competitive on the British scene, and Shane was committing lots of time to him. Even if I thought about it, all these factors didn't really matter to me. I was going to race for the win and set this as my goal for 2002. I didn't know exactly how I was going to deal with all these riders, but I was going to give it my all.

CHAPTER TEN
Success in Italy

As the days went by and with the two UCI teams I had contacted producing no viable offer, it looked like the British WCPP women's road team could be the best option. They did plan to go to a number of European events and maybe I could still ride the races I dreamed about. It was going to mean eating humble pie, after I had told them that I was going to join a professional team.

I could see that on the positive side I would be with my GB team-mates and that regularly racing together would help us build up our tactical knowledge and become a more effective team ready for the World Championships or Olympics. British Cycling's appointment of Peg Hill gave me confidence. The WCPP had enough funding to send riders to races with a full accompanying staff of mechanics and physiotherapists. By comparison, the continental women's teams were often under-funded, and travelling to races meant hours sitting in the car, rather than flying, and most of the time you had to look after yourself.

On the negative side I wouldn't be able to learn from riding alongside an older, more experienced rider who had won a classic or road World Championship. This was the vital ingredient necessary for the next stage of my development. The squad was also seriously weakened. Yvonne McGregor had retired at a natural point in her career, but surprisingly so had Ceris Gilfillan, who was only three years older than me.

I approached British Cycling and had a meeting in December with Peter Keen and Dave Mellor who was in charge of the women's road section. Peter and Dave were both supportive of the idea of me joining the team and we made plans for the 2002 season. At the meeting, I was shocked and disappointed to learn that Peg Hill was no longer the coach.

We then spoke about the Team Agreement. This was the same document that had been used when I was riding as a junior, when I had insisted on a couple of changes. I had brought a copy to the meeting and we discussed it and made notes on it. Peter and Dave were positive about the proposed changes but they would have to seek authorisation before final approval. That same day, I received a welcoming email from Richard Wooles, the coach hired to replace Peg Hill on the women's squad. My only knowledge of Richard was that he was a competent club rider and a GB *soigneur* at Plouay. I amended the Team Agreement in line with what we had discussed and agreed, and emailed it back to them. At last, I thought, I could just concentrate on my training. I was looking forward to riding with my British colleagues and hoping we could form a productive team together in 2002.

Dave Mellor replied to my email, saying that the proposed changes were not acceptable to those in authority above him and that I would have to sign the standard Team Agreement. The standard Agreement included a clause stating that the rider had to 'obey every instruction of the coach'. The problem for me was that I would have no control over choosing the coach, and they seemed to be changing coaching staff at quite some rate, with Richard Wooles the third coach in less than 12 months. Why should I be forced to take instructions from someone who didn't know me and I didn't know? The attitude of some of the staff was far from professional. Meanwhile, the performance of the senior women's team at the 2001 Lisbon World Championship was woeful: 15th, 53rd and one DNF in the road race, and not a single rider competed in the time-trial. What had the WCPP done with Ceris, the rider with 'such a bright future' in 2000? Why should I sign an Agreement to obey all instructions from an organisation that had been pouring Lottery money into the best funded women's programme on the planet and achieved so little? More disturbingly, what had happened to Peg?

In one sense, even though I was only disagreeing about words on a document, I was very aware of the case of Wendy Everson, a track cyclist. She was on the WCPP and objected to some of the things she was asked to do and the way she was being treated, particularly compared with the men. Unable to change the situation through discussion, she decided to take her case to an employment tribunal. BC defended themselves at the tribunal, not by justifying their actions but by simply stating that Wendy was not employed by them; she was actually self-employed, as a grant-funded athlete, therefore the tribunal had no jurisdiction. The tribunal agreed with this argument on the basis that since neither BC nor Wendy were paying employer or employee taxes, the relationship was not that of employer and employee. No doubt if BC were a private company and had demanded the degree of control over individuals that the Team Agreement sought, the Inland Revenue would have been interested in addressing the relationship at the heart of the case, but since BC was a publicly funded body they had no interest in following up. It did not stop the relationship imposed by the Team Agreement being one-sided.

The changes to the Agreement we had discussed in Manchester were in line with the revised Agreement that I had signed for the previous two years. If they had agreed once, maybe if we could move the case high enough in the organisation we could persuade them to agree to some 'reasonable' changes. So I asked Dad to write to the CEO Peter King and to the president Brian Cookson. The reply was emphatic. I would not be eligible to train or race with the WCPP, or Great Britain, unless I signed the standard Agreement. No changes were allowed.

At this point, it is worth considering that the grant money was irrelevant when compared with what was really at stake: the whole relationship between the athlete and the governing body of their sport. No one was going to any World or Olympic Games without selection by, and support of, their governing body. If I, or anyone else, was going to be able to perform, it was vital that such support was effective, or at worst neutral. I'd already had my experience of negative support in 2000, at each of the events I had ridden with the national team. After my recommendations in late 2000, the organisation had gone out on a global search to obtain a top-notch women's coach. They had recruited Peg Hill from Canada. She was there during the spring and summer of 2001. I met her at the British Championships in Oakley, and the last time in Lisbon 2001.

Peg Hill wrote about Lisbon 2001 and of the squad she was working with:

Most of the women didn't belong at that level yet. It was a delight to work with Nicole who obviously did know what she was doing, wasn't afraid to say what she needed from the support staff, and got the racing results. I thought it was a breath of fresh air but other staff seemed to grind their teeth about it. I always say that had she been American, her forth-rightness would have been viewed as being normal for an elite athlete.

The next time I encountered Nicole was at the 2001 World Championships in Lisbon. She had already won the Mountain Bike Cross-Country World title. Again I saw a happy athlete.

Before the road race, the staff asked her what she would like for breakfast. Nicole answered with no hesitation. Staff seemed to grit their teeth when dealing with her. I found it entirely refreshing – an athlete who knew what she needed and produced results!

I found her very easy to work with. Since I co-authored a book on Sport Psychology for Cyclists, I offered sport psych sessions which seemed to be tolerated by the Endurance Squad. Nicole embraced it and we had a one-on-one relaxation and visualisation time the day before she won the road title. I would have liked to continue to work with Nicole, but I know now that I was in the wrong camp, and my time with the WCPP was abruptly ended, even contravening the conditions of their contract.

Now in December Peg had been dismissed, and instead a novice male coach, with no experience of riding on the continent, no experience as a professional and no experience of the female scene or coaching female riders, had been put in place. I'd already had too many bad experiences of poor advice.

What could I do if I wanted to question a decision? BC did have its own appeals procedure but before appeal, any appellant had to offer up to BC a deposit to cover the assembly and

Growing up in Wick was always full of adventure. Craig and I are off exploring down a lane.

On our first tandem holiday on the Isle of Wight, with Mum.

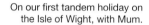

I have now got my first 'racing bike', I'm kitted out in a Z Peugeot outfit and ready to climb the mountains like Robert Millar.

During a stop at King's Lynn – everything we needed for two weeks was in the bags on the back of the tandems.

My first international racing trip to the Helmond Youth Tour in Holland, aged 12. What a way to start – racing in the polka dot jersey!

At the British Cyclo-Cross National Championships in Durham, aged 14.

Aged 15 and racing the GHS 10-mile time-trial.

A successful week at the Manchester Velodrome in 1999, winning a clean sweep of all five British U16 track titles for the second year in a row. Dad and I took great interest in watching the senior women's races that year.

A few weeks later at the British Senior Road Race Championships. I won the sprint after a long break away with Yvonne McGregor.

Riding up from Southerndown beach, part of my daily cycle to school. No bag of books this time.

The first British winner of a World Championship road race in 18 years. After a season of near-misses, the joy on my face is evident.

Winning the time-trial at Lisbon in 2001 made it world titles in three different disciplines. Natalia Boyarskaya (left) took the silver medal.

[Graham Watson]

On my return from Lisbon, Cardiff Ajax cycling club laid on a surprise welcome home party for me at Cardiff airport. Plenty of girls plus Geraint Thomas and the Rowe brothers.

Life at the Deia team was always exciting. Here Fany and I celebrate at the end of a race in Italy. In my first season, I valued Fany's advice and encouragement.

Commonwealth Games road race gold, Manchester 2002, aged 19.
[Press Association]

Winning the Amstel Gold Race was a highlight of my career. I had just turned 20, and was the first British winner of a classic since the days of Tom Simpson. [Corvos]

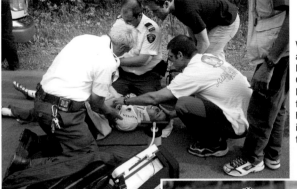

Weeks after the Amstel and Flèche double, I finished second to Genevieve Jeanson in Montreal, and then in the following Tour I had a huge crash. Out of shot is my smashed bicycle frame.

August 2003 Plouay – a World Cup win while I nursed a still injured knee was a great result, but masked long-term problems.
[Getty Images]

San Francisco 2003 – the Americans really did a great job in putting on the race and supporting the women's peloton. It's a great memory of a win in front of huge crowds, but the hills in San Francisco were killers. [Garrett Lau]

My knee never recovered and I needed an operation to fix it. This was May 2004, three months before the Olympics and eight months since my last race.

oved living in Treviso during my three years there. ionna' made us all very welcome and I immersed yself in Italian life.

President and manager of Acca Due O was Maurizio Fabretto. His flamboyant passion always shone through.

Italy, July 2004 – winning the Giro at 21 was a great way to return to the peloton.

April 2005 – shoulder t
shoulder with Oenone Woo
in the Flèche Wallonne, o
my way to my second wi

Descending from the Acropolis
in the Athens Olympics 2004.
[Independent]

The Holland Ladies Tour,
September 2005, following keyhole
surgery on my right knee. I was
caught up in a crash on Stage 3
and had little form. Using tactical
skill rather than strength, I crafted
a great win on Stage 5 which
boosted my confidence.

maintenance costs of conducting the appeal. In the event of the appellant not being successful, all costs, without limit, were to be met by the failed appellant. In the regulations, the BC Board not only had given themselves the unique authority to decide who was on the panel, with no right to dispute that construction, they also required that the panel need not make public their decision but that the decision of the panel had to be delivered to the Board. The Board had to approve any decision of the panel in order to validate it and the Board reserved the right to dismiss such findings the panel may make. That is why Wendy Everson had approached an external body with her grievance, hoping for a fair hearing of her case. Fundamentally, I felt as if this was a collection of insecure men who wanted a sport for men. Peg was the only female coach, and undoubtedly she suffered from the same prejudice as Wendy and me. The ridiculous wording of the Team Agreement – that you had to obey every instruction of whosoever the WCPP decided might be available to 'coach' you – reflected this.

I felt that BC took advantage of the fact that I was without a professional team for 2002 and exploited it, pushing the boundaries back from what Peter Keen and I had agreed previously. As I was getting nowhere with BC, maybe there was another way. UK Sport was the body charged by legal covenant with overseeing the individual sports' federations, and the distribution of Lottery funds to individual athletes. Surely they could help? They could consider the Team Agreement and pass judgement to determine if what I was asking was 'reasonable' or not. Initial approaches to them fell on deaf ears. They said it was not their responsibility, but we reminded them that the responsibility lay with them and not BC. It was going to be a long haul.

Why didn't I simply sign the Team Agreement and then try to work out a sensible arrangement with whoever was my coach or manager at an event? Aside from my own bad experiences in 2000, I had also seen other riders suffer as a consequence of the 'Do as we tell you' approach. Keiran Page was the same age as me and the male 'talent' of his age group. While I stood apart from WCPP, Keiran fully embraced it. After Lisbon, Dad asked Shane Sutton about Keiran. He had come 12th in the 2000 World Junior Time-Trial, and we all hoped he would get among the medals in 2001. Cruelly, the winner in 2001 was the rider one place behind Keiran the year before. 'The trouble with Keiran is, he just does not know how to prepare for a big race. He does not even know how to do a warm-up,' stated Shane Sutton.

Dad then told him that some years before, at a BSCA championship event, Keiran was warming up on a static turbo trainer and his dad Russell had a clipboard with a list of timings and heart-rate levels, in the most detailed and controlled of warm-up routines. Dad told Shane that when we saw this, we upgraded my own routine to match that of Keiran's. If, years later, Keiran's warm-up was inept, it was surely nothing to do with Kerian but everything to do with the sloppy and unprofessional techniques of the BC WCPP staff telling the riders what they had to do and, if ever questioned, pointing at a Team Agreement and saying, 'Our way or the highway.'

The focus was wrong. When they made the rider the centre of what they were doing, then they would have success. Two years earlier, when Dad and I had prepared a report on proposed changes required for the sport to succeed, this had been a fundamental element – that the athlete and athletic performance should be the focus for the support staff, not the other way around. The Team Agreement formalised the ascendancy of the coach, and in my case, a novice coach, who, however nice he might be, knew precious little about women's road racing at this stage of his career.

We reached an impasse. The best female road racer in Britain was not to be supported by Lottery funds. However, the BC team management and support staff would spend their year travelling around the world going to races where the riders would finish totally out of contention or even not finish at all. If they didn't want to have a rider with ambition to win, then I didn't want them. I didn't sign the Team Agreement.

At least somebody, somewhere, thought something of me. UK Sport might not have wanted to convince BC that I should be on the WCPP, but at least they passed on an invite for me to attend a Garden Party at Buckingham Palace.

I needed to find a way to race. I went back to the UCI database and searched for teams that might be suitable. Three stood out as possibilities. I wrote introductory faxes and fired them off that night. The next morning I took the phone numbers of the teams with me on a five-hour training ride to Monmouth and called when I arrived to check that had they received the faxes. The first team said yes and they would get back to me, but Maurizio Ricci, who answered at the Deia-Pragma-Colnago team, was talking so excitedly that it made a huge impression. They were very keen for me to join the squad.

An offer was faxed through that evening – €8,000 for the season – which was a lot better than the €2,200 being offered by the Nürnberger and Farm Frites teams but a long way from the €15,000 I had been expecting from Acca Due O. At least I would be able to afford to fly out and back a couple of times during the year. Faxes went back and forth over the next few days and although they weren't going to improve the money, the team manager would consent to me wearing my own shoes, glasses and helmet from which I knew I could negotiate another £1,000 in personal sponsorship elsewhere. No one could say professional women riders got into the sport for the money, but at least I could exist if I received no subsistence Lottery grant from UK Sport.

I was excited and thrilled that everything was back on track and I would be racing in Italy with one of the top teams after all. The reason I had picked Deia as a potential team was the presence of Spanish rider Joane Somarriba who had won the last two editions of the women's Tour de France as well as winning the Giro d'Italia twice. It meant we would be doing the top-level races and I would have a fantastic champion to learn from; it would be an honour to ride with her and see someone like this in action from the inside of her team.

Although I didn't know all the riders, it was clear that a team capable of winning the Tour de France had riders with different specialities: climbers, sprinters and breakaway specialists. To serve those riders, the rest of the team are composed of *domestiques*. Their role was described beautifully by writer, journalist and cycling enthusiast/historian Roger St Pierre, who wrote:

> It is team tactics that so often win or lose races – and the lieutenants and the dog soldiers who expend their energy blocking chasing moves when they have riders up the road in a position to win. It is they who ride out into the wind so their aces can get an easier ride tucked inside their wheel [close to the rider in front and in his shelter]. Rare indeed is the major victory that cannot be credited in large part to the groundwork laid by the 'domestiques'.

This would be my role in the first season. I knew that, as a young rider, I was an unknown quantity and would have to earn the respect of my team-mates before asking the team to ride for me and sacrifice their own chances. It was a bit much to expect me to have the stamina for the grand tours, but I knew I could be there helping in the one-day races. Then, if the opportunity came up in some of the lesser races, perhaps I would have a chance to race for the win myself. In the days after signing the contract, I was already riding imaginary races during my training rides

I couldn't wait. In mid-February I said goodbye to Craig, Mum and Dad to start my first professional season. Peter King had recently written to me on behalf of the BC Board confirming that until I signed the 2002 Team Agreement, without any of the amendments that were possible in 2001, I would not be riding for GB and 'The Board does not accede to your request that the matter be put before the Sports Disputes Resolution Panel.' I left Dad and Mike Townley, a solicitor who had experience of the sport, to bring the reluctant British Cycling Board and UK Sport to face their responsibilities. I was going racing.

I walked through the baggage hall at Bologna airport expecting to have to search for Maurizio Ricci. I didn't have a clue what he looked like. A middle-aged man in a bright multi-coloured fleece rushed forward shouting out my name. He bubbled with generous enthusiasm throughout the journey to Forli. I was the second to arrive at the team house; French rider Fany Lecourtois had arrived a few days before and greeted me warmly when Maurizio dropped me at the door and said goodbye.

Fany was ten years older than me and had been around the tour since the mid-'90s. She was very nice and wanted to know all about me. A lifelong friendship was born that night as we chatted away, mostly in Italian but occasionally in French, laughing together at my funny accent and unusual word combinations. The team house had three bedrooms, two decked out with bunk beds sleeping six riders in a room, and we took a tiny room with two beds crammed in. The house was full of trophies, just like the houses of Acca Due O, but here they also had a cabinet full of videos. It was a treasure trove for me as my experience of elite racing had been limited to highlights of the men's Tour de France, the most recent World Championships and standing by the side of a mountain road on holiday, watching the women's Tour de France.

The videos went back to the early '90s, covering most of the major women's races, and I was able to take a walk back in recent history watching Fabiana Luperini win the Giro d'Italia four times in a row, along with Alessandra Cappellotto winning the 1997 world title. It was fantastic, but at the same time it brought home the fact of how far removed I had been from the centre of the cycling world. I thought I was quite well informed on riders' statistics and race results, but this gave me quite a sharp reminder that I still had a lot to learn.

Every day seemed to be full of action and discovery, whether it was receiving my new team clothing, or heading out on training rides and seeing so many other cyclists. I would attack every hill on the ride as if it was the critical moment in a race, while Fany would ride the climb at her pace, meeting me at the top before we descended together into a new valley.

After returning from a training ride one day, team manager Luigi Milioni came round and told me I was going to Milan to meet the major sponsor. Ernesto Colnago, the legendary bike manufacturer had decided, seemingly on a whim, that he wanted to build me a custom frame. It seemed someone else thought something of me as well.

Joane Somarriba and my Spanish team-mates settled in the team's second house while my Ukrainian team-mates and the riders of a second team, Raschiani, made up of mostly Italian riders, moved in with Fany and me. The rules state that there should only be one team managed by the same people but, I was quickly learning, many slid around rules when they wanted to. I initially assumed that the reason for having a second team was simply to gain extra exposure for sponsors, but, as I would soon learn, motives are usually more basic.

Until this point everything had been going perfectly. I'd been welcomed into the team, accepted by senior riders like Joane who was friendly, if slightly scary simply because of her achievements, and I was healthy, strong and in good form, raring to do my first race. The GP Castenaso was held on a flat course. The Spaniards were targetting the Tour de France later in the season and we didn't have a top-class sprinter suited to the expected bunch sprint finish. *Directeur sportif* Giorgio Zauli told us that it was just a case of getting in the mix. For me, a valuable learning experience beckoned.

Then, less than 20 minutes before the race, Luigi told me I was to go back to signing on, re-sign and collect a new number. Somewhere, in Italian, there was mention of the GB team. Apparently, I was still to ride in my Deia-Pragma-Colnago kit. Why should I want to change kit? As confused as I was, it was also too late to question so I just accepted what I was told, and went and re-signed on and put on the new number I was given. I tried not to focus on any of this, as I prepared myself for my first-ever race as a senior professional. One of the British team riders came up to me before the start and said, 'Thank you Nicole, for helping us out. You really got us out of a mess.' For weeks I had been conversing solely in Italian or French and much of what was said passed me by, yet here was a girl talking to me in English and I had no idea what she was on about. The race was about to start – my first race for my team.

The pace was fast and the roads very narrow, but I felt good near the front of the peloton. I found Joane and asked if I could make an attack, she nodded back in her calm manner and I went into 'attacking mode', waiting for a move that I could counter, or an opening for me to launch my first attack. As a few breakaway riders were swallowed up into the bunch, I jumped hard down the left-hand side and sprinted for the next corner, leaning in low round the bend before sprinting off again. Two riders joined me and we had a gap on the bunch. I was loving the freedom of escaping the bunch and leading the race. One rider was from Acca Due O and was obviously marking the break, aiming to set up a sprint finish for their leader Diana Ziliute. We were eventually caught a few kilometres later and I spent the rest of the race watching the attacks and choosing counter attacks to follow. I made a couple more attacks of my own, more for the sheer thrill of it and to get a feel of the timing, rather than a calculated bid for victory.

With 10km to go, I got into position near the Acca Due O train at the front with the intention of going for the sprint finish. My team-mates were all staying safely in the middle of the pack and I would have to look after myself, sliding through gaps and trying to get as much shelter as possible from the teams setting up their sprinters. I sprinted to finish seventh behind Diana Ziliute. I was absolutely thrilled with my top ten result, in my first professional contest. After the race, I was buzzing with excitement and adrenaline. My team-mates were also excited for me and Giorgio said a top ten place was a great start and that I had done really well.

I chatted non-stop with Fany and Giorgio all the way back to Forli about the racing, That evening, after sitting down to a meal we all helped prepare, I rang home, excitedly recounting the lead-up and the race in great detail. Mum and Dad shared my excitement and let me finish and then Dad went back to the situation before the race. He wanted to know more about this strange incident with the GB girl and the number change. Had I ridden for Deia-Pragma-Colnago or for Great Britain? I would have been given a number in the series for my trade team. Any other number would have been for another team. What exactly had gone on? Dad told me to confirm a few details with my manager, right there and then.

I rang the manager and then got back to Dad. Apparently, the organiser had approached my team manager before the start. The UCI rules for a Category 1 race stated that only teams could compete and teams must attend with a minimum of six riders and a maximum of eight. We were there with eight but incredibly the British team had flown in especially for this one race, with a team of just five riders but with the full support crew. They could not start. The organiser asked the British manager, Dave Mellor, if there were any other British nationals riding who could be asked if they would change their entry. I was the only other British rider out of the 140 entrants. The organiser said Dave Mellor should ask me, but he knew that BC management had instructed I was never going to ride for Great Britain unless I signed their Team Agreement document. He persuaded the organiser to ask my manager if I would ride for Great Britain on this occasion, and that 'request' became an 'instruction' that I had to get a new number.

You couldn't make it up. Laurel and Hardy were alive and well. So that is why I was thanked for helping them. If I had not signed on for Great Britain, they would have joined the spectators. Well, I didn't mind because now I had ridden for Great Britain and not signed a Team Agreement. The evidence of this farce empowered Mike Townley and Dad in the work they were doing behind the scenes. They had recently got UK Sport to agree that they and not BC were responsible for the distribution of Lottery funds to athletes. This was a crucial legal point to make, as it placed the BC in the position not as gatekeepers but as administrators and service providers, responsible to UK Sport. Regardless that the BC Board had unanimously voted that they were not going to allow the beloved Team Agreement to go anywhere near the Sports Disputes Resolution Panel (SDRP) organisation, UK Sport had agreed that they, BC and I would go before the SDRP. To provide a fig leaf, the details were that it would not be in front of a panel but the SDRP would hire a QC to receive written statements, then convene a meeting to hear the various arguments and then an agreement would be thrashed out. That was one great victory for Mike and Dad. They were setting principles for UK Sport across all sports.

My first race had vindicated my recent decisions: I was with some great riders; I had achieved a top ten result and now had the confidence of all my very experienced team-mates and team management. Furthermore, BC had confirmed that, for all their best intentions, they still had not got their head around the finer details of bike racing, like turning up with the right number of riders in a team to be able to be allowed to start. Morally, their dogmatic stance regarding a Team Agreement was sunk, because as soon as I was essential to them, they let me ride for them without signing it. And, on top of all that, the British team manager did not have the good grace either to ask me before or to thank me afterwards for saving them from wasting a lot of the public's money on flights for staff and equipment from Majorca, where they were holding their second warm-weather training camp. I was ignored.

Mike urged a word of caution, as a good lawyer would, and asked that my manager get photocopies of the signing-on sheet and a letter from the organiser confirming it all in writing. When it was reported at Manchester that we had the authenticated copies of the signing-on sheet showing my name against the Great Britain roster and the written statement from the organiser, the BC senior management reluctantly had to face the facts of the situation. Dad wrote a detailed email to Peter King, who replied declining to respond. Dad then wrote to UK Sport highlighting the hypocrisy and bungling. My first race had been very successful in so many ways.

A week later, we drove three hours to the Trofeo Citta di Rosignano on the coastline of Tuscany. I was excited and nervous because Giorgio told me that I would be the protected rider in the race, but stated it would be wasted if my enthusiasm could not be tempered. I was part of a team, he said, something I was not used to in my junior career when I was racing alone. He knew the hilly 107km course well and insisted that I should sit in behind my more senior team-mates for the first 90km before considering any move. Let them get you in the winning position.

I savoured the experience of being sheltered by my team-mates, including Joane, and sucked along in their slipstream as they controlled the race. A few kilometres from the start of the last hill some riders attacked. I went with them. A group of about 12 formed, including Fany. I shouted at her to work, but she didn't need to be told, she was already on the front driving the break to get it away from the field, while I stayed in the slipstream, saving my energy. She was setting it up for me. As soon as we turned on to the climb, I took off, sprinting up the hill, finally able to unleash all my energy. As I crested the hill, four riders had come back to me, including Edita Pucinskaite, World Road Race champion in 1999, and silver medallist the previous year in Lisbon. We were all committed to working together, like a team pursuit, to try to hold off the bunch who would be chasing us down on the descent towards the finish. Suddenly, the lead motorbike crashed in front of us. In a split second, we had to dodge the motorbike, desperately changing our racing line in a zone where there were speed humps that we needed to bunny hop. We all made it past the motorbike and were back descending at top speed.

The plan was working perfectly. I didn't feel any nervousness; I was already weighing up the strengths of my rivals and running through the various finishing scenarios in my head. I knew there was a right-hand corner with about 400m to go. If I positioned myself at the back, prior to this, it meant I could jump early, hopefully taking the others by surprise. There was a risk that if I went too early they could catch me if I died, but I preferred this plan rather than leading out the sprint. I carried as much speed as possible through the corner and then kicked with everything I could muster. I screamed with delight as I crossed the line two bike lengths ahead for my first professional victory. The bunch came in seconds later. I celebrated with my team-mates and Giorgio, not knowing who was most excited, me or the others, as we crowded around hugging and laughing. It had been a race plan that we had executed perfectly. Mum and Dad were almost speechless when I rang. It confirmed our hopes that I could be competitive very quickly in the elite ranks, but I don't think any of us thought I would win in only my second race, while still aged 18. It looked like I didn't need those 2003 university applications after all. For the foreseeable future, I would be cycling.

CHAPTER ELEVEN
Running on Empty

The Cyclingnews.com coverage of my win in Italy was over the top in its praise, declaring that I was 'formidable' and 'already one of the strongest riders in the elite ranks'. Then again, it was written by Maurizio Ricci, our Deia-Pragma-Colnago secretary moonlighting as a journalist. But it spoke volumes of the confidence that the team had in me after only a few weeks and cemented my position in the team. I was now looking forward to competing in my first-ever classic, the Primavera Rosa World Cup, the women's equivalent of the Milan-San Remo. The race is over 118km, running down Italy's far north-western coast from Varazze to San Remo, just short of the French border. The main difficulties are in the final stages, with the 5km Cipressa climb and the 3km Poggio climb whose summit is just 5km from the finish line, meaning another white-knuckle ride on the descent at full speed before launching almost immediately into the sprint.

The team had been working well for me throughout the race and I was in the lead group of about 30 riders as we descended the Poggio and started jockeying for positions for the sprint finish. I was well positioned as we came into the last kilometre, tucked in behind Petra Rossner, who was leading the World Cup and would go on to win the overall title that year. I was confident I would be up there in the sprint, until Petra caught the rear mechanism of the bike in front of her, which shredded the spokes of her own front wheel and caused her to veer sharply to the left. I was forced to go with her, as I was overlapping her back wheel with my front wheel, and in trying to avoid a collision with her I lost all my speed and contact with the leading group. I finished in 20th place, upset that in such a prestigious World Cup event, the finish had ended in this way.

The drama of the day wasn't over. We set off on the long drive home to Forli, our Ukrainian team mechanic and driver Oleg heading off at breakneck speed. I was chatting away with my team-mates in the back when there was a huge bang and the back window smashed. I swivelled around to see what had happened. In the darkness behind, I could see sparks under a following car and the outline of a wheel. We pulled over, accompanied by the car behind, hissing steam and sparks. A bike had fallen off the roof rack and was being ground away under the car, having holed its radiator. I started squawking like a parrot, repeating over and over: 'That's my bike, that's my bike!'

The two young lads in the car behind were Italian, trying to communicate with a carload of foreigners including two Ukrainians, a Spaniard, French and myself. While we waited for the breakdown truck, we tried to explain that we were on our way home from a race, and they were telling us how they were on their way to a local *discoteca*. Oleg taped over the gaping hole where the back window had been with a black plastic bag and loaded my mangled bike back on the roof. We eventually arrived home in the early hours of the morning.

During the week, I was kitted out with a replacement team bike and we spent time getting to know the course of our next race, the 4th Memorial Pasquale di Carlo, to be held on the roads around Forli. Joane Somarriba and her compatriots had gone home to prepare for some important races in Spain, so it was a weakened Deia-Pragma-Colnago team that was entered for the race, and we could do little to dictate the race tactics.

It was a very different course from the previous races, with 20 laps of a 4.3km circuit. The bigger teams like Acca Due O, who had Rasa Polikeviciute, Diana Ziliute and Nicole Brandli, wanted to keep the race together and force it into another bunch sprint. They succeeded and with less than 2km to go, the field was still together. The finish was up a very shallow climb, it had about four hairpins on the way up and the last two in quick succession at about 400m to go, where the road flattened out for the long straight to the finish. I felt that with the drag to the finish making everyone work quite hard, it could be a sprint I could take on from the front.

I was in about fifth position entering the last two bends and with my main rivals on the left, I felt the moment was right to dive up the inside on the right for the last bend and take the lead. I jumped out of the last corner, hugging the right-hand edge of the road to make it hard for anyone to get any slip-stream from me, and I kept on sprinting all the way to the finish. No one could get up to me and I'd won my second race from four starts.

My team-mates were ecstatic, and others around me kept talking up my victories as unprecedented in the world of women's cycling. I deserved my wins and had raced well, arriving on the scene with no intention of taking it easy in my first season. I had trained for this like a demon and I tried to look at the praise without rose-coloured glasses. The truth was that I had come off a very comprehensive pre-season training schedule and was in good form, while some of the others, like Joane, were still building into the season and would undoubtedly beat me later in the year when most of the big stage races were held. Still, no one could have hoped for a better start in what was a giant leap into the unknown. I'd left home excited and unsure of what lay ahead. I had acquired many friends, immersed myself successfully in another country and delighted in the discovery of the sport's history. I was proud of my achievements in these months but now looked forward to returning to Wales.

I was back home because the residents of Wick had decided that they wanted to put up a plaque in the memorial village hall commemorating my four world junior titles. It was a touching reminder of where I had come from and where my heart belonged. Bob Humphrys of BBC Wales asked, on the morning of the unveiling, if he could do the sports section of *Wales Today* from the hall and could the village turn out then. Of course we could! The hall was packed as we went out live. I celebrated my 19th birthday and then flew out to Belgium to get ready for another of the classics and my first Flèche Wallonne World Cup, including the famous finish up the Mur de Huy, a 1.3km climb which averages 10%, with one corner at 26%.

With a full field of 130 riders, the race started on a steep descent out of Huy. The rough and pot-holed road took an early toll, as I dodged around an obstacle course comprising drinks bottles that had bounced out of bottle cages.

I spent most of the race at the front of the peloton to stay out of trouble and keep an eye on the action over the 'côtes' (climbs). On the penultimate climb, with 15km to go, the two-time winner of the race Fabiana Luperini attacked, followed by Priska Doppmann. I looked around to see who from the big teams might chase them, but no one did. I'd missed my chance, through a tactical mistake rather than physical selection, and it was too late. They were pulling away from us and we were racing for a minor place.

I am used to the pain and burning of climbing hills and can push myself very hard, but the huge crowds lining the Mur made me dig even deeper as I forced myself well into the 'red' in an excruciating finale, played out almost in slow motion up the steep gradient of the Mur de Huy. The last metres seemed an eternity and I collapsed after crossing the line in fifth place. It had been a fantastic race packed with action and super crowds – the sort of race I love – and I made up my mind, there and then, that this was an event I was determined to win in the future.

After getting cleaned up, I was told by the team that plans had changed and instead of going back to Italy to take some rest and then training, they wanted me to fly to Spain for the Castilla y Leon World Cup race, followed by a five-day stage race. Sure, why not. Just go with the flow, I thought as I repacked my bags with everything in full view, in the car park. Belgium one day and Spain the next; the fairy tale just kept getting better. Joining me in Spain was a new C40 carbon fibre bike from the Colnago factory. I struggled in the World Cup race but, as the protected team rider, finished third overall in the stage race, and we were all delighted.

The Spanish girls stayed on, while Oleg, Fany and I took in the realities of life on the circuit, a 17-hour, 1,700km drive in the team van, non-stop other than for petrol and toilet breaks. In the early hours of the following morning, after stopping for something to eat, Oleg forgot to close the back door and as we drove away all the bags fell out onto the road. The way we just pulled over and leapt out, dodged the traffic, grabbed the bags off the road and then continued home, as if nothing had happened, was a measure of the world we lived in. When we arrived in Italy, Giorgio Zauli was waiting for us, wanting to speak to Fany and me privately. He was leaving the team because he hadn't been paid for three months and felt he had no option but to stop. He liked both of us and felt obliged to tell us personally. Fany and I checked our bank accounts and relaxed a little; our latest pay was there, but it was unsettling when things had been going so well. After all, I was barely 19 years old and had known these people three months. Could I actually trust them?

Fany, having been around the scene for many years, must have read the signs because she decided that we should pack up our things and move to the second team house, where the Spanish girls had been staying which was now empty. It would allow the Ukrainian riders to have the house to themselves and give us some sense of reassurance. The alarm bells weren't ringing loudly, but they were certainly there. There was a realisation that outside the glamour and excitement of race day, we were vulnerable.

Meanwhile, the efforts of Mike Townley and Dad finally paid off, when at the beginning of May I flew to London to attend the meeting convened by SDRP/UK Sport to solve the problem over the conditions of the Team Agreement with British Cycling. A great weight was lifted from my mind when all the points I had proposed were accepted. I would be able to join the team to represent Great Britain in the World Championships. From a personal point of view, I was delighted that UK Sport now felt it appropriate to recommend me for a Lottery athlete subsistence grant. I never took the public's money lightly. I felt very proud to learn afterwards that UK Sport asked Mike to review a lot of the documentation for a wide range of governing bodies in addition to BC. If my little challenge and my stubbornness helped move sports administration in Britain from the amateur to the professional so that it might compete effectively on the world stage, then it was worth every bit of the heartache my family and I had to put up with over the months. All I had to do now was show that I was worthy of selection.

Next came a stage race in the French Pyrenees. I felt I was among the stronger riders in the field and, after finishing fifth in the first 108km stage, won by Simona Parente from the powerful Edil Savino team, I had high hopes. I then won the next stage, a shorter 63km course, ahead of Fabiana Luperini, Simona's team-mate. This put me in second place behind Simona and just ahead of Fabiana on the General Classification. I maintained that position during Stages 3 and 4, so going into the last stage Simona was in first place, I was second at 19 seconds and Fabiana was in third place, a further 12 seconds behind me.

The last stage was a mountain-top finish, which I was certain would suit my climbing strengths, so I decided to go for not just the stage win but for the overall victory. It was tantalisingly close and the three of us were again together in a break as we approached the last climb, 10km up the Col du Cauteret. I concentrated too much on trying to beat Simona, forgetting that Fabiana was also a strong climber and that they would work as team-mates. Every time I attacked, Fabiana would bring Simona back up to me and then sit back and rest. Then I would go again and Fabiana would nurse Simona back behind me. I was doing all the work and wearing myself out with my fierce attacks, while they were working together and taking their time to steadily catch me up, using their energy wisely.

NICOLE COOKE

Near the finish, Fabiana attacked and I simply couldn't respond. I struggled after her but she kept pulling away, and then seeing that I was in difficulty, Simona attacked me too. I eventually finished in fifth place. Instead of winning and taking the overall title, I had actually lost a place to finish third overall, although I did win the King of the Mountains title and U23 classification. It was a mistake. I still cringe when I remember that race, although Joane and the others were sanguine about it, insisting that it was a learning curve and that there would be another day.

Back after another epic drive, the mood in the Forli team headquarters had turned sour. The departure of Giorgio had been worrying enough, but now former professional cyclist William Dazzani had been mentioned as his replacement. The name meant nothing to me, but Fany was angry, insisting that Dazzani was suspected of being involved in doping. Her worry was that Luigi could have heard the stories but still hired him; Giorgio privately agreed, warning us to be vigilant and offering to stay in contact.

We were invited to Dazzani's team house in a nearby town to train with Team 2002, a squad of mainly Italian riders he also helped. Neither Fany nor I wanted anything to do with him, but Luigi insisted we went to join the other girls for a training ride twice a week. A few days later, Fany returned from a training ride during which she had met up with some other cyclists who chatted openly about what they were taking and how it made them feel fast, as if this was normal. Fany was furious. 'I spend my life working as hard as I can; looking for every tiny improvement to be a better rider for the team and for myself, and yet there are riders out there who take whatever they want and are getting away with it.'

Suddenly, drugs were everywhere. We watched the coverage

158

of the men's Giro d'Italia in which a number of riders had been kicked out of the race for drug offences and police were raiding team after team, searching for drugs. My most recent race was in Bolzano, in which I had won a stage and finished second to the 2000 World Road Race champion Zinaida Stahurskaya. She had recently returned to racing after a positive test the previous year in the Giro d'Italia Femminile when she had been banned for four months, the first of four failed tests for her.

The first time I met Dazzani he said he wanted the team to have a blood analysis, which, on the surface, seemed reasonable. But I was petrified, sitting on a chair with my results waiting for a doctor to advise me what to do, repeating in my basic Italian, 'I'm a clean rider, I don't do drugs, all I do is train,' like a mantra.

A year later, Dazzani was one of 22 people who were placed under house arrest after telephone taps ordered by Italian prosecutors revealed that he was a suspected dealer in an organised drugs ring. He was not subsequently charged. Doctors and nurses were implicated for assisting in hiding the drug trail, there were claims that a teenager was being forced to ride 200km per day on a diet of apples, and there was a bizarre conversation about women hiding drug use by getting pregnant to avoid testing procedures and then aborting the foetus.

In the midst of these worries and fears, Craig came to visit. Now aged 17 and in his final year at school, he arrived with BBC Wales reporter Richard Owen, who was putting together a television documentary about six Welsh athletes preparing for the Commonwealth Games. After the filming was finished, Richard left and Craig stayed for a week, a calming influence when I needed it. We rode the hills around Forli and mixed a bit of tourism with our training rides. I even braved driving the team car, complete with the widening crack in the windscreen that no one would fix, down to San Marino to show him the amazing cliff-top castle.

The excitement of Craig's visit, and showing my new world to one of my family, helped put my worries out of my mind, not that I had any as far as the racing was concerned. I just wanted to ride every race I could. Next on the calendar, the Giro del Trentino, had a reputation for being one of the toughest events of the season, with three days up and down the Italian Dolomites.

On paper, my result of fourth overall and top in the U23 category was another super achievement. The reality was that on the last two stages I was suffering like a dog, climbing as wheels or riders, who weeks earlier I was riding away from, were now too fast to hold. What was wrong? I overlooked the obvious, that I had been racing non-stop since March, over four months of racing in four countries. I was worn out – over-raced and under-rested.

Back in Forli, Fany and I spoke about my situation. Giorgio would have been helpful, but he was not on the team any more. I felt there was absolutely no way I could speak to Dazzani about my bad form and ask him for suggestions as to how to get better. And to add to the problems with my form, Fany and I had not received our wages for June. Other riders in the team had, and now Luigi was not answering my calls. Just when I needed to rest and recover, the realities of my situation made it hard to get any perspective on what lay around me.

The British Championships were only a few weeks away, and then there was the Commonwealth Games in Manchester at the end of July. I rang my parents, who suggested I came home and prepared for these big races in my home environ-ment. I have never been happier to be home. After a few days' rest, I felt ready for one of my hard training rides to get a guide on where my form was. I did my standard 75-mile route which takes in the Bwlch and Rhigos and finishes by coming back over the Windmills, a session for which I had all the times and data, having repeated it many times over several years. I did my best time, and when I told Dad that evening, we came to the conclusion that the Giro del Trentino had probably just been a few 'off days', affected by all the other things going on around the team.

Overjoyed, I did more training. It was ten days or so later – when my heart rate wasn't responding as it should have during training rides, and, in particular, I was riding very weakly after the first hour – that we realised the problem was much bigger, and in training hard I was actually just compounding the error. By then, it was too late to do anything else but rest up for two or three days before the National Championships, which were being held at Resolven, a short 45-minute drive west of Wick.

My recce of the course – a 40km loop and then five laps of a 15km circuit – a couple of days before did little to boost my flagging spirits. There was only one hill on an otherwise flat course and that hill was in the first loop. As the favourite, I worried that everyone would want to attack me in turn, then sit in my slipstream as I chased down each breakaway. To avoid this, I needed a small group to crest the hill of that first loop and stay away, as a small group of riders, fancying their own chances of a medal, would all work together and the bunch would not be able to catch us.

All I could think about was my poor performance in the Giro del Trentino. I pulled myself together on race day and with a chain of Nana, Mike, Craig, Mum and Dad tactically distributed along the key hill, in case my resolve wavered in the task we all knew I had to execute, I rode at the front and kept the pace high. The race had to split right here. The elastic stretched and stretched. Riders dropped off the back. Over the top, I dragged a little group away from the bunch. On the descent I kept going, needing to make sure we would be out of sight of the bunch once on the circuit. Time checks from Dad on the circuit told me we were safe. By the time we reached the last lap of the finishing circuit, the break was reduced to Rachel Heal, Melanie Sears and me. I attacked them with a kilometre to go. I had won my third title in four years, looked supreme but inside I knew my form was far from good. I felt more relief than joy.

My next event would be the Commonwealth Games. The publicity I received after re-taking the National Road Race Championships at Resolven was excellent. Not having received the cup at the time of my win in 2001, I had taken it along this time. The photographs of me – the 'Welsh Wunderkind' in the sun of South Wales, having ridden everyone off my wheel to win alone, smiling with the big silver cup in hand, the only rider wearing an exotic continental trade team jersey to go alongside the club jerseys worn by the rest of the field – were widely promoted. And to the many who knew little of the sport of cycling and even less about the intricacies of road racing, all I had to do apparently was turn up and Commonwealth gold was mine.

Just when a publicity bandwagon was starting to roll and I was getting attention from the broader press, instead of being overlooked by the cycling journalists who focused almost exclusively on male cycling, my times in training indicated that all was not well and a sense of frustration was rising within me. Only my family and I were aware of this, and we knew the next few days were likely to be very challenging, with little prospect of success. Could more bluff and confidence, and a few days' rest, restore the magic? We all kept on smiling and whistling.

I was down to ride the time-trial on the first Saturday of the Commonwealth Games, the track points race on the Tuesday and the road race on the following Saturday. I had the answer straightaway. In the time-trial, where I had been seeded as a favourite, I was caught after only 10km by Australian World No.1 Anna Millward, who had started two minutes behind me. This was shocking. I was not competitive and I was going to be riding a road race where she and any of the other capable Australian riders would form a formidable team. I needed to have a margin of physical advantage if I was to stand any chance, not be weaker!

It wasn't as if I didn't try, or there were any of the bungling, bumbling Laurel and Hardy routines of previous years to degrade my performance. Here I was with Welsh coach Phil Jones and others who were competent and wanted me to win every bit as much as I did, but I could muster only tenth place. BBC Wales' Bob Humphrys, always so supportive, interviewed me afterwards to find out what went on. He was very gentle on me regarding questions about the time-trial, explaining to the viewers, in terms far more generously than I would have allowed myself, that it was not my specialist discipline. The timing and position of the TV interview could not have been more apt. The medal presentation for the time-trial was going on simultaneously, and while not in camera shot, the crowd and sound were. At a pause in the interview, the Canadian national anthem struck up, and we both listened. Bob asked very encouragingly about the road race. I answered. He then made a comment about the anthem and without pressurising me, gave me an opportunity to answer in respect of whether that same anthem would be playing again in seven days' time.

I knew what he was doing for me. 'We'll sort that one out for next Saturday, Bob.' The defiance and determination were there, but the events of the day would not give confidence to any who were knowledgeable about the sport.

Days later I was on the track at the Manchester velodrome, in the points race. I read the race well, getting in an early breakaway and lapping the field, which gave us each 10 bonus points and should have ensured that our breakaway would fight it out for the podium. All I needed to do was regularly pick up points from the remaining sprints through the race, but when I contested the sprints I simply couldn't muster the energy to score any more points, and finished back in sixth. I knew that it was far below my best and I was being outsprinted by riders who I would normally beat comfortably.

It wasn't looking good for the road race in four days' time, a race I desperately wanted to win for Wales. How many hundreds of times had I run over the race in my mind since my visit the previous year? In none of these did I expect to get to the start line being so far off-form. This was a nightmare scenario. At a national level, the knives were sharp and already the first cuts were being made on the Welsh Wunderkind. The Welsh public, via the good work of Bob Humphrys, had followed my career since I was a young girl and had supported me in my unsuccessful fight to gain a place at the Sydney Olympics. I very much wanted to repay them and this was meant to be the moment.

The race was eight laps of an 11.7km circuit, for 93km total. There was one challenging hill that finished 4km before the end of the circuit. The hill was a series of three steps, each of which were quite sharp, with a little flat for recovery between them. Given my form, those flat sections were starting to look like important features. The field would be only 36 riders strong. However, alongside World No.1 Anna Millward would be five powerful Aussies including Sara Carrigan, who would become the Olympic Road Race champion in Athens. The six-strong New Zealand team included Sarah Ulmer, who became Athens Olympic champion in the pursuit. Several of the other riders were regulars at World Cups and had an excellent string of results to their credit. The Canadians had a team of four, with Genevieve Jeanson pulling out, claiming injury. What was left was very powerful nonetheless, with defending champion Lyne Bessette, and in Clara Hughes, fresh from winning the time-trial gold a week earlier, they had the only person on the planet who had won medals in both winter and summer Olympics, while Sue Palmer-Komar was on the European circuit and riding well. England and Scotland fielded six and five riders respectively.

Objectively, it looked like a three-cornered fight between Canada, Australia and New Zealand. My two team-mates, Penny Edwards and Nina Davies, would perhaps be able to help me in the early stages. My form indicated that going on the offensive would erode my precious reserves. It was pointless to attack, I just had to make sure I was still in touching distance at the top of the final climb, so that I could get myself in contention for the sprint.

I went into ultimate recovery mode, doing two very light sessions riding on the rollers for the next three days. The only exception was practising the sprint with Craig. First of all Craig, Dad and I rode very slowly back from the finish and then towards the finish, so that I knew exactly how it was laid out. We did this a few times. We discussed in detail the small undulations on the run-in and even the run-off at a bend, and the fact that the finish line would be out of sight due to a slight curve as I approached it. Then I did four practice finishes coming from behind Craig. Now I would have to hope.

Relations with Shane Sutton, meanwhile, had been up and down. With just one day to the finish of the Games, the cycling events had been a shambles for the Lottery-funded British riders competing for their various nations. The only gold achieved was that by Chris Hoy for Scotland. It is hard to get a perspective on things now. A couple of years prior to this, Brian Cookson had suggested that with the new WCPP coming on stream and all the resources going into it, there was no reason why the home nations should not win every cycling gold at Manchester. He was right; there was no reason why not. With hindsight, we can see that a lot of good work was being done, but at that stage the management structure was not yet strong enough.

Just before dinner on the eve of the race, Shane decided to call an impromptu meeting of the three of us road girls. At this late point in the preparation cycle, he decided it was very important that he shared with us his professional and detailed critique of our preparation. He gave the impression we were beyond any help he could offer. He did not want us to ride as a team; we were to ride as individuals and we should take a long look at Julian Winn, as he was the only one in the Welsh Cycling team who was professional about his approach.

Shocking as the comments were, the unprofessional nature of the delivery and the timing made it worse. Nina had been doing her best since 2000, with scant little encouragement. My form had dropped off a cliff, but that was nobody's fault apart from mine and nobody knew that more than me. I didn't need to be berated; I wanted someone to encourage me. Shane left the three of us totally deflated, and if his words were meant to spur us on, they had the opposite effect. We trudged off to an evening meal which we ate in silence. Our mood could not have been lower. This race was going to be hard enough without Shane taking away the modest assistance I could have. In hindsight, I should have proposed to the other two that we would race together as a team, regardless of any instructions the national coach was giving us. After all, they both knew they were there to support me; it would not have been a new concept. That I didn't grasp the situation, regardless of the circumstances, was a mistake on my part. It felt as though cycling was a man's world and only their views counted. We all knew that Shane wasn't right, but I didn't rise above it.

After dinner, I went out of the athletes' village for a pre-arranged meeting with Dad, who was staying in a campsite nearby, and told him what had gone on. Dad reminded me that Shane wasn't riding in the race. My main rivals, how they raced against each other and my reaction to them were critical, not Shane's unhelpful rants. I said goodbye to Dad and returned to join 'Team Wales', determined to do my very best.

Next morning, Dad managed to evade the security around the race start to join me at the Welsh team pit and wish me well for the race. He told me that Uncle Chris, Mike, Brian Rourke, Nana, Granddad, Auntie Karen and my cousins, along with Mum, were distributed all around the course at key points. By the start of the race, I could not have been more motivated and had almost convinced myself I could win. Why not? I'd had a great season, I was a great rider and I was as close to riding in front of a home crowd as I would ever get. I could not slug it out with the three powerful teams, but I had just one focus and that was to get to the top of the last hill on the last lap, with the leaders. Time to race.

With such a small field there was no luxury of hiding in a big bunch and being sucked along; I had to stay near the front and be vigilant at all times The pace of the first three laps was

steady, and I felt a little relieved that my race was now effectively down to five laps and I hadn't spent much energy.

Towards the start of the fourth lap, Sue Carter of England
raised the pace. New Zealand made a probing attack, but
Australia and Canada were not yet ready to attack. At the end
of the fourth lap, Clara Hughes from Canada forced the pace.
Then a move formed with a rider from each of Australia,
Canada and England. The girls from New Zealand worked
hard to bring the break back. There was a counter attack that
took a group of six away. The Canadian team did not like the
construction and worked hard to get the splintered peloton
back up to them. Another attack with Sue Palmer-Komar,
Australia's Margaret Hemsley and England's Frances
Newstead formed, and as we approached the hill, it looked like
a dangerous springboard to a possible race-winning split. On
this feature of the circuit, I knew I hadn't been climbing well,
so just prior to the hill, I jumped off the front of the group
together with an Australian rider. Up the three stages of the
hill, various riders made attempts to catch the leaders and
break away from those behind. I had made exactly the right
move going into the hill, although others had passed me on
the climb. I crested the top, still in touch with the leaders.

We merged into a group of ten which then became 12 a
we went through the finish with two laps to go. I looked
around. At this stage of the contest, Australia had the better of
the engagement. Out of the 12 they had four riders, compared
with two each from Canada, New Zealand and England. Just
Caroline Alexander was left from the five-strong Scottish team,
and I was there from Wales. Behind, nobody else was going to
regain contact. Now would be the most dangerous phase.
Australia would undoubtedly play out their advantage in numbers and it would be impossible for a lone rider like me to

cover everyone. I had to look at the other riders and think who was most likely to go in the race-winning break.

I opted not to go in any move with Anna Millward, but go with any move with the other three Aussies and Lyne Bessette. The attacks from the Aussies came thick and fast. Several times I had no option but to chase when a group of three were away. I always tried not to close up too quickly, knowing that as soon as we made the junction, the next attack would come. Caroline Alexander was in the same position and was doing the same thing. A group formed – Margaret, Rachel Heal, Roz Reekie-May and Sue – Australia, England, New Zealand and Canada all represented, but were they the right riders? Caroline and I played poker, not chasing. Four riders, three medals, surely one of the teams knows they have the wrong person up there? The gap went out to 20 seconds. It seemed that four nations were content.

I rode next to Caroline and quietly asked if she wanted to attack together to bridge up. We had to chase or the race was finished. She clearly understood the position we were in and said we should go in the dip ahead where we could at least build up some speed before attacking as the hill began. There was an excruciating wait as we approached our designated point. I made sure I was on her wheel. She jumped at the start of the descent into the dip.

Caroline blasted up the climb. I could not hold her wheel and was passed by others as she powered on after the break. I used up a lot of energy chasing Caroline, who was chasing the break, but gradually I clawed my way back up to her group. We were a group of six riders who were 13 seconds behind the leading four. Now I had no cushion of being ahead of stronger riders; we were chasing the race. I had to measure my effort. Over the top, Margaret Hemsley broke away from the other three and was riding away alone. Our group split up, with me in the middle, but I knew I would have the flat on the top and the descent to get back on, so I remained calm. I needed to conserve my energy for the finish. Now on the descent, three from my group had caught the three dropped by Margaret. I was just about to regain this six when I saw Margaret Hemsley getting up at the side of the road. The descent was very treacherous with patches of water on it. She must have caught one while braking and gone down. But I was back in the group at last. We were now seven riders and it was the Canadians who had the advantage. There was a single representative from the five other nations but two Canadians. In one lap, the Australians had lost three riders and a massive advantage.

As I came through the finish for the final lap, I had a last bite of an energy bar. There was a glimmer of hope. Anna Millward, the sprinter I feared most, was dropped, and the two Canadians had the numerical advantage which would be tricky for me if they tried to break away, but good if others attacked, as the burden would always fall on them to close the gaps. My climbing was not amazing, but with only one more time up the hill I could give it everything, I would not need to save energy for a counter. However, even if Anna wasn't with us, she neutralised the Canadian advantage. She continued to chase as hard as she could. On the flat, she was making good progress. The gap back to her varied between 10 and 20 seconds. The Canadians could see this and both of them, fearing her in the sprint, played out their numerical advantage by countering the chase of Anna. The Canadian duo did not attack us, but took it in turns to drive at the front. I took advantage to have my last drink from my bottle and then disposed of it. I needed to be as light as possible for the hill. I also needed to be in the best position I could be. Lyne was leading as we approached the hill and I made sure I was bonded to her wheel in second place. If I could get to the top of the hill in a position to be able to chase and regain contact, a medal was a real possibility.

Lyne and Caroline set a ferocious pace up the climb. I dug deep, and used every fibre in my body to stay in contact, my riding style losing all coordination. I had Brian Rourke and Uncle Chris at different stages of the last climb both shouting at me to keep in contact; they knew this was a critical moment of the race. At the top of the final climb, there were three of us alone. I'd done it, I'd hung on, and now it would come down to the sprint.

We paused. The group enlarged back to seven and took the descent flat out. We approached the sharp left-hander, where Margaret had crashed the lap before. As I leant the bike over and took my line round the corner, I felt my wheels slide as I was braking. There was water on the road. I had to react quickly if I wasn't also to crash. I immediately released the brakes and straightened up, then reapplied the brakes hard but kept going in a straight line, running off the road and managing to stop. I had to unclip my foot and turn my bike round and start chasing to catch the others.

I pursued the group exactly like any track pursuit specialist but had to make sure that I didn't panic and burn up my precious energy reserves that I had husbanded so carefully during nearly three hours of racing. I needed to catch them but I needed to still have energy left to sprint in a finish that would probably be as tactical as any track match sprint. Then, as I came round a corner I saw them, going under the 1km banner, spread all over the road. My heart rose; nobody had started a leadout, they were too busy watching each other. I was going to catch them! With only 800m to go, I was back in the front group. The gold was still on. I tried to take some deep breaths but I just had to concentrate on the tactical positioning and movement. I went to the far left, watching everyone to my right – I needed to look only one way. With 400m to go, Caroline jumped hard. I was on to her like lightning, into her slipstream and closing her down fast. I carried my speed and blasted straight past her, totally focused on the line.

It was still a way to go and now my legs were in agony, but I had to keep going. I had made my move and there was now no other option. I had a gap, they weren't closing on me. I kept going. My legs screamed 'pain', my brain screamed 'I'm going to win this!' I threw my arms in the air as I crossed the line, I'd done it! It was a magical moment and one I will always treasure.

At the ceremony afterwards, it was fantastic. Rachel had timed her sprint well to come third and Sue was second. Australia, who had packed four into a winning break of 12, were not on the podium. During the interview Bob Humphrys reminded all the viewers what I had said the week before about making sure, today, the flags were in the right order and the crowd sang the right anthem. I think he knew just as well as I did what a punt that had been and I don't know who was happier, Bob or me! Despite my poor showings earlier, the Welsh fans were there in huge numbers. With Welsh flags flying all around, we all belted out 'Hen Wlad Fy Nhadau', which caused John Inverdale, anchoring the show for the BBC, to state that Riverton in Lancashire sounded as passionate as rugby's Cardiff Arms Park.

In the Welsh camp, it was all delight. Phil and Louise Jones came and greeted me, along with other riders and athletes. Penny and Nina were obviously pleased as well. Sadly, Shane did not find time or space to see me or say a single word to me. If he had been brave enough to apologise, we might have been able to move on. I was very pressed for time, with a plane to catch to join my team-mates in France. I was certainly not going to prioritise a possibly fruitless search for Shane over seeing my family. He knew exactly where to find me. I said goodbye and jumped into an official car to race back to the village, pack my bike and head to the airport to catch a plane bound for Brussels to meet my Deia-Pragma-Colnago team-mates for our biggest race of the year.

I was about to ride the race that I had dreamed of since watching Robert Millar attacking in the Alps. I was about to understand what it was like to be a servant of the team – a *domestique* – in the Tour de France. It was time to repay my debt to Joane Somarriba, who had done so much to help me in my first races as a professional.

CHAPTER TWELVE
Humbled by the Tour de France

I arrived in Belgium that Saturday night, reunited with Joane, Fany and the rest of the Deia team, who were all very excited for me, knowing how much I'd told them about the Commonwealth Games all season and what the win meant for me. I spent the evening examining every detail of the Tour de France race manual; there were two stages the next day, a road stage then a team time-trial, followed by three stages all in excess of 160km. An individual time-trial on Thursday led into three serious days of climbing in the Alps before a much-needed rest day. Then the race would go to Le Mans, there was another TT and eventually on to Paris in two weeks' time. My job was to help Joane, who was aiming to win her third Tour. The management seemed to have everything in place. We had a campervan so we could stretch out our legs to help recovery on transfers and use the cooking facilities to have food after the stages. Luigi had also hired an extra masseur, as there would be eight pairs of tired legs at the end of every stage to deal with.

We rode to the start from the hotel with Joane resplendent in her yellow jersey as defending champion. The crowds and people cheered our team when they glimpsed Joane's jersey. I felt the magic of the Tour. As we rode, I also felt an uneasy tightness in my legs, that didn't get any better with each kilometre.

I ignored my concerns. In Stage 1, my job was to go for the sprint to try to get a high finishing position that would seed our team higher, and therefore later, in the team time-trial that afternoon, giving us more time to recover. However, I would have no support in the sprint as my team-mates needed to save themselves for the team time-trial. As we left Brussels, the pace was frantic, with 120 riders all wanting to be to the front where it was relatively safer. In the sprint, I had to gamble on the wheels to follow. I was disappointed with 13th and felt I had let Joane down. My team-mates and the management were satisfied with the placing and pointed out that I was first U23 finisher and got to wear the blue best young rider's jersey in the team time-trial that afternoon. We finished fourth, and that evening Joane was happy enough with her start. I looked forward to the relieving massage of my very tight legs.

The second stage, 159km to Valenciennes, featured long stretches of cobblestones in the closing stages. My job was to work as Joane's *domestique*, supplying her with drinks and food from the team car and keeping her out of trouble until the cobbles started, which I did. All day the tightness in my legs remained. Stages 3 and 4 were theoretically 154km and 156km respectively. The UCI set limits on stage 'race' distances. The mercurial organiser Pierre Boué would always do his very best to put on the grandest Tour stages possible, taking in iconic cities and areas of outstanding natural beauty. With this in mind, he sometimes became quite inventive with the stage route. So on Stages 3 and 4, Pierre came up with the idea of adding in neutral or 'non-race' sections. These enabled the peloton to ride out of a busy city centre with a parade and fanfare. Pierre thought nothing of making some neutral sections

20km long, and once you added in the odd 'miscalculation' in the race manual, we were racing more like 180km. Pierre wanted to create a spectacular Tour, and frankly I'm glad he did.

Each day the dead, tight feeling in my legs became worse. After long stages we had long transfers, sat in the campervan driving for hours to the hotel. On one transfer, our campervan got a flat tyre on the motorway and Dazzani and our new masseur had to fix it. We had to get all equipment out of the back to get at the spare wheel, change the wheel with the camper balancing perilously on a tiny jack, and then repack the equipment before continuing our late, long journey. On Stage 4, I was really struggling to hang on to the peloton. As the gradient increased on a long drag, I was at the back, in among the team cars of the race convoy. Out of nowhere, my Deia team car appeared alongside me. 'What do you want, what is it, does Joane need something?' I didn't know what to say, I couldn't bring myself to say I'd got dropped, but they quickly jumped to the conclusion that Joane must have needed some energy bars so they stuffed them in my back pockets, gave me a massive shove and I had to somehow get back into the bunch.

I was just about on the back of the bunch, when there was a screeching of brakes and some riders crashed. I tried to avoid them but someone fell on top of me, and the next thing I knew I was in a ditch; it had been raining so at least it was a soft landing. I clambered out and then pulled my bike up after me. I got going after the bunch again, my mission being to get these bars to Joane. I sprinted up the side of the bunch and handed her the bars and checked that she was okay, after which I slid to the back of the group before grovelling my way to the finish.

That night there was lots of screaming and shouting in Italian. I did my best to keep up but thought it not the right time to ask my team-mates for a literal translation. Our new masseur threw a tantrum and packed his suitcase. 'That's it, I quit!' he wailed, before leaving to sit at the front of the hotel, his suitcase at his side, with his arms folded in a huff. I don't know what the masseur was expecting but Luigi was hardly flustered. I looked around. Most of my team-mates found something very interesting to concentrate on and pre- tended to carry on as if nothing odd was going on. After about an hour, perhaps it dawned on our masseur that no one was going to take him to the station or drive him home and we'd probably leave him there the next morning when we left. He got over it, and quietly got back to work.

The following day was the 31km time-trial and I finished in 94th place, more than eight minutes slower than the winner. I'd been told to take it easy to save myself for the next day, and to the casual onlooker it might have seemed I carried out the instructions perfectly. In fact, I had been riding flat out to make the time cut. Each day the tightness in my legs was worse than the day before, my strength ebbing away. Each journey back to the car was followed by a chase to the pelo- ton which seemed longer, further and more frantic each time I made it.

Stage 6 was a very hilly 127km between Lyon and Villard de Lans. My legs just wouldn't do what I wanted them to do and my reactions and brain power were ebbing with them. I was involved in a crash and although I somehow stayed up, my front wheel had lost spokes and would not turn, so I stopped for the team car and a spare wheel. A few of us formed a chase group; we worked hard and had the tail of the bunch in sight on several occasions but could not quite make the shelter of the race convoy. The chase went on for what seemed like an eternity, and I was running on empty. Next, were two mountain stages in the Alps. I could start but I would not be of any use to Joane and the rest of the team – this was not something I could ride through. I knew my Tour was over. I told Luigi I was exhausted and that I couldn't continue. I think he was expecting it, as he asked me to hand him my numbers off my jersey and he would withdraw me from the race.

I found Joane and apologised for my bad form and for not being able to help her. She was very understanding. At the hotel that night, Fany – who had also abandoned that day – and I talked about the race and the exhausting and crazy events of the season so far. While I had been back in the UK for the British Championships and Commonwealth Games, part of the team had ridden the Giro d'Italia. It was not surprising that Fany was exhausted as she had ridden both grand tours working as a *domestique* for the team leaders.

There were other problems than my form. The Spanish riders had their wages ring-fenced from the team via the Spanish newspaper sponsor; our erstwhile Ukrainian housemates were also being paid, but neither Fany nor I had received our salaries for a few months. It was not the biggest thing on our minds because the money was poor anyway. Even worse, Fany and I were both very disturbed by the blood tests and help being offered by Dazzani. In the Giro, our Ukrainian team-mate Nataliya Kachalka finished eighth overall. Some of the quality of rides we were seeing had both of us incredulous. Zinaida Stahurskaya had finished second in the Giro and was now smashing everyone in the Tour including Joane, who was in superb form. Was Zinaida 'reformed', having been banned from racing during the winter for PED abuse? From where Fany and I stood, it looked like the actions of the authorities had precisely the opposite effect on the peloton from that they were meant to achieve.

If ever anyone excuses Lance, Tyler, Ullrich, Riis, Millar, Hincapie, Barry or any of the other dopers by saying they only did what they had to do to level the playing field, then they need look no further than Fany Lecourtois.

Burnt into my memory for life will be how she felt that night. She had ridden as a professional for ten years, plus all the years before she had put into preparing for that career. She lived the life of a professional athlete every day, watching what she ate and how she rested, sacrificing so much. She gave her all for her team-mates and helped me achieve wins. Her team managers didn't pay her and she turned the other cheek. Our sport came up with meaningless out-of-season penalties for that tiny minority who actually tested positive. She, like me, would never resort to taking drugs. She stood rock solid, her personal integrity intact. Nature had blessed me with physical characteristics which, in an injury-free season, allowed me to take on all-comers. Fany didn't have that level of natural ability and simply strived as hard as she could, but was now realising that the system, which should have been designed to protect those of us who would never take drugs, did not; and those at the top of the sport who should have acted, failed to do so.

She was exactly like Peter, who I spoke about in my retirement statement. It is these unknown riders who are the victims of Lance, David Millar and the rest of the liars. I will value my friendship with the team-mate I met, on my first professional team, for the rest of my life. Peter and Mlle Fany Lecourtois are each worth a thousand Lances.

Fany and I helped out the team as best we could, washing clothes, handing up bottles and preparing feeds. On the

Sunday, we were at that same summit at Vaujany where I had first seen the Tour three years before. The conditions couldn't have been more different: fog and freezing rain, with visibility barely 10m. It was a different experience watching the soaked and shivering riders traipse in at the summit, holding bottles and clothing ready for Joane and the rest of the team.

Zinaida Stahurskaya has her name in the record books as winner of the 2002 Tour. In 2003, she would again test positive and receive only a two-month ban from competition.

After a week of total rest in Forli, it was back to Wick where they had planned a big party for me. The village hall was bursting with people, spilling out onto the road and park outside. The organisers asked me to ride around the village on my race bike wearing my Commonwealth gold medal. Bob Humphrys covered the event for BBC Wales and it was fantastic to re-live the race. After everything that had gone on at the Tour, I loved being surrounded with such genuine people, happy to share in my achievement, and it restored my confidence in human nature. It seemed like I was a million miles away from Ms Stahurskaya, my unpaid wages and the whole circus that surrounded the worst of professional cycling. Still in recovery mode, I went to Mildenhall, camping with Sean and Kathryn McClelland's family. We had a wonderful time watching the grass track racing and doing some marshalling for the kids' duathlon and the cyclo-cross race.

Around this time, I had wished to address Shane's behaviour at the Commonwealth Games with the WCU. He certainly had a great deal to offer in terms of his knowledge of the sport, but he was in a professional position, working for the WCU, and he needed to learn to behave in a manner appropriate to his position. While I was on the Tour, I asked Dad to represent me in a meeting with Bill Owen, the volunteer president of the WCU. On the day of the meeting, Dad heard that Shane was no longer working for the WCU but was now a full-time employee of the BC WCPP. Dad asked Bill if this was true, but neither Bill nor the secretary of the WCU (who maintained the personnel records) had been told about this and had to check with his new employers to find out. This meant there was nothing more to discuss. It seemed that I was not the only victim of Shane's lack of respect.

Finally, at the end of August, I was refreshed and ready to build up my training for the last part of the season, so I returned to Forli keen to race, with the World Championships not too far away.

First up, in September, was the Giro di Toscana. I was now rooming with two new girls, but when I got back to my room one night after dinner, I walked in on what looked like a hospital ward. My two room-mates were sitting there with drips hanging out of their arms and there was a collection of bottles of milky liquid. I was absolutely incensed. What the hell was in those bottles? Knowing my anti-doping stance, how dare they do this in my room?

'What's going on?' I demanded.

'We're recovering from the stage,' came the lame reply. 'We're using amino acids and sugars, medicines.'

'Not in my room you're not, I'm not putting up with this.'

I found Luigi and told him the girls were injecting stuff in my room and I wanted to change rooms. He came up to my room, mumbled a few words and the two girls got up, needles still in their arms, picked up their bottles and walked out into the corridor and off to another room. I lay on my bed seething. I felt I was surrounded by aliens. I didn't want this.

I thought back to the celebration in Wick and the fun of Mildenhall. I struggled to match the pictures of Wick and Mildenhall against riders who had needles in their arms, and Luigi who seemed to have no conscience about not paying his riders. Was there something wrong with me? No, but there appeared to be plenty wrong in cycling.

I tried to focus on racing the Giro di Toscana and looked forward to the following season when I could make a fresh start with a new team. Joane did not race. Our team formed an odd assortment of personnel bonded mostly by simply wearing the same jersey. Given the fact that I was virtually riding alone, and the state of the peloton at the time, I am immensely proud of my riding in that Tour. I finished best U23 rider and eighth overall.

My last race of the season with Deia was the Giro della Romagna. After the race, I handed my bike and kit bag over to Dave Mellor and the British team who had also raced, so that they could take my things to Belgium for the World Championships in Zolder. I set off to Forli and would travel lightly to Belgium a couple of days later. I was glad my time with Deia was finished. Then Dave Mellor called. 'Hi Nicole, your team manager has just picked up your bike.'

'What?'

'He came along, we'd already put it on the roof and he said something in Italian like he was going to take it to Belgium. I didn't know what he was trying to tell me.'

'And you just took it off the roof of the GB team car and handed it over to him. Thanks Dave.'

In the run-up to Romagna, Luigi had stopped answering my calls and I had suspected something was up. After Mike Townley had contacted them on my behalf, the UCI had taken action; they had written to the team to ask about my wages, and now I had no wages and no bike. I called Luigi again, but still got no answer. Just as I thought my nightmare with Deia was finally over, Luigi had yet another trick up his sleeve. I had no bike for the World Championships.

But before then, I had one more race in Holland. Perhaps feeling guilty at giving away my bike, Dave rang to say I could use one of the many spare bikes the Lottery had funded for the WCPP girls to race on. Looking back, I just can't see how I did it. For the race at Westerbeek, which I won, I must have been running on anger rather than energy.

Meanwhile, a contact made a discreet call to the Colnago factory to explain what had happened, but apparently Ernesto was at a bike show in America. Surely Colnago would want the British star on the Colnago bike that they had supplied to Deia at the forthcoming World Championships? Two days later, Luigi turned up at the GB team hotel with my bike. He smiled as I came out to see him, as if there was nothing wrong. He insisted on making a public scene about wishing me luck and said that he wanted to make sure the bike arrived safely for me. I was just wishing the moment would come when he would have no more impact on my life.

After two wins at the last two World Championships, I should have made a big bang here. There was a kind of bizarre camaraderie at Deia, such that when we got on the bike, regardless of what crazy things were going on elsewhere, at least we knew how to race and what we were there for. With GB, I entered the twilight zone where David Millar was fawned upon by the staff, while I was with Dave Mellor and the WCPP girls, for some of whom cycle racing seemed to be a necessary but unwanted diversion from comparing air travel and the hotels they'd stayed in. They made all the right noises about how they would help me, but I felt like screaming, 'You don't

know how to race at the top level, how could you help me?'
Rachel Heal, in particular, was willing and sincere, but with
some of the others, I just felt like I was a meal ticket. The
uneasy looks of so many of the support staff towards me told
a story. Since Peg Hill had been ousted, I doubted any would
be sad to see me go the same way.

It was a flat course at Zolder, so I knew it would finish as a
sprint. I hid in the bunch, recognising I would need everything
for the finish. None of the British riders would be able to get
me into the top 20 in the last 5km. I don't know what my
team-mates were doing during the race, but those I could
locate in my half of the race looked startled when I told them
a break was up the road and I wanted them to go to the sharp
end and earn their year of Lottery funding. It didn't do any
good. Peg had been right; they really needed to start from the
basics.

With about 5km to go, there was a big crash in front of me,
which blocked the whole course. I tried to get through it as
quickly as possible, but there was no way of catching up the
lost ground and I chased all the way to the finish line. I finished 35th and 27 seconds behind the winner, Susanne
Ljungskog of Sweden.

It would have been nice to say that was the end of an event-
ful season, and now it was time to make plans for 2003. I had
learnt a lot riding with Deia-Pragma-Colnago, particularly
from Joane and the short time with Giorgio, and I had been
thankful for a place on a team. My salary had only been
€8,000 for the year and it took lots of help from Mike
Townley, and action by the UCI, before I saw it in full.

After the Commonwealth Games, I had received a call from
Peter Keen. Despite all the efforts of British Cycling, home

riders had garnered only two golds – Chris Hoy on the track and myself on the road, a small improvement on Kuala Lumpur 1998, when there had been no golds for British riders. By contrast the Australian track team had won eight gold medals and the men's road team had won all three medals in both the time-trial and road race. England was at the bottom of the list of seven nations that had won medals at the cycling events. With the Athens Olympics less than two years away, Peter Keen asked me for my ideas and thoughts. I was happy to share them.

The girls on the WCPP were riding the big races, but they were travelling out from Britain each time. In order to gain real experience, I said it would be better if they could actually live with a team on the continent as I was doing, so they could not only race with top riders but also learn by training and living with them. The Australians successfully used this model to develop their talent. I was not suggesting anything radical.

During the season, Maurizio Fabretto, the manager of Acca Due O, and I had spoken together. He wanted me to ride for his team in 2003, just as I had wanted to ride for his team in 2002. I spoke to Peter Keen about my optimal team placement being with Acca Due O, but also that we both needed my relationship with the WCPP to develop. The arrangements that had come into place since May, to make me a member of the WCPP while riding for a professional team, had worked well; certainly I would have found it very difficult to continue without the generosity of the Lottery funding. Peter was supportive of continuing this arrangement with Acca Due O for the following year. This was acceptable and we spoke about other WCPP riders possibly joining me. Peter also suggested that he could include me with the WCPP girls for the endurance events on the track. If I was prepared to dedicate the time to the specific preparation, then a ride at the 2003 World Track Championships was a possibility.

British Cycling took my suggestion to heart about placing WCPP riders in a continental team and Dave Mellor contacted me about getting a place for Rachel Heal at Acca Due O. The plan started to be fleshed out and Maurizio was willing to take her on his roster.

In October, I attended the WCPP induction camp for the women's squad where the staff identified their aims. Over the next weeks, Rachel and I swapped emails about going to Italy together. Later, I received a call from Dave Mellor that should have rung alarm bells. He had obviously spoken to Maurizio and was trying to sound me out. Dave wanted to know what was being lost in translation.

Some team managers liked playing practical jokes on other managers and GB, with no Italian speakers, were an easy and very attractive target. The way they flew in and flew out and had all the latest and most expensive kit, grated with so many teams who were stretching their resources so thinly. Dave had obviously started asking around the circuit attempting to gain offers for Rachel to ride with a continental team.

Dave said that Maurizio had offered Rachel just board, lodgings, kit and a bike, but no salary. However, other teams he had contacted said they would pay a salary of €40,000 for the year, so he wondered if Maurizio was just trying it on. I told him that €40,000 per year would be well beyond any amount I would be able to negotiate, and that the wages I was still chasing via legal challenges would total just €8,000 for the year. At this stage, Rachel did not have a single win on the international circuit. Dave seemed very confused.

Maurizio wanted me to sign the contract in Italy and meet some of the sponsors. Just before I went to Italy, Dave was in contact again, saying I was not to sign under any circumstances unless it was confirmed that Rachel was to be placed with the team. While I was not going to take instructions from Dave about whom I would and would not sign for, I was happy that Maurizio was sounding positive about Rachel and I could not understand the reason for this bizarre conversation.

Dad and I met Maurizio in his office. Firstly, I made it clear that I would not live with anyone who was taking drugs or any 'preparations' which required to be taken intravenously. Maurizio agreed and replied that he had just the right place to stay; a house looked after by 'Nonna' – an 80-year-old known to be totally drug-free!

We then discussed the possibility of including track racing in my programme. Maurizio wasn't interested. What if I won a track World Championship? 'Track titles!' a gesture of his hand indicating they were of little consequence. Dad insisted I press the point and said if we were to negotiate a bonus for a road world title, surely there would be one if I was to win a track world title. How much would it be? I translated. Maurizio looked at us both and then nodded. With a dramatic flourish he gripped his calculator, stabbed at the keys and noted the result on a piece of paper. He then took a notebook out of his drawer, looked through it until he found exactly the right page – his thoughtful nod confirming he had found what he was looking for – before more stabbing at the calculator and another figure written on the piece of paper. Then he looked at the ceiling and put some more figures on the paper and a final calculation. With a flourish, he wrote a sum on a separate piece of paper and passed it over, face down. This, he assured me, was his single and final offer. We turned it over – €100. We all laughed together. You see, Maurizio explained, the Italian public is just not interested in track racing. The road racers are their heroes, they want to see them when they stand at the side of the road at a criterium or on a mountain pass. On the road is where the great races take place. So it was settled that I would ride a road programme based mainly on Italian races and World Cups in Europe.

With that issue sorted out, there was just the position of Rachel to be confirmed. Maurizio passed me a fax he had received from Dave Mellor and asked me to translate it all for him. It was quite simple and just asked for Rachel to be recorded with the UCI as one of the 12 members of the registered team, and that Rachel was accepting of the conditions Dave had verbally outlined to me. It requested a written confirmation in reply. There was some issue about numbers, relating to a new regulation for the next season that set a maximum of 12 riders per team, probably to avoid better sponsored teams having more riders than other teams. I asked Maurizio whether he would be able to give one of the 12 places to Rachel.

Maurizio waved away our concerns and then described how he was going to deal with the maximum team-size rule. He had a twist. He was going to have two teams, the older riders headed by Diana Ziliute and a team of younger rides with me as captain and Rachel on my team, called Ausra Groudis Safi. When I began raising concerns about which team would be entered in which races, Maurizio reassured me: 'Don't worry, I'll enter both in every race, and you can work as one team.' Those rules were being taken to the limits of their flexibility! Rachel's spot was confirmed. I signed a two-year contract, with my salary €23,000 per annum.

Next was a visit to London at the end of November. Tony Blair was hosting a reception for all the gold medallists from the Commonwealth Games. Chris Hoy and I were there and

of course there were the representatives of the sporting federations, in our case, Brian Cookson and Dave Brailsford. With
Tony Blair just a few metres away, Dave came over and asked
if we could have a quiet word; he had something he wanted
to tell me. I have never been able to find out why this happened and no one at BC has wanted to talk to me about it,
therefore I can only speculate on the motives.

Dave told me his urgent news: 'If you sign for a professional
team, you cannot be supported by WCPP, so you are not
going to get a grant next year.'

All the barriers would be erected against me riding with a
trade team, exactly like they had been the year before. Of
course, I could rip up my contract with my trade team and
ride with the rest of the girls on the BC WCPP and then I
would get full support from them. I was shocked at his timing
and the content. With Tony Blair so close, I could hardly make
a scene. Dave was making sure I understood that their agenda
had primacy. Mum drove me home and we discussed it with
Dad in the early hours of the morning. Peter King had a very
detailed email to respond to by the time he came into work
the next day.

Six months earlier we had been in arbitration with UK
Sport over my WCPP membership, and now we were further
back than before that. I explained that I had gone through my
2003 WCPP membership with Peter Keen in August and
he had confirmed it. I was told there must have been some
misunderstanding, as Peter Keen could not possibly make such
a commitment. I also pointed out that I was not the only British
rider with Acca Due O; there was also Rachel, indeed I had
helped translate her contract and the fax from BC, and helped
Maurizio draft his reply while I was with him, these rather
uncomfortable facts somewhat mitigated against the scenario

they were trying to present. So was Rachel still on the WCPP, or off it like me? But the BC WCPP were never ones to let facts get in the way of a new policy.

Within BC there was little or no knowledge of the women's professional cycling scene. As a matter of fact, there was not at that time a great deal of knowledge of the men's scene either. As a result of this ignorance, rumours abounded, particularly about riders' salaries. If they thought that Rachel could receive €40,000, no doubt they thought that I was on a much greater sum. The fact that my contract registered with the UCI was for €23,000 wouldn't have stopped them thinking I was actually receiving more. They would have been aware that some men's teams registered smaller contracts with the UCI than they actually promised to pay the riders, both to reduce the deposit the teams had to lodge with the UCI and also for 'tax optimisation' purposes. I was never aware of similar practices on the women's side because the salaries were always so small.

Some of the other gossip was relayed to me by Darren Tudor, the Welsh junior coach. Apparently, BC staff wanted to know how I had got such a good sponsorship deal with Jaguar to get a new convertible sports car. Dad had spent the days after the Commonwealth Games frantically putting a new clutch in my 1983 Peugeot that my aunt had given me free as a nonrunner, with no MOT, so that I could go and see everyone camping at Mildenhall. I had tried to get a car sponsorship deal earlier in the year and been laughed at. 'Come and see us after the Commonwealth Games,' one of the more promising leads had said. After Manchester, I saw them with my gold medal. More excuses. It was a bad time of year, sales were down.

Mum and Dad had worked hard and had paid off their mortgage early, and then their original endowment policy had matured. They went mad blowing just over £6,000 on a totally impractical second-hand Jaguar. Now I don't think anyone would begrudge Mum and Dad that. At the time and for years afterwards, their transport was two second-hand cars that notched up over 300,000 miles each! Dad did all the maintenance on them and ran them on a shoestring. I think to offset the disappointment I had after the Commonwealth Games in not being able to trade up from my salvaged Peugeot, they allowed me to use their new treat. So maybe this decision to not allow me to have a contract with a trade team and also receive the Lottery grant awarded to all the other riders was simply a question of jealousy based on gossip, ignorance and myths.

Just when I had finished with troubles regarding teams and thought I could concentrate on cycling, here were the very people paid by the public to help elite athletes creating yet more chaos, playing on the fact that UK Sport didn't keep them in check. Rachel's position was an obvious flaw in their argument, and so they also destroyed her dreams of riding on the continent as she was prevented from joining me in Italy. Maurizio was informed just before the deadline for registration, and at exactly the wrong time of year he had to find a replacement rider. BC refused to recommend me for a Lottery grant and demanded that if I were to ride for GB, for example at the World Championships, I would have to ride a GB bike, not my team bike, which is never the case on the professional circuit.

Ultimately, I wanted support and I wanted some British riders around me committed to winning. The issue was not about the money. BC had tried to stand in my way at the start and now, at the end of the season, they were behaving in exactly the same way. While BC either wouldn't or couldn't seem to accept what was required to become a successful rider, there were individuals who did. Claire Dixon, my junior team-mate at Plouay, had made her own way to Italy and Rachel had also been willing to make sacrifices and take the risk and go and live in a different country. BC preferred pouring public money into a UK-based team which included a whole train of coaches, mechanics and other support staff. Maybe if all the riders were based abroad, they wouldn't be able to justify all these jobs?

Certainly it was not a decision based on success. Following my own path in 2002, I had seven race victories and a Commonwealth gold medal. A quick look at the women's World Cup standings at the end of 2002 indicated that the public were not getting too much value for money, five years into this programme, for all the bikes, vehicles, air fares, full-time staff, grant-aided athletes on the women's programme and its management team. Only three other GB riders had scored any points at all! Twelve months ago, with Peg Hill on board, prospects were good; now GB had gone backwards.

Then BC raised the stakes further. I received a written communication denying that Peter Keen had assured me that they would support me, in that conversation after Manchester 2002. It was obvious that politics and personal power plays within the still evolving WCPP were getting in the way of the organisation doing what the public paid it to do – support good athletes and help them become better. While I had no grant and therefore no support from them, I was confident that my cause was just and the route I was taking was the one they should be urging other riders to go down. Looking back, I'm sure they understood this too.

This second dispute did not worry me. I was confident, despite the posturing by some at BC, that UK Sport would see the sense of my position. Unlike in 2001, when I was portrayed by BC to those such as Peg Hill as a troublemaker who had yet to achieve on the professional women's circuit, I now had a series of senior wins to my name, achieved against the very best in the world. The way they dealt with Rachel's placement in Italy and the sacking of Peg Hill all confirmed that I needed to hold firm to my principles. As currently configured, the BC WCPP needed new direction. It needed a new director.

CHAPTER THIRTEEN
World Cup Triumph

At least Maurizio was more than living up to his commitments. All contact was positive and everything he said he would do, he did. I revelled in the comforting isolation of hard training, where I was my own, rather demanding master. I accompanied Craig on his morning school run each day, my old school bag filled with textbooks and strapped to the bike, which provided an ideal, high-intensity workout. Then in the afternoons I would do my long ride over the Bwlch and other hills to develop endurance, lost in my own thoughts and expectations about what might be ahead. This steady routine, undertaken irrespective of the weather, created a strong base for the season ahead. I wanted to repeat my early-season success of the previous year but – and this was the hard part – ensure that I didn't fade later in the campaign. I looked back on that first year and realised I had learnt a lot, despite the difficulties associated with adapting to a different language and culture.

In early February 2003, I arrived in Cornuda and settled into an environment that was welcoming and homely, although the surreal events occurring almost daily in Maurizio's team were never far away. The house I stayed in was owned by an old Italian widow who lived by herself on the ground floor and rented out the top floor to Maurizio each season. This was the famous 'Nonna' who Maurizio had promised I would live with. She was in her eighties and a real character, with six children and numerous grandchildren who would pop around to see her, so the house was usually a buzz of activity. She kept chickens, had a vegetable garden, made her own bread in a big oven and even produced homemade wine in a garage fitted out with an enormous wine press, with grapes grown in a small vineyard tended by one of her sons. She and I became particularly close. I admired her resourcefulness and resilience, as well as her joyful spirit. I sometimes took her to the village church when she wanted to attend a service, or to the cemetery to lay flowers on the grave of her husband; flowers which she'd grown specially for this purpose.

The other girls arrived within a few days, including Australian Rochelle Gilmore who had the role of a sprinter within the team and was to be my room-mate. We prepared diligently for the next four weeks, riding out to meet up with our team-mates living nearby and making quite a sight on the roads as our yellow and silver train headed out into the quiet countryside. I also regularly trained with a local men's U23 team to get some good sparring partners for the hills and to do my longer endurance rides. My form felt excellent.

For the season opener, the GP Castenaso, I happily acted as *domestique*, supporting the sprinters. Intra-team rivalries, if not managed properly, can cause havoc. The result was disappointing; the sprinters couldn't agree who would be the team's finishing rider to be led out by the other two in the last stages of the sprint train – they placed third, fourth and fifth. The following week, for the GP Rosignano, where I was team leader and protected rider, I felt great again but we made another tactical mess of the finish, and I finished in second place behind World champion Susanne Ljungskog, with Rochelle third.

The first round of the World Cup had been held in Australia. The second round was the Primavera Rosa, and Maurizio was in overdrive with his passion and desire for a victory in one of the biggest showcases for women's cycling, and his team, in Italy. For him, the Primavera Rosa and the women's Giro d'Italia were the highlights of the year.

Russian Zulfiya Zabirova was Olympic and World Time-Trial champion who, due to her lack of a good sprint, would always try to get away on her own and use her time-trialling abilities to solo to the finish. She had won several stages of the Tour de France in this manner. We discussed the possibility of a Zulfiya breakaway in our pre-race talk; Maurizio waved his hands around saying, '*Non mollare.*'

My Italian was getting much better but I was still learning about the subtleties of the language and phrasing. My interpretation of the instruction was not to worry, to relax. I was always being told that I needed to calm down, that I was too anxious and should learn to save my strength during a race. If Zulfiya broke away, then I shouldn't worry because someone else would chase her down.

The race started and despite earlier attacks from different riders, a big group was still together as we tackled the Cipressa with 25km to go. Zulfiya attacked, by the top of the hill she had a gap of 35 seconds and after the descent it was 50 – she was gone. My natural instinct would have been to go with Zulfiya, I had been in a position to chase and I felt great athletically. I was easily capable of matching her move, but I had obeyed what I thought were the team instructions. There were no tactical opportunities for a break in the last few kilometres and so I led out my room-mate Rochelle in the sprint. She finished on the podium in third. In the post-race analysis, Maurizio and I spoke. He explained that '*non mollare*' was a warning not to give in or yield if Zulfiya made a break – in other words, to get after her!

We drove down to Spain to tackle the Castilla y Leon, the third round of the World Cup. It was on a tough course and should have suited me down to the ground. I decided to change tactics and follow my natural instinct to attack on the hills, hoping to break away or at least reduce the lead group to a selection of the strongest riders, and fight it out for victory from a more manageable-sized group, as my team did not have the strength to dictate race tactics on a hilly course.

I attacked several times, only to be brought back to the peloton. On one occasion, with about 8km to go, Mirjam Melchers made a counter. It didn't look threatening at first, but as no one chased her down, her lead gradually increased and she went on to win. I finished 14th in the bunch sprint behind. This left me with a total of just seven points in the World Cup standings after three rounds (a win was worth 75 points).

I could feel a volcano brewing inside me, frustrated that my excellent form was not translating into results, and also because I felt there was a lack of tactical direction from Maurizio and his staff. While I never wanted to go back to Deia-Pragma-Colnago, it was evident that the tactical skill and team direction of Giorgio and the sanguine encouragement of Joane had provided a vital element that was not present here.

My other tactical resource was Dad, but it was difficult to discuss pre-race tactics on a course he hadn't seen and with riders he didn't know. It was obvious that I would have to be far more self-reliant. I committed to building up my databank of knowledge about the characteristics of each rider and how they might respond during a race. I was determined to learn and succeed.

In late April, a week after my 20th birthday, we were in Holland to compete in the fourth round of the World Cup, the Amstel Gold Race. I recce'd the course and rode the finishing hill, the Cauberg, a couple of times to get a proper feel for it. The Cauberg is 1.2km long with an average gradient of 6% and starts in the small town of Valkenburg, near Maastricht. I began to formulate my tactics. The race is known for the succession of climbs over the Limburg hills. If the race was run off at a fast pace, this would lead to a selection from the back, as riders not able to maintain the pace would be dropped. If there was a break, I would definitely go with it, but I wouldn't attack until the final climb.

The Amstel, like the Primavera Rosa and the Flèche Wallonne that follows, was one of the spring classics, held on the same day as the men's race. Both the women's Amstel and Primavera races are now long gone, as the women's sport has declined, even though the men's races remain. As we watched the men line up, my mind was in race mode even though my legs had not yet turned the pedals. Today there would be a different outcome.

I kept near the front as we tackled each of the successive bergs (climbs). As the race wore on, the fast pace reduced the field. Cresting the penultimate hill with 13km to go, Australian Oenone Wood made an attack and I was quickly on to it, with Dori Ruano, my Spanish former team-mate at Deia, coming with me. After we bridged to Oenone, the three of us worked well together doing hard turns. We knew it would be touch and go whether we could hold off the chasing peloton. Coming into Valkenburg, I knew I had to time my move perfectly. If I went too soon, I would die up the long climb, but if I left it too late, the bunch would sweep us up. We had already started the climb and I couldn't afford to wait any longer, so with 800m to go I put in a strong acceleration and dropped Oenone and Dori. I risked a glance back and saw that both had been caught by the bunch. This was going to be very close. Could I stay away to the line or would the bunch sweep past me in the final metres? I had to force my brain to overcome the signals that it was receiving from my body to 'stop the pain', and just suffer. The line was approaching. I was starting to hear the tell-tale sounds of the tyres on the road and the breathing of other riders approaching, but I kept going. Would I make it? Yes! Standing on top of the podium in front of the vast and knowledgeable crowd, I felt my frustrations of the first few weeks begin to abate.

I now had 82 points in the season-long competition and was in fifth place. Australian Sara Carrigan, who had won the first round in Geelong, had finished seventh today and was leading the series with 139 points.

The next round was the Flèche Wallonne, only three days later, just across the border in Belgium. I would now be considered the favourite and all my moves would be marked by the other teams, while their tactic would be to attack and get away from me before the Mur de Huy.

Zulfiya Zabirova attacked several times trying to escape from the bunch, just as she had in the Primavera Rosa, but on this occasion was unable to get away. Others joined in the hostilities, with many attacks coming in the closing 25km as rider after rider attempted to break away before the Mur. On the penultimate climb, the Côte de Ahin, I thought the best form of defence would be to attack and accelerated hard myself, not really with the intention to get away but to whittle the field down and to test the reactions of the other riders. We were down to 20 as we approached the Mur. Passing under the 1km banner, I attacked, opening up a gap. At 500m, I was caught by Sue Palmer-Komar, who I had beaten into second place in Manchester the previous year. Five hundred metres is a very long way on the Mur; perhaps all wasn't lost.

I concentrated on my pedalling action, trying to put as much effort into pulling one leg up as the other was pushing down. Sue matched me stroke for stroke. My legs felt like they were going to explode at any moment, my teeth began to tingle as I kept driving, and gradually Sue faded. As I crossed the line, I barely raised one arm off the bars to acknowledge the crowd. Then I collapsed, having to be attended to at the side of the road with oxygen before I could stand. All sportsmen will know what I mean by the sweet agony of victory.

I wanted to know where Sara Carrigan finished. At first, no one could tell me. Then I found out she had gained just a single point that day, so now I was leading the World Cup standings with 157 points, to Sara's 140, and had achieved a rare Amstel Gold–Flèche Wallonne double. Climbing up onto the top of the podium, the second time in three days, in front of a massive crowd, was everything I had dreamed of as a ten-year-old, charging up and down the hills on my little pink bike.

Maurizio wasn't at the race. He'd been at Amstel but had then taken the other half of the team, headed by Diana Ziliute, to a different race in Italy, the Trofeo Alfredo Binda where, with a flat finish, she stood a better chance of winning. When we stopped for a meal at a service station during the 11-hour, 1000-kilometre trip home in the campervan, an excited Maurizio called to tell us that Diana had won the race. He told us that he had bought a massive bottle of champagne and everyone was having a party to celebrate with Diana. We could hear it all in the background! There were a few awkward glances as we looked at our modest fare in the service station; then Primo, somewhat embarrassed, scurried away and rummaged through the campervan until he found a bottle of Prosecco which we shared. Maurizio knew how to celebrate success and we needed to learn from him.

Life at Cornuda was good. There isn't much spare time when you're a professional cyclist – training, eating, sleeping and racing are pretty much the routine, with socialising limited to the occasional meal at a local trattoria or baking high-protein muffins with team-mates. One day in May, Maurizio's brother Luciano, who was involved with some men's teams in the area, called by with a rider, Peter Baker, and wanted to introduce us because Peter was an English speaker surrounded by Italians who lived nearby in Castelcucco.

Peter was trying to make his way in the U23 ranks of cycling, dreaming of a start in the Tour de France. We became good friends, perhaps because of our common experience, being far from home and immersed in the quaintly chaotic, crazy but always engrossing world of Italian professional cycling. Peter had won the US National Collegiate Road Race Championship while he was studying architecture at the University of Virginia, and had decided to pursue cycling to see if he could make it as a pro. Like me, he loved cycling and the exhilaration of competition. Needless to say, it tended to dominate the conversation if we were out for a ride, having dinner or grabbing the occasional pizza.

Meanwhile, my good showing in the World Cup had called for a change of team plan. We now needed to get across to Montreal at the end of May for the next round. I rested up and by the time we left for Montreal I was feeling refreshed and ready to perform on the hilly course, which was pretty much the same as when Eddy Merckx won the 1974 world title there.

Canada's Genevieve Jeanson, the hometown favourite, had won the event for the past two years (and would win another three times before her drug-fuelled career ended in disgrace in 2006). She was the clear favourite over a course that required 12 ascents of the 2km Mont Royal. Her team attacked constantly and by the time we climbed the hill for the last time, there were only six of us left at the front – Genevieve, Sara Carrigan, Lyne Bessette, Susanne Ljungskog, Judith Arndt of Germany and myself. Genevieve attacked to win alone. I had the privilege of being the last one to get dropped and took second. Sara finished in sixth place, so now I had increased my lead in the World Cup to 44 points with three rounds to go, one each in France, Germany and the Netherlands.

Maurizio was delighted. He told me that now I should focus on the World Cup series and World Championships and that lifted the pressure to win any other races. The events in between were important but not essential, which meant I could enjoy the fun of racing without any pressure. I could also change role from leader to that of supporting my team-mates, knowing I would need their help in the remaining rounds.

Two days later, we started the stage race that accompanied the World Cup event. A lot of European-based riders had travelled to Canada for the World Cup; while most stayed for the subsequent stage race, a good number returned straightaway. The organisers were then faced with a difficult dilemma. They had some of the very best riders in the world present and were putting on a super Tour – they could not have been doing more to showcase their world star Genevieve Jeanson – but the field of high-quality riders was now reduced by absences. Should they run the stage race with a small field, or open it up to local riders of somewhat variable experience and ability levels to keep the field size large? The same situation did not occur on the men's circuit – with larger global participation rates, an equivalent men's Tour would have not seen such a spectrum of standards in one race. We started the race with a staggering range of ability levels within the field.

Genevieve pleased the home crowd by winning the first stage, a time-trial. Three years later, they would no doubt feel differently when she confessed to having taken EPO, in connivance with her coach and parents, since the age of 16. I finished out of contention but wasn't concerned, I was thinking about the World Cup and the rest of the season and Diana was to be our team leader for the Tour. That evening, there was the second stage, a 50km criterium around the town centre. On the last lap, I was looking for Diana but she was not in the front half of the field, so I moved up to try for myself, alone. My positioning for the final sprint was not ideal, so I was happy with my second place.

The next day, Stage 3, was a 111km road race which had some decent hills. Although I was under no pressure to win, I certainly wasn't going to be a spectator or ride 'gruppetto'. So when the pace was whipping up and we were getting strung out by attacks, I was fully committed. We came round a fast corner and were all in a line on one side of the road. Without any warning, the rider two places ahead of me swerved to avoid a stationary motorbike in our path. The next rider caught it a glancing blow and I went into it. My arm had hit the motorbike and my frame was broken into pieces, while behind and around me, bikes and riders were flying through the air. An experienced rider would have indicated the hazard to all behind and moved over well in time. A novice, caught up in the excitement of being in such a race, would not be sure what to do. It was a totally unnecessary crash and one that changed my sporting career.

In the melee of bodies and bikes, I didn't even try to move, the pain in my arm was so acute. I could see faces hovering above me; one of my team-mates asked if I was okay and I just groaned something back to her, saying she should go on and I'd be okay. Then the team car and ambulance arrived and people were tending to me.

'I think I've broken my arm,' I said to my team's *directeur sportif*.

'Your arm? What about your leg?'

I couldn't feel any problem in my legs, so I ignored the comment as I was put in a neck brace, strapped to a stretcher and loaded into an ambulance and quickly taken to hospital, where the very first thing they did was to take all my details to make sure they could send me the bill. Then they attended to my injuries. I still hadn't sat up when a doctor came to see me in the ward. My arm was swollen up in the middle, like a football had been inflated under the skin, and it felt like it was broken. The doctor helped me gradually straighten the elbow and sent me off for x-rays. The good news was that I had not broken a bone. I'd had a lucky escape.

'Now, what about the knee,' he said.

'No, my knee is fine.'

'Have you seen your knee?'

'No.'

The doctor lifted me so I could see. There was a bloody pulp below my cycling shorts. My left leg must have caught the end of the tubing of the shattered bike frame, because it had ripped a massive gash. I got a glimpse of something white inside the mess and immediately lay back down, reeling from the sight. After that I was sewn up with internal and external stitches on my left knee.

Racing for me was finished for some time. It meant I could not ride the two-week Giro d'Italia, which was a great disappointment, as after my poor showing the previous year I really wanted to prove myself and my form in one of the grand tours. Fortunately, due to the Giro and Tour, there was almost three months until the next round of the World Cup, so I did have the time to recover properly. I flew back to Wales to enjoy an unscheduled but relaxing time with my family while I waited for the wound to heal and then gradually returned to training.

My first race after the accident was the two-day Giro del Trentino. On the first climb of the first stage I should have been at the front on the hill, but I was still recovering from the accident and couldn't hold my place. I was in a group of riders chasing down the descent, and as often happens when one fast group catches a slower group ahead, there was a crash. Riders came down in front of me, then I came down. This time I was thrown over the handlebars, landing face-first on the road with my knees taking the impact. There was an immediate searing pain in my legs and I couldn't move, but I could hear the groans of other riders who had been injured. The team car arrived and helped me get up. I looked at my legs: serious grazes, but nothing worse. I was fuming, so I demanded my bike and set off chasing the peloton once more. I caught the rear of the bunch but was dropped on the next climb and finished well down the field. I went to the start line the next morning aiming to get into an early breakaway, since I was out of contention for the overall win. I formed a break with about five riders, but midway through the stage I started to feel pain in my left knee. It had been the same niggle as the previous day, but each minute it now became worse. I then did something I had never done before: I sat up and let the break go. I tried to soft pedal to the finish where I crossed the line alone, behind the bunch and in agony.

I had trained so hard that year and I had got everything right. Weeks before, things had been going so well. Now I'd been involved in two accidents in consecutive races, and the season had gone into reverse. I tried to forget about it the next day when I went for a very gentle ride around Cornuda with Peter. We were happily chatting, but my knee started to hurt and as much as I was enjoying the ride, I had to insist on cutting it short and going home.

I prepared for the British Championships the next weekend, held in Wales for the second successive year. The course at Newport was mainly flat with only one medium hill early on and then three short rolling circuits to finish. Being the clear favourite, it would be hard for me to control the closing stages of the race against a large group. So the best option was for me to force a small breakaway on the main climb and then ride fast enough to stay away and fight out the positions from our small group, where everyone would have worked quite hard, or at least make the bunch work hard to catch us, hopefully whittling the numbers down to a manageable size. Of course an arduous race, with me making it even harder, was not the way to preserve my knee. Mum and Dad were now very concerned for me. Maurizio rang me before the race and assured me that I could beat all the other British riders with one leg anyway, so what was there to worry about! I was not so dismissive.

I attacked on the hill after just 10km, and kept on going,

attacking again and again until eventually I was left with just two riders, Rachel Heal and Vicki Pincombe, a former tri-athlete. Three is the ideal number for a breakaway in a championship race, as it meant a medal for each of us. Rachel and Vicki recognised this and we worked very effectively together for the rest of the race until the finishing circuit. As we started this, Rachel and I dropped Vicki, and now the two of us would have to go head to head on the last little hill to the finish line. The pain had been gradually building as the race went on but I just ignored it, and close to the line I sprinted away, winning by a few seconds from Rachel.

You will recall that there had been no junior or U23 women's titles in 1999, which is how I had been able to ride the senior women's event. In an attempt to broaden the prize purse and reduce the gap with the men, organiser Bill Owen arranged for an U23 subcategory to be created within the race. Club cycling has its traditions and one of those is one rider one prize (no one should be greedy), so here was a chance to encourage some British riders of my own age. Catherine Hare was most reluctant but she was the highest U23 finisher behind myself, so the prize was hers. I stood guard at the side of the podium (with my dodgy knee hurting) to make sure Catherine and the other two medallists got on the U23 podium in the right places. That day, I struck up a great friendship with Catherine and we have roomed many times together since and our parents always spend time together when they bump into each other at a race.

I was thrilled with the victory in front of a home Welsh crowd, and my bluff obviously worked wonders as it was reported: 'Cooke showed no signs of the knee injury that she sustained when she crashed in the four-day Tour of Montreal in Canada.' But all I could think about was what was going on with my knee and how long would it take to recover. This was not like any injury I'd ever had before, so I consulted with the BC doctor and went for an MRI scan two days later, where I was diagnosed with severe bone bruising in the knee cap and femur which would need at least two weeks of complete rest.

In August, after being given the all-clear from the doctors, I returned to Cornuda and had about two weeks to get ready for the next round of the World Cup at Plouay. As he watched my progress, Maurizio decided I needed more hill work to tackle the course. So I rode about half an hour from Cornuda to a 2km hill at Asolo and spent the next three hours going up, down, doing some recovery on the flat and then back up the hill again. I was absolutely exhausted afterwards, but most importantly my knee was not hurting – well not too much anyway. Maurizio's philosophies were endearing and he was always supportive of the riders; and, unlike some managers, he always paid the riders what he said he was going to pay them in the contract.

Peter and I would meet up often, and one night during dinner he spoke about when he arrived in Italy at the start of the season. For many cyclists, arriving on the continent is not the start of the journey; there have been many years of dedicated training before this point. Rules for Italian amateur men's teams stated that there could be only one foreign rider per team, and Peter and another rider were training with the team, both hoping that they would be picked for that spot.

At a meeting with the team management to discuss his racing calendar, they asked Peter about his ambitions in the sport and then they used an analogy. There are cyclists who compete naturally, in the white area, and there are cyclists who compete in the different shades of grey, all the way to black. 'How far into the grey are you prepared to go?' Peter was taken aback and said he wanted to see how far he could get naturally, and was definitely in the white. A few weeks later, the team announced that Peter would not be offered a contract. He eventually found a place on a small regional team based in Bassano.

Peter knew he could not compete. The playing field is not level. He returned to the US with a shattered dream but his integrity intact; he could look in the mirror with pride. Around this time another American, Lance Armstrong, completed a highly lucrative fifth Tour de France win.

I was quite nervous as we set off on the two-day trip in the campervan to drive the 1,600km across Italy and France to reach Plouay. The course was one of my favourites, with plenty of climbs and technical descents to provide opportunities for attacks. My worry was that I had no real reference point as to my form. I was going to have to race very cautiously and try to save as much energy as possible in the early stages. Our next best climber, Modesta Vzesniauskaite, was not up to the level of the climbers from some of the other teams, and even if I was good enough to stay with the leaders, I could be isolated and hostage to teams with more riders in the break able to mark me out of the race. This was all on the basis that my knee would stand up to the strain of the race.

I had special support. Mum and Dad had been holidaying in the French Alps where they had watched stages of the women's Tour and had planned a typical Cooke family logistical marathon, arriving in Plouay at the opposite end of France, meeting up with Craig and Uncle Chris as well as my grandparents and some friends from the Cardiff Ajax cycling club who set up a little tented stand on the course to promote the team and share their support.

Plouay is about much more than just the race itself. The town organises a whole weekend of activities, including cyclo-sportif events for the active members of the crowd. Fans are attracted from all over Europe. The organisers put up mobile grandstands to go alongside the road they built into the town centre specially for the World Championships in 2000. There is a tunnel under the road for spectators to use on cycle race days and there is even a separate stadium with an outdoor velodrome 500m from the finish line. No community in the world has integrated cycling more into its heart than Plouay.

With the help of my agent, I urged the BBC in London and Wales to send representatives to view this spectacle. Surely it would not be too much to ask that in 2003, when Wales had few sportsmen performing on the world stage anywhere, they might spare a cameraman and reporter to hop across the Channel for the day? French TV had helicopters providing full live coverage of the race. At the time, it was perhaps the broadcast which was the most professionally conducted on the whole women's scene. Even if BBC Wales could not get a cameraman there, could they just get somebody to come and watch and get a flavour of what it was like to see the race, with a view to coverage next year? My agent tried her best, but BBC Wales couldn't spare anyone. The drive to Plymouth, a ferry ride and 70 miles the other side of the Channel was a trip beyond them. The message was clear: they weren't interested and they weren't going to expand their horizons.

The race itself was active throughout and a great advert for the sport. The decisive break came on the penultimate lap, and I was the last rider to get across, making a group of nine. On the last lap up the final hill, there was another stinging attack. I was almost fighting the bike to make contact with a group of three that was riding away from the others. Joane Somarriba, still in excellent form after her Tour de France victory, was setting the pace with Mirjam Melchers and Judith Arndt, both still in contention for the overall World Cup. I was just able to follow. As we crested the final hill, Joane came off the front and normally would have come back down the line and taken her place behind me.

Sensing an opportunity, I hung back and left a gap between myself and the rider in front of me, hoping Joane would take the hint that I was suffering and enter the line in front of me. She glanced at me as she slotted into the gap, deliberately giving me a little extra breathing space with 2km to go. This was not a mistake, Joane knew exactly what she was doing and why. This gesture was just the boost I needed. As the sprint wound up, I kicked, looking below my arms behind me to check on the others. The exhilaration of winning a race I thought was going to be a battle of survival is clearly shown by the photos of me crossing the line, arms outstretched like an albatross, mouth open in a whoop of delight, while the others behind still have their heads down sprinting. My family and Ajax club-mates were overjoyed, and it was fantastic to share the moment with them. To make things better, Sara Carrigan had come in 38th and scored no points, so I now had a 118-point lead in the World Cup series, with just two rounds to go. I hugged Joane.

The penultimate event was based around Nuremburg, a flat, sprinter's race, not ideal for me but with team support I could be competitive. It was mathematically possible for my three closest rivals, Sara Carrigan, Judith Arndt and Mirjam Melchers, to get enough points to overtake me in the overall standings, and of course I always had to factor in the possibility of a crash. It wasn't over yet. No one got away and as the finish approached Rochelle Gilmore was up there with me and did a great job in guiding me through the last kilometres to finish fifth. I had clinched the World Cup, the youngest to ever do so, male or female, and the first-ever British rider to achieve such a victory. At that moment, despite all the injury problems, the future seemed as bright as ever.

However, just like the week before, we were quickly into the campervan en route to the next race, in this case the six-day Tour of Holland which began the following day. Here, I would work for Diana Ziliute. The first stage over 118km was a sprinter's stage on another flat, typically Dutch course. With 6km to go, there were around 40 or so riders left in the leading group. It was a finish that suited Diana, but I couldn't see her so I dropped back and found her in last place in the group. I encouraged her to get on my wheel so I could take her to the front, getting her into a position to win before I tucked into the pack to recover from the effort. But, having got her from the back of the bunch to the front once, I was shocked to see her towards the back of the group again as the race entered the last 2km.

There was a lull in the pace and as we reached the long finishing straight, I decided to make another effort, diving up the side and screaming at Diana to hold my wheel, as I charged to the front so that I could lead her out for the sprint. Usually, something goes wrong to block your passage down the side of the group, but for once it went perfectly. I had won the World Cup the day before, Diana was the principal rider in the team and I knew Maurizio wanted the team to do its best for her, so I was going to give it everything I had. I got Diana to the front and she was able to accelerate off my wheel and take the win.

Diana, spirits buoyed by the way we worked together, won again on the second day and I finished fourth. It was a great feeling as we were the best team on the road. When we arrived back at the hotel, I stepped out of the campervan and put my left foot awkwardly on the curb, twisting it and immediately felt a sharp pain. I staggered away, angry with myself for being so stupid, and tried to ignore the pain, but my foot swelled badly. At least it stopped me thinking about my knee.

My foot still hurt the next morning when I walked, but felt okay when I tried riding, so I decided to ignore the discomfort and race on. The team enjoyed a successful week, with Diana winning overall, and I achieved a second in Stage 4 and won Stage 5, beating Susanne Ljungskog in the sprint from a small breakaway group. Next up was Rotterdam and the final World Cup race.

I knew that with the World Cup in the bag, it would be a great opportunity for me to support my team-mates in going for a big result themselves, as a 'thank you' for their dedication to me. It was a grey and wet day and there was not much action until the finish. Mum, Dad and my Ajax club-mates had placed themselves around the course, waving flags, cheering and sounding their car horns as we went past. Given the grim weather conditions on the course, they seemed to outnumber the local spectators, which did make me and my team-mates feel quite special to have such wonderful support. At the finish, I helped set up my team-mates for the leadout, and then eased up, not wanting to take any risks, and rode over the line in 54th place, punching one arm into the air and then being mobbed by my team, including Chantal Beltman who had won the race. It was very special being presented with my jersey and trophy in front of my team, family and supporters.

After Rotterdam, I took up the kind offer to stay with Mike Townley's parents in Athens, spending three days riding the 2004 Olympic course, getting up at 5am to ride several laps before the traffic became too busy. This allowed me to learn about the hills, gradients and the finishing straight as well as taking lots of photos, to remind myself of what it was like when back home.

Another great race of the time was the San Francisco Grand Prix. Rather than go early and attempt to adjust to the time difference, we went late and I maintained my European meal and sleeping pattern, taking full advantage of the 24-hour restaurant in the hotel. At the press conference, I was one of two female stars accompanying the men, as we were given proper coverage. I even had to act as interpreter, as one of the male cyclists spoke only Italian. The race itself was brilliant, with four ascents of the fearsome 18% average Fillmore Street. A small group was left at the foot of the final climb. On the podium, preparing to receive the winner's bouquet, I looked at my hands. I'd been gripping the brake levers so tightly on that final climb that I'd drawn blood.

From there I maintained my hectic schedule and returned to Italy. With no adjustments needed to my body clock, I was racing two days later in the six-day Giro di Toscana, where I won a stage and figured in the finishes of several others. My attention by now was firmly on the World Championships, in Hamilton, Canada, with the GB team. I believed I was capable of a medal, and I really wanted to make up for last year's disappointing performance. The circuit included some good hills and would certainly be different from the last time.

I studied the results of the time-trial, which was held a few days before the road race, to gain any last-minute insights into my rivals' form. I didn't ride it myself, as I wanted to concentrate on the road race, but I was really happy for Joane who won it.

My World Cup win marked me out as one of the strongest individuals in the race. However, it would be very easy for other national teams to use their strength in numbers against me. Once the real racing began, I would effectively be riding alone. I could only think what a difference it could have made if Rachel Heal had been able to be with me all year. By the time the race came, I was feeling frustrated that a lot of people in the British team and media seemed to think it would be a foregone conclusion that I would win. 'Nicole Cooke just has to sit on the saddle and ride round and she will do it.' The hopes of the home nation naturally rested with Genevieve Jeanson. I couldn't match her up Mont Royal earlier in the year and she was going to be a big threat here.

Some weeks earlier, Genevieve had done an interview for Cyclingnews.com entitled 'Killing Them Softly'. In it, she made mention of her very special coach, Andre. Now, on the day before the World Championships in Canada, put on to showcase their global superstar, there was an unscheduled news conference. The UCI required that riders with elevated blood haematocrit levels – those above 50% – must take a two-week 'health rest' (which comedian came up with that title?). Genevieve had been tested and now had to withdraw from the World Championships. After pausing for long enough to assure us all she did not use illegal doping products, never had used illegal doping products, and cross her heart and hope to die, she never would use them, she blamed her elevated haematocrit on an oxygen tent she had been using for months. She left the press conference in tears. A series of tests after-wards were meant to prove to us that she was not using EPO. The test results only proved the ineffectiveness of the testing. Genevieve still had several years left in the sport, but this was the beginning of the end for her and her coach Andre. She was killing us all softly, not least the Canadian races so many of us enjoyed.

The race was a cautious affair; Jeannie Longo made a serious attack with about 40km to go. No one reacted and as her
lead hovered around 45 to 60 seconds, there was a real chance
that she might stay away and win. I wanted to organise a chase,
thinking it would be in everyone's interest to share the work,
but as I realised after the race, it was a big mistake. I did not
realise that my desperation to win showed through so clearly
to my rivals, and as the one favourite without any effective
team-mates, I ended up leading the chase, while some of the
other race favourites, even those with team-mates who could
easily have acted as *domestiques*, just stayed in my slipstream and
watched me wear myself out like a fool. On the final hill, with
Jeannie still up the road, Mirjam Melchers and Susanne
Ljungskog launched an attack which I followed with Edita
Pucinskaite, but rather than holding the wheels comfortably
and considering a counter attack near the top, as I had been
able to do in Amstel or the Flèche Wallonne, I was now
reduced to clinging on to the wheels in front of me, my
energy dissipated by the chase of Jeannie. Even so, others
seemed content to let Jeannie ride alone to the win. I chased
again.

We caught Jeannie with only 600m to go, and using the
rotation off the front, I placed myself in third position as we
approached the final corner. Against these riders, I still felt I
could beat them all in a straight sprint, and I mentally prepared
myself for the kick out of the corner to the finish line. Mirjam
was in front and Edita second as we approached the bend,
when Susanne charged up the inside past me and got onto
Mirjam's wheel, setting herself up perfectly for the sprint. I
wasn't expecting the move or the force with which Susanne
made it and was momentarily thrown out of my ideal position
round the last corner. I kicked as I came out of the corner,

forced to go to the outside of Edita and only just managed to get my front wheel in front of her's with a final lunge for the line. Third and a bronze medal: I'd made a series of tactical errors during the race and fought back tears on the podium, as I tried to come to terms with having just thrown away a world title I could have won.

If someone had come to me at the beginning of 2003 and offered me a season in which, aged 20, I would win the World Cup and finish third in the World Championships and win two classics and a number of other races, I would have taken it in a heartbeat, but now I felt really disappointed. An athletic career is short and in cycling, where a mechanical failure or crash, neither of which you may be able to control, can rob you of a great result, an opportunity not taken may never come around again. Every 'champion' always wants to be a winner and has an immense inner drive, but what can be a blessing in one situation can also be a curse in others. I was very hard on myself and at the time could see only disappointment. As I flew back from Hamilton, I was grappling with all these emotions, I was also aware of a noise in the background. The clock was already ticking towards Athens 2004.

CHAPTER FOURTEEN
Under the Knife

For a second year in a row, Mike Townley and Dad had been busy writing, with highly detailed and well-formed arguments being made in my case against British Cycling, but UK Sport had been intransigent for many months, continuing to back the BC position. We had to ask our local MP Win Griffiths to get involved and he spoke to the Minister for Sport and met with the CEO of UK Sport, Richard Callicott. Critical to all this was the discovery of an email sent by Alison Livesey, Peter Keen's PA, in late 2002 confirming BC WCPP support for me during the 2003 season when it was known that I was at Acca Due O – exactly as Peter Keen and I had verbally agreed earlier. This written confirmation totally undermined the position that Peter and British Cycling had adopted since the time of the Tony Blair reception in late November. Dad sent a series of recorded delivery letters to UK Sport. Within 24 hours, UK Sport put out a press release announcing that Peter Keen had resigned as performance director of British Cycling, later taking up a post with the pharmaceutical company GlaxoSmithKline.

Following Peter's departure, I much appreciated the fact that Liz Nicholl, the director of UK Sport Elite Performance, took the time to ring me up to confirm that they had changed the decision and would be asking the BC WCPP to support me and that they would be backing me all the way to Athens. While I was left entirely confident that at least UK Sport would be supporting me, I worried about the legacy of another major clash with BC management. I had a wry smile when, in the lead-up to London 2012, Dave Brailsford stated that it was very important to get the key riders in the same trade team for the run-up to the Olympics. In that case, it was all the GB male riders at Team Sky. Nine years earlier the official line was quite different.

I was always confident in Mike and Dad representing my case to success, but I was so sad that in all the posturing and hubris, a golden opportunity had been lost. What would have happened if, exactly as planned, Rachel Heal had ridden alongside me at Acca Due O for the 2003 season? As it was, Rachel developed very well through the year to become the clear No.2 GB rider. However, we didn't work together in races. What could we have achieved had we both been riding together on the same team, working every day, sharing tactics and practising them together in race after race? Others could have joined us for the following season. Frustratingly, 2003 had been yet another year when no junior girls were sent to the World Championships. Where was the support that really mattered?

Liz Nicholl also took the time to ring Dad and ask his opinion about the way ahead for cycling and the WCPP. Dad offered his opinion that Dave Brailsford would make an excellent replacement for Peter Keen. Whether this had any bearing on the decision we will never know, but we were delighted with the appointment and the working relationship soon improved. Dave introduced many changes to the way the WCPP operated and had many long conversations with my father about operating methods, although Dave was always his own person and made his own decisions. Another topic of conversation was the situation regarding the use of performance enhancing drugs in cycling. I have recorded most elements relevant to this issue in one chapter. However, relevant to the timeline is that Dad was relating my experiences and concerns to Dave, and foremost was the need to address the fact that cycling was just one of two major sports that had failed to sign up to the World Anti-Doping Agency (WADA) code. The sport continued to pay lip service to addressing what was the key issue to its future.

Meanwhile, I happily reconfirmed my contract at Acca Due O for another year. Maurizio was only running a single team this year. As British Cycling had embraced the idea of WCPP riders joining continental teams, I asked if he could find a place for any other GB girls. The answer was a definite no; he couldn't forget how he was messed about the previous year. I can't say I blamed him. Thankfully, Rachel was able to negotiate a place with Dutch team Farm Frites for 2004.

In the meantime I was invited to attend the BBC Sports Personality of the Year. They did a terrific piece with Lance Armstrong, who had notched up Tour win number five. The lengthy eulogy was effusive, as they awarded him BBC Overseas Sports Personality of the Year. *Sunday Times* journalist David Walsh's excellent book, *LA Confidential*, was still one year away at this time. That book recorded what many of us in the sport suspected. Days before the show, I had sent out an open email to all the girls on the WCPP urging them to support and actively participate in a voluntary programme of out-of-competition drugs testing by British Cycling of its athletes. Dad had spoken to Dave about introducing this and he needed strong support for this worthwhile initiative. At the time, the cheats were obviously winning by a large margin.

Gasping for the little oxygen left after so much programme time was spent genuflecting before Lance, the main domestic cycling story at SPOTY was David Millar's win in the World time-trial at Hamilton. Just like with Lance and Genevieve Jeanson, we were all later to have it confirmed that Millar's was the 'drug assisted' performance it appeared to be. To rub salt into the wound, for the ten seconds that they decided to speak about my performances for the year, which included being the youngest-ever and first British winner of the season-long World Cup – in fact no home-developed rider, male or female, had ever won a single round – they showed a picture, not of me, but of Jeannie Longo, the rather generous clue being the word 'FRANCE' on the side of the kit. It was bad enough that they showed the wrong picture, but even worse when Dad didn't notice!

It was late 2003 and time to get back training. The hills around Wick are quiet at the best of times, but as autumn turns to winter they become almost deserted. I was looking forward to those long winter rides which would allow me to build the foundation for next year's racing. On my first ride over the Bwlch, after about 90 minutes, I started to get a niggle in my left knee. This came and went. It then became more persistent. As the ride reached the three-hour mark, my knee was very painful, I eased up, pedalling gently as I crept home.

I rang the BC doctor in Manchester who directed me to Dr Rod Jaques at the English Institute of Sport Medical Centre in Bath for appraisal. We reviewed everything that had happened since July 2003. Rod asked if there were any other accidents; I mentioned my painful foot after going over on my ankle when getting out of the campervan in Holland, so Rod arranged an MRI scan and some x-rays. The scan showed that the bone bruising on the left knee had improved, but there was a problem in the plica membrane (the remnants of foetal tissue in the knee), which serves little useful purpose in the normal function of the knee but can be debilitating if it becomes irritated. And mine was very inflamed. Then, he put the x-ray up on the screen and showed me a very obvious fracture on the outside of my left foot. The bones were clearly displaced. My eyes popped out of my head. That incident going over on my ankle when stepping out of the campervan had caused the break. I had ridden out the end of the season, including the World Championships, with a broken bone in my foot.

The puzzle was why my knee had flared up now. The diagnosis was that I was over-compensating for the fracture in my foot and putting extra stress on the knee that eventually led to the inflammation of the plica membrane. When sightseeing with Rochelle in San Francisco during the GP event, it was obvious I was walking with a limp and favouring one leg. Now, seeing the x-ray, I realised I had been compensating for the injury for months. The solution was, firstly, rest and then a rehabilitation programme with physiotherapist Chris Price. Cycling was out for the time being. The staff encouraged me – it was only November, so time was on my side. I looked at the clock on the wall. I heard it tick.

I concentrated on work in the gym, strengthening the stabilising the muscles around the knee. Some weeks later, when I got back on the bike to go for my second training ride of the off-season, within an hour the pain in my knee had flared up once more. I stopped all riding again and gave it a rest, before building up slowly, starting with shorter rides and then hoping to get to the four- and five-hour rides. But each time, once I got to around one hour, the same thing happened, my knee hurt and I couldn't ride. On Christmas Eve, I went back to see Rod and Chris in Bath where we devised a new strategy based on doing shorter rides to try to train up to a point that would not irritate and further damage the knee. It would be an even slower build-up and there were no guarantees. There was no ready answer as to why it was not responding to the rest and rehabilitation.

At Bath they gave me a large exercise ball and I spent Christmas Day using my new present in the lounge doing the stretching and rehabilitation exercises I had been set. It had been over two months since I had last completed a single decent training ride, the longest period of not riding so far in my life. I was on the eve of what might be my greatest season ever. I had a good team, British Cycling had a new director of the WCPP, around me things looked better than they had ever been – and I couldn't ride my bike. On 31 December, the clocks all struck midnight. Early the next morning, Dad drove me to Bath for our 9am appointment with the team there. My Olympic year had arrived.

Finally, I could now get back on my bike. I was to do three short rides rather than my one long endurance ride each day. Every time I went out, I held back from sprinting for a '30' speed-limit sign or charging up a hill, in case I aggravated my knee. This was not the training I had done for the last two winters which had resulted in a successful start to the season.

Despite my 2003 success, I had received little coverage in the British media. They were being fed press releases from the British Cycling press office, who were more focused on the male riders, especially the track riders who were total products of the WCPP. This was a fact of life. The Olympics were different. Once every four years, exploits would be seen by the public at face value, rather than metered out according to unnatural bias. The nation's mums and dads and budding stars would see me, not ten seconds of a French rider. This was the year I needed to be at my best. I was on the countdown to my 'high noon' in August, and I was forced into a much tamed-down version of the training programme that I knew I needed. Each room in the house had a clock and each one of those clocks seemed to have developed a very loud tick that I had never heard before. Why was this happening to me now? I was beginning to get a clear insight into why caged tigers pace up and down and are so angry. Mum and Dad learnt to put the tops on toothpaste tubes every time; and certainly every cereal packet now had the lid folded back on properly.

The days went by, the clocks marking every single second. By late January I was, at last, tackling some of the longer routes over the hills, albeit at a very steady pace, so in early February I decided to take part in the annual 100-mile 'reliability' trial organised by the Cardiff Ajax. I had taken part in the event a few times before, but this time, after about only an hour, the niggling pain in my knee started again. As I rode on, it gradually got worse and I soon came to realise there was no way I would complete the course. I waved goodbye to my club-mates as they continued. The Olympic prospect got off her bike in Abergavenny, from where she phoned home from the town's leisure centre. That was one very long wait in which the helplessness of my situation was thrown into deep contrast with the opportunities ahead. Dad arrived an hour later. It was a quiet drive home. I visited the medical team at Bath, where 'rest' was the only prescription.

I flew to Cornuda to join the team in mid-February. This had been planned long ago and for the 'caged tiger' it was a release. I had kept in contact with Maurizio and he assured me that the team doctor was used to treating this sort of injury. It seemed the right thing to do; I would be at Nonna's big, happy house and in a cycling environment, and on top of that I would have Italian sunshine rather than Welsh winds and rain.

A few days later, we had the team presentation where our new name was unveiled, Safi-Pasta Zara. This year our wine sponsor, Astoria, produced a bottle of Prosecco with my picture from the Plouay victory on the label. Once again, Maurizio was celebrating in style.

Italian cycling sponsors were typically the medium- and small-size companies on which Italy is built. The sponsors of famous men's teams like Mapei, Fassa Bortolo and Saeco were from this category. Maurizio, bless his heart, had decided that he didn't have enough money to sponsor a men's team, but having gone into women's racing he was totally committed. He did not jump in and out each season but tried to keep a consistency over the years. Of course, although there were other sponsors, he put in significant sponsorship from his own company. It was his team and so he made the key decisions. This is why he could turn up on the eve of a big race and decide to change the team. At times this behaviour could be maddeningly frustrating, and like many males with a group of females, he had his favourites, but we knew that he was really passionate for the team to do the best.

The physiotherapy and swimming programme devised by Maurizio's doctor seemed to be working, as I did short training rides through February and into early March. Maurizio accepted that I was going to miss some of the early races, but it would all be worth it if I could be strong and healthy again in time for the Giro in July and Athens in August. The plan was to travel with the team to the Primavera Rosa, the second round of the World Cup, where I would not race but ride the course as a training run. I would then travel with the team to

Spain for the next World Cup round, the Castilla y Leon, where I would ride. His logic was that I could not risk starting a race in Italy and failing, but doing so a long way away in Spain would be less noticeable.

Another of my team-mates, Zita Urbonaite, was also having a slow start to the season and therefore was not riding the Primavera Rosa. We set off together to ride the course an hour or so before the race started, so we would be at the finish before the riders arrived. I was barely 20km into the ride when my knee started hurting. I knew from experience that once it had started hurting in a ride, it never got better. There was still 100km to the finish, so Zita went on by herself while I turned around and rode gingerly back to the start, arriving back at the campervan just as the others were leaving for the race. I put on a brave face and brushed away their concern, but as soon as the others left I sat in the back of the campervan and alone, where no one could see me, started to cry.

The Italian rehab plan had also failed. I rang Mum and Dad, got a flight home and Dad took me to Bath where again we tried another variation on the rehab plan, which allowed for periods of training but, inevitably, we ended up back at square one. By April, I was desperate. It had been more than five months since the problem was diagnosed, there was no real improvement, and it was now just four months until the Olympics. Mum and Dad did their best to cheer me up on my 21st birthday. All I could hear was the crashing sound of the clocks marking out each second.

Then a new option emerged – surgery. The plica membrane, or at least some of it, would apparently have to be removed because it must have become 'pinched' by the kneecap, causing an irritation that was perhaps thickening the membrane, making it more likely to be pinched again and

inflamed in a vicious cycle. The specialists insisted it was possible to have the surgery and be ready for August, but could I
really be racing to win by then? There was so much unknown,
and it wasn't just the Olympics at stake but now my whole
career. When I explained the decision to have surgery,
Maurizio was very supportive and said all the right things, but
I sensed a trace of resignation in his voice. I could understand
his position. His star rider had missed all the early season classics. The World Cup was already lost, surgery meant a gamble
and those sorts of gambles for high-performance athletes do
not have a great track record of success. I vowed to myself that
if I could come back, I would come back stronger than ever.
Surgery was set for 13 May with Dr Jonathan Webb, the
former England rugby full-back.

I was less than an hour in the operating theatre. The first
thing I did when I woke up a couple of hours later was to
clench my quads to check if my massively swollen knee was
still attached. Jonathan assured me that it had gone well and
gave me a DVD of the keyhole surgery. It made ghoulish and
difficult viewing. There was the white membrane and then
from the edge of the shot, these crocodile-like clippers appear
and snip the membrane into pieces and away from the joint
where it had been continuously pinched and causing me pain.
Next to enter the show was a miniature vacuum cleaner thing,
sucking up all the white bits. It looked disgusting. Would it
work? I had to lie down and do nothing. I had to wait.

Within a week, I was doing rehab work and back on the
bike, riding in the countryside around Bath where I was now
based so that I could see the medical team for regular check-
ups. Soon I was even able to test my knee with sprints. Eureka!
The surgery had worked – in every training session after that
I was planning my comeback. By early June, the medical team

gave me the all clear. I was back in Cornuda pleading with Maurizio to let me ride the Giro d'Italia. Maurizio, understandably, wasn't so sure, and suggested that I tackle the shorter Giro di Trentino before making a decision.

I was certain of my plan. Instead of racing in Trentino, which for once was a flat course and therefore a waste in terms of preparation for the mountainous Giro, I wanted to train more specifically for the Giro and in particular for the most critical climb, the Passo del Ghisallo. This was on the penultimate day and would undoubtedly be the decisive stage if the leader's jersey was still in contention. 'Maurizio, I need to train for that stage. I need to train for that climb.' Dearest to his passionate Italian heart were the great Italian cycle races, the Giro and the Primavera Rosa. To Maurizio these were beyond any Olympic medal. He had never had a winner in the Giro, Diana achieving a second place in 2001 being the closest the team had ever come. The counter was obvious. If he agreed to my plan, it meant that he would give me one of the seven precious places in the team built around supporting Diana in her bid to win the race this year. I would get just one race outing before the Giro to prove my form – the British Championships. My last race had been in October the previous year.

Maurizio probably thought I was mad but eventually agreed, and while the rest of the team went to Trentino, I trained alone in the mountains before heading back to Wales for the British Championships. The course was the same as the previous year, and this time I felt very strong and won alone by nearly three minutes. Looking back, this was the most emphatic and dominating win of all my ten British road titles. In terms of competition, second-placed Rachel was now firmly based on the continent, and with a stage win to her credit in the Tour de L'Aude she was now performing at a level well beyond that seen by the other British girls for a long time. As I came up to the finish, I gave my left knee a big kiss. I jumped up onto the podium and took my one prize and one jersey. Back home that night after the race, I noticed something strange. The clocks all seemed remarkably quiet. The next day, I flew back to Italy, where my second race in eight months would be the Giro d'Italia.

The women's Giro d'Italia is the most prestigious stage race on the women's calendar, first held in 1988 and still running now. For 2004, there was no women's Tour de France, with accusation and counter accusation flying between organiser Pierre Boué, the French Cycling Federation and the UCI. Beyond organisational difficulties, it was obvious that cycling in France had been shaken to its foundations since the Festina revelations of 1998. The French cycling media and population did not appear to be as gullible as many elsewhere in accepting the story of Lance Armstrong's unbelievable rise. With waning interest, sponsors were lost. While the men's Tour had more margin for loss, events already operating at their limit were sunk. Women's cycling in France crumbled away.

So the 2004 edition of the Giro was undoubtedly the star in the calendar that year. It was to be held over ten consecutive days, without break, and as always included some of the fiercest climbs. Favourite would be Fabiana Luperini, a four-time winner supported by a very strong Let's Go Finland team which included Priska Doppmann and Zulfiya Zabirova. Another strong contender was the previous year's winner, Nicole Brandli, riding for the Michela Fanini team, who also had a very strong team-mate in Edita Pucinskaite, who had won three medals at road World Championships including the title in 1999 and the Tour de France. And of course there was Joane Somarriba, who with no race in France to defend would view this as the worthy alternative. Other strong riders included Susanne Ljungskog, Zinaida Stahurskaya, Mirjam Melchers, Russian Svetlana Bubnenkova and Oenone Wood with a good Australian team.

Safi-Pasta Zara fielded Diana Ziliute as the historical favourite and rider with current form. We also had Regina Schleicher as the team sprinter targetting a couple of flat stage wins. In a world of my own, I felt frustrated that I was not the obvious team leader, but I was saved from most of the *domestique* duties, with Maurizio going with my plan to get me to the penultimate stage in contention. Then on the climb to the Ghisallo, all talk would cease, and the 2004 edition of the Giro would be decided.

The race started with a short individual time-trial. There was also a team time-trial on the sixth day which could prove critical. Fabiana Luperini's team were so strong that Diana and I could potentially lose much time to them, particularly if by then we were so weakened by injuries or exhaustion that the deficit could be too large to make up during the rest of the race. Therefore, it was critical to get to the penultimate day less than one minute behind my main rivals.

As I waited for my turn at the prologue start house, I had time to think. I had only ridden one race all year and in my last big stage race, the Tour de France in 2002, I had not even made it to the finish. I was meant to be here testing out my Olympic time-trial bike, a tangible asset from the much vaunted 'marginal gains' BC WCPP programme, and clear, irrefutable proof that BC had changed direction and were now backing me. But where was my bike?

The previous November, Dave Brailsford was keen to promote the first two members of Team GB selected for any sport for the Athens Olympics – David Millar and me. So dominant were we that our positions in Team GB were indisputable. Dave convened a special press conference at FA headquarters in London to stage the event and promote his two stars. That World champion David Millar was given pride of place, while I was there as some sort of gesture to feminism by an overtly male sport, was uncomfortable but to be expected. That nobody seemed to question the ability of Millar to ride effectively against the likes of products of the East German sporting past, such as Jan Ullrich, while EPO use was endemic in the peloton, seemed illogical to me.

Looking at the press coverage of that event now, it is laughable, the male journalists paying all their attention to Millar, while I was seen as an afterthought. In a 400-odd word article in Cyclingnews.com, the unbelievably good David got blanket coverage, while just eight words in a part sentence were left for me. This contrasted somewhat with the website's reader poll at the end of 2003, in which I was voted female rider of the year across all disciplines. I was the only female to make the top ten of readers' rider of the year. That list was topped by Lance Armstrong, with fellow luminary Tyler Hamilton also up there. David Millar did not make that listing. As the sexist attitudes of the time dictated, most sporting journalists wrote about the male first, then the female – if there was any space left.

I don't regret that my role was marginalised, as being associated with Millar was not something I wanted. Just before the British Championships the previous week, news broke that the French gendarmerie had gained a warrant to search Millar's house while he and Dave Brailsford were enjoying an evening meal together talking strategy and plans for Athens. The gendarmerie had found empty phials of EPO. This was a shock to Dave Brailsford and many others, though the news was greeted very differently in the Cooke household. That Dave chose to ring up my Dad in the days that followed to talk to him about the ideas we had about anti-doping programmes, was most eloquent witness to where we stood. While Dave had been firming up final plans with Millar over a glass of wine, nothing had been done to prepare a TT bike for me, the other 'first' selected member of Team GB, at the Giro.

Dave gave Dad the go-ahead to visit the factory at Derby that produced the special TT bikes for the squad. On the Saturday of the first weekend of the Giro, Dad was discussing frame sizes and bottom brackets with the manager of the company. The specification was agreed and Dad asked when the machine would be ready. Apparently, the earliest time this could possibly happen was September – my clock struck 12 noon in August! (*Déjà vu* on the cunning BC plan for solving Olympic age restrictions four years earlier.) It was not that the company was busy on other jobs, rather all free production time was committed to the British Cycling Olympic bid. Apparently, in the ovens and laid up in the moulds were the spare machines for all the track riders. The track riders already had their No.1 machines and these had been tuned and modified some time ago during the programme of marginal gains – they were simply preparing the back-up bikes. That Saturday morning, Dad called Dave while still at the works office with the manager stood alongside him. Priorities were changed and a bike was produced; however, the first I saw of it was a few days before departing for Athens, and I had my first competitive ride on it at the Athens TT.

Back at the Giro, I was delighted with my eighth place in the prologue time-trial against the best riders in the world in the No.1 race in the world that year, even if it was 'marginal gains free'. Diana Ziliute showed that she had superb form and won, which put her in the pink leader's jersey. The benefit of this was that it took the attention away from me.

On the second day, Stage 1 proper, Diana was challenged for her jersey by some attacks, notably from Zulfiya, but we worked well as a team to keep the race together. The stage ended in a sprint won by Oenone and Diana retained the leader's jersey. On Stage 2, there were two Category 2 climbs in the last 30km. Other teams wanted to break up the race. We were under instructions to keep it together to make sure Diana retained the pink leader's jersey. We all had to work hard chasing down break after break. Eventually, Edita broke away to win the stage but only by seven seconds, so Diana retained her lead. Stage 3 started from our home base of Cornuda, so there were many familiar faces in the crowd. Maurizio wanted us to put on our very best show for the sponsors he brought to the race. The crowd's genuine enthusiasm and support reached out to inspire us that day, as we were all at the front, apart from Diana, to set up a perfect leadout train for our sprinter Regina to win the 132km stage. Diana stayed a bit further back in the bunch, away from the dangerous jockeying at the front with the risk of crashes, and kept the leader's jersey. We tried to repeat the success the next day, but Regina was pipped to the line by Annette Beutler.

Stage 5 was the big test we were all worried about, the team time-trial. This was no ordinary time-trial course. We had travelled across the border to Switzerland and the stage started in Brig and went along the valley before turning off up the mountain to finish at 1,400m above sea level in Leukerbad. The team's time was going to be taken on the third rider to cross the line, but any rider finishing slower than the third rider would receive their own actual time. The Let's Go Finland team was very strong and sure to take time out of us if all eight

NICOLE COOKE

of us tried to stay together. Instead, we decided that we would sacrifice part of the team. Diana, who needed to defend the leader's jersey, together with Modesta Vzesniauskaite and myself who were the best climbers, would be the three to go together up the climb. The others would effectively ride a shorter race by riding flat out along the valley, leaving the three of us fresh for the climb, while those who had done the work on the flat would have to make their way up the climb as best they could. It was a high-risk plan, because there was no back-up fourth rider in case anything went wrong.

Having the race leader in our team meant we were last on the road and could receive time checks on our rivals ahead. Our team-mates rode flat out while we slipstreamed behind them, and by the start of the climb we were level with Let's Go Finland. Diana is not a great climber, but she knew that she was going to have to give it everything. Modesta and I needed to ride ahead of Diana, fast but avoiding accelerations which would put Diana in difficulty. We received a time check – our strategy was working, we were only a few seconds down on Let's Go Finland. Then at about 8km to go, I heard that tell-tale hissing sound. I bounced on the bike slightly to see if it was a front or rear wheel puncture. It was the worst, a rear wheel, especially with a hill start. I shouted to Modesta to keep going at the same speed; she needed to ensure Diana rode at an even pace up the whole climb. I was going to be the one who did the chasing.

Primo got a replacement bike off the team car in record time and I launched into a chase. With about 4km to go, I closed up to my team-mates. As I caught them, the road started to flatten out and we immediately changed from climbing mode to each doing short hard turns on the front, with the other two taking temporary shelter, like a team pursuit on the track. It nearly killed me; the maximum pace on the climb was at least continuous, but now we were doing short high-power intervals and the pressure was on Diana and me to keep the speed as high as possible. We were both good time-triallists, whereas Modesta was a climber and was struggling with the fast speed on the flat. We crossed the line; all of us exhausted, and heard the result: second place but only 17 seconds behind the Let's Go Finland team of Fabiana Luperini, Priska Doppmann and Zulfiya Zabirova.

Diana had lost the Maglia Rosa to Priska but only by five seconds. Diana was second on the same time as Zulfiya, I was fourth at 22 seconds with my main rival for the overall victory, Fabiana, fifth, one second behind. The really good news was that we had ridden so hard that the Michela Fanini team of Nicole Brandli and Edita Pucinskaite were over four minutes down and out of the running for the overall title. In contrast Rachel Heal, with whom I would be riding together in the GB team a few short weeks later in Athens, had proved just how much she had come on in the last two years, and after a superb ride with Farm Frites was in eighth place only 1 minute 25 seconds down. Maurizio was delighted with the result, knowing how well we had ridden as a team and that without my puncture we might have actually beaten Let's Go Finland.

The next stage was tricky, with difficult twisty roads. As a team, we had to stay alert and help Diana counter the attacks from the other teams and make sure that she was in contention for the win, which carried a ten-second bonus. It worked well, Diana won and got the bonus which put her back into the pink jersey, and I also picked up six seconds in intermediate bonuses so now had seven seconds over Fabiana on GC. The next day was a hilly stage. Both Edita and Fabiana used it to try to get away, but the whole team were motivated and committed to keeping Diana in pink. I led her out in the sprint at which more precious bonus seconds were available. She finished third behind Olga Slyusareva and Zinaida Stahurskaya.

I had predicted that the stage up the Ghisallo would be critical, and here we were on the eve of that stage with five riders within 30 seconds of one another on GC. Ever since I had been able to resume training earlier in the year, this stage and this climb had been my focus. I spent the evening driving up and down the hill, making notes on the hairpins and gradients, which I then studied back at the hotel and again in the morning. To my delight, Mum and Dad arrived on the morning of the stage. Today I was the team's protected rider. My teammates helped me and controlled the race until we started the Ghisallo. On the climb they were dropped, tired from their earlier successful efforts to get me safely to this critical point. As the group at the front of the race became smaller, Joane Somarriba rode alongside me and whispered 'testa fredda, Nicole' ('keep a cool head, Nicole'). She then moved in front of me to protect me so I could follow in her slipstream. Soon we were into the first set of hairpin corners. As Joane set a steady pace, Fabiana sprang from behind to launch a stinging attack. This was the crucial moment of the race. I went after Fabiana. I was straight on to her as we rode away from everyone else. I came up alongside her and took a long hard look at her, as if to say 'You are going to have to do better than that.' The psychological element of racing can be very important. She might have won this race four times before, with complete mastery in the mountains, but I was not going to be dismissed out of hand.

Fabiana is a very experienced rider and was not going to give up after only one attack, so she went again. I was able to match her, so my confidence grew. A few riders got up to us as Fabiana rested, restoring her strength for another attack. We marked each other.

I had anticipated that I could have been in trouble if all three Let's Go Finland riders were still with us, but Zulfiya had been dropped and I sensed that Priska was at her limit. It was all down to Fabiana. She tried a few more times, but each time I was able to match her. I was now biding my time until I made my own attack. From my recce, I knew that with 1km to go there was a steep section; this was where I would attack. I jumped hard. Fabiana and Priska couldn't go with me, but Edita and Nicole B, who were going for the stage win, kept pace. I now knew that I could take the overall lead but I also wanted the stage win, so I went again and this time they couldn't match me. I kept on driving all the way to the line, the crowds and in particular the fans of our team going wild seeing me in the lead. I crossed the line and was mobbed by our team staff and all the photographers at the finish, swept up by a whirlwind of excitement. Maurizio was finally going to have a Giro winner. Edita was second at 14 seconds and Nicole B third, a further four seconds back. I had taken the stage win and the overall race lead, Fabiana was at 32 seconds and Priska at 1 minute 11 seconds.

The last day would finish in the centre of Milan where the sprinters could show off their skills. Barring accidents, the Giro was as good as won. My team-mates, Mum and Dad, and all the staff as well as Italian *tifosi* were all ecstatic and I could not have wanted a better place for this to happen than in the shadows of the Madonna di Ghisallo, the patron saint of cyclists. After the stage presentation and still wearing my Maglia Rosa, we paid our respects inside the chapel. I was amazed by the bikes, jerseys and memorabilia representing the history of cycling and our greatest champions. It was a truly remarkable and special day.

The last day was a formality through the streets of Milan, ending in laps around the majestic Castello Sforzesco just like the men's Giro d'Italia and similar to the Tour de France finish up and down the Champs Élysées. As the whole peloton started preparing for the finish, I went to the front of the bunch to show the pink jersey and lead the peloton before then working with the team to provide a leadout for Regina.

Then the celebrations started. I was the overall winner, we had won the team classification, we had won four stages and between Diana and myself we had worn the pink jersey for eight of the nine stages since the prologue. I jumped into the fountain with my team-mates, still dressed in my Maglia Rosa and splashed around, savouring every moment. I was the youngest-ever winner of the Giro and it was run at the fastest-ever average speed. I was, of course, the first-ever British rider to win a major grand tour on the continent – male or female.

Maurizio threw a massive party that night when we got back home to Corunda. It was a huge event for the cycling-mad community. All the sponsors and local companies, who each year contributed to this, and their team of professional racing cyclists, of whom they were so proud, were there. I felt so privileged to be able to reward all their years of devoted support. The mayor made a speech, the Alpini mountain reservists tended the bar and Nonna and her family joined in. The night was all about the Giro. Some may have celebrated long into the night, but I knew the next day it would be time to focus on Athens. A clock had gone quiet for the last week; it was about to start ticking loudly again. I had been able to hear its faint beat when I stood in the cool of the fountains that afternoon.

CHAPTER FIFTEEN
Riding Under Athena's Gaze

I had a week in Italy, enjoying the status of winning the Giro before heading back to Wales to get my knee checked. I was in such good form that all I needed was to maintain my health through the next few weeks. I had beaten the world's best in Italy; bring on Athens.

When I got back to Wales, I was invited to BBC Wales who wanted to discuss how they were going to cover me at the Olympics. They were probably trying to make up for the fact that they had given me no coverage during the Giro d'Italia. BBC Wales later purchased some RAI footage of the race and *Wales Today* ran a small section in a regional sports programme, but for the nationwide BBC I did not exist. However, now BBC London wanted to give me a camera so that I could produce a video diary for the breakfast programme. They also thought it would be a good idea to cover Mum and Dad out in Athens as well. This synthesised my problem. In Italy, I was greatly appreciated and their sincerity was touching, but women's cycling was a financial basket case and there were no sponsorship deals for foreign riders in Italy. Maurizio was able to pay me but my career was going to be short, and if I did slightly better than break even, I would have done far better than most other female cyclists. In the UK, my profile was

controlled, as 2003 had shown so clearly, not by my performances but by cycling journalists, British Cycling and the BBC.

The twin themes that run through my cycling career in relation to the English-speaking cycling journalists of the time are
their failure to question the Lance story and their sexism in
reporting. On the former point, only David Walsh and Paul
Kimmage come out with any credit. Week after week, all that
Cycling Weekly could put out were magazines full of eulogies
to Lance.

While satellite TV showed plenty of men's cycling, my only
race on TV each year in the UK, and therefore my only
chance to shine, was the World Championships. But there
were two problems. Firstly, I was effectively riding alone in a
team sport against very strong teams, and secondly was the fact
that the male commentators never followed the women's sport
on a regular basis, and so instead of being able to instantly
recognise riders and describe the action and finer tactical
points, they wasted time trying to identify riders from glimpses
of their numbers. To get around this uncomfortable unfamil-
iarity with the riders, the commentators tended to talk about
something they knew about – the men's race coming up next.
Beyond TV, the British Cycling press office remained in the
hands of Philip Ingham. The shadows of events in 1999 would
still be dark four years after Athens; I could not expect fair
coverage from that source. A World Cup win might take the
headlines for a short time on their website, but soon there were
the dramatic events of a domestic club race to knock it off the
front page.

The BBC was undergoing change as satellite channels
outbid them for so many of the sporting jewels they took for
granted. The Corporation started trawling for sports that were
easy to cover and did not come with a high price tag and in

which, no matter how small the competitor pool, British success was frequent. Track cycling was about to fit the bill perfectly. British Cycling and the BBC would together promote track cycling in a powerful way that would not be matched anywhere else in the world. Therefore, a fact of life for a British female road race athlete was that only the Olympic road race counted. This was where the BBC would cover women's road cycling and my exploits could be relayed direct to the public without somebody imposing arbitrary censorship.

However, it was not all negative. At the Olympics, the UCI's sexism acted to offset my team disadvantage. While men could have five riders in a team at the Olympics, for women the maximum team size was three. Once every four years, I would get an opportunity where the odds were not stacked so steeply set against me. A win in this race was crucial to how I was perceived, and hopefully the spectacle of the event would shine through the ineffective commentary. Without it I would always be that woman, riding abroad, for whom a clip of a rider with 'FRANCE' on the kit would do as a backdrop while giving her an annual ten seconds' air-time. Not many other people understood my predicament. I felt it only too keenly.

My first day of training when I got back to Wales was a long ride in the hills – and that's where I made a mistake. Instead of being sensible, I went out into the pouring rain and cold and trained myself into the ground for four hours, driven by a voice inside which kept telling me that if I wasn't completely exhausted when I got home, then I wasn't working hard enough. The next day and the next were more of the same. More! Harder! There, that would drown out that clock.

A few days later, I started to recognise the symptoms that

were so evident two years before, when I was so overtrained and exhausted before the Commonwealth Games. I would get back from a training session knowing that the intensity was missing, my instinct confirmed when I downloaded the data from the heart-rate monitor. My performance at the Giro had made me forget that I had no proper base of winter training. I flew back to Cornuda and the heat of Italy and a more appropriate acclimatisation option than the unseasonal cold of Wales. I competed in a team time-trial in Germany but raced badly. I clearly needed a rest. But would there be time to rest and build again in the days towards Athens? Rachel Heal, who had been selected in the GB team alongside me, came over to train with me, while the third member of the team, Sara Symington, decided that optimal team preparation was achieved by going to the Team GB Olympic holding camp in Cyprus. An earlier request to BC management asking Sara to prepare with Rachel and myself in Italy had merit, but was met with a verbal shrug of the shoulders. It was good to have some time with Rachel before the Olympics, as during the Giro there had only been time for a snatched 'Hello, how are you?' We went training together and bounced race scenarios and ideas for tactics off one another while we rode.

The Athens 'experience' started with a comical episode which proves conclusively that you can't take your parents anywhere! Firstly, you need to be aware of cycling's long tradition of painting the names of the fans' favourite riders on the roads, on climbs or key parts of the course. I'm sure you will have spotted it if you have watched any of the major continental races on TV. Mum and Dad were keen to write 'GO NICOLE' on the road. Accompanied by BBC Wales' Richard Owen, Dad chose an unusually quiet stretch of road race course. However, the reason it was quiet was because it was in the embassy district. Some armed guards from a nearby embassy spotted them and called the police, suspecting that they were writing some political slogan. The police arrived and were not unduly concerned; other cycling fans had also written names elsewhere but must have avoided being spotted by the guards. However, once called to an incident, the police would have to report it, so they asked Dad and Richard to show them their passports or other identity documents as required under Greek law. Neither Dad nor Richard had such an official document with them. The solution was for Dad to wait at the police station while Richard fetched his passport and then for Richard to do the same. Somebody decided such important news merited transmission via the international press agencies!

It's possible that this had something to do with the fact that Greek athletes Konstandinos Kenderis and Ekaterini Thanou, whose faces were plastered across the billboards of the city, were about to miss their appointment of carrying the flame into the stadium during the opening ceremony. They had gone into hiding in a hospital, claiming that they had both been riding on a single motorcycle and had been involved in an accident. They were recovering in hospital and could not speak to anyone. In fact, they had been keeping one step ahead of the drug testers who had been chasing them for weeks, trying to catch up with them across several continents. Earlier that day, a story broke about the accident being a fake and that the motorbike was undamaged in a garage. A distraction was needed: 'Cyclist's Dad Arrested for Creating Disturbance in Athens' was obviously picked up by someone.

Once I knew the true facts relating to Dad, it came as a bit of light relief to the seriousness of preparation. I only wish winning a big race garnered me a quarter of the coverage Dad was able to get that night for 'being arrested'. Meanwhile, Kenderis and Thanou withdrew from their home Olympics.

I had been staying away from the Olympic village, with the Townley family who lived near the time-trial course on the peaceful coast. This was ideal, away from the intensity of the athletes' village with a bit more freedom to ride on the quieter roads, and in those final days I had begun to feel the magnitude of the occasion. I was constantly on edge, paranoid and tetchy about most things. Do my legs feel okay? How is my resting heart rate? Is my heart rate as expected in my last training ride? Am I resting enough? How was the course recce? Did I feel good? Question after question about detail – could I recover fast enough was the only question that mattered. That clock in my head was now booming again at every tick. I was convinced that this was a race I could and should win and anything less would be a failure.

The Olympic road race, with teams of three riders, would be very different from the professional races. If I attacked, the other teams would make sure someone chased me, but when they attacked, how could I tell if it was to be a winning move when they had two or even three riders capable of winning? I couldn't afford to use my energy chasing every move, and conversely I didn't want to miss the right move. The very fact that I wasn't in a move could cause impromptu alliances to arise that could turn it into the winning move. Looking back now, my Giro win is one of the highs I treasure most from my career. It also ensured that every other athlete viewed me as the principal favourite for whom there was the obvious counter: 'Let her do the work, she is without strong team-members, if we isolate her, she will have to chase and she will fail as she did at Hamilton.' Therefore, by winning in Italy weeks before, I seriously degraded my chances for Athens.

The temperatures were predicted to hit 40 degrees Celsius, and in the city centre where there was little wind, it would be like an oven. The race was nine 13.2km laps, making almost 120km of what was practically a criterium course with plenty of sharp turns, as well as the zig-zag climb up to the Acropolis, a cobbled section and a tricky descent.

The last couple of days leading up to the race seemed eternal. Sleeping was difficult, despite the absolute tranquillity of my surroundings and hospitality of my hosts. The day before the race, I did my last ride in the morning along the coast, nice and easy, and then made sure all my equipment, my helmet and shoes were spotlessly clean. I also double-checked we had my favourite type of pasta ready for my pre-race meal. Mum and Dad joined me at the Townleys and we watched the men's road race, run the day before mine, on television. The Italian team rode a superb race, placing a strong rider in every move, and duly had a man left over to win.

That afternoon, the British staff came to collect my bike. The rest of the evening was spent watching other Olympic competitions, which was a distraction from thinking about my race, but it only served to remind me of the triumph or disaster that awaited me. I just wanted this excruciating wait to be over. After a glance at the clock, I went to bed early, my dreams full of race-winning scenarios, visualising myself sprinting across the finish line.

I woke up excited; finally my day had come. The morning seemed to fly by. I ate my pasta meal then seemed to be constantly checking I had my shoes, helmet, mitts and heart-rate monitor all packed in my bag. The team officials came to pick me up, the Townleys wished me the best, promising to be cheering the loudest on the course later on.

The pits were small tents where we changed, got ready to

race and somehow tried to stay cool in the afternoon heat. Sara, Rachel and I went through our plan for the race and what we would do if I had mechanical trouble; we were all ready, and all visibly nervous. There was not much space for warming up, and with all the media, team cars, officials and riders in the narrow side streets, it was hard to find anywhere to even hear myself think. I asked to sit alone in our team car so that I could have a few moments of quiet and collect my thoughts. I looked at the clock on the dashboard, got out of the car and went to the line.

In the first part of the race, everybody was twitchy and nervous. I paid special attention to my rivals: how were they riding? Did they appear to be better or worse than when I last rode against them? How were my team-mates doing? Everybody was more nervous than normal; everyone riding knew the same thing. This was our one chance to shine in the gaze of the wider public. The next opportunity was four years away.

The early attacks came from the French and Spanish teams trying to set up something for Jeannie Longo and Joane Somarriba respectively. These attacks and successive accelerations were having an effect, as riders were shelled out of the back of the bunch. Rachel was doing a great job of making sure that I was getting enough to drink, providing bottles for me, and keeping me in a good position in the bunch.

Going into Lap 6, Sonia Huget of France was ahead on her own when Judith Arndt launched a massive attack. It was a dangerous move. I went after her of course and this caused an immediate reaction from my other rivals. I caught Judith and then we reformed as a group of about 13 just as we caught Huget. Ominously, all three Australians made the selection. I was on my own, as were a few others. If the Australians wanted this move to stay away, they'd best do some work. As we came through the finish line to start the next lap, defending champion Leontien van Moorsel, who had been riding tempo on the front for a lot of the race, looked back over her shoulder to check the situation behind and rode into the Spanish rider, Iturriaga in front of her and came crashing down, taking other riders with her including Canada's Lyne Bessette. They were both now out of the race.

This crash and consequent easing allowed the chasing group, which included Rachel, to rejoin us. I was pleased to see her as we still had three laps to go. Then Sue Palmer-Komar escaped off the front. We dawdled, and Sue's lead grew to over a minute. On the climb, Joane was forcing the pace with Mirjam Melchers and me following. The gaps were starting to open. I went to the front to help Joane create the selection. It worked; we were now a group of five, Joane, Oenone Wood, Susanne Ljungskog, Mirjam Melchers and myself. We started taking turns to make the pace at the front, all except for Susanne. Mirjam and Oenone saw that Susanne was not working and then they stopped coming through as well. Joane and I were the only ones left working, so we slowed. Judith, for whatever reason, had not managed to come with us on the climb but was now chasing hard by herself. As she caught us, she immediately attacked. Sue Palmar-Komar was still out front by herself; if Judith got to Sue before we could catch her, they would almost certainly make it to the finish. This was one move I couldn't risk taking a chance on. I chased very hard.

As I was one tactical bound behind Judith, so Oenone was one tactical bound behind me, each chasing the other like a track pursuit, then virtually simultaneously a selection of five formed, with Sue still out in front while Susanne had lost contact from our group.

Our pace eased, with everyone wary of the other. Russian Olga Slyusareva had jumped from the group behind to bridge across to us, so now we were six. Judith was driving on and remonstrating with Oenone, who was now not only not working but hindering our efforts by riding in second place and not going through. Olga, a sprinter, was not working, but at least was not hindering as she sat at the back. I had used a lot of energy and was swiftly recalculating. There were only four of us working but we pressed on, catching Sue by the end of the penultimate lap. Seven nations now each had a single rider in the lead group. Our pace eased, every one of us thinking how we were going to act out the finale. Judith was clearly the strongest.

Behind, Australian Sara Carrigan had jumped away from the group like Olga had done earlier. She was in no-man's land, chasing and hoping. She played the cards she had in her hand, as many another rider has done in identical situations, and this time they came up; there were not enough of us working hard and she caught us. Now the Australians could call the shots.

As we crossed the line to start the last lap, we all looked back down the wide finishing straight and could see the chasing group, just 20 seconds behind. If we continued messing around, we would all lose out; I 'suggested' to Olga to start working, we needed to stay away, but it had no effect. Olga was following wheels until she saw the 200m sign.

On the wide drag after the finish, Judith made a probing effort. I jumped after her, as I could not let her go again, and Joane jumped after me. We chased again, reformed again and eased, pausing to catch our breath. The others caught us. Sara saw the opportunity and attacked, but neither Judith, Joane or I were capable of immediately responding to her. Even if we could have, Oenone was riding shotgun, and should we catch

Sara, Oenone would immediately counter. Sara was quickly opening up a gap; we all recalculated. We paused, watching Sara just ahead of us.

The trick is to attack when your rivals are distracted. I was on the right of the group and Judith was on the left. Behind us there was a new sound, the heavy breathing as riders caught us. I manoeuvred to see who they were; others in our group did likewise. Judith went and I'd missed the moment.

In a twinkling we had become a group of eight, chasing two lone riders. Of our eight, only Joane, Mirjam and myself were going to work. Edita Pucinskaite and Kristin Armstrong, who had just crossed to us, couldn't, and neither could Sue. Olga was saving herself for the sprint and Oenone was actively disrupting any chase. Joane and I looked at each other and together with Mirjam we did our best, biding our time until we got to the hill. Ahead, Judith quickly caught Sara and swept on. At the hill, Joane and I gave it all we had left. Oenone was strong and Joane and I could not get rid of her; Mirjam stuck with us as well. By the top, the gap to Judith and Sara was tantalisingly small, but we had not made it. Oenone was excellent, always riding second wheel, disturbing our group to the maximum. I would have done exactly the same in her place. She earned the duo ahead those precious metres that were needed.

Joane and I descended as if our lives depended on it. I don't remember it like this at all, but writing now after I have watched the video of the race, first I can see myself remounting after I slid out of control into the barrier on a corner. I'm not hurt and the impact was minimal. Next, we see Mirjam braking, out of control, and she goes into the same barrier, independently of me. Finally we see Edita, doing exactly what Mirjam and I had done. Somehow, on one corner, once in the race, all three of us, independently, overdo it! All three of us had already ridden the same bend eight times, yet now, this last time, we all make exactly the same mistake and overshoot.

In the fracas after the corner, any chance of catching Judith and Sara as they played out tactics on the run-in to the finish is gone. Not that Judith is worried about that. She is a woman on a mission, she drives the last couple of kilometres, storming to her own special ending for which she needs time and space. Judith signals to Sara that she is ready for the finish by coming off the drops and putting her hands on the hoods of the brake levers and sitting up, exactly the opposite of what she should be doing. After Sara takes the 'hint' and goes for the line, Judith takes her mitts off, no doubt savouring every penny of the fine imposed on her, after she had sent her own special message to her very special friends in the German Cycling Federation, as she crossed the line.

We catch the little group ahead, but I am exhausted. Olga has been saving herself for the sprint, so I position myself on her wheel. Oenone sees me there and leaves it as long as she can before jumping, but neither of us can match Olga. I'm still battling with every last ounce of strength in my body as I cross the line.

I was fifth and felt devastated. The way I viewed it for a long time was that I'd put everything I had into it and got nothing out. I'd failed in what had been my ultimate aim in life since I was 12. There had been so much expectation and although I don't think I wilted under the pressure, in 2004 I viewed it that my training disaster three weeks before Athens had ruined my form, and my desperate desire to win had clouded my tactical judgement.

Watching the video now, I see it differently. Fundamentally I wasn't strong enough. If I could have taken the form I had at the Giro into the race, I would have been able to get away with Judith on one of several occasions. With the form I had, I made sure I was in every move that counted and several times took the initiative at exactly the right moment. You can't make it happen if you don't have the legs. The Australians, like the Italian men the day before, had played their hand superbly. There was a huge gathering of British media at the finish, all with high hopes they would witness the first British medal of the games. I had to face them. There was not much to say, I'd blown my chance and failed. They were sympathetic, but it did not ease the pain, and later on I finally cracked, crying as I got changed alone. I had never contemplated what would happen after the Olympics. While others went on with life and the world kept turning, I wondered what I was supposed to do now. The clock had stopped. There was no ticking now. All was silent.

I still had the time-trial three days later and was determined to try to salvage something from this Olympics. The reality was that with the disruption to my training and the delay in delivery of the bike, I had done precious little specialist preparation. Certainly nowhere near as much as in 2001, when I won the Junior World title. Now, I was only ever going to have an outside chance against the specialists, but I ignored the statistics and went straight into resting and recovery, clinging on to the totally unrealistic hope that I could pull a big ride out of the bag.

The time-trial was won by Leontien van Moorsel, who had so many wonderful results in the mid '90s. Set off behind me was Deirdre Barry. She caught and passed me, leaving me for dead, on the way to silver. She would find a walk-on part in the Lance Armstrong scandals of 2012. Long-term team-mate of Lance, husband Michael Barry had been hired by Team Sky. He confessed to the US Anti-Doping Agency (USADA) that he was guilty of using EPO. Deirdre was named in the testimony of a young rider David Zabriskie, working with Lance, who stated that he received EPO injections at Michael Barry's apartment, and that after taking injections he states 'that night Michael and his wife Deirdre and I had a conversation about EPO and its wide use in the peloton. They proceeded to come up with justification for drug use.'

Thanks to USADA, you can read the whole testimony online. It makes a very sad contrast to the honourable and decent attitude of Peter Baker, the American I had met in Italy trying to progress honestly through the sport. Poor David Zabriskie, who had lost his father early in life, lost his way and met people who he really should have walked away from – Michael Barry confessed that he kept the drugs in the fridge! His wife, however, has never been convicted of doping. Zabriskie was entranced with the sparkling, 'win at all costs' brigade – the people who cannot contemplate honour in defeat, going down, having given absolutely everything you have. The unspoken tragedy of PED use within the peloton is one of the reasons I felt I had to make such a powerful statement on my retirement and why I include such evidence here.

Karin Thürig came third in Athens. Later, I would be on the same team as Karin for two years. I have the utmost respect for Karin, I admired how she raced and her ability to both win and lose with grace. I am confident she is entirely deserving of her bronze medal. I finished 19th, and spent the next three days in the Olympic village. I put my disappointing results to the back of my mind and took in the 'Olympic experience', visiting the Acropolis, watching other competitions and touring the food hall in awe of the assortment of athletic specimens and quantity of food on show. Even going around the village on the bus was a cultural experience, seeing the different athletes jump on and off and passing the headquarters of all the different nations, with their huge flags and decorations to display their national identity and traditions as well as making their athletes feel at home.

I was back in Cornuda by the time the second week of the Olympics was underway. Away from the bustle of Athens, the feeling of despondency hit me again and I decided I had to do something to try to deal with my thoughts so I could move on. The answer was a bike ride and I chose to ride to Lake Garda, 180km to the west, with no distractions, to sort my head out. I told Nonna about my escapade, packed a few belongings – toothbrush, money, shorts and a pair of trainers – and set off with the intention of riding six hours there, staying the night and then riding six hours back the next day.

The unfamiliar roads and beautiful surroundings gave me something new to think about. I got there in time for an afternoon walk around the lakefront and that night watched Kelly Holmes win the 800m back in Athens. The next day, riding back, I tried to deal with my race in Athens, and set new goals, trying somehow to move on.

The rest of the season went by in a sort of blur. I was out of the running for the World Cup, having missed seven rounds, but my form recovered a little. I defended my title in the San Francisco Grand Prix and I won a stage and finished second overall in the Giro di Toscana. At the World Championships in Verona, the lack of a training foundation at the beginning of the season displaced my preparations once again, and on the wane, I finished 24th behind winner Judith Arndt. At Athens I had missed the target, but considering where I was in early May, I still believed I could win the Olympics. I looked forward to 2005; perhaps I could have a good winter and a full season.

CHAPTER SIXTEEN
New Approach and New Goals

I needed to work out how I was going to get from the Athens failure through the next four-year Olympic cycle to be capable of winning in Beijing in 2008. It seemed my biggest issues were how I evaluated my training and the tactical limitations of having little British team support. I was determined to address both.

I needed a coach, someone independent who I could trust to tell me when to train harder and when to ease off. I knew I was prone to selecting a default mode of try harder, train harder, race harder. Dad had guided me through my early years, although his judgement, like mine, could also be compromised by being so close to the daily intensity and pressures. Now I was older, would I really listen to him? I approached British Cycling and Chris Boardman, 1992 Olympic Pursuit champion and three-time winner of the Tour de France prologue, was proposed as a potential coach. Chris could provide an independent perspective on my programme, help analyse the data and would be someone I would listen to when he advised me to ease off and I wanted to keep going.

Regarding team support, I couldn't have asked any more of Rachel Heal at Athens; she rode wonderfully, but she'd had only one year living and riding in the continental peloton.

Where were the others? Sara Symington was the best of the UK-based WCPP riders and she was a DNF at Athens and then retired. British Cycling had not sent any junior women to the three road World Championships since my win in Lisbon 2001. I was spending my time in the winter visiting clubs and I saw a great enthusiasm from the girls. The WCPP might be producing male track riders but it certainly wasn't looking after the potential female road riders of the future. Why was this talent not coming through? Dave Brailsford was good enough to listen to my ideas for how we could deal with this and assurances were made that British Cycling would make efforts for the World Championships in Madrid.

For the media, one Olympic gold medal was pretty much the same as another. Maybe I should widen my horizons and look at some of the other events? In the time-trial you were not dependent on a team. Mountain biking was an even more interesting prospect. It demanded a high level of physical ability and still offered tactical challenges yet did not require a team. But I loved road racing. Races are held in all weather conditions, from the sleet and snow of the spring classics to the summer heat of Provence. The roads can be as smooth as an autostrada or as rough as the Belgian cobblestones. I had experienced winning in a massive shoulder-to-shoulder bunch sprint over the last 200m, and having ridden all day to victory in a solo break. Every single race you start is different. You can win (or lose) by pretending to be the strongest, when in reality you are feeling terrible, or conversely you can be strong and kid everyone that you are having a bad day. Each race was as tactically interesting as it was physically demanding. I loved living in Italy, in this world that I understood and understood me. However, I had to face reality if I dreamed of an Olympic gold.

I decided that my 2005 programme would include road

racing, time-trialling and mountain biking. I began working with Chris Boardman on a pre-season training programme that combined mountain biking sessions, lengthy road rides for endurance and intense sprint sessions at Newport velodrome. In mid-February, I returned to Italy for pre-season training with the team and then flew to Cyprus for my first test in mountain biking. The field was of a moderate international standard and although I won all of my four races, and was able to dedicate time to my technical development, I was not going to get carried away. Even so, I quietly hoped that I'd got the formula right.

Back in Italy, there was a new team house in Montebelluna and sadly it meant Nonna had lost out, although I would often go round to say hello. There were five of us living in the team house, which made for an interesting cultural mix with Rochelle Gilmore, Gessica Turato (an Italian who would go on to win the European U23 Championships that season), Mexican Giuseppina Grassi and Miyoko Karami from Japan. This was Giuseppina's second stint on the professional circuit, having ridden as a *domestique* in the mid-'90s with a major team but cracked under the stress and worked harvesting apples to pay for a ticket to get home. She spent some years back in Mexico, then decided to return to Europe to try again. Miyoko was embarking on her first season in the professional ranks and we all liked her pluckiness and the way she dealt with the new challenges of life in a foreign country and the wacky everyday events of the cycling world.

The season got off to a great start when I won the GP Rosignano, the scene of my first professional win three years before. I went into the Primavera Rosa World Cup with high hopes of a win. There was still a group of 15 riders as we started the final descent towards the finish, which included four riders from the Nürnberger Versicherung team – Judith Arndt, Trixi Worrack, Oenone Wood and Regina Schleicher who had been our sprinter last year but moved back to a German-based team, perhaps with an eye on the World Championships later that year.

You could see the logic from the Germans: this year's World Championships were likely to finish in a bunch sprint, and Regina could ride all year with her German team-mates, who could then deliver her to a sprint finish in Madrid, having practised it all season. Everyone was a winner as the team and sponsors benefited, and so did the riders who could share the races during the season and repay the favour. How I envied such forward planning.

As we approached the finish, the 'Blue Train', as the media later referred to the Nürnberger team, upped the pace, occupying the first four places. It was a classic leadout for a sprinter. I fought my way onto Regina's wheel ready to do battle with her in the final 200m. We went round a bend 400m from the finish, and the pace seemed to ease off slightly. As we came out of the bend, I saw the reason why. Trixi, who had been on the front, had accelerated round the corner while her team-mates behind her had eased, allowing her to get a gap, and now she was making her bid for victory.

I was trapped, with no team-mates to chase her down. If I jumped after Trixi, I would simply be providing a leadout to one of her team-mates; being the only Safi rider, I was reliant on other teams to chase Trixi. It was a clever move on their part. I did the only thing I could do in that situation and won the bunch sprint for second place. But I was seething inside that I had lost out yet again on such a prestigious victory, foiled by a stronger team with some very smart tactics.

The following day, our team presentation took place back

at Cornuda and I was again honoured that Maurizio had chosen my win in the Giro d'Italia the previous year as the photo for the team's Astoria Prosecco bottles. My good form continued the following week when I won the Trofeo Alfredo Binda in Lombardy, before we headed to Belgium for the Tour of Flanders World Cup.

I had missed the inaugural women's Tour of Flanders the previous season through injury and was looking forward to riding one of the great spring classics. It includes many notorious climbs and for good measure also has many cobbled sections, a real test of bike handling, tactics and physical strength. I made an early break that was reeled in by the bunch before the main climb, the Muur de Geraardsbergen. Mirjam Melchers of the Buitenpoort-Flexpoint team broke away before the Muur, then Susanne Ljungskog attacked on the climb, catching Mirjam, and the duo stayed away to finish first and second. The race for third place ended in a farce when my group of 20 riders were led off course by an official race car about 2km from the finish. We ended up riding through the finish line in the wrong direction and being disqualified.

We stayed in Belgium and I won the GP Roeselare in a bunch sprint ahead of Oenone Wood, which set me up nicely for the Flèche Wallonne three days later. It had turned into my favourite race with its steep finishing climb, the Mur de Huy, and although I was struggling on some of the longer climbs, my good run continued with a very satisfying victory, with Oenone second and Judith Arndt third.

This was my fourth win from six starts, and was a terrific antidote to any hangover from Athens. Other good news to look forward to was that a round of the World Cup would be staged in Newport, with the ever-industrious Bill Owen at the heart of the organising group, I was delighted at the prospect of being with my team as they came to Wales. As the team returned to Montebelluna, I went to Spa in Belgium to compete in the first round of the Mountain Bike World Cup, wondering if it was possible to win two World Cup races in separate disciplines in the same week. The answer was a resounding 'no', as I finished in a respectable but uncompetitive 11th place. My limitations riding off-road were shown up at the second round in Madrid a fortnight later, where I finished way down the field. If winning World Cup mountain bike races meant giving up road racing in order to concentrate on them, then the answer was simple. The road was where my heart was and where I belonged. While in Madrid, I took the opportunity to recce the course for the road World Championships, which appeared certain to finish in a bunch sprint, so I adjusted my training to suit.

I had been back in Italy only a few days when I felt a niggling pain in my knee in training, but this time the pain was in my right knee. I recognised the pain immediately as similar to what I had felt before in my left knee, so I eased off, heading back carefully to the team house where I spent a nervous night hoping it was just a blip. When the same thing happened the next day, I booked a flight back to Wales, as I wasn't going to delay this time, and I went straight to see Dr Rod Jaques in Bath to get an assessment. It was the same problem – an aggravation of the plica membrane – and surgery was still a last resort. I stopped training and began a rehabilitation programme, which we estimated would take four weeks, and that meant I would be out of action until the middle of June.

The rehab programme completed, I flew back to Italy for the Giro del Trentino. I finished second in the first 120km stage, admittedly a fairly flat course, and then as we headed into the mountains the next day I was riding well and in the leading group of six riders. Then, the niggling ache returned and I limped to the finish in sixth place. Reluctantly I pulled out of the race before having a frank conversation with Maurizio. If I couldn't do two days' consecutive racing, there was no way I could do the Giro, which was our main goal for the season. I needed surgery again but first asked the doctors if I could race the British Nationals. Jonathan Webb said it wouldn't do any long-term damage and that actually causing further irritation would make it easier to see the inflammation during the operation. It was just a matter of whether I could stand the pain.

Of course I could. I really wanted to win the National title and wear the champion's jersey for another year. It was a rolling course at Ryedale in Yorkshire, and I decided that my best chance was to form an early breakaway group of a manageable size, establish a lead over the bunch and then hang on as best I could and hope the group came to a finish in a sprint where I could be confident. As I attacked, Rachel Heal, Helen Wyman (née Saunders, from my early years), Emma Davies and Emma Pooley, who was riding in her first British Championships, came with me and, as planned, I managed to control the race, resting the knee as often as possible during the three hours and sprinting away in the last 400m to take my sixth victory. Rachel was second, for the fourth year in a row.

I went into surgery two days later. It appeared to go well and the early recovery was as promising as my left knee a year earlier. However, I got a minor infection in the cut which delayed things. Then, just as I was about to build up to full training, the pain in my knee began again. The complications seemed never-ending. My knee had to be strapped to lift the kneecap slightly on one side to ease the pressure on that area, while the internal wound continued to heal. The demons of Athens were still lurking in my mind and now that I was injured and couldn't race, I felt that I wasn't only letting myself down but the team too and doubted whether I would ever reach my full potential after the operation.

I decided to put the enforced time off the bike to good use. At the end of 2004, the UCI set up a commission to move women's road racing forward. I had joined straight away and was selected to be part of the eight-rider committee. During 2005, a topic of debate was the Olympic programme where two track events (the 1km for men and 500m for women) were to be removed, so that BMX could be introduced, leaving seven track events for the men and just three for the women. A group set up a petition calling for the reinstatement of these two events, though I thought this did not go far enough. I proposed to the UCI commission that we should lobby for equality of cycling events at the Olympics and was very disheartened that some members of the women's commission did not want to support such an initiative.

I wrote to the UCI, highlighting the inequality and asked them to address this. It became clear that there was no support or desire to listen to the women's commission on this or many other issues and it was disbanded by the UCI before the end of the year. I was delighted when the inequality of the Olympic track programme was addressed for 2012, but the sexist bias could have been sorted out four years earlier.

Chris Boardman and I had also parted company. His contribution had been of valuable benefit to me, but we both agreed: why discuss the fine details of training data if I was not on a training programme but a rehabilitation process that needed doctors rather than coaches to guide me? I visited the World Cup when it came to Newport, but the day, watching a race in which I should have been fighting for the win, was a miserable experience. I doubted the race would ever be repeated in my career. It was now August, and I was struggling to see any positives. I was also alone, as Mum and Dad had gone on their summer holidays to ride the Alps, and Craig was now studying in Melbourne.

My home, normally a place of sanctuary and support, felt like solitary confinement, until I hit on the idea of asking Miyoko to come and stay with me, which Maurizio agreed to. She couldn't speak much English and her Italian was still limited, but we spent a happy fortnight doing hard rides in the hills. We also spent some time exploring the area, visiting the beaches and going to the Glamorgan agricultural show where we watched sheep-shearing competitions and sampled Welsh Cakes. Her sunny disposition, appetite for training and ease at trying something new lifted my spirits, particularly the day she noticed me mowing the back lawn. She was captivated by the noisy machine, childlike in her excitement as she begged to have a go, finished the job, and then offered to do the front lawn too!

Miyoko and I joined the team in early September for the six-day Holland Ladies Tour, giving me about one month of racing before the World Championships. With a field of 164 riders, everyone who was likely to feature in Madrid was here: the last two World champions, Judith Arndt and Susanne Ljungskog, plus Oenone Wood, Mirjam Melchers, Kirsten Wild and others. Regina Schleicher had spent the season riding with her German team-mates at Nürnberger and they would be putting the finishing touches to their leadout practice. I was delighted to welcome fellow Brit Amy Hunt, a rider three years younger than me, who was with us as a *stagiaire* with a view to joining the team the following year. Phil Griffiths, a former top British amateur rider and now running a business distributing Italian cycle parts and accessories, was trying his hardest to help ease other British riders into the Italian scene to support me. There was another British rider in the race, Jacqui Marshall, one year younger than me, who recently had had a win in a Belgian criterium, ahead of a 60-plus field. She was in the same team as Helen Wyman, and Emma Davies was also riding. It was encouraging to see their initiative; maybe things would improve for British Cycling thanks to these girls, but they, like me, were doing it outside of the WCPP system.

Rochelle offered to lead me out on Stage 2. She did an excellent job and I should have rewarded her efforts and those of the rest of my team with a win, but I misjudged Regina's late surge, relaxing too early, thinking I'd done enough to win. At the line, the judges consulted the photo finish equipment for a long time before declaring Regina first. It was my fault; they should not have needed to look. I had made the mistake of a novice. Despite being infuriated with second place, being so close to a win was encouraging and perhaps I could salvage something from the season after all.

By Stage 3, I was happy with how my knee was holding up to the continuous days of racing, so I was very angry with myself for getting caught up in a big bunch crash as the roads narrowed on to a cobbled section. I fell heavily, gashing my elbow, but luckily not my knees. My handlebars had been twisted and I had to wait for the team car with my replacement bike. I chased and caught the peloton quite quickly, but within a few kilometres my saddle started to slide down into the frame. I was now pedalling with my legs in a crunched up style and it was hurting my right knee. The team mechanics had repaired my crashed bike and rejoined the race convoy, so I stopped and changed to my original bike, even though it did look somewhat the worse for wear. I chased again to get back to the peloton, and exhausted from the effort, I spent the rest of the stage worried about my knee and the damage I might have done.

On Stage 4, I strapped my knee, hoping to prevent any further aggravation or pain, and tried to take it as easy as possible in the bunch, not getting involved with the racing action. The 125km Stage 5 was a similar story, and when a small group broke away I hoped that the bunch would ride steadily to the end. As the stage went on and my knee was giving no signs of pain, I began to relax. With 15km to go, the time checks indicated the break was less than a minute in front of the bunch, and several teams who did not have any riders in the breakaway group began to organise a chase. I hovered near the front, watching to see what would happen and take advantage of any opportunity which might present itself.

As we entered the finishing circuit, the gap was 25 seconds. We had to do three complete laps of the 3km circuit. As we approached the finish line with one lap to go, the gap was about 20 seconds and I decided to take a gamble and jump across to the group alone, without any of the sprinters currently in the bunch coming with me. I chased like crazy, catching the break with just 400m to go, and I used my momentum to immediately launch my sprint to win the stage. Joyously, I held my arms outstretched as I crossed the line wearing my British National champion jersey, bandages over my arms, strapping on my knee and a wonky-looking bike. It was not the most glamorous of shots, but with the bunch six seconds behind the break it was a win which had combined all the necessary ingredients: tactics, pursuiting and sprinting. Coming as it did after a season ruined by injury, in my first race back after surgery and rehabilitation, it was a critical moment which convinced me that I could still dream of great victories.

NEW APPROACH AND NEW GOALS

At the last two rounds of the World Cup, I supported my team-mates, with Anna Zugno fourth at Rotterdam, behind winner Ina Teutenberg. One week later, at the final round at Nuremburg, Rochelle was the sprinter we were all supporting. She had not been picked by the Australian selectors for the World Championships, so we wanted to help her send a message to them. We worked hard to get her to the line, but she came second, narrowly beaten by Giorgia Bronzini. All the sprinters were testing themselves for Madrid. Oenone Wood won her second World Cup series in succession, and despite my disjointed season I finished ninth overall.

My final race before the World Championships was the six-day Giro di Toscana. By Stage 3, as a result of my lack of strength in the hills, I was well down on the GC and no threat for the overall win, so I escaped in a breakaway. In the closing stages, we received time checks indicating that the main group were chasing hard and would probably catch the break. I attacked the others to go it alone, I pressed on in time-trial mode for the last 5km, with the bunch swallowing up the breakaway and now breathing down my neck. I held off the charging pack to win by a couple of seconds; this was now the second time in a couple of weeks that I'd created a winning chance, despite not being the strongest in the peloton.

During the Giro di Toscana, I received visitors. Dave Brailsford had come to Tuscany to meet Max Sciandri, a British-born and Italian-raised former professional cyclist and bronze medallist in the 1996 Olympic road race. Dave was really taking to heart my message of 'get them onto the continent'. He had visited Max with an idea of setting up a house in Italy for the U23 men's academy as a base for them to ride continental races. Now they both talked with me about the idea of a house for the British women. The discussions were positive and at last I felt that things were moving in the right direction.

After the Giro di Toscana, the British team of Rachel Heal, Helen Wyman, Catherine Hare, Charlotte Goldsmith, Emma Pooley and me had a training camp in Tuscany. Of these, only Helen had been at the Holland Ladies Tour, so although we discussed tactics and practised manoeuvres for Madrid, we all understood the difficulty of translating these gestures into race-forming moves. Then, after our final pre-race briefing, at my suggestion, we watched a video of the Zolder World Championship men's race which Mario Cipollini had won following perfect, race-long, support from the Italian team.

With lots of encouragement and Helen assisting, the girls sensed that this was a race where they could help me. We knew that we didn't have the strength for the girls to do anything to counter the big teams in the last 5km, but if they could help me get there, it would be a plus, and if Rachel could do more, that would be a bonus. Sitting with the whole team watching a video and having a sensible discussion about tactics together with the coach was a new experience for me in a GB team. It had taken six long years of struggle, but things were changing. Dave Brailsford was bringing a new dynamism to the race strategy and preparation. The fact that I was being consulted rather than told what to do, was a major change which I appreciated greatly.

The squads from Germany, Australia, Holland, Italy, Russia and Lithuania all had plenty of capacity for delivering their sprinters to the final 200m, but it wasn't their only option, as in their teams of six they also had riders capable of going the distance in a breakaway. Other nations like the USA and Canada would need to break up the race. Susanne Ljungskog was always a danger and there were about half a dozen other riders who would have the strength and desire to cause an upset. Joane Somarriba would be extremely motivated to win on home soil and would give everything she had. I knew from the Giro di Toscana that my endurance form was fragile, but in the sprints in Holland I'd been able to match the pure sprinters.

The course featured one long hill, so each lap I positioned myself near the front before the start of the climb so that during the climb I could allow myself to slide backwards through the bunch. What started as a tactic to conserve strength became a matter of survival after the halfway stage, as the serious attacks started coming. In the last three laps, the big attacks started from those who did not want a sprint finish. I only know that from reading the reports after the race, as it was all I could do to make sure I got back into the bunch after the hill each time. On the last lap, Joane launched a big attack on the final climb, not that I knew it was her at the time. All I knew was that I was really suffering just to stay in contact.

We were really stretched out from the action at the front. I had to pray that no one ahead of me was letting a gap open in front of them. As we crested the hill, I was still in contact. Rachel came alongside and led me up the side of the bunch until we were in the leading 12 riders. This was a terrific help. The German team appeared the strongest and Regina was their sprinter, so I knew I needed to get onto her wheel. The only problem was that I was not the only one who had worked out that this was the best place to be! After quite a bit of jostling, I was there with just under 1.5km to go.

With 1km left, Judith Arndt had taken over at the front and was going flat out, with Trixi and Regina tucked in behind. The finish was on a dual carriageway and to provide spectacle we rode past the finish on the opposite side before doing a 180 degree turn with 400m to go. As we went into the turn, Judith was riding too strongly and as she powered out of the bend she opened up a gap. There was a call from Trixi, so Judith eased and the German train stalled. This hesitation allowed other riders to start challenging, led by the Lithuanians who were leading out Diana Ziliute and the Australians leading out Oenone. If I waited behind the Germans, I could be over-whelmed by the other leadout teams and get nothing. The line was less than 400m away and getting closer every second.

Up the side came the Lithuanian train. I should have been following an ever-accelerating German leadout all the way to 200m and now that they were being passed, I was being passed. I was in no-man's land. I knew if I waited, I could never win. I went for the line myself. It was a long drag. Trixi got going again, so Regina had her leadout and powered over the line to win with me in second place. I stood with clenched teeth during the medal ceremony. The pictures show a happy Regina and Oenone and an unsmiling Nicole. My desperation to be a World champion wouldn't allow me to be satisfied with second, regardless of the circumstances and being beaten on the day by a very fast sprinter, led out by her national and trade team-mates.

Looking back, I am very proud of that ride. Behind me was Australia with Oenone, Italy supporting their sprinter Giorgia Bronzini and the Lithuanians supporting Diana. I was delighted with our new-look GB team. At long last, we had worked as a team and even though we had a long way to go, these were good first steps. For the first time ever, a GB rider had helped me in a worthwhile manner in the closing kilometres of a race. Rachel's help was critical. Earlier in the race, my team-mates gathered around me as best they could, to help me get back into a good position in the bunch, as I slid out of the back on the hill. Without this support, there would have been no silver medal for the GB team, the single medal of these championships for Britain. Rachel had come through for 2005, despite those missed opportunities at the end of 2002; together, we were one step away from the top position. We needed to arrest the cycle of riders coming to the team only to leave a couple of years later, disillusioned by what they saw around them. With Peg Hill there had been one opportunity lost; here, four years later, another opportunity presented itself to British Cycling. Rachel and the others needed careful nurturing.

I may have always thought that the women in British Cycling were getting a rough deal, but an incident in the men's race showed that it could be just as bad for the men. Roger Hammond was the team's best rider; with a third in Paris-Roubaix to his credit. He wasn't an out-and-out sprinter, more a fine classics rider. During the race, the crowds were treated to the strange sight of two GB riders riding on the front for several laps to close the gap to a breakaway. These tactics were not in the interest of the British team, as one of the stronger teams such as the Italians would normally have done this, as there were no Italians in the break. Tom Southam and Charlie Wegelius were effectively riding for Italy and not GB or Roger. Later the collusion between the Italian team and these riders was exposed, and they, along with British team manager John Herety, were permanently excluded from ever performing with a GB team again. For far too long, the team officials had thought that they could do what they wanted; after all, the riders had signed agreements telling them they must do as instructed so the chance of them complaining was very limited . . . apart from that 'troublesome' Nicole Cooke.

Looking back, this was clearly a turning point in the way British Cycling operated its road teams and would lead to the eventual success achieved by Team Sky. At the time, I simply knew that at last, after all my years of demanding improved standards of behaviour, changes were now happening in British Cycling.

I had been giving a lot of thought to the following year. I had seen how well the Nürnburger team was organised, not simply having good riders but the support staff, equipment and general race organisation. When Maurizio started his team in the '90s, he was the best. Now the other teams had caught up and gone past him. While I had been concentrating on my build-up for the World Championships, some people had been working on my behalf discussing options with other teams, even including the possibility, which Dave Brailsford had mentioned, of a GB team house in Tuscany. When I got back to Montebelluna, I told Maurizio that I would not be re-signing with the team. He was good about it, telling me I would always have a friend. He asked if I had already signed with another team and actually, although those working on my behalf seemed confident, I admitted I had not received a contract or even a written proposal.

Together with my team-mates, we organised a big end-of-season party and then I headed back to Wales, ready to prepare myself for the future.

I hadn't quite finished for the year. The mountain bike trial had not worked out, but there was no reason why I couldn't target the track for the Commonwealth Games in Melbourne in March 2006, particularly now that Wales had an indoor velodrome in Newport. I would ride both the road race and the track. I entered the British National Track Championships and went into the races with nothing to lose. The 15km scratch race was an attack fest in the closing stages, with move and counter move, and I came in third behind Victoria

Pendleton and Rachel Heal. The following day, in the points race, I dominated every sprint, winning my first and only senior National Track Championship.

Looking at the long term, I still needed to work with a coach. The coaching stint with Chris Boardman had ended because of my injury. British Cycling then recommended working with Dan Hunt, who I knew from the Welsh Institute of Sport although I had never worked with him. He was now with BC WCPP and together we formulated a programme targetting road and the track points race. My first test on the track would be the Manchester World Cup in December, with an eye on the Commonwealth Games, now just five months away.

I also needed some riders in the Welsh road team to defend my Commonwealth Games title. In 2002, as a first-year senior, I had been able to take advantage of the rivalry between the Australians and Canadians, but it was certain that this time they would use their six-rider teams to mark me out of it. In the winter of 2004–05, I had gained agreement from the Welsh Cycling Union to run a programme similar to the one being run for the men to develop girls specifically for the Commonwealth Games, and during 2005 the girls travelled all over Britain to designated races. Unfortunately, there was still a dearth of races for women and it was a big commitment for them to travel so far each weekend.

Mike Townley and Dave Brailsford were putting together a deal with Bob Stapleton, an American multi-millionaire who was about to take over the men's T-Mobile team and wanted to run a women's team alongside it. The idea was to get some of the British U23 men and GB female riders on the team. Negotiations were going well. I also met with Julian Winn, the latest WCU coach, who was also still a rider at that time and had his own preparations for Melbourne 2006 to optimise. We met to discuss the winter programme through to the Games, as I needed to train and race with the girls over the next months so we could practise our teamwork. Julian and I agreed a programme and we informed the girls so that they could plan time off work with their employers.

Just before I set off to travel to London to finalise discussions with my prospective new team, the WCU informed me of the selection decisions for the forthcoming Commonwealth Games. They had decided that I was to ride alone. I enquired about the men's team supporting national coach Julian Winn. What had they decided to do for the men? That had a full quota of six riders. Just why did I waste my breath asking?

Chris Landon was chairman of the WCU and of the selection commission. He explained that it was the recommendation of the coach. I pointed out that only a few days before, the coach had held a very different opinion and how, after speaking to him, I had sent emails to other riders reflecting that position. It was irrelevant. The selection commission had made a decision and there was to be no going back and changing it now as that would look weak. I could have understood it if the men's team stood a better chance of bringing back a medal than the women's, but in fact the opposite was the case.

The girls were devastated. They had been working towards this aim for 12 months, training, travelling to races, giving up their normal social life and dedicating themselves to this goal. They had suspected that something was amiss for some time, as they could see the attention that the men's squad was receiving, while they were practically ignored. On one occasion, when Julian was meant to watch their performances at a selection race, he turned up, went for a training session by himself, didn't see them race and left without talking to them. As the

WCU refused to budge, I went to the Commonwealth Games Council for Wales (CGCW) and the Welsh Sports Council. Eventually the WCU were brought to a meeting and forced to reconsider their dogmatic stance by the CGCW, which resulted in the WCU changing their decision and sending a letter to the girls.

But it was too late. The three girls – Michelle Ward, Rebecca Jones and Alex Greenfield – politely declined and decided to move on with their lives. British women's cycling had just lost another three talented riders to add to the many others over the years. What a terrible and avoidable waste of time, effort, ambition and talent! By their decision, the WCU had gifted Australia, Canada, England and New Zealand my head on a plate. Not only was a full men's team being sent to the race itself, but even more money was to be lavished on two warm-weather training camps, no doubt accompanied by a full complement of support staff. No wonder they were trying to cut down costs by not even sending the women to the race itself!

What was the result of all this expensive preparation for the Welsh men's team as Julian, with Shane Sutton behind him, optimised marginal gains for them? Of the six male riders who started the road race in Melbourne, not one of them finished. Even riders from those well-known cycling superpowers Mauritius, Namibia and Malta rode with dignity and passion and at least managed to finish.

As I travelled to London trying to take in this news from the men who ran Welsh Cycling, I could predict all the events that would come to pass in the next few months. When I arrived, I was in no fit state to have a critical career conversation with anyone. My mind was raging with the injustice and duplicity of it all: the WCU treatment of me and women in general, and the fact that the coach said one thing to me and another thing to the commission two days later.

In London, I met Bob Stapleton of T-Mobile. Bob wanted to negotiate some points of the contract with me – I'm sure he did – but I was currently having an 'off period' with anything that resembled an alpha male, particularly if he wanted me to negotiate. We couldn't come to an agreement and parted ways. It was November and I now had to start again looking for a contract for the 2006 season.

Giancarlo Ghillioni, the scout who had organised my first meeting with Maurizio after I won the Junior World road title in 2000, called me. Maurizio no doubt had told him that I had left Safi and hadn't yet signed a contract. Giancarlo, knowing even better than me the world of cycling teams and contracts, was calling to check how I was getting on. Would I be interested in meeting Thomas Campana, a former amateur cyclist who ran the Univega Pro Cycling team? The team had been around the previous year as a Swiss national level team.

I called Thomas, who told me that he had plans to boost its ranks for 2006 and was keen to add me to the list. The only problem, as usual, was money, but he had a plan. Univega was a sister company of the British Raleigh Bikes firm, so he suggested a deal under which my salary would be paid by Raleigh UK and I would race on a Raleigh frame, while the other team riders would use the Univega frames. I asked if I could arrange personal sponsorship. Yes, this would be okay, as long as it didn't conflict with anything else and was agreed in advance, so I extended my contract with Nike for racing shoes and glasses. A Cardiff businessman, Del DelaRonde had from time to time over the years helped me out in different ways. I spoke with him and he got in touch with Thomas and he agreed to become a part sponsor of the team.

Thomas organised a press conference to announce the signing during the World Cup track meet in Manchester. It would take place on the day after I competed in the points race. First, I had an innocuous qualifying round to ride. Early in the race, I scored enough points to book my place in the final, so I was taking it easy riding low on the track. I was then hit by a rider from above me and crashed heavily. I was rushed off to the hospital where x-rays confirmed I had broken my collarbone. Luckily, the bone had not completely separated into two parts so there was no need to operate, but it did not save me from excruciating pain that night.

The press conference went ahead the next day to announce my new team for 2006 and sponsorship deal with Raleigh. Thomas was there with his partner and fellow rider Priska Doppmann. He also introduced me to the *directeur sportif* Manel Lacambra who had also made the trip, showing their belief in me that I was the person to lead the team to be one of the best in women's cycling. I refused to wear a sling for the photos and gingerly held the bike with my good arm, trying to smile for the publicity shots.

Inside I was turning over. Time and again it happened; just as things were looking up. After the blow about the Welsh team, here I was again, having to deal with a serious upset to my plans. I would need to rest the shoulder for at least a month, and training for Melbourne and the early season was washed out. Sitting at home on the turbo trainer, with my arm now in the sling, I had more than enough time to wonder if I would ever be able to string more than a few good weeks together. How I wanted to get out on the road and feel the rain on my face and the burn in my legs, and suck in the clean, salt-tinged air blowing in fresh from across the Atlantic.

CHAPTER SEVENTEEN
Living the Dream on Mont Ventoux

Thomas wanted to do things differently at Univega. He was hard working, committed, capable, and understood women's cycling. He had great ambitions and wanted to get the team started with a bang. Cycling was currently bringing me its fair share of problems, including difficult, prejudiced people, but such challenges are present in all walks of life; it's how we rise to the challenge that is the critical factor. Now, at a low moment, cycling gave me a wonderful new experience.

Thomas decided that we should all meet together for the first time at Engelberg in Switzerland. It was a winter wonderland I shall never forget. I flew out in late December, was met at the airport and took a ski lift up to a mountain resort. Once all 12 riders and five support staff had arrived, Thomas assembled us in a private meeting room and started by giving us the most fantastic presentation on the team's ambitions and plans for the year. He then asked us to introduce ourselves and talk a little about our ambitions for the year ahead. It was great! And it got even better. We were to stay in a giant snow igloo which had several rooms where even the tables and chairs were carved out of ice. There was also a room without a roof which had a jacuzzi so that you could relax by simply looking at the stars above. It was a magical experience, and being there breathing in clean mountain air was certainly banishing the blues of my broken collarbone. It was a great way to bond the team together. None of us were novices, so having seen what went on elsewhere, we could all appreciate what Thomas was saying and doing. New to the line-up this year were Sarah Düster from Germany, Joanne Kiesanowski from New Zealand and myself. The rest of the team had ridden with Univega in the previous year when the racing programme was less international.

By January 2006, I'd had enough of the turbo trainer and, against doctor's orders, I was back on the bike. My shoulder was still very weak, which meant that it was very painful to ride out of the saddle, as I needed to for climbing and sprinting. I was forced to ride everywhere staying firmly seated. I graduated from 40 minutes up to a five-hour training ride in the space of a week. I'd overdone it and now it was not the shoulder but an aggravated left knee that was the issue.

When would I learn? In my urge to make up for the lost time of the broken collarbone, I had rushed too quickly into heavy training. Once again, I was going to have to start the season without the solid basis of steady endurance miles.

In February, more in hope than with a definite plan, I flew to Australia to join the rest of the team who had gone to Melbourne to prepare for the first two rounds of the World Cup, the first in Geelong and the second in Wellington, New Zealand. All this obviously slotted in perfectly for the Commonwealth Games, which were due to be held in Melbourne in March.

The reunion with Craig and the new team was invigorating. I really hit it off with my new team-mates, squeezed into our team house. Thomas and Priska took the main bedroom with five of us sleeping on an array of bunks and floor mattresses in the other two bedrooms, while the *directeur sportif*, Manel, slept on the sofabed in a small room with all the bikes. My fitness was low compared with my team-mates' and it showed. On a six-hour ride the others took a break at a café and had to wait for me. As I worked hard in training, my knee flared up again, but Thomas was understanding and sat with me to discuss how to manage what was clearly going to be a continuing issue. He had brought me onto the team knowing that I had knee injuries and stated that I was under no pressure to perform immediately. I was heartened by the conversation. In contrast, I had felt abandoned two months earlier when I broke my collarbone and the British Cycling coaching staff told me to call back when it was mended and I was able to do full training. Now, here was someone with expertise who saw me on a daily basis and could be the extra set of eyes I needed, so I accepted Thomas's offer to be my coach

I travelled with the team to Geelong, just outside Melbourne, in late February and taking Thomas's advice didn't compete in the three-day stage race that preceded the World Cup, but instead I continued my training programme. I still wasn't race fit, so we came up with a decoy plan to try to mark one of my biggest rivals for the World Cup out of the race, and give me an easier ride in the bunch until the finish. My Austrian team-mate Christiane Soeder, who had won a stage of the Geelong Tour and was in good form, would make an early attack and hopefully take some of the race favourites with her. They would be working hard, while I would try to save as much energy as possible in the bunch. It was unlikely that the break would stay away, and I would be able to contest the finish with what little firepower I had still intact, while the riders in the break with Christiane would be a spent force, unable to contest the bunch sprint.

It worked a treat. Oenone Wood, my most likely contender for the World Cup series this year, followed Christiane and a couple of others in the break. There was a tantalising chance they might stay away to the finish, but they were caught by the bunch with just 2km to go and Oenone finished down the field and out of the points, while my team-mates led me out for the sprint finish. Eighth was a good result in the circumstances, but for myself and all the other girls the most important point was that we had a great feeling of confidence in our management. We were part of a team with strategy and tactics, Thomas and Manel were totally committed, and together we were going to achieve great things.

We travelled to Wellington for the second round, where again I needed to limit my losses until I had made enough progress in training to be able to dictate tactics. After two laps of racing, we were on a fast twisty descent through the city when I rounded a bend in first place and to my horror there was a white van parked smack bang on the racing line. It certainly hadn't been there on the previous lap. Someone had opened the barriers to let the van onto the roads, and rather than continuing its journey the van had simply parked on the corner. I braked, skidded and tried to adjust my line and avoid it, but I hit the side of it at 50km/h.

Other riders came down in the ensuing crash. I jumped up, remarkably suffering only a few bloody grazes and a shredded jersey and shorts, and looked for my bike. The forks and front wheel were totally detached from the rest of the frame and only the cables held the bike together. I contrasted the state of my bike and clothes with the state of my body and I felt very lucky. My race was over as we didn't have a spare bike, and all

I could do was watch from the sidelines as Sarah Ulmer, the local favourite and Olympic Pursuit champion of Athens, attacked alone and won the race. I was grateful to some extent because Sarah was unlikely to be a threat for the overall World Cup and I would rather her win the race than my main rivals, like Oenone, who won the sprint for second. Later, Sarah would carry the New Zealand flag in the opening ceremony at the Commonwealth Games. She had also won gold on the track in Manchester in 2002. Her country was proud of her and backed her completely. I could only compare and contrast her treatment with my treatment by the Welsh Cycling Union.

While most of the Univega team, other than Aussie Emma Rickards and Priska, now headed back to Europe, I returned to Melbourne and moved in with Craig, sleeping on a mattress on the floor. I had planned a three-week training programme with Thomas through to the Commonwealth Games, and each morning I went training with Priska and Emma, whose family was a great support during my stay. Then I'd spend the evenings with Craig, cooking meals for him and his house-mates and learning about his new life. Craig took me on a tour of his university just down the road, and he would buy bags of ice for me so I could have ice baths to help my recovery. We did a couple of rides together and he rode with me to evening criterium training races in the local suburbs. He would watch and give me high-quality feedback on my performance. On the night of the opening ceremony, I was running late with no way to get to the stadium except by train. Craig ended up giving me a 'backie' on his bike; me sat on the saddle with my legs outstretched so I didn't get chain oil on my nice cream suit trousers and Craig standing up pedalling through the evening traffic.

Melbourne is a sports-mad city and put on a wonderful opening ceremony for the Commonwealth Games. I felt very proud walking into the huge stadium with the Welsh team. Back home, the Welsh media were asking why the WCU had not provided any support and put me in such a disadvantaged position, as I was going to have to race alone against teams of six riders. Even the Australians, smarting after the World Championships, were discussing it openly. Oenone had secured her second World Cup win and had been the world's No.1 ranked rider. They had put a full-strength team into Madrid to support Oenone winning the World Championships, but instead, a superbly drilled German team and a determined British individual had turned gold to bronze. She had selflessly sacrificed her chances at Athens and worked hard to help Sara Carrigan, but this would be a showcase for Oenone in front of her nation.

The Australian Institute of Sport was a well-formed and functioning operation, leading the world. Their staff followed the road circuit and gathered information to help their riders. They knew how I had come into Madrid and the relative strength of the riders I had around me compared with those of the leading cycling nations and the measure of what I had achieved in beating their accomplished star Oenone. They paid me the highest compliment by not underestimating the lone Welsh rider. They acknowledged that it would be me against their six best riders. This was going to be a unique situation, due to the position the WCU had put me in, and maybe the answer was to make it a unique race. It was clear that the Australian team would dominate. I had beaten Oenone in Madrid, so they wouldn't dare allow a situation where I was still with a smallish leading group. They had tracked my progress from when I arrived in Melbourne through to the club criteriums that I had been doing two times a week up until a few days before the race. From their point of view, there was nothing to indicate that I was on anything other than good form. To be certain of gold, they needed an Australian up the road, or Oenone in a group without me present, and they would achieve this by using their numerical advantage to attack me and wear me down, so that eventually I would be unable to respond to their attacks. My chances of gold were zero; my chances of any medal were tiny.

Was there a way I could still pick up a medal, accepting that gold was out of reach? The breakaway that would work would be the one without me present. Once one Australian got away, the others would not chase. That would give me an easier race and I would then still have strength at the end of the race to take on the rest of the Australians, whereas if I was active the whole race I would be too weakened to be competitive in the last few miles. To ensure the success of this plan, the rider from the Australian team needed to be one of the weakest so that she would not be able to create such a large gap on the field that the remaining riders could still attack me, knowing that we would never close on her. My job was to influence that selection. I needed to chase all attacks with strong Australian riders but let an attack with a weak Australian rider go away.

I lined up for the start, proudly wearing my Welsh national jersey with the No.1 pinned on. Numbers 2 onwards are taken by the team supporting the defending champion. In this case, thanks to the failure of Welsh Cycling over the intervening four years, numbers 2 to 7 were the Australian team that crowded around me. Other countries that could field only one rider were Malta and Bermuda. There were a couple of early attacks and then New Zealander Toni Bradshaw attacked, was chased by Australian *domestique* Natalie Bates and then joined by riders from England, Canada and Malaysia. This break suited my purpose well, since there were riders from the four countries fielding full teams, so their respective team-mates wouldn't chase. Everyone looked to me to chase, but I didn't. The gap grew quickly as the bunch dawdled and the riders in the break worked together. Once the break reached a lead of over two minutes, Natalie stopped working.

Even in the live commentary, the Cyclingnews.com report states: 'The peloton looks like it's out for a Sunday morning club run. Several Australian riders are on the front and cruising.' Yes, that is exactly what I needed them to be doing. When the lead went over three minutes, I felt that I needed to keep the time gap in check. I attacked and of course was followed by all the Australians and then the rest of the bunch. I chased until the lead was down to just over a minute and a half. I didn't want to bring them any closer, in case someone got the idea of attacking the bunch and bridging across to the break.

In the break, England's Emma Davies did most of the work until Natalie, who had been resting at the back of the break, felt she was close enough to the finish to make it alone. She then attacked the break and headed for the gold medal. I was still in the race for a silver. With just about 10km to go, we caught Natalie's erstwhile companions. The heart seemed to have gone out of them once Natalie had left them. Now we could have a race – it would still be uneven odds, but the short distance to the finish reduced their ability to wear me down. I made attacks to try to get away but was easily neutralised by the Australians. With just under 3km to go, Sarah Ulmer put in an attack on the last small hill, and again the Australians marked it. Sara Carrigan led out Oenone for the sprint and I made sure I was on her wheel. As we came into the last 200m, Oenone came off Sara's wheel beautifully and although I was drawing level with her I just didn't have the strength to get past her. I had won the bronze.

The podium shot is one I treasure, demonstrating what their manager had said before the race, that it was six Australians against Nicole. The Australians had ridden a great race and I always look at my bronze medal as a success. The Australia coach Warren McDonald also recognised the situation: 'The bad thing for Nicole is that she was on her own and you always feel sympathy for someone when you see that. When she went in the middle of the race and brought the lead back to a minute-and-a-half, it showed her quality. She's a class act and she's got an exciting future because she's so young.'

The Welsh men raced in the afternoon. None of them even finished the race, including Julian Winn, who then refused media requests to discuss the controversy about my lack of team-mates, other than to say that my medal had been 'against the odds'. In four years, Welsh Cycling had done nothing but thwart the talent that followed me. Would the 'men only' Board of Welsh Cycling manage the next four years any better? My hopes were not high.

In October 2005, things had been looking good for the women riders at Madrid as British Cycling examined various options for supporting them. A house was set up in Italy for the U23 men. and the beneficiaries of this included Mark Cavandish, Ian Stannard and Geraint Thomas among others, all of whom went on to achieve success afterwards. However, it was decided that plans for a house for the women in Italy were not to go ahead. To make matters worse, after Rachel Heal had shown she could provide effective and tangible support to me in a GB jersey at the sharp end of a World Championships, straight after the Melbourne games the WCPP decided to remove her Lottery funding. There was no way that she could survive on the road circuit without a living wage, so she left the country and went to America. Other girls also had their Lottery support removed, and I felt for Rachel and some of them. If 2001 was the zenith of GB coaching support for me at the World Championships, then 2005 was the zenith of GB rider support. Another brave 'new start' had been snuffed out.

After my triumphs in Lisbon in 2001, 2005 marked the fourth year in succession that there had been no junior girls sent to the World Championships. All those girls who had followed me to Helmond and elsewhere had left the sport. In conversations at events when I returned to the UK, many parents, often long-term club cyclists, expressed their opinions that not only weren't British Cycling supporting the girls but by failing to select anyone to represent Britain, they were actively blocking the road.

At the time, I was unaware of their plan for Rachel, so I returned to Wales in a far better frame of mind than when I left. I felt that I could challenge for both the World Cup and the women's Tour de France, which I had not ridden for four years. I rejoined my team in Belgium for the Tour of Flanders, where our team plan was based around Christiane and myself as joint leaders. Christiane finished in second place, a just reward for sacrificing her chances for the team in Geelong, while I won my group sprint to finish sixth, not a big points score but I finished ahead of my World Cup series main rivals and closed the gap slightly to 78 points on the leader, Germany's Ina-Yoko Teutenberg, who had won Geelong.

After the race, we set off in our team cars for the seven-hour drive from Belgium to Zug, Switzerland. We moved into our team house, a tiny flat on the fourth floor of an old building with a jewellery shop on the ground floor, emblazoned with the word 'schmuck' – which for those who don't know is

German for jeweller. It was a tight fit for four people, with privacy at a premium given that the shower room was in the kitchen, but we happily adapted to our new home in the heart of the old town, where the daily training rides began and ended with views of the lake against a backdrop of beautiful green hills and snow-capped mountains. This was heaven. Even unseasonably bad weather and snowfall did not slow me down. My bag was packed and with it on my back, I rode down to the station, jumped on a train and travelled two hours south to Lugano, on the border with Italy. Giancarlo lived there with his wife and had offered it as a training base for me. I trained in bright sunshine for three days and couldn't have been happier on my 23rd birthday.

I was fairly confident going into the Flèche Wallonne. I was strong and healthy for the first time in three years, but as always in road racing, I was also keenly aware that my rivals would be planning a strategy to thwart me. Oenone was two places and eight points ahead of me in the World Cup standings and she was going to fight to retain that lead.

In the middle of the race, my team-mates and I had a challenge on our hands. Russian Olga Zabelinskaya was away with more than a one-minute lead and we were forced commit our riders to a hard chase. Olga was caught with 25km to go, but then Team Nürnberger, who now had the most riders in the lead group, started setting up the finish for Oenone. They set a furious pace before the Mur, and Oenone attacked right from the bottom of the climb. I was now going flat out and could not stay with her. As the climb went on, the other riders dropped away so that Oenone was leading and I was in second place, but now so far back that the commissaires let a motorbike into the gap between us.

The Mur is a terrible climb, but I wasn't going to give up.

At 400m to go, there were some hairpin corners with a 20% gradient. I still didn't seem to be closing, but as the gradient eased I changed up a gear to somehow pick up my pace and started to close, very slowly. With 100m remaining, I finally drew level with her and as I came alongside I clicked up another gear, willing myself to drive all the way to the line, and pulled away. This win hurt. It hurt a great deal. I was now second in the World Cup rankings, just three points behind Ina-Yoko Teutenberg.

I took over the World Cup leader's jersey a week later, although my race in Berne, Switzerland, wasn't very good. I missed a breakaway by the eventual winner, Zulfiya Zabirova, and then sprinted badly to finish fifth behind Oenone, Olga Slyusareva and Judith Arndt. However, I now had a 14-point advantage over Oenone and a 24-point lead over Ina-Yoko. This year it was going to be a close fight.

Thomas suggested that my next race should be a time-trial. I had a very mixed record in time-trial rides, and to be frank I had decided that I wouldn't ride any more World time-trial championships. Thomas reminded me that stage races included time-trials and I had to face up to the fact that I needed to ride them. Besides, the course at Lausanne was hilly with lots of turns and much more suited to my style of riding. In addition, he would provide me with a special time-trial bike, made by the Swiss frame-maker Andy Walser. Andy provided specialist TT bikes for several of the men's teams and they had been used to win world titles. I was measured, the machine appeared and when the last fittings were completed, I started training on it. A week later, despite my reservations, I was on the start line for the Magali Pache time-trial against a very strong field. I won and Thomas had restored my confidence in my time-trialling ability.

The sixth round of the World Cup was the Castilla y Leon in Spain. Thomas worked with us to plan the tactics. Priska launched a series of attacks to keep reducing the lead group. Then, when it came to the finish, our sprinter, Joanne, led me out. I held off Judith Arndt and Susanne Ljungskog to take the win and finish off the excellent work of my team-mates. I now led the World Cup by 74 points from Judith, with Oenone third, a further five points back. It was a happy team that returned to Zug to prepare for the UCI's oldest female stage race, the Tour de L'Aude.

It was the middle of May but snowing hard in the foothills outside Zug. I kept going, hoping it would ease, but as it became colder my left knee began to ache and throb. Please don't let this be happening again. I eased up and looked for a spot to turn around and head back. The ride back was awful; racing through my mind was that injury was again about to ruin my season just as things began to look settled. Reluctantly, I told Thomas the news and he immediately referred me to the Cross Klinik in Basel, which specialises in sports injuries. In desperation to hold on to my fitness, I did three daily swimming sessions, swimming like 'a dead dog' according to Karin Thürig, who watched my pathetic attempt at front crawl with a float between my legs while she trained for triathlons. I had a tentative ride a week before leaving for the seventh World Cup round in Montreal, but it did not go well and I travelled with great trepidation.

Thankfully, the Montreal World Cup event was a fairly tepid affair for most of the race, my rivals unaware of my knee problem, thinking I had missed the Tour de L'Aude in order to save myself for this race. Perhaps their tactics would have been different if they had suspected but, as it was, my team-mates patrolled any dangerous attacks and looked after me, until it came down to a battle between Judith Arndt and myself as we raced up Mont Royal for the last time for the hilltop finish. Judith sprinted away from me and there was nothing I could do; I crossed the line in second rather pleased that my knee had held up to the race and I had not lost too many points. My World Cup lead had been cut to 49 points over Judith. Oenone Wood did not finish.

I flew back to Switzerland and could not wait to get out on the roads around Zug. My knee appeared to be holding up. I was back in Britain at the end of June, my recent results ensuring I was once again the rider everyone else wanted to beat for the British Championships. Since I had turned professional in 2002, as British champion I had worn the white jersey with the blue and red hoops on it every year and I was easily recognised in it. I was always pleased to ride World Cup events in the jersey of the leader of that competition, but each time I pulled on the British champion's jersey was a special moment in my life. This time, the course around Beverley was rather tricky with narrow roads, where you couldn't get more than three riders abreast, which put the onus on staying at the front. It was also a rather flat course, with one very gentle drag that was only about 400m long. Rachel had come second for the last four years, but naturally given the recent blow to her confidence by the management of British Cycling, her form was seriously reduced this year. With no anvil on which to crack open the race and no really strong second rider, I knew I would have to attack the rest of the field every lap on the 'climb' to wear down the others.

Going into the last lap, I had still not managed to break the invisible elastic holding the bunch together, so I put everything into my attack the last time up the hill. I got a few metres' gap and kept going and twang, the elastic finally snapped. There is a special feeling about a solo victory compared to a victory in a sprint. You have more time to savour the moment and when you come into the finishing straight the crowd is already applauding rather than holding their breath to see who will win. I really enjoyed this victory, which meant I could wear the British champion jersey going into my next race – the women's Tour de France.

In the race for the men's British Championships, Roger Hammond was clearly the best in the field, but with a sense of *déjà vu* I watched the other riders simply gang up on a solo rider. Roger tried time and time again to get away but was faced with riding against the whole bunch by himself. Hamish Haynes went into the record books as the men's British champion of 2006. Roger rode a fantastic and brave race that day but was defeated by negative tactics of riders not trying to win but simply riding to prevent someone else winning.

We had a great team of five riders for the women's Tour de France in 2006. There were my flat-mates and now close friends, Joanne and Emma, and two of our Swiss riders, Sarah Grab and Pascale Schnider. The Tour began with a time-trial in Font Romeu high in the Pyrenees, which I won, vindicating Thomas's decision to reignite my interest in time-trialling. I started the next day in yellow, dressed just as Joane Somariba had been in 2002. As the field was not as strong as the Giro, we felt defending yellow all the way was an option. I suggested that in that case we could also take advantage of me holding the jersey by letting other riders of the team go with break-aways and try to go for a stage win for themselves. During the second stage, Sarah got in a two-rider break in the closing kilometres and just missed out on the stage win. There were two stages that day, and in the afternoon I led out Joanne for her to achieve the win, a thank you for her leadout at the

Castilla y Leon World Cup. Then Emma won the fourth stage on day three while I carefully controlled any threats for the yellow jersey.

Since the age of 12, I had dreamed of winning the Tour de France. On the TV, I had watched Robert Millar climbing the mountains. I had ridden the French Alps on our family camping holidays, dreaming as I was climbing that I was on my own ahead of the pack, heading to victory. Now I was standing on the start line wearing the yellow jersey, about to begin a stage that was going to take us over the famous Mont Ventoux, a climb of special magic to all British riders. The stage was not going to end at the top, there would be a further 60km after the summit until the finish line.

As we assembled on the start line, I heard nothing. Instead, I saw this quiet figure of a 12-year-old wish me well; she would be watching me from her TV in her lounge, and she would be with me every pedal stroke today. The crowd behind her seemed not to be French nationals but her friends, Sophie and the Jameses, her schoolfriends and teachers, and Geoff Greenfield, Walter Rixon and Ron Dowling. This was the day I owed to her and all those standing behind her. Her TV had a special camera that would follow me every second of the race. I was going to do everything to make it the most special day I could for that innocent little girl with so much hope in her heart. Today was the day, above any other in my life, which I owed that little girl.

As soon as we reached the first steep slopes of Mont Ventoux, I attacked hard. I wanted to ride this one on my own, ahead of all my rivals, wearing the yellow jersey, just as I had seen in all the old magazines and books. As I emerged from the trees, I got my first glimpse of the strange lunar landscape. I still had over 7km of climbing to reach the top. I pushed on, wanting to gain as much time as I could. I crested the top and started the descent flying round the bends; I made sure I was within centimetres of the edge of the road at every bend, trying to gain every second. It was a long way to the finish, but I pressed on, never doubting myself. This was going to be a day I would remember for the rest of my life. I crossed the line six minutes ahead of the next rider. I had done it.

In the last few kilometres, that little girl came up to me again. This time she was leaping about, trying to show me something. She had a picture frame in her hand with a photograph in it. It was of a rider in a yellow jersey, on a bike. There were no other riders around; she was alone with just the motorbikes and official cars. The mountain background of the picture was a moonscape. The 12-year-old was just so happy. I told her she could have a present as soon as I was finished. It was a bit sweaty and had a couple of pin holes in it. It was yellow. We both smiled. The little girl gave me the picture I treasure so much.

The race finished the following day, no one was challenging me and I couldn't have been happier. We were a perfect team, the riders were all great friends and we had excellent support. I was leading the World Cup and had just won my dream race in a wonderful manner – I had ridden from beginning to end in yellow. I was the first British winner of the Tour de France.

Our focus now returned to the World Cup, as it became clear that not only was I leading the individual title but that Univega was in with a strong chance of taking the team title. Thomas and I carefully planned the events leading up to the final at Nuremberg in September.

First up was the Thüringen-Rundfahrt der Frauen in

Germany. A year earlier, the cycling world was deeply shaken when the Australian team were out training on the morning of the first stage and a car lost control and hit all six riders, with Amy Gillett losing her life. I had not been at the race in 2005, and it still gives me shivers thinking about that night when I received the text from Rochelle informing me of this terrible accident.

The Australians, and particularly their coach Warren McDonald who was following the riders in the team car when the accident happened, showed incredible strength. The Amy Gillett Foundation was set up in her memory to promote road safety and safe cycling, and every year there is the Amy Gillett Ride in Australia. To mark the first anniversary, a memorial was unveiled at the scene of the accident, with a ceremony on the morning before the first stage. It was optional to attend and my team-mate Emma Rickards went with her fellow Australians. I personally felt it would be too upsetting to go to the ceremony, and rode there alone a few hours afterwards to see the memorial and pay my respects. It was covered with the flowers of the ceremony, and I spent a quiet moment taking it all in.

This certainly put things in to perspective. Our Univega team came to the race with possibly its strongest line-up, with Karin, Christiane, Jo, Priska, Emma and me. After a third in the prologue, each stage was executed with tactical precision. I broke away on Stage 2 winning the stage and took the lead in the GC. As a team, it was a commanding performance and I won three more stages on my way to sealing the tour against a top-quality field.

We then travelled to Sweden for the Open de Suède near Gothenburg, a new addition to the World Cup series. The local hero was double World champion Susanne Ljungskog, who had missed Thüringen to rest up for her home event. There were 11 laps of the 12km circuit with one main climb of about 800m. The circuit was lined with cheering Swedish fans having barbeques in the fields next to the course. They had really taken the race to heart and had even constructed huge figures out of hay bales and dressed them in Swedish national costume, complete with Viking helmets that towered over us from the fields.

On the penultimate lap as we approached the hill, Susanne attacked, I jumped straight on to her and the two of us broke away; then a few kilometres later, without warning, Susanne sat up and refused to work. It was a calculated gamble on her part, that I would either sit up and we would drift back to the peloton and she could take her chances on the last lap, or that I would do all the work while she sat on my wheel in the slip-stream waiting for the sprint. I sat up myself, prepared to play Susanne at her own game, but Thomas, watching from the team car, called me over the team radio: 'Keep going, you can beat her in a sprint even if she sits on.'

I wasn't happy, but he had made some good calls in the past and I kept going. I tried to drop Susanne on the last hill but couldn't. I motored to the finish with Susanne glued to my wheel. I hoped my sprinting would still save the day. Susanne jumped first and, being so much fresher than me, she finished a length ahead of me. It was a tough moment; Thomas and I had made the wrong call and letting a win slip away always hurts. Far more serious was the fact that my knee pain had returned during the race. In just two days, we would compete in the Team Time-Trial World Cup in Denmark; could I ride with so little time to rest my knee?

We blasted out of Aarhus, and after one third of the distance we got our first time check: we were leading Susanne's

Buitenpoort-Flexpoint team by a handful of seconds. We kept on going, now down to five riders, having lost one, and it was starting to get very tough. Some riders had to miss a turn every now and again, which is perfectly normal in team time-trials, but it means there is less recovery for the riders still working. There was also the issue of size, and being rather small on the bike, I was happily sitting in the slipstream while Karin Thürig was getting very little shelter behind me. I did the longest turns I could to try to compensate for her lack of cover from me. Thomas was shouting encouragement and instructions from the car. He had a megaphone, but we could only just hear him under our aerodynamic time-trial helmets.

After two-thirds distance, we were still just a couple of seconds ahead of Buitenpoort-Flexpoint but really feeling the effort, and we started to make silly mistakes, confusing the calls and instructions. Then, the noise of the megaphone changed. Thomas was now leaning out the window of our team car and screaming at us and thumping the side of the car with his fist. He was desperate. We were giving absolutely everything we had in our legs and after 52km we won – by just two seconds. We were elated but absolutely exhausted. Later, we surveyed the damage to the side of the car. Thomas's passion was adorable. Oenone's Nürnberger squad had finished fourth and T-Mobile third. With three rounds to go, the World Cup standings were looking good: I was on 354 points, with Judith on 197, Susanne on 197 and Oenone on 170.

Back in our little flat in Zug one evening a few days later, Joanne started jumping around on our creaky floorboards and telling me to look at her computer screen. I had just taken over as World No.1 on the UCI rankings! I rummaged around under my bed and pulled out a bottle of champagne, a prize from one of the races, and cracked it open so we could all celebrate. I went to bed that night and shut my eyes. I was 23, I was the first-ever British rider to be ranked No.1 rider in the world, I had won the Tour and had the World Cup in my grasp. I could not have been happier.

I had been totally absorbed in racing and keeping fit. The flare-up of the knee problem was a worry but the doctors were confident I could manage it through to the end of the season, provided I was careful. With three weeks until the next World Cup event in France, Priska and I were sent up to St Moritz for a high-altitude training camp, which sounded great but it snowed heavily. I managed to last a week, my knee aching in the cold, before fleeing back to Zug to rest and warm up before heading to the GP Plouay.

Away from our world of cycling, the men had been getting more coverage than they expected. Thomas had ambitions for the team and had been courting various sponsors to support his and our vision. Early on, after the spring classics, he prepared some super presentations and had a couple of major sponsors talking seriously. Negotiations developed and as we kept coming up with the results, the deals looked to be on as we aimed to be the No.1 team in the world.

However, our success in France was totally overshadowed by revelations taking place as the men's Tour assembled. It was a new era. Lance had won his last Tour the year before and was now relaxing, lying back on his sofa, under his seven framed yellow jerseys (mine are in bags in my parents' loft). On the eve of the race to find his replacement, news regarding Operation Puerto broke. Spanish doctor Eufemiano Fuentes had his collection of bags of blood seized by the police. He coded them with names chosen seemingly more for comical effect than security: 'Son of Rudy', 'Birillo' and 'Goku' caused those who had come second, third and fourth in the men's Tour the year before to be eliminated from the race on the day before it started. The exposé had fully occupied the shocked cycling press at the time of my Ventoux stage, so there was practically zero media coverage of our event. Later, my GC win did make the BBC website and a few short notices in some of the press.

The summer of 2006 was one of sporting flops for the UK. The England football team went out of the World Cup on a penalty shootout. Elsewhere there was similar gloom. The BBC Radio 4 *Today* programme conducted a poll of its listeners asking them to vote for a British sportsperson whom the nation should support. I came top of the listener vote. That was very good of them, particularly as the hourly sports bulletin always reported the stage winner and yellow jersey of the men's race but never reported a word about my performances.

That was a little 'high point', but a second drugs scandal lay ahead. Sometime later, Thomas was close to finalising with a major sponsor for 2007, then the devout Mennonite from Farmersville, Floyd Landis, who, weeks earlier, had all the world's cycling press agog with his entirely unbelievable riding to win the men's Tour, was declared 'positive'. This second major cycling drugs story was too much. No one could blame the prospective sponsors for pulling out – the sport was a joke.

Floyd had way more time on the Radio 4 *Today* programme than they could muster for me during my whole career, telling them how he was not positive, that he had won fair and square, and basically running an advert encouraging gullible listeners to contribute to his 'Floyd Fairness Fund' for his legal defence against doping charges. As Floyd grabbed the headlines, keeping the 'omerta', the pact of silence among the drug-taking professionals, for his 'best friend' Lance, Thomas was rightly livid as his sponsors for 2007 walked away. It is very difficult to think about the consequences.

Floyd Landis can have no concept of the havoc he wreaked in the lives of people he will never meet. All the efforts of the riders in our team, all that we achieved in the sport, was brought close to zero because the press were transfixed on a liar from Farmersville. While the public donated over $1 million to the 'Floyd Fairness Fund', Thomas could not raise a small fraction of that for the best women's team on the planet. I would still be dealing with the direct fallout of that in 2011, but the first strains were clearly felt in late 2006.

It should have been a joyous affair – my third placing at Plouay virtually assuring me of the World Cup crown – but Thomas, on edge, frustrated and tetchy, was livid afterwards because we had not followed team tactics and covered the moves of other key riders as we were supposed to do. We had let Nicole Brandli, from the rival Swiss team Bigla, ride away to a solo win. There was a six-day Tour of Holland between Plouay and the penultimate World Cup race in Rotterdam, and I managed to write my bike off for a third time in the year, although thankfully with no serious damage to the rider. I placed fifth to secure my second World Cup.

Post-race celebrations featured another Thomas blow-up. Manel had spoken to me before the race, asking if I would speak to the manager of Équipe Nürnberger. What could be the harm in that, I naively thought. Maybe I could get some leverage for next year's salary negotiations. After all, while having the luxury of a living wage, I was not actually making money, and I knew that there were riders in the peloton earning several times my salary. What I didn't know was that I was just one of three riders who Manel was masterminding to move across, along with taking up a position for himself as *directeur sportif*. Thomas ordered Manel into the team camper-van, where they had a blistering argument, after which Manel was sacked. When we got back to Zug the next day, Thomas demanded an explanation from me and the other girls, threatening to disband the team. It meant a lot to him and it meant a lot to us. We riders were all reduced to tears. The next day, he appeared with a new contract for the following year.

Having secured the individual title, the season continued apace in Nuremberg for the final World Cup race of the season. We needed to ensure Univega won the team title, and there was the extra incentive of a trophy organised by the German Cycling Federation, with big sponsors backing it for the best overall performance by a rider in Germany during the season. We won the team title and, although Regina won the bunch sprint finish, I finished fifth to win the German Federation trophy too, the only time a foreign rider had prevailed.

All year I had worked on my time-trialling and for the first time in my senior career I entered the World Time-Trial Championships that took place in Salzburg three days before the road race. I was fifth, with two USA riders filling out the podium alongside Karin, but I was within a minute of the winner and did beat Zulfiya Zabirova and Judith Arndt. My form was still good.

The road race was six laps of 22km, based on the hills around Salzburg and with practically no flat roads on the course apart from a passage through the finish line. After the purge earlier in the year, I had three GB team-mates alongside me: Rachel, Tanja Slater and Catherine Hare. Tanja and Catherine were still developing, so I could only expect them to help in the early laps, but Rachel was very keen to do what she could. We decided that my best chance would be to create a split on the penultimate lap. Rachel would lead me out up the main climb where I would launch my attack and hope to create a break with a smaller group of good climbers. Hopefully there would be only one rider, or at most two, from each nation, thus putting me on an equal footing with the others for the last lap. Again it was a good thing that we were planning race tactics; it was just sad that it was effectively only myself and Rachel.

In response to earlier attacks, Zulfiya Zabirova was ahead of the group as we reached the main climb, then Rachel made a huge effort leading me out up the hill. I attacked and only Nicole Brandli and Marianne Vos of Holland came with me. We caught Zulfiya, then over the top, a number of riders bridged and we became a group of about 15. When I looked around at the composition of the group, I saw that the Swiss and Germans both had three riders while the Dutch and Austrians each had two. I was now alone.

Judith Arndt attacked with just over a lap to go. I was bridging up when Marianne Vos used me to jump up and join Judith, a smart move and a tactical mistake by me. I had thought Marianne, sat on me, didn't have the strength to come through and help me chase. Judith and Marianne were a race-winning partnership, so I was grateful of the work of Svetlana Bubnenkova, who did some big turns to get the pair back, despite Judith powering away at the front. Then more attacks came, with Judith and Theresa Senff of Germany particularly active, working to wear me out before the finish.

On the last time up the main climb it was my turn to attack, and once again only Nicole B and Marianne came with me. The three of us worked together and quickly formed a nice break. Then, to my and Marianne's utter disbelief, Nicole B suddenly stopped working and sat on us. It seemed completely stupid: if she kept going, the worst she would get was bronze, and in road racing you never know what might happen – by continuing to work at the front you've always got a better chance. Apparently, she was obeying instructions she was receiving on her race radio. Marianne and I eased off, not wishing to carry a passenger to beat us in the sprint. A small group caught us from behind.

It looked like being a sprint finish. Trixi had two riders to lead her out, then Marianne took Trixi's wheel and I took Oenone's wheel for the sprint. The four of us launched our sprint at the same time, Marianne came off Trixi and took the lead and won the sprint convincingly. I passed Oenone, but I could not get alongside Trixi and finished third. I was upset on the podium and tried to see some sort of positive in my third medal in a World Championship behind riders backed up with team-mates in the finale. The international press were gener-ous in praise of how I rode the race. I was World No.1 and World Cup winner, I was alone but I had repeatedly taken the race to the rest, despite the odds. This was admired by those knowledgeable enough to understand my situation.

At dinner that night, Rachel was as unhappy about the state of affairs with the national team, as I was. Once again, my bronze medal was the only medal GB took away from the road World Championships, and my fifth place in the time-trial was the next best finish. There was no women's national coach and had not been one since Madrid the year before, when so many positive options had seemed to present themselves. Elsewhere, at long last a GB women's junior team competed for the first time since I won in 2001, and among the support staff there was an air of a more professional attitude.

Perhaps because of all the doping controversies, Thomas was struggling to find sponsors and staff for 2007, so I pressed Dave

Brailsford for support. I gave him the benefit of the doubt, in that he was achieving great changes with the track squad, and hoped that after the purge good developments would follow for the women. Dave committed to meeting Thomas in the winter to see what support British Cycling could offer him during the next season, so as to develop riders for the Beijing Olympics of 2008 and also to support me. This seemed a very positive initiative.

Dave, though, was not without problems of his own. At the end of October, Dave spoke about his situation at British Cycling to Dad. The success of the BC WCPP was now evident on the track. However, like any success in life, there are always many who wish to claim it as their own. Dad was never any part of the structure at BC, and thus was free from the political manoeuvrings at Manchester, but we had first-hand experience of this project and had seen it evolve since 1998, which gave us perhaps a unique perspective. Dad wrote to Liz Nicholl, director of performance at UK Sport, giving our view on who was responsible for the changes, championing the work Dave did and urging her to speak to Peter King and Brian Cookson and clarify their understanding of Dave's effectiveness. Liz responded positively.

Returning to Zug after the World Championships, my season was now over. I headed to Italy to attend the wedding of a former team-mate and another of a friend. Life was moving on, and I was getting tired of the lack of privacy in team houses, especially the unexpected arrival of team managers. I had spent only three days in Lugano training, but the city and its location seemed ideal, a comfortable train journey from my team-mates. Furthermore, the 2008 World titles would be in Varese, just 30km away over the border in Italy, and the 2009 Championships would be 14km away in

Mendrisio. I enjoyed living in Switzerland and Lugano seemed to offer the advantage of Swiss efficiency, beautiful surroundings for training while being in the heart of the cycling world.

I was delighted to find a two-bedroom apartment with a garage and a small garden in the foothills on the outskirts of the city, and signed the contracts to move in in late December. In the meantime, I attended the German Sports Press Ball in Frankfurt where I was presented with the award I'd secured in Nuremburg a few months before. It was clear that there was a great deal of respect for what I'd achieved and it was a great occasion.

Just after Christmas, in my modest and entirely comfortable apartment, I joined that 12-year-old again. Together, we pulled a bag of jerseys out from a cupboard. She had watched me as I moved all my possessions into my cosy little flat. We gave ourselves a treat. We spread a jersey out on the floor and looked at a photo of a dreamer riding in a yellow jersey up a giant mountain. Puerto, Fuentes and Floyd had grabbed the headlines all year, dealing blows to women's cycling from which parts of it would never recover. Soon there would not be a race for a women's yellow jersey. That little girl gazed at me. She told me I had given her all she wanted. She told me she was very proud that I had faced down the demons that the weak gave into. I had started 2006 with my arm in a sling, but I finished it as the only ever British World No.1 ranked rider, sat on the floor with a cup of tea, looking at an adorable yellow jersey. I wanted to get a couple more jerseys for that 12-year-old. There might be some new kids on the block, but on my day I could match them.

CHAPTER EIGHTEEN
Unfulfilled Commitments

While I was moving into my new flat, on 29 December Thomas Campana flew into Manchester for a meeting with Dave Brailsford, Dan Hunt and Dad. One year on from our fantastic introduction camp in the igloo at Engelberg, our team had achieved more than we could have hoped for: World No.1 rider, World Cup winner and three riders in the top five at the World Time-Trial Championships, with Karin Thürig in silver and my bronze in the road race. We were the top team in the world; however, Floyd Landis and Operation Puerto were still creating victims across the continents. While Pierre Boué lost sponsors and shortened the Tour further, Thomas was facing similar problems and had parted company with Univega. He was casting around for sponsors with little luck.

There was another underlying challenge around us. Many a women's cycling team had spiralled off into oblivion fuelled by personal relationships between the male manager and female team members. Priska was Thomas's life-partner. In the previous year's World Championships she had finished fifth in the road race and had beaten me by 0.59 of a second in the time-trial. Without me in the team, she would be the star and an ideal team scenario would feature herself as the unchallenged leader and Thomas the manager.

The previous year, I had ridden a Raleigh machine and had my wages paid by Raleigh, while the rest of the team rode Univega bikes. As a result of my publicity, Raleigh were keen to extend their relationship with me. In addition Cardiff businessman Del DelaRonde, who had part-sponsored the team, wanted to do all he could to help me. Thomas explained the financial situation to Del. Despite its success, the team would not run in 2007 unless new sponsors could be found.

Del fully understood the nuances of the complex situation. He had followed my career for ten years and had seen how the talent behind me had been lost to the sport. Like me, he knew that I needed at least one other British rider in that last 15 of the World Championships or Olympics if I was to turn silver or bronze into gold, and that British Cycling had to be able to claim a portion of the success as of their making if ever they were to support me. Del recognised the opportunity as a canny entrepreneur would. He introduced me to two of his business associates, Michael Jankowski of Creation, a sports car racing team, and Heather Bird. Both were complete stars and fully engaged in what Del proposed. Raleigh would widen their sponsorship and be joined by Michael, Heather and Del. So exactly as in late 2002 and the ill-fated attempt that so nearly came off to get Rachel to Italy, here we were, Del, Dad and me, four years later, attempting the same thing and trying to get some British riders into my trade team, only this time I held a few more cards.

For Priska there was a reality – without my presence, her team would have to revert to Swiss national status and would not get starts in all the big races, so her own ambitions for Beijing would be thwarted. I think both she and Thomas accepted this in the most positive and professional manner. A critical question was: who would replace Manel? On a women's team, the *directeur sportif* not only developed tactics but had to be involved in all the logistics in preparing for the race. Directing and helping the mechanics preparing the bikes, organising the meals and food and drinks in races, as well as liaising with the media to promote our results – it was a very hectic and varied job. Manel was very good at this, as well as superb tactically. He was going to be extremely hard to replace.

In a deserted Manchester velodrome, an attempt was made to thrash out a deal. Dave Brailsford stated that he needed to develop some British riders to form a women's team and that was best done on the continent. He also needed a British women's team manager who did not 'fly-in, fly-out' but was familiar with the riders and staff of other teams. The post had been vacant for over a year, after he stalled on the women's team house in Italy while progressing the U23 men's version. Thomas needed sponsors' money and an effective *directeur sportif*. He did not have a need for riders, but he fully understood the need for me to have GB riders with me at a World Championships.

I had to keep this very good team intact, but I also needed British riders to be developed alongside me. I could bring a dowry of sponsors but I needed it to be used wisely. Thomas was effective in what he did and was motivated for team success, and therefore I had no worries about his commitment. But I had had several years of observing British Cycling doing wonders on the track and for the U23 road men, but somehow opportunity after opportunity fell through their fingers when it came to the women's road team. I needed Dave Brailsford to be locked into a commitment that extended to others beyond myself. Surely this modest proposal, so much less than he was doing for the U23 men, and partly funded by British sponsors – because I was there – could be supported by the WCPP? After all, Dave was very keen to tell me every time he saw me that he wanted to support me through 2007 to Beijing 2008. Here was a golden opportunity to make good that commitment.

Of the girls available, Thomas agreed that Tanja Slater and Anneliese Heard would join me, but he did not want to work with Emma Pooley, who he had seen compete and did not impress him. Ironically, later, after he recognised her talent, she would ride for his team for several years. Anneliese's career had stalled after her Junior World Triathlon titles. I had great sympathy for her plight. She was a competent cyclist and fierce competitor as a triathlete in her youth, and the prospects of becoming a good road rider were high if she could concentrate on that discipline alone. Due to the lack of sponsorship for the team, Thomas could supply only board and lodging, so British Cycling would recommend the two girls for Lottery grant support. To have two British riders in the team alongside me was a great start. The other part of the plan would be for British Cycling to develop a team manager who could manage the women's road team in time for Beijing. Therefore, it seemed an ideal opportunity for BC to supply a manager to work with our team and understudy Thomas. Some financial support would also be given in relation to transport and other activities that could be attributed to supporting the development of the British riders by the team.

As a consequence of this happy coming together, it seemed like British Cycling, Thomas, Priska, Tanja, Anneliese and I would all be winners. At best, one could only describe the benefits accrued to the companies run by Heather, Michael and Del as 'indirect', but their contributions were greatly appreciated. Was this grand plan going to work? Thomas backed up his commitment straightaway. Tanja and Anneliese came out to Switzerland and were immediately taken with some other team-mates to Italy to get measured up for their full set of racing kit. On the way back, they stopped off in Lugano. Spirits could not have been better, as I met up with Tanja, Anneliese, Thomas and various other team-mates for an evening meal together. I was overjoyed: at last, I was going to ride with some British girls in my team and we could develop together, and behind us we had a team manager who had fully engaged in the plan.

Around that time, I read in a cycling magazine an interview conducted with one of the U23 men, saying how little he had to do apart from ride his bike, based out of the house in Italy. I could only contrast that with the hours I spent talking with and meeting potential sponsors and talking to the press. My presence, or Dad representing me, were intrinsic to negotiations, whether we liked it or not. If I was to win a World or Olympic title, I needed to have the support of a good British team, and if the system wouldn't support me, then I needed to work to put something in place. Doing all this was difficult, but it was about to get a whole lot worse.

Over that winter, going out on the bike was the easiest thing I was involved in. I trained harder than ever before. The gym had now become important to strengthen the stabilising muscles around my knee, as I wanted to overcome the knee injuries that had blighted 2004 and 2005 and threatened to ruin the 2006 season. I also incorporated weight training to build up sprinting power, as Marianne and Trixi had beaten me in the sprint in Salzburg and I had to raise my game. In January, I travelled to Melbourne, met up with Craig and prepared to start the defence of the World Cup. I threw myself into endurance rides, building up the volume to new levels, and continued with my programme of gym sessions. I also rode a few local criteriums to test myself and felt stronger than ever before on a bike.

The team members had all arrived by the end of January in our new team house, near the beachside suburb of Brighton. Thomas was more than living up to his part of the arrangement, by agreeing to manage the Great Britain National Team for the Geelong Tour and World Cup. This allowed Tanja, Anneliese, and Emma Pooley, who had self-funded her winter training in Perth but was still without a team, to get a ride in these top-class events, when team number restrictions would otherwise have precluded them. We crammed a dozen riders and support staff into the four-bedroom house, some of us sleeping on mattresses on the floor, with Thomas on the couch. The human crush served as a bonding agent, as we all pitched in to play our part with rotations of cooking, shopping and chores.

Of the promised British Cycling team manager, there was no evidence. Thomas was now running two teams, Raleigh and GB, by himself, so he hired two local Australians to act as a masseur and mechanic. However, there was so much to be done for the two teams that the masseur hardly had any time to massage anyone, but we got by wonderfully. The GB track team were also in Australia, hotel-based with a full support staff. I doubt that Shane Sutton would have settled for sleeping on a couch like Thomas did.

Unlike the previous three seasons, when my winter had been wrecked by injury, I was primed for the opening events at the end of February and wanted to send out a clear message that, despite the bronze medal in Salzburg, I was the World No.1 rider. However, I had a major challenge. The T-Mobile squad of multi-millionaire Bob Stapleton was immune from the financial strictures present everywhere else in women's cycling. Stapleton was doing exactly what he had set out to do and more signings made his squad the dominant force for 2007, by some clear margin. One of his new signings was my great rival Oenone Wood.

The Geelong Tour had been a prestigious feature of the women's pro circuit for many years. It attracted a field of around 130 riders. Unfortunately, the last edition took place in 2008. In 2009 it was converted to a men's five-day stage race. At the end of the first day of racing, I had the leader's jersey after finishing third in the time-trial and third again in the criterium. Day 2 had a wonderful climb up Mount Wallace through the You Yangs, which, while a lovely location for an attack, was way too far from the finish to go alone. I showed my relative strength and then I let the bunch catch me and finished in the leading group to retain my lead. On the final day, the overall victory was far from secure, with time bonuses available at intermediate sprints. The whole Raleigh team rode with cool composure to contain some aggressive racing from T-Mobile, Colavita and the German national team, all of whom had riders within a handful of seconds who could win. Several times, T-Mobile attempted to smash the race apart and put one of their riders into a race-winning break. Quoting the Australian report for Cyclingnews.com:

> Twenty-three year-old Welsh cyclist Nicole Cooke made history today, becoming the first non-Australian to win the UCI women's season-opening Geelong Women's Tour as the race reached a dramatic climax at Barwon Heads on the Victorian coast.
>
> It was a smashing effort from the Brit, who, despite being

under siege on a number of fronts, showed pure class to stave off a series of determined attacks from the magenta train of T-Mobile, not to mention fighting for every available second in the intermediate sprints.

T-Mobile rider Alexis Rhodes was quoted: 'Today we were trying to go for the overall and we got on the front and did a bit of a team time-trial and managed to shell most of the bunch ... The girls were awesome but we couldn't shake Nicole [Cooke], she's a class rider.'

Certainly I was very proud of the result, and spirits in our team, along with the GB national team managed by Thomas, were very high.

Although the Geelong Tour had been an important season opener, the real target was the Geelong World Cup race two days later. It usually ended in a bunch sprint, and last year's winner, Ina-Yoko Teutenberg, who had just won two of the stages in the Tour of Geelong, was in great form and part of T-Mobile, who were described by the press as 'holding the aces for the Geelong Tour and the World Cup' and having 'one of the most impressive team rosters ever to be assembled in the sport of professional women's cycling'. They had three of the world's top ten ranked riders, with Judith Arndt, Ina-Yoko Teutenberg and Oenone Wood, supported by Danish champion Linda Villumsen and Australian champions Alexis Rhodes and Katherine Bates. Their attempt to lure me into personally marking them, and wearing me down, had not succeeded on the last stage in the Tour of Geelong, but with the best sprinter in the race and on a course so suited to a sprint finish, they had the advantage.

Thomas and I were fully aware of T-Mobile's relative strength and we executed a perfect counter, a break in which we placed Sarah Düster, forcing T-Mobile to chase. Judith,

Katherine Bates and Alexis Rhodes made a ferocious pace to close the gap, so that we caught the break at the start of the last lap, with about 14km to go.

My moment had finally come. I attacked on the main climb with 7km remaining and Oenone marked me. I kept on attacking all the way up the climb and forced a break with Oenone and another Australian, Nikki Egyed. Initially, we all committed to working while the bunch was regrouping and organising a chase, but soon Oenone eased. Thomas was yelling into my race radio to keep on going. I was totally committed to the break, but even if we held off the bunch, how would I deal with Oenone? With her team-mate Ina-Yoko in the bunch, Oenone could sit behind me and save herself for the sprint, not worrying if we were caught because then Ina-Yoko would be fresh and do the sprint for T-Mobile. While Nikki and I had to keep going, Oenone prepared for the sprint.

The peloton was closing on us fast as we turned on to the Geelong waterfront and headed into the last kilometre. We couldn't ease up, it was going to be a fast sprint. Nikki jumped first, Oenone and I were on to her straightaway and I kicked again, taking the lead and holding it to the line. The bunch was led home by Ina-Yoko just a few seconds later.

This is one of the victories I take most pleasure in. When the Welsh Joint Examination Council asked me for a picture to go on the cover of their new PE textbook, I chose the photo of me crossing the line with the pack looming behind us. It shows the dynamic of the race, the joy of winning, but also the dirt and grime visible on our legs, jerseys and faces after the downpour earlier in the race. Afterwards, Katherine Bates was quoted as saying: 'I think we got beaten today because Nicole Cooke's just better. We rode really well as a team and we're really pleased with what we did, we just have to figure out a new strategy to knock Cookie off her perch.'

While I knew this was just the start of a challenging season, I had no idea the true challenge was going to come from events off the bike. In early February, Tanja, Anneliese and I were so alarmed with the lack of commitment from British Cycling that we wrote to Dave Brailsford to ask what had been done about providing the manager to support the team. We were informed we were not going to be supported by the member of staff who was initially provisioned at that December meeting, because he was going to work full time with the three U23 girls who had gone to the Junior World Championships the year before, the first time British Cycling had sent any girls since 2001. This would not have been a problem if there was someone else, but there wasn't. We were told: 'Leave it with us.'

That a manager at British Cycling was needed was evidenced a few days later when Tanja, Anneliese and I received an instruction from the BC WCPP that demanded we attend an 'all rider' conference in Manchester. Nobody had consulted the calendar to discover we were on the other side of the planet, about to race in the Geelong Tour. Our race calendar obviously didn't come up on anybody's radar. I was the No.1 rider in the world, and two other British riders were on the squad of the No.1 team in the world, and an integral place in the management was being held open for a member of staff from British Cycling. Where was the problem? Marginal gains were not in much evidence from where Tanja, Anneliese and I viewed things. Knowing that we were a lesser priority than the U23 girls was not a comforting thought. In Australia, Thomas had done what he had to and filled the gaps by spending money he did not have, hiring in local staff.

In Australia, we were there to do a job and the squeeze in the house and hectic nature of what we were doing carried us along. How would we shape up once back at base? Well, on the bike at races we carried our good results forward. We headed to Italy for the GP Costa Etrusca, two separate races on successive days. In my jet-lagged brain, I didn't make the connection between the heat of Australia and the still thawing European winter and began the first race in light clothing. It began raining as we started and then snowed. I went back to the team car to get more clothing, then had to stop at the side of the road to do the zip up on the thermal jersey because my fingers couldn't feel anything. I chased back to the bunch and finished fifth, barely able to ride because I was shaking so much from the cold.

On Day 2, I made sure I was properly clothed and was in the leading group of nine riders that had formed on one of the climbs. Fabiana Luperini attacked, joined by another rider. I'd missed the move, but then made a probing move and when no one followed, I drove hard up the climb to the finish, chasing to join the leaders. As I caught them, I attacked straight past them, continuing alone to victory. I added the Trofeo Alfredo Binda the following week, again attacking on the last climb and winning alone.

Back in Lugano, I began to meet other cyclists. One was Mauro Giacomazzi, who lived across the Italian border. Mauro competed in Gran Fondo events, where riders complete long and difficult courses, and he made the perfect training partner for me, being one of the few who enjoyed tackling the climbs I sought as a necessary part of my training.

The Tour of Flanders was my next target, the most significant race outside the Olympics and the World Championships that I hadn't won, and it would also be my first meeting with

y only senior time-trial World Championships.
route to fifth place in Salzburg, 2006. [Getty Images]

1984 Tour de France with winners Laurent Fignon and Marianne Martin. A rare sight – recognition of the women's winner alongside the men's.

What a team! Sarah Duster, Karin Thürig in the jersey as world time-trial champion, Priska Doppman, Joanne Kiesanowski, Christiane Soeder, the Austrian TT champion, and myself in the jersey as World Cup leader. We have won the team time-trial World Cup and I am about to become world no 1 ranked rider. [C J Farquharson]

Oenone Wood and I sprinting it out for the Geelong World Cup, 2007. The grime from the road after the earlier downpour is evident on my face.

[C J Farquharson]

...he women's Tour de France of ...006. I am 23, riding in yellow, alone ...the head of the race over Mont ...ntoux. It was a childhood dream ...me true. [Getty Images]

A critical moment at Flanders, 2007. I pause towards the top of the Muur Geraardsbergen for Karin Thürig, shouting encouragement so together we can take the tactical advantage on the run into the finish. Zulfiya Zabirova was second and Marianne Vos third.

Beijing 2008. The final metres. [Independent]

I'd dreamt of this moment for a long time [Michael Stenning]

A fantastic welcome back in Wales at the Welsh Assembly. [Huw Evans]

A day like never before in the tiny village of Wick. Houses were decorated and there were many times more people present than the population of 700.

A shot of me not actually riding a bike!

...arese, 2008 World Championships. ...lid-race, the break has a lead of ...early two minutes. I have to wait ...nd be patient. [Getty Images]

The climax of the World Championships. After 15 minutes of constant attacks I pull away from Marianne Vos in the last few metres. [Getty Images]

2008 World Road Race podium, with Marianne, myself and Judith. I am World and Olympic champion in the same year – the first time ever for a male or female. [Getty Images]

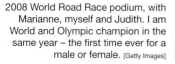

Collecting my MBE at Buckingham Palace. Andy Walser's support and advice helped make 2008 a dream year.

Celebrating my 10th British National Championships, with Lizzie Armitstead second and Emma Pooley third. [Chris Mayer]

The 'curse of the rainbow jersey' held me in its grip for most of the year, but here was a great win on Stage 2 of the Emakumeen Bira in Spain.

The Vision 1 Racing team in a pre-season training camp. While it would not work out, the riders were fantastic and I am proud of how we raced and what we achieved in 2009.

2010 World Championship road race – Geelong. So close yet so far. Judith and I were caught right on the line. [Press Association]

In a dark season, my win at Verona on Stage 5 of the 2011 Giro was a great lift. I drove to the line like my life depended on it.

London 2012 brought me lovely memories to cherish for the future, with people so kind in what they said. The population of Great Britain made me proud to compete on their behalf. It was a great way to sign off. [Reuters]

3:32:23

FINISH

Ω OMEGA

SWEDEN

The Olympic road race, Beijing 2008.

[AP/Press Association]

Marianne Vos since the World Championships the previous September. With 9km of cobblestones and ten climbs in its 122km, it was a classic all-round test. The action started on the first climb, the Molenberg, after 41km when Marianne blasted up the cobbled hill and we pulled her back. Over the top of the Valkenberg climb, with 40km to go, Karin Thürig attacked for us, as per the team plan developed by Thomas. She got away alone and went into time-trial mode and steadily built up a lead over the next two bergs. Our first move had worked. When Karin's lead reached 50 seconds, T-Mobile put Oenone Wood on the front of the bunch to bring the gap down. My team-mates and I watched. At 20km to go, the famous cobbled Muur Kapelmuur in Geraardsbergen was a decisive part of the race and with Karin still 45 seconds in front, I attacked at the start of the climb. I got a small gap, and kept on going. The plan was for me to drop the bunch and jump up to Karin. The pair of us would then time-trial to the finish.

The crowd roared and the noise was deafening. Fans had pressed in on the road and I had to ride between people lining either side of the hill. I caught Karin just before the steep section near the top, encouraging her to keep going. I needed her! Alone, we would both be caught easily. I waited for her, freewheeling and shouting encouragement. Over the top we raced on together. Could we hold off the chasers behind? Looking behind, we could see that a group of four were chasing, with the main group in sight behind them all lined out. This was going to be some team pursuit, two v four v a large chasing group! As we approached the Bosberg, with 11km to go, Karin told me to go on alone. She would be more help to me now by easing up momentarily and slotting into the chasing group behind rather than staying with me, as she would not be able to keep up with me on this last hill. By the top, I held a 20-second advantage over the chasing group of Marianne Vos, Trixi Worrack, Susanne Ljungskog and Zulfiya Zabirova with Karin sitting in last spot, watching and recovering from her 30km in the lead. They would have to take her as a passenger.

With about 6km left, I was caught but Karin knew exactly what to do, and having rested, she immediately launched a hard attack. Zulfiya sprinted to cover it. Assisted by Marianne and followed by Susanne, they closed. I slotted into the slipstream and planned my next move. As they caught Karin and we reformed, Karin and I glanced at each other; we did not need to speak. Karin attacked again, and was again covered by Zulfiya. Perhaps Zulfiya could see that if she got away with Karin, I would not chase and it may be her best shot at victory. She certainly wanted to win.

Whenever we glanced behind we could see the large group not far behind still actively chasing us. If we eased too much, we would be caught. This race was still a long way from being decided. Karin didn't give up, she went again with 2.5km to go. This time, there was a lull as everyone looked at each other. Zulfiya was not going to chase for a third time, she played poker. Marianne cracked and sprinted after Karin, with Susanne and Trixi in tow; I followed with Zulfiya in last spot. Just inside the 2km banner, as we reformed on the left of the road, approaching a section where a central reservation divided the carriageway, out of the right corner of my eye, I spotted movement from behind. Zulfiya had attacked down the right, I dived across to get after her, aware that the others were about to be trapped on the left of the central reservation. I sprinted straight past Zulfiya to take the lead and draw her away with me; she needed to know I was happy to go with her to the finish. Here was our chance. None of the other three could switch into our slipstream. We both knew this and we both totally committed to this break. Inside the last kilometre, I checked behind and could see that Marianne was chasing us, now alone. We could not ease up. Zulfiya jumped early, but I was on her immediately, I waited for the right moment and then kicked hard for victory. A win in the Tour of Flanders is the dream of all classic road riders and one that I will treasure forever.

Karin had ridden a fantastic race. We had a basic plan but a lot of the tactics had to be worked out on the spot and Karin was great. Everything played a part in this race, including tactical cunning, the equipment for the cobbles, teamwork and physical strength. Karin and I both played to our different and complementary strengths. We could only do it together as part of a team. We celebrated together, right then, Karin and I; we were on top of the world.

Dad had been on the course watching the race develop and filming it. He was worried about Marianne Vos. 'She was very angry at being beaten, and that anger is going to burn. She's going to come back hard after you.' Closer to home, there were other concerns. Thomas was burning the candle at both ends and the middle attempting to keep the show on the road. He was clearly more than living up to his part of the agreement thrashed out in December, but it was not fair. Priska had sacrificed her own position as leader on the team because of me, and right now, I was British and British Cycling was placing her whole project in jeopardy. On the way back to Switzerland, body language indicated that our success was not universally appreciated within the team.

Dad was right about Marianne, and I wouldn't have to wait long to get a sense of her determination. The next World Cup was the Ronde van Drenthe, in the Netherlands, Marianne's home territory, and we were so busy watching each other that we both lost sight of the bigger race with Marianne finishing third and me seventh.

The off-the-bike strains now produced real cracks in the team as Thomas continued to wait on British Cycling. Back from a very different time in Australia was Shane Sutton, who paid the team a visit for a day on a fact-finding mission for Dave Brailsford. In our different ways, both Thomas and I were left demoralised and disappointed after his visit, with little hope of the support Dave had committed to in late December arriving. Had Thomas known that no one was ever going to show up, he could have made other plans. As it was he tried to do too much himself and as a consequence corners were cut. Thomas and I had worked well together as coach and rider, but right now he no longer had enough time to coach me effectively. Bikes were not being prepared properly and communication deteriorated. I definitely felt my form was dipping a little, but first I had to get through the next round of the World Cup.

The Flèche Wallonne and its steep finish had become my fortress; I had won here three times and was determined to make it four as the race reached its predictable finale at the base of the Mur de Huy. I attacked midway up the climb, confident about taking the race on. Marianne stuck with me. No problem, I was riding flat out, but I also knew how to dig very deep. We got through the hairpin corners and Marianne was still with me, so I upped my pace, giving everything and hoping to break her, but still she was there. With the line in sight, we were shoulder to shoulder and then Marianne went. In about four pedal strokes she opened a gap and I could only watch as she pulled away. My reign on the Mur had come to an end.

The trip back to Switzerland from Belgium that night was uncomfortable and poorly planned; I was in the back of the car wrestling with my demons, while Priska, who had now recovered her sense of humour, cracked jokes from the front seat. I tried to ignore her. When we got back to our team headquarters, I was told that I would have to get back in the car the next day with Andy Walser and drive back up to Büttgen in Germany, to do time-trial bike testing. I couldn't believe it: two enormous car journeys, straight after a demanding race when rest should have been my only priority, all to put me back within a few kilometres of where I had been the day before! I was livid.

The conversation driving to Büttgen was also disturbing, Andy was pondering about the number of women on tour who had found form suddenly. He had worked with male professional teams and it was clear he believed that some were doping, that it was systematic and that team managers and perhaps medical facilities were implicit in the cover-up. 'I don't think you understand how many people are involved in doping. Be careful,' warned Andy.

It was not as though he was telling me anything I didn't know, though Andy was as much at a loss as to what to do as I was. Dad had taken my observations to the head of UK Anti-Doping and had come back totally demoralised. Both he and I had continued to press after the positive tests from the Athens Olympics produced no outcome. However, for me at that precise moment, I considered it was the wrong time to be putting in time and effort when my resources were needed elsewhere. Having quashed T-Mobile, and thinking my problems were over, my focus was on what I could do to beat someone who had just borrowed my crown in my backyard. It was hard to get Marianne out of my head as I returned to Switzerland, hoping that a much-needed rest and a few weeks of solid training would sort me out.

It was now the end of April. While we were at the Flèche, Thomas was paying for Tanja, Annaliese and a hired-in manager to go as a second team to a race in Italy. Just like my two-way car journey, this trip proved a logistical disaster for them, with a long journey resulting in no race. Thomas was clearly attempting to fill the holes created by the lack of an understudy from British Cycling. Not only was he spending money to little avail, but reimbursement from British Cycling was not arriving, and while they asked him to provide lots of documentation to justify the expense, he simply wanted a pair of hands on the ground to help him.

Thomas took on a Swiss junior national coach to help out part-time at the team and requested that he be funded by British Cycling, as they had not fulfilled their part of the deal thrashed out in December. Now, looking at the correspondence, I read that Dad was urging Dave Brailsford and Thomas to communicate with each other and for Dave to at least send out a member of staff to see us at a race and gain a measure of what logistical pressures the team was under. Dan Hunt came out for one visit and Shane Sutton made another trip that had a similar effect to the previous one.

Matters came to a head in early May. Various things provisionally planned for the GB girls were not happening. Dan had spoken to Thomas, who was raging, complaining about lack of money for expenses he'd incurred but mainly that there was no manager. One further bone of contention was a training camp proposed for the British girls for mid-May. With no British coach around, Thomas agreed to facilitate it and presented a project proposal to BC. Eventually, approval was forthcoming from British Cycling for the camp, but approval was way too late for the plan to be executed.

This was the final straw; Thomas was finished with British Cycling. He was running his own show and I and the rest of the British girls could take part or walk away. Anneliese packed up and went home, never to race again. Tanja persisted. She would win a stage of the women's Tour, but by the end of the season the racing was all over for her. She did one winter camp and then left the sport forever. Both Tanja and Anneliese gave the project everything. Looking back, the fact we were so concerned in February about the lack of commitment from British Cycling that we decided to write a collective letter to Dave Brailsford, and the nature of the response, really did only point to one outcome. Undoubtedly, marginal gains only applied to those they wanted it to apply to, and that they didn't even know which half of the planet we were in, said it all. That we didn't count was obvious. British Cycling was prioritising virtually everything, including the U23 girls, above the road women. After our stellar start to the season in Australia and the early races in Europe, I wondered if our independent 'candle' was burning too brightly. The fact was that Thomas, Anneliese, Tanja and I, along with Raleigh, Del, Heather Bird and Michael Jankowski, could not have been giving it a better shot.

What could I do? I was committed to the Raleigh team and so were the sponsors. My best efforts and plans to create a solid foundation for British riders and British staff to work together towards Beijing had been ruined. I would just have to get on with it. I had every sympathy with Thomas, but in the eyes of both Priska and himself I was now the embodiment of British Cycling, who they viewed as the cause of their current difficulties. He was trying to run a team and develop his commercial affairs with Cervelo at the same time. He was ambitious and competent, but as a consequence he was now trying to do too much. At the same time, he lost the services of Andy Walser, which now stretched logistical support beyond breaking point. Another casualty of this situation was the coaching sessions I had with Thomas. One time, without prior notice, Thomas was unable to make a motor-paced training session, then at another my bike was wrongly equipped. Reluctantly, I decided to ask Thomas to step down as my personal coach.

On 16 May, I flew into Birmingham airport and had a meeting with Dave Brailsford, Shane Sutton, Dan Hunt, Steve Peters and Dad. I am sure there was a box on a Lottery spend authorisation form headed 'Project Cooke' that needed to have a tick in it. We spoke about dieticians and equipment provision and lots of pointless trivia, but the real issue was the lack of a British women's team manager. Dave Brailsford announced that he was going to apply himself to this.

Towards the end of May, I was asked if I would work with Julian Winn. Five months into the 'job search', this was the only name Dave Brailsford had come up with. So now, after it had all fallen apart at the team, I was asked to work with the person who had presided over the 'preparation' of the Welsh team for the 2006 Commonwealth Games. I am very proud of the way I conducted myself. I set aside all my past differences, did not focus on what the motives were for such a suggestion, accepted the proposal and just looked ahead.

Julian's role was to coordinate and support the activities of Tanja, Emma Pooley, myself and those on the periphery, such as Rachel Heal, now in America, Catherine Hare, and the girls at Helen and Stefan Wyman's Global team. This person would also have to liaise with the manager who was working full-time with the U23 girls. I was never going to be best friends with Julian, but I did believe that he would be competent in this role and would not make the same mistakes he had made previously. Certainly, he had a first-hand understanding of the pressures of being a rider expected to deliver, and I'm sure he had felt under pressure at Melbourne in 2006. I agreed without any reservations. He worked effectively and was committed to the programme and myself. He did what was asked of him, without needing to be asked again or needing constant reassurance. At this time, seeking to replace the loss of Anneliese, I was also aware of the problems Emma was still encountering. Dad pressed British Cycling to speak with Emma and support her at the Specialized team. This was one suggestion they did take up and complete successfully.

A short block of racing followed – fourth at the Magali Pache TT, fourth at the World Cup race in Bern and then fifth in a sprint at the Montreal GP with Marianne Vos taking fourth, so by the end of May I was still leading the World Cup but Marianne was slowly closing the gap.

The women's Tour de France was held in the middle of June, and once again looked set to be a great race for our team with Karin, Priska, Tanja, Pascale and new addition to the team this year, Caroline Steffen. The race was a shadow of its former glory, as each hammer blow of drug abuse on the men's scene drove sponsorship away from women's cycling. As a consequence, it no longer attracted all the great names from the sport as it used to. Nevertheless, it was a prestigious race and the last stage, with climbs up the Tourmalet and Col d'Aspin, would be a classic to any aficionado. That huge Pyrenean stage effectively ruled out Karin going for the overall, and at early season calendar meetings it was pencilled in as a chance for me to repeat the win of the year before.

Due to his business commitments, Thomas did not come with us. With four stages to go, Priska was in yellow, because I had gifted her the stage after the two of us broke away.

'I've got the yellow jersey, Nicole. Are you going to let me win this race?'

I was puzzled. 'The only reason you've got the jersey is because I gifted it to you, not because you're the better rider. I've had the Tour marked down all season. We all know that.'

The next stage was an individual time-trial. Karin would win but would lose so much time in the mountains that she would not take the GC. Priska wanted me to ride easily in the time-trial so that she could have an advantage to carry into the mountains and take the overall win. It was a pan-flat 20km, rectangular course with straight roads and four corners. Exactly the sort of course that suited me least. It was undoubtedly the best time-trial I ever rode in my life. I won, beating Karin by six seconds, Priska was at 47 seconds with Emma Pooley at 2 minutes 2 seconds, just four seconds clear of Tanja. I was now leading the GC and in yellow. The next morning, Priska made another plea, insisting that Thomas, who was back in Switzerland, had told her that she could win, even though he'd told me that I could go for the win. Since the team meeting the previous day, I had been calling Thomas to get the situation clarified, but hadn't received any response, which only frustrated things further.

The penultimate stage settled nothing as Priska and I watched each other in the bunch, so I still held a 37-second advantage going into the last stage which would be raced over the Tourmalet and Col d'Aspin before descending to the finish in Arreau. Buoyed by my time-trial win, I was fairly confident I would be the strongest rider and could control the race by marking Priska, who clearly wasn't going to back off. But all this trouble within the team was putting my mind into a whirl and I was clearly not thinking properly.

On the early slopes of the Col du Tourmalet, Emma Pooley made an attack and I followed. The two of us built up a nice lead, which seemed to solve my problem with Priska. I stuck with Emma, a fantastic climber who wanted to win the iconic stage of the Tour. But something was wrong. I started to suffer badly and I shifted down the gears, easing off, while Emma rode away from me. Had I managed my eating and drinking properly early on in the stage? Why was I so weak now? I needed to eat some energy bars and recover, otherwise this could turn into a disaster. The time gaps to the group behind containing Priska showed they were closing on me, and with about 5km to the summit I thought it best just to ride easy until the group caught me and then continue with them. It meant Priska would be in a position to attack me, but I didn't have much choice.

The group caught me and I slotted in with them but was immediately struggling to stay with them. I had nothing in my legs and slid out the back of the group. Priska needed no invitation. She was riding away and in to the virtual yellow jersey. I could see the summit, I could just see Emma, now minutes up the road, and I could see Priska's group in front of me. I put everything in to the next kilometres, desperately going as fast as possible and yet pedal stroke by pedal stroke losing more and more time. At the summit, I was about four minutes behind Emma and two minutes behind Priska. I had not conducted a recce of the course and I had never been over these Pyrenean climbs.

I sprinted down this unknown descent, my Tour de France lost unless I could catch Priska. I took the first corner at full speed, and realised, way too late, that this was a tight corner and the road kept on turning to the left. There were no barriers and I wobbled on and off the edge of the tarmac with one foot out of the pedal, trying to keep my weight towards the road. The road straightened and I was still on the road! I clipped my foot in and sprinted off. No time to dwell, I was still in this race. Three years later, a man came up to me at the GP Plouay and began telling me how he watched my descent that day from an official's car travelling right behind me: 'Oh, that corner!' he wailed, putting his head in his hands. 'I don't know how you managed to stay on, and then you descended, you descended like a cannon ball!'

I took risks and never eased up; how would I live with myself if I threw away the Tour de France on the last day? Halfway down the descent, I caught up the group that had been with Priska, but I could see she was not there. Priska was clearly descending as fast as she could, as well. They could follow me or continue descending at their best speed, but I had a rider I needed to catch. No one decided to stay with me.

Near the bottom of the descent, I spotted a race motorbike and rider ahead. I was closing very fast. This would be Priska.

No! It was Emma. Priska was now first on the road and first in the race. Some thinking was needed. I had been dropped by Emma and passed by Priska and a group of other riders. Priska was leading, with the final mountain ahead, up to 1489m at the top of the Col d'Aspin, followed by a descent to Arreau. I eased up as I passed Emma and encouraged her to get on my wheel. Emma was still hunting for the stage win and if Emma helped me catch Priska, I would certainly like to see Emma win the stage. I took nice easy lines through the corners, started braking early, leading the way for Emma, keeping her with me.

As soon as we finished the descent and headed towards the Col d'Aspin, we worked together to try to catch Priska. Emma did most of the pace-setting on the climb as I was still not feeling great. We now had some time checks, we climbed steadily, and the times came down. Now Priska was only 30 seconds ahead; we could see her. We caught Priska on the climb. If looks could kill, I would have been dead on the spot. Our trio, led by Emma and with Priska and me marking each other, crested the Col d'Aspin and began the descent towards the finish, but hostilities were not ended. Priska set as fast a pace as she could, and as much as I wanted to help Emma, I had to match Priska, so Emma was dropped. Priska sprinted for the finish and stage win, I just eased up and crossed the line with my hands raised in relief, happy to have salvaged my Tour from an almost impossible situation, hoping that by not taking the stage win, it might be an element in later rapprochement. I was very grateful indeed to Emma for helping me catch Priska; without her I doubt that I could have done it and I would not have won the race.

It was the end of June and I headed back to the UK for the British National Championships. Although to the press all was well, I was beginning to feel very uneasy and quite down. It was hard to concentrate on anything. I had replaced Thomas on the coaching side with Gordon Wright and Dad, but they were both UK based, and looking back it is easy to see that despite the very best will by all of us, it was never going to be effective. The British Championships were postponed due to flooding caused by the heavy rains of that summer. Then, on recovering after the women's Tour, my knee began hurting when I resumed training. I went to Bath to work with Dr Rod Jaques on building up my knee. The prognosis was that with rest and care, I should be fine.

As July turned to August, I had to steel myself for the Open de Suède World Cup when I would have to face Marianne Vos again, something I would relish if I was injury-free but that I dreaded in my current physical condition. Again, Marianne and

I marked each other out but she was 10th and I was 12th, so while the points damage was minimal, and my overall lead intact, the cumulative impact of being beaten by her was wearing me down – a nightmarish Groundhog Day in which I was not going into races to win anymore. I had never raced like this before.

Early August, an event planned the previous December, organised by British Cycling, did take place. Julian ran a four-day GB training camp in Quarrata, Italy where British Cycling had based the men's U23 academy. For four days, we had access to the motor-pacing scooters and all the facilities the Lottery had provided for the men. Present were Emma Pooley, Tanja Slater and Rachel Heal, along with Nikki Harris and Lizzie Armitstead from the U23 girls' squad. The coaching team supporting the men, Rod Ellingworth, Dan Hunt and Max Sciandri, showed an occasional interest in the temporary visitors. The camp was good, giving a fleeting taste of what could have been. Julian supported all my requests for the types of training I wanted the team to do. We spent our time there as an initial bonding session, training, doing leadouts and talking about the 2007 World Championships and the Olympic Games, now just 12 months away.

I probably shouldn't have raced at the rescheduled British Championships. I knew I was risking aggravating my injured knee, which had got worse in the past two weeks. It was a flattish course in Essex, the rain was torrential and my knee started to ache after just an hour, but I gritted my teeth. I attacked on the last climb, more of a drag than a hill, and got a small gap and went on to win alone. It was my eighth victory, the last seven in a row. Girls from the training camp filled five of the first seven places in the race. We were beginning to build a solid group as the World Championships started to dominate our thinking.

After the British Championships, my knee was so bad I decided to head to the doctors and get treatment before making a decision about my next races. I spoke with Julian and explained the situation with my knee. He was highly supportive, with his true athlete's perspective shining through. A few days later, I travelled to Germany for the Albstadt Frauen-Etappenrennen which I rode with Raleigh, while the other British girls rode as the British Team. I performed terribly in the first-day prologue. I rode with tactical skill and willpower to win the second stage but was almost non-existent in the racing on the last day. The GB riders then travelled to Stuttgart to recce the course for that year's World Championships. It was my kind of course, complete with an uphill sprint finish – if I could return to anywhere near full fitness, I felt this one could be mine.

However, before then, the World Cup needed to come to a conclusion and I wanted to be the first person on the planet to win three. I was not going to give up. The penultimate round was in Plouay, I would need to draw on every scrap of experience to try to reverse the losses to Marianne. None of my rivals knew about my knee problems, which I'd kept very quiet. I spent the first part of the race riding cautiously, and then on the last lap I attacked with 18km to go. I was joined by three others, including Oenone, while Marianne was in the peloton behind. Italian Noemi Cantele got away from us on the last climb. I put everything into beating Oenone in the sprint for second place, while Marianne was back in seventh.

I had an 80-point lead with only one race to go, the GP Nuremburg. In other years, I would have been the champion already, but this season the UCI declared there would be double points in the last race of the women's World Cup. So instead of 75 points for the win, it was 150 for this one race, so I could still be beaten if Marianne won or got second, and I finished outside the top five.

There was a two-week gap to Nuremberg and after more treatment the doctors at Bath concluded I needed another operation to clear more of the plica membrane. They were ready to operate there and then, but I was determined to be there in Nuremberg and do everything I could to win the World Cup.

My gift of the final stage at the Tour was futile. Thomas and I spoke and we knew that I would not be part of any team plans Priska and he had for the following year. For Nuremberg we had a strong team, three riders would finish in the top nine at the World Time-Trial Championships two weeks later and there was any number of ways we could have blocked out Marianne from getting the top two finish she needed to overtake me. A sacrificial break driven to the finish was the easy solution, but Thomas did not see it that way, possibly because he did not want me go to another team as World Cup winner. Besides, we led in the team competition as well and he did want to win that.

Thomas felt we should not let a breakaway go. The race would be contained for a bunch sprint – my individual title sacrificed for the good of the team. I pointed out that if we had riders in a winning break, the team competition would also be won. Thomas was having none of it. I got through the first of ten laps before the pain began. It grew with each of the next nine laps as the breakaways were all quashed. I was near the front but as the pace picked up in the final kilometres the best I could do was 34th. Marianne rode superbly and her team delivered her on the day, winning the race and the World Cup. Of our team that had preserved every ounce of resource for the sprint finish, only Jo Kiesanowski made the top 20. She came eighth which, by pure luck, was enough to make sure Thomas had the team award.

Dispirited, I left the team. I bid a fond farewell to several of my team-mates, with whom I had many happy memories of two years together. They had witnessed at first hand what went on, but they knew the facts of life relating to a women's professional cycling team, every bit as much as Fany did years before. It would take three years and a court case for me to recover the money owed to me, and in every race thereafter, Priska and Thomas ensured there was one rider they wanted beaten. They also had another plan to extend their impact on my career, which was a cruel twist, but that was another slow burn.

The following day, Mum was with me in Bristol waiting by my bed for me to come out of general anaesthetic after the operation on my knee. She drove me home very carefully and looked after me. I had lost the World Cup in the last race, having led the competition from the start to the last metres of the final finish line. The next year and thereafter, the UCI removed the 'double points on the last round' rule.

I watched the World Championships on TV. At long last, there was another GB rider who could finish in the lead group. The GB team comprised Lizzie Armitstead, Catherine Hare, Rachel Heal, Emma Pooley, Tanja Slater and Helen Wyman. Emma was 10th, with Catherine 30th and Rachel 57th; the others did not finish. Two things shone through. Emma had made more progress this year than could be hoped; and at the vital time in the race, the Italians played out their superiority in numbers. Subsequently, the other nations let Marianne and her Dutch colleague Chantal Beltman do the work. No one was going to help the favourite. Welcome to the club, Marianne. Hanka Kumpfernagel won the time-trial with Emma in eighth.

Wendy Houvenaghel – who, earlier in the year, when I was requesting the presence of her undoubted talent and professional attitude, only to be informed by coaching staff that she could not possibly come off her track programme to join in any road activity – was given a berth in the British team. She finished a creditable 25th in the time-trial. I did not even think 'what might have been'.

The year had started so very brightly, but Marianne was now World No.1. It was ten months to the Olympics. A clock was ticking again, a clock I hadn't heard for three years. Alone, the year's events gave me much to think about. I had another yellow T-shirt for the person I held most dear, that little girl with the bike too big for her but with lots of determination, who came back to see me at quiet, critical times. Despite my very best efforts, an awful lot had gone wrong; I had a lot of bad news for her. She squeezed my hand and told me she was proud of me.

CHAPTER NINETEEN
Rock Bottom

I had always set out to show that I could win different races in all types of situations: one-day classics, stage races, winning alone or sprinting to the win from a group, or even a big bunch sprint, whether on a hilly or a flat course. I had also set records for being the youngest winner of the World Cup and Giro d'Italia. But with more injury and the collapse of the Raleigh team, I felt that my star was waning while Marianne Vos's was firmly in the ascendance. Marianne was driven and confident; she could climb, sprint and had a smart tactical head. She had a team around her that was well funded and built totally around supporting the star whose presence created it. Marianne had finished her season with silver in the World Championships, having displaced me as No.1 in the world rankings as well as winning the World Cup series. The Dutch understood road cycling, and her support structure was only going to get stronger as her success confirmed they were backing a winner.

Following my latest knee operation, I returned to Lugano where I attempted to draw a line under the events of the previous season and put aside my disappointments. It was time to focus on the biggest prize of all: the Beijing Olympic road race. Julian Winn's appointment eased the communication problems within the GB set-up. I was a little concerned about the lack of definition about the time-trial selection criteria, but a discussion produced a confirmed, written conclusion that Steve Peters would have responsibility for resolving that with the relevant riders.

Then a most curious situation presented itself. Halfords were keen to work with British Cycling and promote their range of Boardman bikes. Dave Brailsford came up with a plan to register a UCI trade team, made up of the U23 girls that BC had supported the year before, under the Halfords' name. I would join it and bring my UCI points, so the team could then get into all the big races. Julian would be manager, assisted by Simon Cope, the full-time U23 women's manager. There would be BC mechanics and support. In the team would be myself, the U23 girls and British girls who were not getting a ride elsewhere. The sponsors would pay me a good salary and other expenses.

I was disappointed that we were not joined by Emma Pooley, who was staying with the Specialized team, but if that worked for her, she needed to stay there. If we did a race that her team could not get into or did not attend, she could join us and then we would enter as the GB team. Halfords would have only GB nationals on the roster. Of course, the downside of this was that this would be the weakest team I had ever ridden for. I had to park up any ambitions of a World Cup campaign or a race win where I could not survive for the significant period of the race on my own. But as the year drew to a close, I was not bothered. My health was poor, I was in for a legal battle with Thomas Campana, and scarred deep into my soul was the memory of my last race – being with a strong team who were directed, specifically, to race for an objective that was contrary to my interest. What was the point of being with a strong team?

My training progressed over the next few weeks, back with Mauro in the hills. Then during a modest training ride in mid-November, my knee began to ache. I eased up immediately and gently headed home, hoping an overnight rest would resolve what might only be a niggle. After a night of wrestling my demons, I set off gingerly the next morning, but within 20 minutes it was hurting again and every worst-case scenario was now running through my head. I was distraught, I'd done the best-ever injury prevention programme and it hadn't worked. I'd had an operation and followed the rehabilitation to the tiniest detail, and now that hadn't worked. There seemed like no way out. I rang my parents to tell them about my knee, managing to hold myself together for a few minutes before breaking down in tears. I could not take it anymore; I wanted to stop and end my career there and then.

Mum and Dad were both so supportive. If I wanted to retire, then they would totally respect that and stand by me. Cycling was not everything in life and there are lots of other things I could do, it was up to me. I was convinced that was it: five seasons with knee injuries was too much, and to have the pain return so soon after the operation that was meant to fix it, left me desolate. The one thing that had kept me going through all the chaos of the last year was the belief that I was capable of becoming Olympic champion regardless of all that happened off the bike, but with my knee looking like it was unfixable, I touched rock bottom.

I needed time to make such an important decision. I thought about cycling almost every minute of every day and I needed to hit 'pause' and consider what life would be like without it. I had found comfort in talking with Mum and Dad and sharing my feelings and fears – so I texted Andy Walser, the only other person who I felt could understand my situation and cared, rather than seeing me as a name on a result sheet, or a medal prospect. He telephoned almost immediately and we ended up talking about the ultimate rewards of doing something that was difficult. He also wanted me to meet a friend of his, Doctor Fabio Bartalucci, who might have some fresh ideas about my knee injury.

I also emailed Steve Peters. If ever a sports psychiatrist was going to be able to help me, it was now. He was able to put things more into perspective. There was only one goal for the year and it was almost nine months until the Beijing Olympics. If I took time to recover from my injury and began training perhaps as late as March, I could still be ready for the games in August. Then I headed for Tuscany to see Andy's doctor friend who, after listening to the long history of the injury, asked me about my training and what I did in between races during the season. Fabio suggested that I could be doing too much, pushing the knee beyond its limits too often.

Back in Lugano, I reflected on what had been said. Julian and I had already planned the recce of the Olympic course in Beijing to coincide with the Track World Cup held in December. I hadn't ridden my bike for two weeks and was struggling to believe that I might actually be at the Olympics, but the tickets had been booked so I made the trip with Julian, meeting the British track team in Beijing. The road race course started with an 80km flat section before swinging onto a hilly circuit, which had to be completed twice. It began with a 10km climb, followed by a descent and then an uphill finish. This course would create a selection on the long climb for pure climbers, yet it needed a sprint to finish the race. On the second day I decided, regardless of whether my knee might hurt or not, that I wanted to ride the 10km climb, and sprint the 750m of the uphill finish. My physical condition was appalling, but it allowed me to get a feel for the gradient and the gear ratio I would need.

I spent December in the UK, mostly in Manchester, having intensive rehab for my knee. Here we spent time confirming the programme for the year and key markers. I took part in a GB training camp just before Christmas at Abergavenny, where my knee prevented any serious training. Tanja Slater was with us here but she then left competitive cycling forever; 2007 at Raleigh with Thomas had exhausted us both.

January 2008 was horrible. We had the official launch of the Halfords team and Dave Brailsford had added in a couple of male riders – Tom Southam, last seen in 2005 being banned from ever representing GB again, and Rob Hayles who had been to the three previous Olympics but who would be quietly dropped weeks later, forced to take the prescribed sanction of a 'health rest' due to an elevated haematocrit level. For a team apparently built around supporting my Olympic bid, many features left me entirely baffled as to their purpose. I never saw either of these two again. The media conference was one of the hardest I had ever done. There was no way I could put a dampener on the celebrations and, despite having done no training and my knee hurting, I tried to behave as if everything was on schedule and I would be ready for Beijing. They even wanted to get shots of me riding the bikes that Halfords were providing. I couldn't tell anyone that I was barely riding.

The full squad was: Jess Allen, Lizzie Armitstead, Katie Colclough, Katie Curtis, Wendy Houvenaghel, Jo Rowsell, Emma Trott, Catherine Hare and me. Despite this large roster, we would, bizarrely, find the need to 'guest-in' other riders when we couldn't get a team together to attend the events planned into our so meticulously prepared calendar.

The British Cycling medical team, led by Phil Burt, were genuinely supportive. There was a theory that with the onset of pain in my knee, nerve messages were being sent to the surrounding muscles to switch off in a response to protect the body and reduce the cause of the pain. So to switch these muscles back on, they stuck electrical pads attached to a battery on my gluteus muscles. When the battery was turned on, small electric shocks were sent through the pads every six seconds to spark my muscles into action. I was riding for 20 minutes, three times a day on the rollers, during which I had to endure hundreds of these shocks. It was unpleasant and soul-destroying. At dinner one night with my parents, a tune came on the radio, 'Vinceró' by Luciano Pavarotti, which is a positive, rousing number, but to me the phrase 'I will win' caused tears to well up in my eyes. At first, I tried to hide it from my parents and then there was no point. I was now just seven months away from what should have been the most important day of my career. I was still at rock bottom.

By the end of January, I had progressed to the point where I was doing three, 45-minute sessions each day. Andy Walser had previously suggested that I could use his house in Tuscany and make the most of the milder weather. I hadn't trained properly for the best part of five months, so my fitness levels were the lowest they had been since I had started competitive cycling. I began training by blowing up spectacularly after an hour and having to stop. Mauro remained a great support, waiting with me by the side of the road whenever my knee needed a rest and pacing me on climbs regardless of how slow I was going, or how hard I was breathing, as I tried to follow him. Slowly, I increased the duration, in five-minute segments day after day. At the beginning of March, I completed a long ride, pain free, for the first time in seven months.

My season and debut race for Halfords began with the Trofeo Alfredo Binda, a round of the World Cup in late March. My expectations for the spring classics were low. If I could finish with the bunch that would be an achievement – a total contrast with my thoughts 12 months ago. The intensity of racing would be a big test for my knee. Gordon Wright and Dad were keen to protect my knee by racing less and resting more. Having just one British sponsor meant we could design a racing programme to meet my needs, rather than doing a lot of local races to satisfy a collection of minor sponsors needing local publicity, as is normally the case for women's teams.

Emma Pooley attacked alone on a hill 40km from the finish and stayed away from the peloton to win comfortably, which made a good statement about her own ability. It was a win exactly like her Stage 3 win in Thüringen the year before. Other riders noted the performance. I rode well, considering my circumstances, in the main group but was not competitive in the sprint, finishing 20th. I was relieved to have completed the race; however, the media decided I was 'riding deliberately low on form due to a season-long build-up towards the Olympics'. If only they knew.

I was defending champion in the Tour of Flanders and had completed two more weeks of training, so I hoped to see some improvements. Irrespective of my form, I missed the race-winning attack by Kristin Armstrong and Judith Arndt and then made a futile attack in the latter stages trying to secure third spot, only to be caught and passed by the whole of the leading group, finishing 16th.

At the Flèche Wallonne, we entered as the GB team so that Emma could join us. A new addition to the team was Sharon Laws, who had been living in Australia and won numerous mountain bike races and performed well in testing. She was offered a place on the Halfords team and moved to Britain. Here, we were to have our first race as the provisional Olympic team of Emma, Sharon and me. My GB team-mates delivered me in prime position at the base of the Mur de Huy, but Marianne Vos claimed her second victory on the Mur, while I could manage only eighth place. Emma finished sixth and had led me out; I'm sure she would have finished higher had we been leading her out instead.

The first significant milestone of the season, where I expected to perform competitively, was the Magali Pache time-trial in early May. The importance of the race was heightened because Sharon Laws had decided she wanted to challenge me for the second spot for the Olympic TT event. After her top ten finish in the 2007 World Championship, Emma had been given one of the places. Out of contention was Wendy Houvenaghel, who was now concentrating only on the pursuit.

I finished 12th, just behind Emma, which was a very frustrating result. Gordon had travelled out to see me race. It was a key point in our programme and had been since we confirmed it in December. We had put a taper in for the event, so I should have been performing to capacity, challenging for the win. Instead, I was well off the pace. Gordon and Dad were working on my daily training, and Andy was with me as I was riding one of his machines.

I talked it through with Andy. Gordon and Dad were doing their best, but both had full-time jobs and neither saw me regularly. Fabio Bartalucci's strategy for the knee had been working very well and he was still suggesting I reduce the volume of training. Importantly, Fabio was within easy reach, he could go out for rides with me and could see me climb and sprint. My best years with Dad had been when he saw me every day and could tell me to ease up over the next few days or go hard. Training feedback, hours later, over the phone wasn't even third best. This prompted Andy to suggest changing coaches and asking Fabio to take me on. Gordon and Dad were both very good about it.

With Fabio, the training rides were shorter and had a greater variety of interval training. He also introduced strength training on the bike by riding up hills with a low cadence. We did many rides together. At first, the training triggered knee pain but within a fortnight, with Fabio fine-tuning my training depending on how my knee was responding, I could sense an improvement. I felt like I was starting to get stronger. The day before travelling to France for the ten-day Tour de L'Aude, I realised in the middle of my ride that I actually enjoyed riding my bike again.

We rode as a GB team comprising Catherine Hare, Sharon Laws, Emma Pooley, Jess Allen and myself. Guesting with us, due to the unavailability of any Halfords rider in this, one of our two major races before Beijing, was Leda Cox. Also present were Helen Wyman's Swift team, featuring three other GB riders. They were now regulars on the continental circuit, with Helen and Stefan doing great things with little resource.

In the prologue, I was pleased with 13th in a field of over a hundred; it wasn't great but it showed I had made progress. The first test would come straightaway on the 107km Stage 1; there was a big hill where a group of four broke away – Susanne Ljungskog, Trixi Worrack, Judith Arndt and Sharon Laws. I could not go with them and was in a group of a dozen or so riders chasing close behind. At around 5km to go, the gap had reduced to 30 seconds. I launched an attack, took no one with me and then started the individual pursuit to close on the leaders, latching on with 2km to go. Sharon and I now had the numerical advantage and were in a position to take the initiative. Sharon led out the sprint immaculately and I was delighted to reward her effort by timing my kick perfectly to win.

This was a very big moment. Alongside us in the break had been two recent World champions, so this success was right out of the top drawer. I had waited eight years for this privilege, being in a break and having another GB rider riding with me. Over the rest of the tour, I didn't add any more wins but could feel my strength and fitness returning and was pleased with my fourth overall. Much more importantly, my knee had stood up to ten consecutive days of racing. I was a long way from daring to dream, but at least I was looking forward to the next day.

CHAPTER TWENTY
Defeat and Victory

My preparation for the 2008 Olympics, while not perfect was now back on track; I was racing and training and had a very good win under my belt. A lot is now noted about the techniques of 'marginal gains' used by the British Cycling team and their efficient use of public money to support their riders in the build-up to and completion of competition. British Cycling and Team Sky are very keen to promote the story that it was Chris Froome who exorcised the ghost of Tommy Simpson on Mont Ventoux, riding in yellow past his memorial to win at the summit of that fateful mountain. In 2006, two years before the events I now describe, I had already done it, riding alone at the summit in yellow in that year's Women's Tour de France. No doubt there are many individuals who would prefer the efficacy of 'marginal gains' and the 'Froome did it first' account to hold firm.

Fifteen years after Robert Millar's heroic defeat, I was on that same mountain, also riding to defeat, my dreams shattered. I was deliberately deserted by British Cycling's 'marginal gains' machine, the system that was cosseting and looking after every whim of its chosen stars. Mum and Dad were there of course, cheering me on every yard, even as I lost my crown, despite all that the childhood friend and her team could do to assist and deny the inevitable. Olympic team-mates were not in evidence. Deadliest of enemies on the road that day were my team-mates the year before.

From early on in the winter, Team Halfords had planned that the women's Tour de France would be my last major race, apart from the British Nationals, ahead of the Olympics, not least because it had a 40km TT which was similar to the Olympic course and the last two days in the Alps were very demanding. After the team finished the very successful Tour de L'Aude I went back to Lugano to prepare. Five days later, a short email arrived from Julian Winn informing me that the team was now not going to the Tour. I went straight to the decision-maker, Shane Sutton. Apparently Shane had decided that I was not going to race the women's Tour and Team Halfords was being withdrawn. He did not consult me before changing the team plan on something I viewed as vital to my preparation. He simply didn't seem to care about what I thought

Shane suggested I join Julian, Emma and Sharon, who were now going to do some club races at Abergavenny, where perhaps I could ride an evening club time-trial. While I had been recovering from surgery and had no form, he had not appeared interested in what I raced. But now, when I had form and might win the women's Tour for a third time, was the time he decided to take an interest. I had won the two previous editions and had a yellow jersey to defend. I protested the decision. The management were men, the cycling reporters were men who wrote about men. I was a girl. I could scream, but the scream would not be heard. The management could ignore me and they knew nobody would know.

If Team Halfords, launched to the public to prove that the BC WCPP were fully committed to the best GB road cyclist, weren't going to the Tour, I knew some long-time friends I could rely on who were. I joined up with Helen and Stefan Wyman's Swift Racing team who had gathered around them a close-knit group, her brother Greg and long-term unpaid stalwart of cycling Martin Eadon, for Pierre Boué's 2008 edition of the women's Tour de France. The race, shorter than in previous years, was on life support, with just one more edition left before it became a silent victim of the drug-taking liars, too self-centred to contemplate the carnage they inflicted on others.

However, the race still included classic stages. Stage 1 started in Ghent, Belgium and raced over the Hoogberg and Kruisberg to Wattrelos. Stage 2 included the famous cobbled section from the Paris-Roubaix race, Arenberg Forest. Here, I finished second in the bunch sprint. In Stage 3, I finished second again in the sprint. The next day, we raced in torrential rain and the bunch was all together to contest the finish. I crashed as we went round the last corner with 800m to go. I remounted and finished, then surveyed the damage – just cuts and bruises. We all quickly got changed, put our soaking racing kit and shoes in black bags and tried to get some warmth back into ourselves. The race was moving 450km south to the Alps. As we drove there, I had an ice pack pressed on my hip all the way. When we got up the next morning, our *soigneur* Martin Eadon had been up all night and had cleaned and dried our shoes and had the kit laid out and all ready for us on the day of the long individual time-trial. I came third to my former team-mates Karin Thürig and Christiane Soeder, riding for Thomas Campana's Cervelo team.

I was now nearly two minutes down on GC. My Swift Racing team-mates were excellent, doing absolutely everything they could, but they were not capable of an aggressive, attritional battle with Cervelo. The penultimate stage finished with a climb to the ski station of Villard-de-Lans, terrain which could provide opportunities for changes on GC. However, I was unable to reclaim any significant time from the Cervelo duo, as we finished within a few seconds of each other.

Prior to the final stage, we had another long transfer. At midnight, our happy band, cramped together in the camper, peering through the dark, was looking for the first glimpse of our accommodation on a mountainside. We were on the eve of a classic showdown in the most dramatic of settings, with three riders still capable of winning the Tour in a final stage comprising three giant climbs: first the Col d'Izoard at 2,361m, then Montgenèvre at 1,850m, before the final 12km climb to Sestriere, finishing at 2,035m in Italy.

The contrast could not be greater. Over 1,000 miles away the track stars, in their final build-up for the 2008 Olympics, were staying at the five-star Celtic Manor hotel, accompanied by the GB team manager, near the newly constructed Newport Velodrome, a building project that was cancelled until the plans were taken out and dusted off following my success on the world stage. Meanwhile, I was surrounded and supported by genuine friends. They were doing all they could to help me, not because they were paid, but because they wanted to.

I thought the time gap was small enough that I could leave my attacking until the final climb up to Sestriere, hoping that Karin and Christiane would be tired by then, and if I saved my energy for one big attack, I would still have a chance to claim the yellow jersey. On the first climb the field splintered with much aggressive riding. A small group of riders crested the Col d'Izoard together – including Karin, Christiane, myself and

Jolanta Polikeviciute. During the descent, both Karin and Christiane were losing ground, so I pushed on, splitting it down to just Jolanta and me. By the bottom of the descent, we had nearly a minute lead. Straightaway, the ascent of the Montgenèvre started and I pushed on, dropping Jolanta. The slope of the climb was benign, not the gradient I needed. Behind Karin and Christiane worked together to haul me back. Jolanta sat behind them to make us a group of four over the summit. I had taken a gamble, spending quite a bit of energy in my early attack, but it had failed. I could only hope the chase had also taken something out of Karin and Christiane.

Jolanta and I descended as fast as we could, taking turns to lead each other, again dropping Karin and Christiane. Jolanta and I started the climb to Sestriere with a 30-second lead over Christiane, who had also dropped Karin. On the early slopes, I dropped Jolanta and made my bid for victory. Instead of pulling away from Christiane, the time checks showed she was steadily closing on me. I tried to dig deeper but was on my limit. I passed Mum, who shouted me on from the side of the road, but behind, Christiane was about to catch me.

Should I ease up to recover and go again, allowing Karin to get back up to us, or keep going, knowing Christiane would just sit on me, and resign myself to go for second place? I kept on going, thinking there was always a chance that Christiane may blow up. I passed Dad, who cheered me on, his video camera recording my impending defeat. I was nearly exhausted. Behind, Karin had caught Jolanta and together they were closing on us. Since Christiane was sitting on me, I was now one against the two of Karin and Jolanta.

With 1km to go, Jolanta and Karin were only 15 seconds behind and then Christiane attacked me. I pushed on to the line, desperate to stay clear of the pair behind. I lost 29 seconds to Christiane, finishing just five seconds ahead of Jolanta and Karin. Christiane won overall by 12 seconds from Karin, I was third, at 2 minutes 29 seconds. I had lost the yellow jersey, but had made Christiane fight for it over every inch of three great cols. Christiane had ridden a superb race and deserved the jersey. To Helen, Stef, Martin and the girls, I owed this fantastic group as much as I owed Emma for the victory the year before.

I started the race believing I could make it three in a row and I had been defeated; the winner inside me was bitterly disappointed. But the spirit of how we went about it and how some sincere, long-term friends had so readily come to my aid and done all they could to help me, contrasted with my treatment by the BC WCPP and fired up my passion. In the weeks before Beijing, instead of being downbeat I became more determined. Back in Britain for the National Championships, held in Yorkshire, the race settled into a match between Emma Pooley and myself when we broke away from the bunch with about 20km left. We worked well together. Emma is a very strong rider, but lacks the speed required for the last finishing burst over the final 200m. I won and we came in three minutes ahead of the rest.

The other match race didn't occur. The previous year, I had a written commitment from Dave Brailsford, agreed by all parties, that Steve Peters was in charge of deciding how the ride-off for the time-trial places was conducted. During the time I was racing in France, I was aware that Emma and Sharon were practising on a course near to where Julian lived and suspected a ride-off being arranged, at minimal notice, on a course with which I was not familiar. I wrote an email to

Steve with a copy to Shane and Julian suggesting a far better course that featured a single big hill and single descent similar to what we would face in Beijing – my training run over the Bwlch. Within minutes Shane had responded, stating that he was in charge of selection and that *he* would choose the course. The response was exactly what I expected. Shane simply walked over previously confirmed arrangements. However, within 24 hours the problem had disappeared. Sharon Laws cracked her tibia during a filming ride being conducted for the BBC. She would be recovered for Beijing, but could not ride a TT selection event.

Later, Shane called a team meeting in Manchester to discuss tactics for the Olympic road race. Once again, I felt that my views were irrelevant. Before I had arrived, Shane, who had not been to a single women's race all year, had decided that Emma was to look for an opportunity to sneak away to a solo victory. So once we got to the circuit, I was to remain in the bunch, the false decoy for the others to watch. If this did not happen and it was a sprint, I could compete. Sharon was to go with any early break that occurred on the run from Beijing to the circuit. I felt an anger building inside me. I had come all this way without a team and constantly had to take on the might of the cycling world, single-handedly, and had delivered in virtually every race I rode for my country. Now, when there was finally some support on hand, it was being denied and my role relegated to that of a lure. Not only that, but this kind of tactic was doomed to failure. Emma had won continental races and always in the same way, a long solo attack. Her use of this tactic was now known and there was no way the strong teams would simply let Emma ride away to the win the biggest prize in cycling.

My fear was that if we actually went with this scenario,

Emma would attack and then be joined by four or five other riders. If the break stayed away, she would not be able to get gold, as her sprint was not good enough. Even if Emma could get away alone on the final climb, there was still a long way to the finish and her chances of staying away from committed chasers would be very slim. My only option would be to piggyback on anyone bridging up to the group. Sharon was as good as she could be. She only wanted to help Emma and me, but was new to this level of road cycling and we needed to have practised as a team much more.

I was enormously frustrated with this plan, and felt that my views were being ignored. The culture within British Cycling was always that the coaches knew best. I could challenge them, and repeatedly did, because I knew that my place on the team was secure. The other girls knew that the gatekeeper to their place on the team was the coach, and you did not need a degree in psychology to work out that an alliance with me was not a ticket to a long-term future on the team. I spoke out against Shane's plans but I was irrelevant. Great Britain's first serious Olympic women's road race team would ride as individuals wearing the same jersey.

I left the meeting and travelled back to Wales. The GB team were due to ride the Ras de Cymru amateur race to practise our 'team tactics', but the result was that we rode as three separate individuals throughout. At least it was a good block of intense racing. I spoke with Dad and we watched the video I'd made of my recce in Beijing and discussed the situation. We both agreed that the counter attack would come either towards the top of the climb or somewhere on the descent to the finish, and then the final 700m uphill sprint would be critical.

During the Ras de Cymru it hit me how much support there was for me in Wales. On one stage, we raced through a village where an entire school was lining the road cheering 'Go Nicole!' and holding out posters they had made depicting me in Beijing. BBC Wales interviewed the children on TV that night as they expressed their innocent support of me. I felt tears down my cheeks. It's amazing how inspired that can make you feel. I packed away any negativity and determined that I would just have to race the smartest race I could.

I was on a mission. Firstly, I went to Andy Walser's house in Tuscany for five days. I was riding around looking for a certain type of hill. After a ride in the morning, I set out in the late afternoon with a can of spray paint in my back pocket and found my 'Beijing Hill'. I used the speedo on the bike to measure and spray lines at 100m intervals up the hill. Then I got stuck in. I would ride steadily to the bottom of the hill, and then sprint flat out to the finish at the top, from the different distances, 100m, 200m, 300m, 400m, 500m, 600m and 700m. I was leaving nothing to chance. This was going to be the most important 700m of my career.

As I drove back to Switzerland, I saw all the team cars and race vehicles of the Giro d'Italia going the other way on the motorway, and it brought home the risk I was taking by not racing against my competitors there. But it also made me more determined than ever. I believed in my plan and was absolutely focused on the remaining four weeks, balancing hard sessions with recovery days, something that would not be possible for my rivals taking part in a long stage race. Just before getting home to Lugano, I stopped off at another 'Beijing Hill' that I had found and got the spray can out again. I matched this with another hill that replicated the 'long' hill on the circuit. Over the next three weeks, I followed a fairly standard pattern with Mauro pacing me up the 'long Beijing Hill', while in the evenings I did sprints to the 'finish' on the 'short Beijing Hill'.

Each Wednesday evening I raced the RB Brugg club criteriums.

One Saturday, Emma caught the train from where she lived in Switzerland and joined me at Lugano to train with me, in particular leading me out. It was a very nice and much appreciated gesture. We did it ourselves, away from any official camp. Maybe we would be there at the real finish together and we chatted and discussed what might happen. Both Emma and Sharon were late converts to cycling, Emma from triathlon and Sharon from mountain biking, and they had great physical attributes but were still developing race awareness. I had been racing practically my whole life and had honed my race instincts over many years. Not for the first time, I reflected that we should have been practising leadouts in real races for the past 15 months: the signals, the shouts, recognising the threats and opportunities, our positioning on the road. The last 800m of an Olympic road race is not the place to try out some new tactics for the first time. None of this was the fault of Emma or Sharon.

My race bike arrived in July and I tested it out on a four-hour Gran Fondo. I felt strong on the climbs, fast on the flat and also kept the intensity up all the way to the finish. I was ready. After crossing the line, I went in search of Mauro to see how he'd got on, as he was always on or near the podium. Mauro had won! We were so delighted together. Mauro had been fantastic and I couldn't have completed my training in this period without him. His everlasting good humour and warm-heartedness were a great strength throughout. It was a memory I shall never forget, seeing him so happy, taking his first prize at the Gran Fondo. Mauro never wanted great things for himself, so it was wonderful to see his face as he walked up to collect his award.

I was excited that everything seemed to be coming together at the right time. Mum and Dad came to meet me in London and spend the night with me. The next morning, my grandparents Maurice and Hazel arrived, together with Aunt Karen and my cousins Stephanie, Dan and Sean. We had a leisurely breakfast together before Mum and Dad took me to the airport.

After waving goodbye, I felt that I had entered an 'Olympic Bubble'. There were seven days to go and I wanted everything to go perfectly. The flight to Beijing went quickly and before long we were in the Olympic village. It was very compact, with high-rise apartment blocks and flats on each floor with two rooms, each with two beds. Sharon and Emma shared one flat, having a bedroom each to themselves, and I had the flat opposite, with my bedroom and lounge space which I quickly made to feel homely by laying out my good luck cards. I tried to stay awake as long as possible on the first evening and slept well, adjusting to the new time zone straightaway. I did a light session on the rollers and spent my first full day finding out the locations of the food hall, Team GB offices, medical zone and anything else I might need over the coming days.

Now that I was here, I wanted to get out on the course and test out the real Beijing hill. As it was over 80km away and I was the only GB cyclist who wanted to ride the course, I went with an official driver and interpreter who took me to the finishing circuit where they would wait and watch as I did my training. I did medium- and high-intensity intervals on the long hill and practised different ways of tackling the finishing hill. I knew that the race was going to be decided on that final climb to the line and I wanted to be as prepared as I could be. On the journey back to Beijing, I ran through the details of the course, the gradient, the corners and the changes in road surface, trying to memorise as much of it as possible.

Three days before the race, Sharon, Emma and I went to the official training session on the course. We had not practised a leadout train together for a sprint all season and certainly not attempted one in a race. I asked to practise a sprint. Julian led us out, followed by Sharon, then Emma and finally me. As I powered through the finish line, I felt very strong. It was an immense feeling; it was as if I could push harder and go faster, as if there were no limits. I had got my form spot on: *I could win*. Then an icy feeling came over me; this was not just a race I could win, but one that was now mine to throw away. I sought out Steve Peters and I told him things were so good that I was now very nervous, and I didn't know how to deal with the emotion. His advice was simple: I had done all the work so I could relax, I was an instinctive competitor and this would kick in once the race started. I should look after myself, make sure I was ready and enjoy it.

The next two days we did some very gentle rides, barely forcing the pedals round, just to make sure our legs were spinning nicely. I was robotic when it came to food and sleep, aware that I needed the right fuel in my body and my batteries fully charged. I passed the days writing postcards to friends and, when I had finished those, I had a look around what was on offer in the athlete zone of the village. There was a variety of low-stress activities, presumably designed to occupy bored or nervous athletes like me. I passed the time learning to write some words in Chinese. With the cycling road events so early in the programme, the GB cycling team watched the opening ceremony together on television, resting. We marvelled at the choreography and scale of it. Truly we were taking part in the greatest show on earth. It made me feel very humble and very grateful. I thought of those children at the side of the road in

Wales so far away, holding their posters, and knew that they would be watching as well.

The men's road race took place on the Saturday, and the women would race on Sunday. The last lap of the men's saw the bunch catch a long solo breakaway and then the attacks up the long climb saw a rapid selection in the bunch. The finale was contested by a group of six riders, with Samuel Sanchez of Spain taking the gold. There was no GB rider in that group, nor for that matter in any of the groups. Not one male GB rider finished.

That evening Shane took us through the tactics as he saw them, again. 'Sharon, cover the moves on the flat . . . Emma, attack on the main climb on the last lap . . . Nicole, be ready for the finish.' This meeting, led by a coach who had still not seen a single international women's race all year, was far removed from a proper professional team meeting prior to a critical race, where the talk would be as much about competitors' likely moves as our own plans. I looked on. For weeks I had been running through many different scenarios in my head weeks, storing away lots of permutations and processing the likely outcomes. The meeting was a different distraction.

The main thing I was telling myself was to save my energy as much as possible. In Athens I had raced well, but rather than be the rider making the attack that splits the race apart, I would follow the moves and save my energy for a big move of my own late in the race. Emma, having recently won the Tour de Bretagne, would be watched and reaction to her bid for glory would be guaranteed.

I was aware that riders were going to rise to the occasion; people will ride out of their skin for the biggest prize in cycling and also take more risks. The field was small, restricted to just 63 riders, with countries limited to three riders maximum. However, in terms of the Olympics, this was the event with the largest number of individual competitors and of the longest duration.

I packed my bag during the day and checked it again in the evening. I had food in the fridge ready for breakfast, which would save me a journey to the food hall, and I was about as ready as I could be. I rang Andy and then rang my parents, touching base for the last time and checking to see if they had picked up on anything new after watching the men's race. I went to bed, falling asleep soon after; a clock was running but I was not disturbed by its tick. I woke up to grey skies and puddles around the village. We knew it might rain and Andy had prepared my 'rain wheels' for this eventuality, to complement the dry wheels he had designed with wheel-builder Haider Knall of Haico. I had breakfast, listened to music then went over to the food hall for my pre-race pasta meal. I was quite happy in my own world, not being distracted by what was happening around me.

At the course, we found our tent and got ready. I had to decide if I wanted my rain wheels or dry wheels. The staff at the finish circuit said it was raining, while at the start it was overcast but not raining. A lot could change in three hours, so I decided to go with my dry weather wheels as they were lightest and I didn't think the thin tread would cause me any problems. I wanted every advantage I could get.

I looked at my watch; silently, it indicated that it was time. On the start line, I gathered myself and went straight into race mode, all my senses heightened and taking in everything, watching for every little sign of body language from the other riders. The gun fired and we were off. I wanted to be near enough to the front to watch what was going on and stay out of trouble, but at the same time find some shelter behind other riders to avoid tiring myself out too early. Although the course made its way past the historic sights of Beijing, Tiananmen Square and many temples, we were almost unaware. Sightseeing could be left until afterwards. We had 80km to ride until we reached the circuit, and it was not long before it started raining and we were soon soaked from the rain as well as the spray off the wheels around us.

Those who had been expecting sweltering temperatures like the previous day might have been upset. I didn't care, I didn't feel it; my mission was to win this race and I was certainly no stranger to riding in the rain. There were a few exploratory attacks on the way to the circuit, but nothing that stayed away. I stayed near the front as we rode out through the big puddles to the circuit. Before the feed zone, I made sure that I was at the front; it was raining and there was a high possibility of a crash. As we started the circuit, Team USA rode hard at the front, causing riders to get dropped from the back. Eventually, they eased, and as they did so my old sparring partner from that first Junior World Championship in Plouay, Natalia Boyarskaya, attacked. Who would respond so far from the finish?

The security was tight for the road race course and the whole of the main climb had no spectators on it, creating an eerie and creepy atmosphere. We could hear each other's breathing and every gear change, sounds normally drowned out by the crowds. We were on the finishing circuit, so I made a quick resumé of the situation. Were my rivals riding as I expected? Were there any potential threats from riders who don't ride the European circuit, such as the Chinese? I needed to watch out for any places where there was a sudden change of course due to the positioning of security barriers. It seemed that I was not alone in carrying out an appraisal of the situation, as nobody decided to chase Natalia.

The circuit was 23km, and basically consisted of a long 11km climb followed by a descent on a wide new road, at the bottom of which were toll booths to negotiate followed by the 700m climb to the finish. The feed zone was located just after the finish. Natalia did the whole of the climb by herself and the gap grew, time checks indicating 1:04, then 1:46. Everybody was watching each other as we crested the climb. As a lone rider, Natalia was going to lose time on the descent, as a big group taking turns to provide slipstream to each other would easily move faster on such a wide sweeping road.

On the descent I watched Emma move to the front, preparing for her moment. We were coming down to the toll booths and there were plenty of white lines on the road, which can be treacherous in the wet. Then I heard a crash behind. Unfortunately, Sharon was caught up in it. Watching the video afterwards, it was a bad fall, but true to character, Sharon got back up and chased hard, pursuing the peloton and passing stragglers for the rest of the race. Emma rode to the front and as others took their bottles in the feed zone, she rode away to launch her bid for victory. It was a good move, she now had the whole of the climb to extend her lead before the descent, and she could pick up Natalia ahead and they could work together.

Ahead, Emma tapped out a steady rhythm, pacing herself; she was riding well and the gap opened. Then Tatiana Guderzo of Italy cleverly jumped away from the bunch, taking no one with her. If I jumped up to Tatiana, I could sit on her, but with two Brits up the road the peloton would recognise the danger, combine forces and chase us down and Emma would have fired her best shot to no effect. I had to sit tight.

Soon Tatiana, Emma and Natalia joined together and were riding as a trio at the front with still most of the climb to come.

This was now the dangerous situation I had tried to explain at the team briefing. Emma would not be able to win from this group, as Tatiana was the better sprinter and Natalia was probably as strong as Emma. They were good riders, and being only three, they would work together to get a medal each. However, it wouldn't be gold for GB. Four years earlier at Athens, the team had the specific goal of working to support me, but unfortunately there was no one capable of helping me in the last couple of laps. Four years later in London, the team would be working to support Lizzie Armitstead. Now in Beijing, with a strong team, we had been told not to work for one rider. Sharon had crashed and Emma was up the road in a move that would definitely not bring a gold medal.

However, the peloton saw the danger of the new situation and knew that those three were perfectly capable of staying away. Judith Arndt for Germany responded, so I moved onto her wheel with Trixi Worrack, Judith's team-mate, following me. I needed to stay in this spot to disrupt the two working together. Trixi then went to the front and this time Tatiana's Italian team-mate, Noemi Cantele, slotted in behind Trixi, helping disturb the chase. Judith was behind Noemi, with me riding fourth. I was feeling good and ready for the next phase of the race as the Germans powered on the chase. All around I could hear the sound of heavy breathing, as the pace set by Judith was taking its toll. I was puzzled that Judith did not try and jump across on her own, which could only mean she was riding for Trixi today. If Trixi was to be led out by Judith, then she would be a possible wheel to take in the sprint. Judith drove on and made the junction to the breakaway. Emma and

I glanced at each other as the break was caught. It was clear that her race was now finished.

The pace had been fast as the Germans chased, but it had at least been steady. Now, everyone left in the front group was back in with a chance, and so there was attack and counter attack which caused constant accelerations that opened gaps in the string of riders. I made sure that I was always near the front; even though many of my efforts would be wasted, I could not afford to have any regret about missing the right move.

Zulfiya Zabirova attacked, countered by Judith with me following. Then Christiane Soeder attacked and Trixi went after her. I immediately reacted – no need to hesitate with those two. Tatiana joined us, but then there was a slight easing from Christiane and we were caught. Zulfiya tried again, and once more Judith was the first to react.

All the time I had to have my eyes everywhere, watching out for an attack but also checking on the response of others. The Swedes, Susanne Ljungskog and Emma Johansson, were near the front but had not made a single move. I remembered Hamilton where Susanne had done nothing all race and then attacked into the last corner. The Australians had already lost Katherine Bates and maybe they were weakened from the earlier chase. I hadn't seen Marianne Vos at the front; she was obviously riding further down the group, relying on her teammates to close down any breakaway that looked threatening. There were also other individuals who still hadn't made a move.

Modesta Vzesniauskaite rode hard on the front, Emma J followed and I followed her. The strange sensation of riding the finale of such an important race without crowds emphasised the sounds of heavy breathing all around me. We were approaching the top of the climb and time was running out for the breakaway specialists.

Tatiana attacked again. She was certainly on a mission today; she had been in the break with Emma and Natalia but was still trying to get away. Emma J jumped around Modesta to chase her. I went with Emma J but saw that Susanne was on my wheel. Emma J pulled over to signal for me to take up the chase, but with Susanne on my wheel it was a move that would have left me open to a counter attack by either one of them. Tatiana was powering on ahead by herself. Then Christiane came from fifth wheel back, with Linda Villumsen of Denmark, so I chased and Emma J followed me. Behind was Modesta, but she was losing contact. We swung right and left onto the motorway and a gap had opened up behind. I shouted to the others that this was our chance. I did a really hard turn on the front to try to increase the gap and make sure the others knew I was committed to this. We soon caught Tatiana and there were five of us, one each from Italy, Sweden, Denmark, Austria and GB. The key missing countries were The Netherlands, Germany, Australia and Switzerland. Judith had been extremely strong earlier on the climb. Was she running out of strength? If Marianne tried to jump across to us, could she still be strong enough in the sprint to the line?

We had gained our initial lead while out of sight of the bunch as we went round the bends, but we would now be easily visible on the wide three-lane road. We couldn't afford any hesitation, we had to totally commit ourselves and we couldn't afford a passenger. Fortunately, everyone understood that three medals out of five was much better odds than three out of 20, if caught. Although in theory the numerically superior group behind us could have caught us, they were not able to use their numbers effectively, while we five were fully committed to staying away. I had to look at the video to see exactly what went on behind. Susanne and Noemi are to the fore, often lying in second wheel in the line, particularly Susanne, disrupting the chase with a team-mate in the break ahead. After that, Judith does a huge proportion of the chasing behind. Zulfiya helps and Trixi does a bit, along with one of the French riders. It was road racing at its fascinating best. It was going to be a close-run thing between the riders who had missed out on the move and we who were in the break, but 'fortune favours the bold' and we now held the advantage.

Going down the descent flat out demanded total concentration, and I only dared the occasional slightest glance backwards. At least the gap seemed to be remaining constant; we weren't gaining but neither was the bunch. As we came down towards the toll booths I indulged myself with another glance back to check the gap. It seemed to be about 20 seconds; we were not going to get caught now. This was the part of the circuit where Sharon had gone down on the slippery white lines. I wasn't going to repeat my Athens error and decided that I would be better off going through this part on my own, away from the others, especially as I was on my dry weather tyres.

I was confident that my absence would not trigger an attack, because anyone going from that far out would just be providing a leadout to the others. As I came round the bend into the finishing straight, I needed to catch the others before they started their sprint. It was going to be a very long sprint for me. I was catching them quickly and took the risk of taking the lead and the inside line around the last bend. There was just enough room for me and it would be shorter than going round the other side of them. I needed to carry my speed to get through that gap before anyone noticed and closed it.

I was through on the right-hand side and was now leading out the sprint. There was still 200m to go; Emma had got on my wheel. My legs were already burning from the effort I had made to get into this position, but I wasn't going to let the pain stop me. This was the moment I'd been dreaming of since I was 12, fighting it out for the Olympic gold medal. I had taken a risk in leading out so early, but I was ready to push myself to new levels of physical pain to win. Whatever the others had, I would have to match it.

I focused on a point just after the finish line and gave it absolutely everything I had. I sensed that Emma and Tatiana were just behind me, getting ready to sprint past me. With 150m to go, I made an extra effort. I kept going, going, going, my eyes locked on to that point just after the line. They were still behind me, but I was focused on giving everything to get to that line, my own personal battle to get every ounce of energy out of my body as I concentrated on each pedal stroke.

I crossed the line. I looked right and I looked left, double-checking with my eyes what my senses were telling me.

I had won! I was Olympic champion!

I screamed with delight, my hands still clenched on the bars, and I looked down.

'You did it!'

This moment meant everything to me. My whole body was exploding with emotions: the joy of winning, the burning in my legs, the tingling in my teeth, my rib cage searing with pain and the wonder of a dream coming true. I collapsed off my bike on to the barriers, gasping to get some air into my lungs. After about three breaths, the realisation hit me again that I had done it. I was swept up by the British staff, jumping around and hugging everyone. I looked for Emma and Sharon and gave them a huge embrace.

The rest of the day was a blur of excitement. Soaked but all beaming smiles, Tatiana, Emma Johansson and I lined up for the medal ceremony. A medal at an Olympic Games is a huge feat, whatever the colour, and we were all pleased for each other and enjoying the moment. I was struggling to take everything in: the flash of photographers, the scenery, with the Great Wall of China looming around us, the rain, the colours. It was all perfect. When the medal was hung around my neck, I knew it was for real. I took the medal in my hands and looked at it. It was huge, so shiny, and the detail of the engraving on the front with the Greek goddess of victory was very special. I'd never seen an Olympic medal up close before.

I applauded Emma and Tatiana as they received their medals and then the British national anthem was played. It was emotional, I felt like I was going to burst with happiness. I called Andy and my parents – it sounded like half the village was inside the house. I was then whisked off to the media centre for interviews and found out I had won the first gold medal of Beijing for Team GB, and the 200th in history. I like round numbers, but as far as I was concerned, I had won the only medal that mattered to me. At 10pm we called an end to the interviews and headed back to the village. There was a joyous welcoming party to greet me as I got back to Team GB headquarters, including Dr Rod Jaques who had been treating me and my knees for the last five years. I went back to our apartment block and the whole cycling team had waited up to welcome me back. I felt slightly overwhelmed; it was wonderful to share the moment together with everybody and I hoped that they could fulfil their dreams too and experience the feelings I had.

In the time-trial, Emma Pooley did a great ride to take the silver medal, 24 seconds behind American Kristin Armstrong, and actually was faster than Kristin on the climbing part of the course. Karin Thürig was third at 59 seconds. Although I had improved since the Grande Bouclé and finished 1:20 behind Karin, that was only good enough for 15th place, one place behind Marianne Vos, who incidentally had won the sprint for sixth place in the road race from the chasing group behind us.

Sharon, Emma and I then enjoyed a glass of champagne that night to celebrate our success. Over the next few days, I tried to take in as much as possible of the Olympics. I was fortunate that Clare Dixon, the first girl to follow me to a team in Italy and a fellow rider from the Junior World Championships in 2000, was there covering the games for Channel M. We spent time together sightseeing in Beijing, taking in both the culture and the games.

I had another very important race coming up – the World Championships – which were to be held in Varese, Italy. So I left Beijing and flew back to Lugano to join Andy and start training again. We headed to Tuscany for five days of training including a Gran Fondo. I then travelled to London, arriving at Heathrow to meet the rest of the Olympic team flying in from Beijing, and joined in the post-Olympic celebrations. I was the only gold medallist who had come out of the Games and resumed training, and so I was the only one in London waiting with Gordon Brown, the prime minister, for the team to touch down. My mind flashed back to the last time I was talking to the British prime minister. Nobody ruined my day this time.

There were many highlights for me. Being reunited with Mum, Dad and Craig, all together for the first time in three years, was very special. The 'Welcome Home' in Cardiff for the Welsh athletes, where the endless crowds filled the area in front of the Welsh Assembly in Cardiff Bay, was incredible. I was asked to speak to the crowds on behalf of all the athletes and then again, once inside the Assembly, to respond to the first minister of Wales.

Perhaps best of all were the celebrations in Wick, where the village turned into a carnival for the day. We started with an open-top bus tour around the local villages, escorted by well over 100 cyclists from the local cycling clubs. I stood on the top deck, waving and being waved to, while behind me a brass band played. I saw that so many people had made such an effort to decorate their gardens and houses in an Olympic theme to celebrate my achievement. I remembered those children who had stood at the side of the road before I went to Beijing, many of them now dressed in costumes with Olympic motifs, and I was so pleased that I had been able to live up to their hopes and expectations.

Then there were speeches and the national anthem, followed by events for the kids in the park with bike races, climbing frames, water slides and endless activities. The villagers had all donated into a fund and every activity was free for children. The County Council generously provided a marquee, in case it rained. The day ended with the unveiling of a plaque in the village hall that hangs next to the plaque unveiled in 2002 marking my junior world titles. Family, friends and so many who had helped me in the past came from far and wide. In a UK summer notorious for its appalling weather, that one day we were bathed in glorious, warm sunshine, from beginning to end. It was the most perfect occasion.

I returned to Lugano very focused on the World Championships. During my 'rest' in Wick, I had still trained every day, for example getting up at 5.30am to do two hours' training before going to Cardiff for the celebrations that day. I was deadly serious about the World Championships. I met up with Mauro to drive round the course and make a DVD for my British team-mates and myself. The next day, we rode the course and I started to get a feel for the hills and the final kilometres; in fact the close proximity to Lugano meant I had probably never recce'd a course so intensely, riding it two or three times a week. World Championships in Italy are always very special, as there are huge, knowledgeable crowds with fan clubs for the individual riders. The course featured two climbs each lap, and I was sure that it was going to come down to a sprint from a small select group. Neither of the hills was par- ticularly long or steep, so would not by themselves be decisive, but they certainly would allow riders to make attacks.

We had an excellent preparation race planned, the Tour de l'Ardeche. We would be riding as a GB team – Sharon Laws, Emma Pooley, Jess Allen, Catherine Hare, Rachel Heal and myself. I spoke to Julian and advised him that I wanted to practise sprints all through the race and needed the leadouts to perfect them. Julian consulted, and the instruction came back that both Emma and Sharon were to ride for GC and so were not to participate in any sprint training supporting me, but Rachel, Catherine and Jess could. I could not have asked any more of those three girls. We did brilliantly. I took a sprint stage win and we contested many prime sprints. Emma rode splendidly to come second overall.

Our national ranking was now such that GB qualified seven riders for the World Championships, so there was even room for another rider to join us in Varese. The British Cycling coaching staff then decided not to select Catherine or Rachel, who had worked so tirelessly to support me through this Tour. They did select Lizzie Armitstead, which meant we had two vacant places. Despite winning Olympic gold, it seemed that old British Cycling habits would never die. The GB men, who had not finished a single rider at Beijing, were qualified with six berths and took a full complement of riders, including drug cheat David Millar.

There were another couple of unhelpful events leading up to the World Championships. When I finished the Tour de l'Ardeche, the headset on my bike needed replacing. This is basic bicycle maintenance, but apparently there was no spare available and no one could make a decision to go and buy one. Despite my urgings, it continued to remain unrepaired.

There is a photograph of me during my first time in Holland in 1995, aged 12, when I'm riding against Joost van Leijen, who has a race skin suit. I took the message to heart. Four years later, for my ill-fated British Championship, I had a new race skin suit, which gave me an advantage over the Lottery-funded WCPP riders that year. In 2000, when Dad was told that all I would have would be a standard GB jersey and shorts for the World Championships, he stated he would pay to get one made in GB colours, pointing out that 12-year-olds in Holland understood the advantages. Then, embarrassed, BC did get one produced. For Athens and Beijing, I had insisted on a skin suit, as on many other occasions, but despite asking for a skin suit for Varese, there was none. Fortunately, I had brought my previous GB skin suit with me, so if they couldn't supply the new one, I said I would wear that instead. This was not acceptable to Dave Brailsford, who was protecting the new sponsor's rights, and so we got into a stand-off.

In the past, Mum had sewed logo badge after badge onto Mick Ives's jerseys for me, as sponsors failed to match their side of the bargain, but this was now post-Beijing 2008. There were TV programmes investigating how British Cycling and its 'Secret Squirrels' maximised each 'marginal gain', with vast quantities of the public's money spent on technical investigations to ensure the country's finest had the best chance. Fortunately, Emma Pooley had her sewing kit with her and came to the rescue; a Sky logo was cut out of a jersey and sewn onto my old skin suit.

I put to the back of my mind these injustices. I needed to concentrate on the forthcoming race. We were going to be in for a great contest, there were many potential winners and most countries had six riders, so it was a big field. On the very first lap, there was an attack which, unusually, included some big hitters. Kristin Armstrong, the Beijing time-trial gold medallist, attacked with former World champion Diana Ziliute, who had won a stage at the Tour de l'Ardeche. There was a reaction from the other teams and a 13-strong group formed which included Lizzie Armitstead for GB, three Germans, although one then dropped back to the bunch, and representatives from all the strong nations, with the notable exception of the Swiss and Dutch.

This was a very good move for me, as it forced Marianne Vos's team-mates to chase as the rest of us looked on. This was no ordinary early race break and there was a real possibility of it going the whole distance. Diana had her Lithuanian team-mate Jolanta Polikeviciute with her, and the rest of her team were very active in constantly going to the front of the bunch and disrupting the Dutch and Swiss chase. In fact, the lead was increasing so much that even the teams who had riders in the break had, in the end, to help the chase, otherwise we would have gifted the race to Kristin or Diana.

The break stayed away until the last lap. As we caught the break, I asked Lizzie to take me up to the front of the bunch, so that I could be there for the start of the climb. I latched onto her wheel and she drove smoothly past many riders, taking me to the front. It was a super effort on her part, and just at the right time before Marianne attacked. The attack was so hard that only the strongest and those near the front were able to respond. We were a group of six: Susanne Ljungskog and Emma Johansson for Sweden, Judith Arndt and Trixi Worrack for Germany, Marianne Vos for the Netherlands and me. Noemi Cantele, riding in front of her home crowd, had missed the move and would spend the rest of the race trying to catch us. Unfortunately for Susanne, she caught her front wheel in the rear mechanism of Trixi's bike and lost some spokes, so we were down to five, with the Germans having superiority in numbers.

No one was waiting for the finish and there followed one of the most exciting finales to a race that I have ever had the privilege to participate in. Each rider was capable of winning and each had a deep-seated motivation to win. Trixi had been beaten for the gold by Marianne in 2006, Judith had sacrificed her own chances at Beijing (she finished 41st), Emma had narrowly lost out to me in the Olympics and of course Marianne had been the red-hot favourite for the Olympic road race and had finished off the podium, a feeling I knew only too well.

From the formation of the break to the finish, there was not a single moment where I was not either attacking or responding to the attack of someone else. Every one of us put in a potential race-winning move prior to the finale. Every single move was countered. All senses were fully alert. It was necessary to constantly monitor your position in relation to everyone else and to our place on the circuit. Each move required a calculation: do I react immediately and give an easy ride to the person on my wheel, or wait to see if someone else will chase instead? I knew that any of the others was capable of going the distance to the finish if you gave them more than a few seconds' lead.

Marianne made another strong attack on the second hill. She had completely changed her tactics since Beijing and was going to try to make a lone break, or at least further thin down our group. She managed to get a ten-second gap and only through the dedicated efforts of the Germans was she brought back.

It is impossible to describe what followed in a blow-by-blow account. It was simply the five best riders in the world battling it out for the honour of being able to put on that World champion's jersey at the end of the race. Every time an attack was nullified, I would take a look at all the others. Who was starting to suffer, who seemed fired up and ready to attack again? If one attacks, who will respond? All the time we were getting closer and closer to the finish. It was a good job I had been training on the circuit for the last few weeks and knew every bend and turn of those final few kilometres and could concentrate on the tactics.

I was on the front when Emma attacked with just over a kilometre to go, but instead of chasing I simply moved sideways as if to say, 'I'm not chasing. Someone else can.' Marianne, Judith and I watched each other as Emma pulled away. As we slowed, Trixi attacked from behind us to chase Emma. Still, Marianne, Judith and I watched each other. It was the coolest manoeuvre I had ever made in a big race, the desperation of previous World Championships not there. I was not cracking. None of us were, but if we stayed like this we would be riding for bronze.

Finally, Marianne cracked and attacked, and I dived for her wheel. Emma was still alone ahead, with Trixi about 50m behind her, and the three of us about 50m behind Trixi. As Marianne caught Trixi, it brought Judith back in play. She attacked from the back and I jumped straight on to Judith's wheel with Marianne now following me. Judith was now bearing down on Emma. As we turned left into the finishing straight, Judith stormed past Emma and it was now going to come down to a three-way sprint for gold.

I had gifted Marianne the best position of being on my wheel, but for once I was coming into the finishing straight not having spent the last lap chasing down most of the attacks by myself. I had remained cool and forced Marianne to do much of the work. I was watching closely for signs that Judith would kick and launch the sprint, while also glancing back and checking on Marianne, in case she jumped first from behind while also anticipating my own opportunity. I didn't need to maximise shelter now, I needed to leave a gap so that if Judith didn't go, I would have enough manoeuvring room to avoid being closed in by Marianne, or accelerate into Judith's slip-stream if I made my own move.

The road bent round to the right at 200m to go, and as it straightened out Marianne made her attack. She made a really hard acceleration and was in front going for the win. The line was coming up fast. Was there still time for me to accelerate, catch her and then get in front? At 100m to go, I was along-side. The current and previous world No.1s were battling it out in the last few metres, just the sort of heavyweight battle I had dreamed of. I gave it absolutely everything and passed Marianne in the last 50m, with enough time to fling my hands in the air in a victory salute.

I had ridden the best race of my life. The elation and joy of winning came flooding through me, and all this in front of a crowd that was as close to a home town as I could possibly get;

the passion of the Italians and their love of cycling reached out to me. All those years of frustration and disappointment were finally laid to rest.

On the podium, I wanted to absorb every single moment. I looked at that jersey and medal as they brought it across to me. There is a photograph of me slowly pushing my head through the neck opening of the jersey. I was pulling on the jersey very slowly and deliberately. Under the jersey, my eyes were shut tight. I was ten years old, charging up and down the hills after watching Robert Millar's heroic ride, daring to dream. Now I was the first person ever to achieve the double of Olympic and World champion in the same year. I was savouring this moment every bit as much as pulling on that first polka dot jersey in Holland at my first international race. It had been a very long, very hard journey.

CHAPTER TWENTY-ONE
Vision 1 Racing and Beyond

I spent the evening in Varese where there was a fantastic World Championship Festival. We British girls went out and found a nice restaurant to dine in and Andy joined us. A number of riders were retiring and I sought out the Aussies, and Oenone Wood in particular, as I wanted to congratulate her on having been a fine competitor and rival throughout our careers. It was a great evening.

That night I didn't sleep, I was so excited and thought of the race and our celebrations. I remembered the time the British official stopped us going out after I won my first World title. I recalled giving my Mick Ives jersey and badges to Mum and reminding her, as I went to bed, where to sew them on to cover up the logos, then waking up to find it at the foot of my bed, all perfectly done. Mick was sincere, stretching a tiny budget to achieve more than could ever have been expected, always enthusiastic and helpful.

I was World and Olympic champion, British Cycling was receiving millions of pounds of Lottery money for the administration of the sport and yet they cared so little that they could not get me the right kit to wear, kit that a 12-year-old could have at the Helmond Youth Tour and all the other things. They couldn't sort out a replacement headset on my bike, while my bike for

Beijing had not arrived until July – at least it was earlier than the time-trial machine for Athens, but it was still too late.

We couldn't get a whole team entered for the World Championships, leaving two women's places blank. Why? By comparison, not a single man had finished from the full male team we had at Beijing in the road race, while Sharon had crashed, but cut and bleeding she had chased alone to the end. At Varese the next day, a full team of GB men would line up comprising professional riders Chris Froome, Geraint Thomas, David Millar, Ian Stannard, Stephen Cummings and domestic rider Russell Downing. Of this illustrious list, Russell was the only one to finish, crossing the line in the main group in 28th place, 4:53 down on the winner. He at least recognised that when you wore a national jersey you were representing your country and not yourself. He wouldn't get rich and nobody would write about his efforts in the newspapers, but that was not going to get in the way of him giving it everything he had, just like Sharon.

And what about that change in my programme for the build-up to Beijing? Right from the start, it was obvious that Team Halfords was not going to be a team that would enable me to complete a road season. Why was Rob Hayles in it? It enabled British Cycling to place a tick in the box that they had supported a women's road programme and satisfied an incurious press, preoccupied with men. But if the calendar had started the season looking thin, the cancelling of the team going to the women's Tour de France and replacing it with evening club time-trials exposed the reality. Why didn't they want me riding at the Tour de France?

After my second Tour win in 2007, the organiser of the women's Tour de France, Pierre Boué, always keen to follow up any possible avenue of promotion to keep the race going, approached London. In 2007, the men's Tour de France had started with the 'Grand Départ' in London city centre. Boué obviously thought that with the women's Tour having a two-time British winner, they might want to follow up the 2007 start for men with a 2008 start for the women's Tour in London. I have no doubt that the budget Boué would have been talking about would have been a fraction of that lavished on the men. Apparently, he made an excellent presentation to London and received a good response from the Mayor's office. They would just need to check it out with British Cycling. The answer came back to London from British Cycling at Manchester that they should not support a London depart for the women's Tour. The project was dead.

From where I was at that moment in time, it was obvious that British Cycling was organised by men for men. The critical roles at BC all went to men, and the 2001 experiment with Peg Hill was just a distant memory, a forgotten high point. On the track, a single female to pose with the men and whose star could not in any way be a threat to their collective machismo, a star whose glow could only enhance the aura around the men, was fine. But if they gave oxygen to me, it only served to bring attention to the woeful performance of the men on the road, and the primacy of the road scene over track was probably not something either British Cycling or the BBC was keen to promote to the public. The BBC had a long-term deal for televising track events and BC was riding high, maximising publicity for its track riders, so my story did not fit well with that narrative. In the months following Beijing, it was almost like an industry had been created, as day after day the papers were full of how 'marginal gains' of the track cycling team should be applied to every facet of enterprise, but that was only a part of the whole story.

Now, in the 'holiday' atmosphere of these championships – where I was doing everything to win a gold medal and so many of the British team seemed more interested in enjoying a social event at the public's expense – all the talk was of the massive Sky sponsorship that was coming into the sport and plans for what they were going to do with the money. I didn't need a crystal ball back in 2008 to predict that, by the time of writing six years later, while millions have been poured into a system to convert the male non-finishers at Beijing and Varese into world beaters, virtually nothing has come the way of the female road riders, whether it was Emma, Lizzie, Sharon or me.

Post-Beijing some media pundits, those who ignored all that the British girls achieved on the road, criticised British Cycling, denigrating their achievements on the track as being peripheral to the sport, due to the fact that so few countries had a serious attitude to track racing. Undoubtedly, British Cycling were somewhat stung by such criticisms. These pundits would state, when Mark Cavendish won the World Championship Road Race in 2011, that this was the first time a British rider had achieved such a feat since 1965 – thus ignoring the achievements of Beryl Burton in 1967, Mandy Jones in 1982, and my own exploits.

A similar account would follow in respect of the Tour. Some within British Cycling would foster the convenient narrative – 'we cut our teeth with success on the track and then moved our skill set to the road' – because it placed the management team at the centre of all success. To sustain that account they had to diminish the independent successes of both Emma Pooley and me. Even if Team Halfords ran into the next year, I would be a fool to think that it would be backed to run a serious continental road season. The last 12 months had shown that, even if a tilt at a major stage race was planned into the team calendar months in advance, those in charge thought nothing of cancelling the trip at virtually no notice, and substituting it with a club evening ten-mile TT, without any consultation. These were unassailable facts of life. Well, I would never have a better chance to do something to change it, so that night I decided to give it my best shot. Unfortunately I would fail miserably.

The most obvious thing to do would have been to use my status as World and Olympic champion to negotiate for the best year's pay of my life and join an established team. I might even have been able to persuade them to allow me to bring a couple of GB riders, but I couldn't expect them to create a team composed mainly of GB riders. My dream was to create a team that would act as a development opportunity for young female British riders. I wanted others to have an easier route than I had. So much talent had been lost, ground down by the attitudes of British Cycling. I knew I would only ever have this chance once to do something this big in my life, and I wanted to take it, regardless of the men in the sport around me and regardless of the risk to me. They didn't care, and I knew I would be finished in the sport before they would be replaced by people who would care.

I felt that with a good number of British riders we would be able to attract some UK sponsors. I had plenty of experience from riding with teams on how to organise one, and sitting there on the border of Italy and Switzerland it seemed to me that all it needed was to find some Italian enthusiasm, combined with Swiss organisation and British determination, and we could have a world-class team. Not wanting to assume that British Cycling would be completely uninterested in my idea, I set up a meeting with Dave Brailsford. He listened politely, wished me luck, but there was no interest from BC. The men's road team, Team Sky, was taking shape.

Andy had many good ideas and was a great driver for the project. Helen Wyman joined in straightaway, with her husband Stefan as *directeur sportif*. I had great memories of how they had both supported me earlier in the year in my ill-fated attempt to retain my Tour title. Stefan had a good way of working with riders and did not let his relationship with Helen get in the way of what he needed to do to support others professionally. We attracted a mixture of young and experienced riders from Britain, Holland, France and Australia.

The three youngest riders were headed by Dani King, who had just turned 18. She had been on the BC Olympic Development Programme as a sprinter but was then removed and not offered any way forward in the sport by British Cycling. I was as grateful she could join us, as was she for the opportunity provided. She has since gone on to win Olympic and World gold medals in the team pursuit. Katie Curtis was turning 20 and had already finished eighth in the World Track Championships, while Jackie Garner was 19 and had won a collection of Welsh junior road and track titles.

Gabriella Day, a cyclo-cross rider and quite handy on the road, joined along with French rider Christel Ferrier-Bruneau, who had finished 13th in the Beijing road race and fourth in the Cyclo-Cross World Championships. Eighteen-year-old Aurore Verhoeven, also of France, who was fifth in the junior world road race, was so keen to ride with me that she had given me her CV the previous year at the women's Tour, telling me, if ever there was a spot for her on a team in which I was riding to let her know. Vicki Whitelaw had been Australia's road cyclist of the year in 2008, in a season that included victories in stages at the Giro d'Italia and the Tour de

L'Aude, while Debby van den Berg was a hard-working *domestique* from Holland. The assembled team represented great potential and everyone who joined us was fully committed and could not have been more enthusiastic.

Finding financial backers to provide the money we needed to pay for logistics as we moved around Europe from race to race, was a different matter. There was plenty of interest, telephone calls, emails and meetings, but no commitments. The media interest following the Olympics had dried up, and the enthusiasm with which we launched the project was turning into the realism that finding sponsors was going to prove much more difficult than we imagined.

The problem was countering the perception that no one was interested in women's cycling. Sponsors want attention on their products in return for their money; not just great results from the riders but media attention, and in particular television coverage. Women's cycling, like so many female sports, did not receive the same media attention as the men and the only televised events were the world titles and the Olympics. It was a chicken-and-egg scenario: we needed the coverage to increase interest and convince sponsors, but the media always cited lack of interest, and sponsors would always fail to commit until the interest was proved.

I met with the BBC sports department and discussed how they might follow the road scene. I even explained that the UCI TV rights to the women's World Cup were available and that they would not have to invest very much because each race was already covered by the national broadcasters in each country. The result was a polite refusal. They felt that their coverage of track cycling gave quite enough time to cycling as far as they were concerned. As I write this, I can only marvel at how the nation and the BBC have now taken the sport to their hearts, better than even I could have imagined, but unfortunately in 2008 and 2009 my voice could not be heard.

To add to the problems of finding sponsors, we were hit by two major events. The financial crisis of 2008 affected everyone, but in particular it led to companies cutting back on their easiest variable cost, marketing and advertising. It was not the time to ask companies to try a new medium of communication, sports sponsorship.

The other was yet more doping scandals in the men's cycling scene. Among that year's highlights was Riccardo Riccò. Riccò had come second to Alberto Contador in the Giro and then won Stage 6 of the Tour at Super Besse. The sporting press were full of it, a classic ballet in the mountains. *Cycling Weekly* eulogised about Riccò and how he had stormed to a great win. But then came rumours that he had failed a standard haematocrit test. Riccò and his team stated that he had a naturally high haematocrit level of 51%, and like all good individuals so unfortunate to suffer with such an entirely natural condition, he had a certificate issued by those responsible for the governance of the sport, giving him exemption. All was well.

The year before, as Emma P, Priska and I were giving absolutely everything on the Col d'Aspin, virtually nobody from the cycling press thought our denouement on the final mountain of the final day was worth a column centimetre. Now one year later, on that same mountain and three days after his initial heroics, Riccò produced another magic moment to have the cycling press filling their pages with superlatives describing his second stage win. Four days later, it was announced that Riccò had tested positive and he became the fourth rider of the Tour to be evicted from the race that year for doping violations.

Of course, like the rest, he couldn't go without the whole circus. First denial, then 'honest' contrite confession and a statement that 'it is only fair that I pay'. His lawyers persuaded the Court of Arbitration of Sport (CAS) to get the now 'contrite and reformed' Riccò's ban reduced to 20 months. Needless to say, despite reform, Riccò continued to lie and cheat. In 2011, he was admitted to hospital in a life-threatening condition after a blood transfusion, that he was administering himself, went wrong – he was using 25-day-old blood that may have been past its 'inject before' date. Apart from this mistake, he would have been able to complete his career with the full charade as reformed repentant, having learnt from his mistakes.

We worked with various specialists in sports marketing and sponsorship, and time and time again we were told of the corrosive effect on potential sponsors not familiar with cycling of googling 'cycling' and coming up with all the recent stories. Particularly galling was the effect on women's product sponsors. As we attempted to attract sponsors outside the norm, who might have a commercial interest in women's health and fitness, we were left with the understanding that no worthwhile brand was going to risk becoming contaminated by contact with a sport where lurid and fantastic tales of bags of blood-dominated search engine results.

In 2006, I had spoken out against the return of David Millar to the GB road team. David's sister Fran was now promoted by Dave Brailsford to handle PR and potential sponsorship enquiries into British Cycling and direct them towards riders. That I seemed to receive only those enquiries turned down by other British Cycling Olympians did not surprise me.

Direct, and not via BC, I was invited to the London Bike Show to speak. At the entrance, above the kiosks, hung five giant, far larger than life-size, double-sided posters of British cyclists at the Olympics. There had been eight gold medallists, and on the ten available sides, every gold medallist was featured – apart from me. There was even room for pictures of riders who had been there and not won a medal, and other Olympic cycling scenes. While I spoke in a lovely Q&A session at the show, taking lots of great questions from the public, Dad made gentle enquiries to speak to the manager of the show. The manager stated that he asked the British Cycling press office for the artwork of the Beijing gold medallists and he had no idea they had not featured me. The manager came up to me afterwards, expressing his sorrow. I had been good enough to be one of just three Olympians to come to the show, and not only that, but I had spent time with the public who had paid to come into the show, away from the Q&A session. He was very sorry and keen to show me the emails asking for the artwork from BC, to prove that the omission was not his fault. I never thought it was.

Andy and I pressed on against the odds; something would turn up surely? Although the first season was important, our sights were firmly on the 2012 London Olympics as the generally supportive media coverage noted. I paused in mid-December, wondering if I should abandon the idea and opt instead for a well-paid place with an established team, but I had come too far to turn back now.

Vision 1 Racing came together for the first time at a training camp in February. Resplendent in our team jerseys, white and blue, emblazoned with a star designed to resemble the spokes of a bike wheel, we prepared for the season ahead.

I had sacrificed much of my pre-season training to get the team up and running and as we approached the first races, the three-day GP Costa Etrusca, I knew that without the block of endurance work, I had little hope of a strong showing. In the circumstances, Vicki's eighth and 13th, and my 12th, fifth and ninth places were a good start, and when I followed it up with a good showing in the Tour of Flanders, finishing fourth, and the Flèche Wallonne in sixth, we seemed to be on track. Vicki and Christel were riding well, with Vicki winning the sprints jersey at the Tour de L'Aude. The younger girls were still learning, as was to be expected given that they were making their first tentative steps in the elite ranks.

But it wasn't enough. The cost of accommodation during races was met by race organisers, but the cost of everything else – transport and food as well as hiring staff like mechanics and masseurs during races – was coming out of my pocket. Any modest earnings from those few post-Olympics endorsements and appearances that did manage to find their way to me were all being ploughed directly into the team. To compound matters, I was also in a legal battle with Thomas Campana over unpaid wages and prize money relating to the 2007 season. The issue would eventually be resolved in my favour, but it was an unnecessary and time-consuming distraction. Without the finances and logistical support needed to mount a serious challenge in such a demanding event as the women's Tour de France, it was a disappointment to have to withdraw the team and miss it.

Wearing the rainbow jersey of World champion is a very special feeling. It always gave me a boost when I pulled it on. At races, it stands out from all the other jerseys and there would be exclamations of 'Wereldkampioen', 'Championne du Monde' and 'Campionessa del Mondo' following me around wherever I went. I had earned the right to wear the rainbow jersey, but had still not yet won a race wearing it. This is referred to as the 'curse' of the rainbow jersey, since often riders who were prolific winners in the year they took the jersey fail to win a single race the following year. I was desperate for this not to happen to me.

My special moment of winning while wearing the rainbow jersey finally came in the Emakumeen Bira stage race in June. I had notched up a number of second places over the season so far, including Stage 1 on the previous day to Judith Arndt. Stage 2 was heading for a sprint finish – there were a few corners in the last kilometres forcing the bunch to line out – and I got the timing spot-on to sprint to the win. Perfect! The team was on a high, leading the team classification, and now that I had the winning feeling back I was on a roll. The next day, the stage finished 100m after the brow of a steep climb. I was shoulder to shoulder with Judith as we crested the hill and then pulled away over the final metres to claim another win.

We were still in Spain when the van broke down; the gearbox had failed. We crammed our bikes and equipment onto the team car and hitched a lift back from a friendly Belgian photographer, William Meertens, who happened to be travelling behind us in his Land Rover. More money, more time wasted, as we prepared for the Giro di Trentino. Life seemed to be providing more than its fair share of distractions.

After all my tough races at the Giro di Trentino over the years, I really wanted the team to do well here, and I sprinted to second on Stage 1. On the final stage, first Christel sacrificed her race to make the other climbers work hard in the mountains classification sprints and then, with 20km to go, Vicki and I attacked over the top of the main mountain, creating a break of five riders. Vicki did the majority of the work, setting a fast pace and establishing a lead of almost two minutes on the peloton. I had rarely experienced this situation in my career, and now it was happening in my own team. Vision 1 Racing had become a force to be reckoned with. I prepared myself for the final climb, immensely proud with our team's performance, and determined to finish the job. I attacked and won by seven seconds, winning both the stage and the overall title as well. As Vicki rode towards the line, she fainted from her efforts. She had given everything.

I capped off the month by winning the British national title for the tenth time, beating Emma Pooley and Lizzie Armitstead in a sprint. This was organised by the ever-active Bill Owen around Abergavenny, and provided a rare photo opportunity to see a British national jersey being put on over a rainbow jersey! On this occasion, Colin Clews applied the one rider one prize principle, that I had insisted on years before at the Celtic Manor, to the youngsters in the U23 medal ceremony. There was then a quite unseemly event as Colin was overruled.

While it gave me great pleasure to ride in the World champion's jersey in Wales, the best bit was seeing all the youngsters who came to watch, in particular so many girls. They cheered and shouted, just as they had done 12 months before. I wondered how many of their hopes I had carried with me to Beijing; I hoped I was living up to their expectations and that they would have the opportunity to live out their dreams sometime in the future.

Across the Channel, Christel won the French national title, giving Vision 1 Racing two national champions in its ranks. We reconvened in July for a team camp in Luino, just across the Italian border from Lugano. My form was still good, and I even competed in a men's points race at a Zurich track where, like the good old days in junior ranks, I held my own and got my photo on the front page of the sports press. A couple of the girls' boyfriends joined us in Luino and we trained together. Evenings were wonderful, dining together with the food spread on a big table outside in the garden. They were good times, as we enjoyed the best of team camaraderie.

Sadly, it was not sustainable. I caught a virus and was laid low by splitting headaches and nausea. I reassured myself that after a few days' rest all would be back to normal. We rode the Carnevale di Cento in Italy, four of us finishing in the top 20, another great result for our team, but it was clear that I was ill. I tried to battle on as we headed for Germany to compete in the six-day Thüringen-Rundfahrt. I struggled for three days before pulling out, which was made all the more frustrating by the good form of my team-mates, with Vicki up in eighth place.

I was at breaking point, physically and psychologically. I had spent the whole time since the World Championships the previous year organising the new team and finding the riders. I had tried as hard as I could to find sponsors, but it was me who was contacting the organisers to persuade them to give us free accommodation, or dealing with the broken gearbox in Spain. While I had energy and could jump out of bed every morning raring to go, I could cope. Now that I was ill, the enormity of what I had taken on hit me. If I didn't do it, the show stopped.

I headed back to Wales for a family event for my grandfather, George. Being away from the cycling scene, I tried to plan for the last months of the season. I was ill and exhausted and the next block of racing was going to involve a lot of travel, which would completely drain what few financial resources I had left. I realised I had to close down the team, so I rang the girls one by one. They were all devastated, but I made arrangements for them on other teams. In hindsight, maybe that was another bad call. Perhaps we could have made it through to the end of the season. Certainly, I know that my state of mind was greatly affected by my poor physical state. I decided to finish my season riding with the GB U23 team.

I should have just sat out the rest of the year and got well, but instead I pushed on. The thought of not riding the World Championships with the race No.1 was something I simply could not contemplate. Goading me was all the press talk of what Team Sky were going to do for the British men in the next year; I wanted, once again, to remind the world what the British women could do. At the GP Plouay World Cup, I put myself in the five-up break riding for second place behind Emma Pooley but punctured with 1km to go. I then struggled in a couple of stage races in France. I knew that I was still not well, but I couldn't bring myself to withdraw gracefully from the World Championships. I had my spot, I knew I wouldn't do myself justice, but I just hoped I would feel better on the day. I was stubborn and I was wrong. I woke up on the day and felt exactly as bad as I had felt all week. I had no strength in my body. I started, was wished luck by my team-mates and wished them luck. It needed something quite different to luck. I should not have been there and dropped out halfway through.

Vision 1 Racing had seemed such a good idea, but we should have put in some break points to call a halt if we hadn't hit the required sponsorship targets. Looking back, a critical point was the news from a professional agent whose opinion was that Dave Brailsford would not recommend us to any sponsor were they to approach British cycling. It seemed that, as with the idea of a start in London for the women's Tour de France, British Cycling's influence spread itself further than I had thought.

The only bright spot was that in early September, I was contacted by Alexander Oppelt, manager of the Nürnberger team, who wanted to sign me for the 2010 season. They had been in existence for many years and had an excellent reputation. It was one of the top two choices I could wish to make of all the teams on the circuit, with Trixi Worrack and Amber Neben, defending World Time-Trial champion, on the team roster. We quickly finalised the deal. After a year of spending my own money to keep my team afloat, I was happy to be back as a salaried employee, without any responsibilities other than winning.

In October, everything was looking positive as I attended the Nürnberger launch of its new sponsor, yacht-chartering company Skyter, and then went to Buckingham Palace to receive the award of Member of the Order of the British Empire (MBE) from Prince Charles in recognition of my services to cycling. I then drew a line under the experiences of 2009 and flew out to Australia for a two-month pre-season training programme, staying with Craig in Perth where he was now living. We made a trip to Geelong to recce the course for the following year's World Championships.

During December, I was starting to enjoy life again when Alexander Oppelt telephoned. The team's sponsorship with Skyter had fallen through. The deal was off, they had signed riders and staff without a guarantee of money and they were now struggling to find a new financial backer. Alexander told me I was free to leave and race for another team, or join a new team that he was forming, but I would have to ride for free. Legally, I had a contract that should have been enforceable, but once again the UCI showed it lacked both resolve and the capability to do the things that really matter – protect the vulnerable. Instead, the UCI granted a racing licence to the 'new' team, and allowed the management to transfer all the assets from the old team to the new, while all the liabilities like signed contracts conveniently remained with the old team. A long trip down the German legal system finally proved that they were wrong. The 'curse' of the rainbow jersey was certainly reaching out further than I expected.

On the eve of the new season, my team options were limited as all teams had filled their rosters. British Cycling said I could ride with the U23 squad where I would receive my Lottery grant, but I could not have any personal sponsors. Despite the fact that I would ride in a jersey emblazoned with the Sky logo, I would receive nothing for this. Sky were also now sponsoring a men's road team and all the riders received a salary. They also sponsored track riders, who received personal sponsorship. If the track riders and male road riders had a windfall, good luck to them. Dave Brailsford was in charge and set the conditions. With the only other realistic choice being exiting the sport, as Amber Neben did at this time, I had no other options. It wasn't like I was getting rich before anyway.

I resumed training back in Lugano alone, looking ahead and hoping my problems of the last 16 months were over. Mauro had a serious crash in a Gran Fondo and broke his leg, so throughout 2010 he couldn't partner me on training rides. Then the dispute with Thomas Campana escalated into a court case. The effort to progress this was made all the more wearying as Thomas would do all he could to stop me winning races. He recruited Fabio, who had been coaching me, and also, knowing how much the British Championship meant to me, he recruited Lizzie Armitstead and Sharon Laws to join Emma Pooley at Cervelo.

The ongoing doping scandals of the men's scene were bringing women's cycling close to collapse. At the beginning of 2010, there were only two main teams: Nederland Bloeit (led by Marianne Vos) and Bob Stapleton's HTC, with Judith Arndt and Ina-Yoko Teutenberg. Thomas's Cervelo was the next strongest team and after that it was just small teams struggling to find the funds to race the full season. The races had also been severely reduced in number and length. The Tour de France and HP Challenge had gone, the Tour de L'Aude was about to run for its last-ever time and the Giro d'Italia was reduced in length. The World Cup had lost the races outside Europe and classics like San Remo and Amstel Gold. Naturally, there were fewer riders in total, with many of the older riders retiring. The 2010 season, for which I was now preparing alone, was certainly not the type of season for which I had left home and gone to live in Italy in 2002.

My early-season form was good, but this was not shown in any results. The duopoly of either HTC or Nederland Bloeit controlled the races, and I wasn't given any latitude and was heavily marked in every race. Emma Pooley had also wintered in Australia and was in sparkling form. I came to the Flèche without any enthusiasm and hope. Marianne had now won it three times in succession and was looking to pass my number of wins. At least it was a finish I knew well, and by my own efforts I could get a reasonable result. On the run-in to the Mur de Huy, HTC were lining it out for Evelyn Stevens and Judith Arndt. Nederland Bloeit were setting it up for Marianne, Cervelo likewise for Emma Pooley, while Emma Johansson's Red Sun outfit were doing their best for her. For the U23 girls, this was a fight for positions they were not used to, so I did what I could myself. I couldn't see what was going on at the front so just pressed on as best I could up the Mur. I moved through some of the second-string riders and then, to my surprise, went past Marianne as I continued overtaking riders. Ahead, I could now see the two Emmas fighting it out. Emma Johansson was fading, so I kept going and managed to pip her for second place behind Emma Pooley.

A British 1–2 in the Flèche Wallonne was unprecedented. Sadly, the performance went virtually unnoticed by the mainstream British press, who seemed to be becoming devoted readers of Team Sky press releases. I thought Emma deserved far more coverage for this and later results.

The result encouraged me. Unfortunately, it just reinforced the idea among my rivals that I needed marking all the more closely. I was back in Lugano training for the next event, the Tour de L'Aude, when I got a call. I could tell straightaway something serious was wrong, and I felt cold shivers as I was told that the other GB girls had been caught up in a horrific accident while out training in Belgium. They were riding as a group of five when they came to a crossroads and were hit by a car that had ignored a 'Give Way' sign and ploughed into them. At that moment, they were all being taken to hospital. Hannah Mayho broke her left leg and right arm, Lucy Martin had a cracked vertebra, Katie Colclough was knocked unconscious, Emma Trott broke her collarbone and Sarah Reynolds split her chin.

I retreated to training rides and competing in Gran Fondos while keeping up with the progress of the girls' recovery. Amazingly, by mid-June Katie and Lucy recovered and resumed racing. We travelled to Spain to race the Emakumeen Bira, where my season finally looked to be on track when I won the third-stage time-trial, my first win of the season, with Judith Arndt second at 15 seconds and Marianne Vos at 25. At last, I could beat the best again. It had been a long time.

The next day, I crashed spectacularly during a descent on

wet roads. I was out of the race and in agony, with gashes and bruises on my ankle, hip and elbow, all filled with embedded gravel, each tiny piece of which was the very devil to pull out. Another team-mate, Nikki Harris, tore the ligaments in her shoulder in the same race. I felt like a contagion was spreading from me.

A fortnight later, I returned to Britain for the national championships, attempting to win it for the eleventh time. Two weeks earlier, Lizzie Armitstead, racing for the Cervelo team with Emma Pooley and Sharon Laws, had been quoted in the written media as saying: 'The main thing is that we work together to beat Nicole Cooke, who's the big threat.' I made an enquiry to the chief commissaire, as to his opinion in respect of team tactics. However, although the relevant rules had not been altered from the previous time this issue had arisen, the UCI had changed the part which stated that 'National championships shall be run according to UCI rules' to 'Every cycle race shall be run according to UCI rules'.

This bungling alteration allowed for confusion. National championships provided no team competition, only individual prizes. For virtually every other event on the professional circuit, entry was only via a team. For this one race each year, individual entry was accepted. I received his written reply, spoke to him, and was confident that we would have a fair race on the day, with the best individual rider winning. However, the chief commissaire seemed to undergo a serious change of opinion on the rules on the Saturday afternoon before the race. At the riders' briefing, which was given once we were assembled by the start line, I heard a quite different version from the one he had committed to me days before. With no time to debate the niceties of the rulebook, we were invited to start the race. However, there is a difference between a race involving riders and one which includes the team manager taking an active part.

Each lap featured a big, steep climb followed by a flat section, then a steep and twisting descent. A rolling section then took us back to the start–finish area. On the first lap, there was a crash after a corner at the bottom of the very steep descent. An official car stopped to attend. A series of riders then crashed into the car, one rider breaking her elbow. This caused the race to be stopped while they cleared the course. It was the second time in the year any problems of my own were put into perspective.

Once we restarted, a group of four soon formed. On the hill, I could shake off Lizzie and Sharon, and temporarily drop Emma before she would get back to me, but then she could sit on me, which would not have been too bad. Normal practice is that when the gap between riders, or groups, is less than 30 seconds, no vehicles are allowed in the gap. Once the gap is above 30 seconds, a single neutral service vehicle drops in behind the leaders. When the gap is greater than a minute, the riders' team cars can drop in the gap. It is the commissaire's job to monitor this rule, to make sure the team cars do not provide slipstream, allowing the chasing riders to catch the leaders.

When I was away with Emma, I saw the Cervelo team car behind us and behind the team car the two helmets of Sharon and Lizzie. The team car was effectively towing them back to me. I tried several more times to get away, but eventually worn out, Emma got away and then Lizzie beat me in the sprint. After the race, I attempted to find the chief commissaire in order to make a formal protest. I was quite keen to look him in the eye as I did so, but he was nowhere to be found. I handed my written protest to another official. Later on in the week, when I wrote enquiring if I should ever receive a reply to my protest, I received the most brief of responses indicating that the result on the day stood, and that if I wanted any more information I should contact the British Cycling offices at Manchester. I didn't. Emma Pooley rode superbly well all season and could probably have won without the special help, but the way Cervelo did it without reprimand from the race officials left me very upset.

My motivation went to pieces. I was going through the motions. I went out training, but could not see the purpose in racing or training. I had won only a single race all year. Was it time to stop or would everything be okay if I found a proper team for 2011? I decided to return home to Wick. Picking up the familiar routine of family life had a beneficial effect. After a few days' rest, I began to train well; my times up the Bwlch were among the best I had ever done. I began to think about the course at Geelong for the World Championships, which would suit me. My spirits rose with each training session on the hills and I finished five weeks of solid training on a high. Helping lift my spirits late in 2010 was the fact that I won my court case in Germany regarding my Nürnberger contract, making it two legal wins in a year – more than on the bike!

The 2010 World Championships would be run off on a variation of the old Geelong race course where they used to hold the World Cup and associated Tour. These races were long gone, but the location brought back happy memories of my wins here earlier in my career. Emma Pooley was in great form and the press were talking up Mark Cavendish's chances for the men's event, although few people realised how tough a course this was. Nobody was talking about me, which was fine. Emma started the week in great style by winning gold in the time-trial, beating Judith Arndt and Linda Villumsen. It was an excellent and well-deserved result.

The main contenders for the road race were similar to 2008, with Marianne Vos the favourite. The Germans and Italians were fielding strong teams; Emma Johansson was there but without Susanne Ljungskog. After that, however, the remainder of the field had changed greatly since 2008. During the season, I had noticed a significant change in the way races were being run off. Due to the duopoly, the races became very negative. Riders in those two teams rode in a set plan to cancel each other out and the rest of the field seemed to ride to just get a good placing behind them. Any aggressive move seemed to initiate a frantic and mindless chase, followed by riders sitting on, waiting for the next move by one of the main teams, rather than using the attack and counter to move the race onto another level.

Great Britain fielded a full team of seven riders – the three Cervelo girls (Emma, Sharon and Lizzie), Catherine Williamson (née Hare), Lucy Martin, Katie Colclough and me. The race was eight laps of a 16km circuit with two hills on it, the last one 6km before the finish. It was not going to be a large bunch sprint, but the size of the group at the finish would depend on the activity in the race.

The pressure on Marianne was significant. She now had three silver medals from the last three World Championships. I knew how difficult it must be for her and how much pressure there would be on her to win. We had several options: Emma was clearly on form and if she was away by herself, we were now a strong enough team to disrupt any chasers. Lizzie had been riding all year with Emma and Sharon, so should have had plenty of opportunity to practise sprint leadouts, and certainly there was no reason why all three shouldn't be present in the finale. I felt good and, although I lacked recent competition, I certainly believed that I had a chance, particularly from a small group.

The team meeting was a strange affair. Shane Sutton led it and was obviously trying to encourage Emma to ride for the win, but she was having none of it. She was going to ride for Lizzie, as was Sharon. This did not seem unreasonable, as they had raced all season together and should be highly accomplished in helping each other. Shane gave me a free hand to do my own thing to go with any breaks on the last lap and counter or make attacks as I saw fit. He wanted it to be a hard race, banking rightly on the fact that in the final selection, the British team would be there in numbers.

A board, clearly marked and held aloft in the British pit, reminded Sharon of the lap she had to stir it up for the 'hard race'. She did that and then settled in the lead group. As we began the last lap, there were fewer than 30 riders remaining at the front, with most of the favourites still in contention. Italy had three riders, the Dutch, Canadians, USA and Germans two each. There were four British riders left: Emma, Sharon, Lizzie and me. Marianne then lost team-mate Annemiek van Vleuten to a puncture and was isolated. This was the ideal time to attack, but nothing happened. Couldn't they see that Vos was now on her own, as I always used to be? She was desperate to take the gold and would be forced to react to any attack. I was frustrated by this negative thinking, couldn't they realise that by not attacking, we were actually helping position her to win the race? As we crested the penultimate climb, the negative nature of the race meant there was nothing for it but to make my own attack.

My objective was not to attack to stay away to the finish – Emma would have been much better for that – but to create a situation where there would be the fluidity of attack and counter attack where it would require strength, skill, courage and cunning to pick the right moves. I worked hard enough on the descent to make the front group chase, all the while keeping something in reserve for when I was caught. They reeled me in halfway up the next climb, but amazingly there was no counter attack. So as we went over the crest of the final hill, still 6km from the finish, I attacked, this time a full-blooded attack to stay away. Judith Arndt came with me and we quickly established a lead of 15 seconds. We left behind a group of about 20, followed by a long strung-out line of stragglers trying to get back on.

Judith and I worked extremely well together, both fully committed. We knew the drill: flat out until 600m to go and then it was down to each of us. We didn't expect it to be easy, but logic told us that apart from our own team-mates the only real sprinters left in the group were Marianne, who was by herself, Emma Johansson, also alone, and Giorgia Bronzini, who still had two team-mates. Of course, there were individual riders who could attack to try to go by themselves, which by itself would inject pace into the chase, but we also had our team-mates who should try to disrupt the chase.

As we took the final right-hand bend and entered the finishing straight with 800m to go, we had a gap of about six seconds. Should I launch an early sprint and ensure a medal but give Judith an easy leadout, or should I wait, and gamble it all for the win, choosing my moment to make sure I beat Judith?

I waited, watching Judith in front in case she jumped, and looking behind to see how close the charging bunch was to us. At 400m, Judith went for home; I responded and I knew I could beat her. I kicked for the line, passing Judith just as Marianne came past us, towing Giorgia Bronzini and Emma Johansson in her wake. I could not match them. Giorgia came off Marianne's wheel and passed her in the last 50m, while I was fourth and Judith fifth. It was heartbreaking to have been so close.

Afterwards, Marianne explained the reasoning behind her tactics. She could see us ahead and although she knew that Giorgia was on her wheel, she knew that if she didn't go from a long way out, they wouldn't have caught us and then she would have been racing for bronze. She, like me, had gambled on gold and lost. Watching the video after the event I saw that after Judith and I had escaped, there was a regrouping and then a very strange move from the two Canadians. They were going flat out chasing down Judith and me, giving a free ride to the rest of the group, and ended up finishing well down the field.

What concerned me is how GB had placed behind me: 9th, 16th and 20th. These were the three Cervelo riders, all three seconds behind Giorgia, who had been in the same group as them up to 600m from the line. Behind the chasing Canadians, GB's three Cervelo riders had two options: they could either have got to the front and disrupted the chase of the Canadians to increase my chances of gold, or they could have manoeuvred into a train to set up Lizzie with a leadout, from which she would have stood every chance in a sprint finish. They had had all season to practise for this moment, and in Emma Pooley they had the World TT champion to drive onto the trio of Marianne, Giorgia and Emma Johannson. In the video, I can't see that they worked together at all, and the result was that we had four placed in the top 20 but had no medal. I was not a scapegoat for their collective failure that year, and no inquest was held by British team management as to why they didn't work to help either Lizzie or me.

Judith and I shook hands with each other as we rode slowly away from the finish. We had many great battles together, attacking each other and trying to break the other one. This time we had given everything together.

I can look back now and see that set against all the trials and tribulations of the last two years, I should have been proud of how I had turned it around and how close I had come to winning that World Championship. After all, in the first year of Team Sky, Britain's men once again did not finish a single rider. At the time, all I knew was that I had been just metres away from winning gold. I had lost and was devastated. But I couldn't just slope off; there was a Commonwealth Games road title to contest.

After the farce of 2006 I did not want a repeat, so Dad had worked with the WCU to come up with a support programme to develop Welsh girls and send a meaningful team. There were many Welsh girls entering the sport, and after my success in 2008 it was agreed that a non-paid coach would be put in place and Lottery funding would be available for the expense of running training sessions and supporting riders going to distant events and gaining experience, working with the coach. This was all coming to a nice conclusion in late 2008. However, internal politics within the WCU once again put the first spanner in the wheel. By July 2009, a selection process had been conducted and Courtney Rowe, father of Team Sky's Luke Rowe, was appointed and the preliminary programme was issued for the Welsh development squad preparing for Delhi 2010. I was really looking forward to working with Courtney and the selected girls. For once, we were going to have a coordinated and focused plan. I was asked to produce a press release to accompany the announcement of the programme. It was now August, we had lost virtually all of one UK season, but we had a winter and the following season to do something tangible.

Within only a week, the programme was cancelled. Shane Sutton spoke to Huw Jones at the Sports Council for Wales and told him it could not go ahead, and Huw agreed. It was incredibly depressing. Just how many individual Olympic gold medal winners had Wales produced over the decades? The answer was at that time, just me, since 1972. That I was not consulted until the decision was made was another saddening feature. It wasn't that the Welsh girls could even be left alone to get on and do our own thing, regardless of any bureaucracy. No, British Cycling had insisted that only they would hold accreditation for cycling events at Delhi, and they would not allow Courtney access to any of the events or facilities, even though he offered to do the job on a completely voluntary basis. Further, they and only they could be engaged in coaching any talent, with the WCU forbidden to run any talent development programme for Welsh women. I needed no crystal ball to visualise what the future might bring. The men at British Cycling were so pre-occupied with their Sky project that they did nothing of value to help develop any of the Welsh road girls.

The Sports Council for Wales refused to challenge British Cycling's directive to them. After the debacle of the summer of 2009, Welsh Cycling and I did not speak to each other until just before Delhi. At the last minute somebody remembered the awkward questions asked at Melbourne – 'Why hasn't the gold medallist from Wales got any team-mates?' – and suddenly Wales fielded a team of four. The riders were doing their best, but they did not have either the experience or the capability to help me. A couple had attended the British Championships but were not in the race. With a programme that supported them from February 2009, we could have done wonders. Instead, yet again I felt like I was a punchbag for the Australians, England and, most of all, British Cycling. Those Welsh riders were there only to save consciences.

The girls selected were fabulous; it was not their fault they were caught up in the wrong place at the wrong time. Jess Allen was excellent and gave me her wheel when I crashed, which meant that her race was over, but it enabled me to chase back to the bunch and stay in contention. Unfortunately, I just didn't have it in the sprint and my old colleague Rochelle Gilmore took the gold, with me in fifth position. As for BC and their much-vaunted support, they suddenly decided that riders had far better things to do than go to Delhi, and many excuses, such as preparing for European Championships and risk of illness, severely reduced the presence of their teams.

I would probably have retired at this point if there hadn't been the lure of the London Olympics, just 18 months away. I still loved riding out in the countryside and feeling the freedom of riding under my own power, I enjoyed getting ready for races and going head-to-head against my rivals, but it was hard trying to believe I would ever get another even chance at a major race.

Others still rated me. I was flattered to be sought by a number of teams. Walter Ricci made effective overtures. He was forming a women's team that was to run alongside an Italian men's team sponsored by a bike manufacturer, using Mario Cipollini as the brand name, and clothing manufacturer Giordana. It was all very promising, with a decent wage and the chance to have individual sponsors where there was no conflict of interest. Fabio, my former coach, had dropped out of the Cervelo operation and called me to ask if I wanted to work with him again. Thinking of London, I cast my mind back to the good days of 2008 and accepted his offer.

The year started with the Tour of Qatar held on the flat, windy desert plains. I played my part for the team, which celebrated when Monia Baccaille won the third stage. I was off the pace during the early spring races, occasionally scraping into the top ten, and had to miss the Tour of Flanders due to illness, although I was back for the Flèche Wallonne, where the team supported me but I didn't make the most of the opportunity and could manage only fifth.

It was an improvement, but I couldn't see the positives as I continued to fall short of podium places, and once again fell into the trap of overtraining. I ignored Fabio's advice and made sure I pounded myself in training each week, arriving at the next race overtired.

Going to the British Championships in June, I was already resigned to facing another one-against-three scenario with the Cervelo girls. Emma, Lizzie, Sharon and I made a break early on in the race, and I then had to respond to a series of attacks by Emma and Sharon over the next 80km. The race came down to a sprint, which Lizzie won comfortably to take her first national title.

It was interesting to see that the Team Sky 1-2-3 on the men's podium, later the same day, had one or two informed commentators asking about the format of the competition: was this still really a competition for individual riders? With so many of the British Cycling staff receiving wages from both the public purse and Sky, this was not going to be a question that would get a sensible answer.

I was encouraged with the way I rode and headed to the Giro d'Italia, which I hadn't raced for a few years, in better spirits. It didn't start well, as I lost large amounts of time over the first few days. On the fifth stage to Verona, we would be finishing in our sponsor's home area and there was a lot of expectation for our team to deliver a big result. The sponsors would be coming along to the finish to meet the team. Walter was as nice as anyone could be about wanting one of the team to get a win and yet not demanding or trying to interfere with wacky tactical contrivances. He was so supportive, and this attitude was exactly the right way to go about it.

I had been trying all day to get into a breakaway and nothing had stuck. One big group with two team-mates in had just been caught, and with 10km left to go, it looked like we were destined to finish in a bunch sprint. However, I never give up, so I launched an attack. At least we would be able to tell Walter and the sponsors how hard we had tried. A few riders came with me and I kept going flat out, trying to drag a group away from the bunch. A few more riders joined us and we were now a group of 11 with a lead of around 30 seconds; there was a slim chance we might be able to stay away. There was a mixture of riders wanting to work while others were sitting on, making it hard to keep a steady tempo of regular strong turns on the front.

With 3km to go, we rode under the walls surrounding Verona and there was an attack countered immediately by Sarah Düster, my former team-mate now riding with Marianne Vos. This looked like the perfect launch pad for me, so I let the other riders chase Sarah, bringing us closer, then I attacked from the back. I sprinted past the chasers and then straight past Sarah so she could not get on my wheel, but there was still just over 1km to go and the bunch had us in their sight. This was going to be my 1km individual time-trial, and a close-run result. I was already riding flat out but nevertheless dared a glance back; the break must have been caught, as all I could see was the bunch strung out in a long line. That meant their objective was to catch me. I churned a big gear, riding the shortest line possible, counting down the distance to the finish. At 200m to go, the road turned onto the cobbles of Piazza Bra and I knew I was going to win. I crossed the line in front of the Arena and screamed with joy.

A few weeks later, I finished third in the Open de Suède World Cup from a breakaway group. After Sweden, Lizzie and I went to recce the World Championship course in Copenhagen with Simon Cope. I asked to practise a leadout and Simon dutifully led me out, while Lizzie did not participate. I discussed potential finish scenarios with Simon and we came up with a plan for attending a series of Belgian and Dutch criterium races to practise sprint finishes. The idea was to get other girls that might be in the team involved, so that we could practise together. Simon asked Shane for approval, but Shane wouldn't agree with this initiative and instructed that this was not to go ahead.

I spent the rest of 2011 grinding myself down with overtraining, desperate to turn my poor performances around. Fabio was constantly telling me to take more time off after races to recover, but I had stopped listening, thinking that I knew better.

The World Championship course in 2011 would be the flattest championship course I would ever ride. Mark Cavendish was the best sprinter on the men's circuit and this was a sprinter's course. In 2002, on a similar course at Zolder, the Italian team had controlled the race to allow their sprinter Cipollini to win. British Cycling were now going to do the same for Mark in the men's race. The whole squad was drilled with one single game plan and practised during the GB team camps held throughout the year. Mark was not delivered quite as well as Mario in 2002, but he did a fantastic sprint to win the title. While British Cycling had created a professional team for the men and had run a series of training camps to prepare for the World Championships, there had been nothing similar for the women. The modest plan Simon and I had attempted to put together was cancelled by Shane.

When you see the last kilometre of a bunch sprint on TV, it may seem relatively easy. You spot a group of riders wearing the same jersey riding in a line and maybe two or three other lines operating similarly. In reality, the bunch is forever a moving mass of riders, and in the last 20km there are plenty of riders who know that they don't have a chance in the sprint and will attack. Each attack draws a response and this changes the order of riders at the front. If a team is strong enough, it can simply eliminate the attacks by riding so fast that it becomes virtually impossible for anyone else to attack. The risk here is that the riders run out of power before the finish and their sprinter is then left to fend for him or herself. The other aspect to be careful of is sprinters without strong teams. Their tactic will be to take advantage of another team's lead out and get in the string themselves, or even more simply just take the wheel of the sprinter who is being led out. To avoid this, teams use 'sweepers', whose job is to ensure that one of their own is behind the sprinter. All these manoeuvres are being carried out in a bunch of riders going at 60kmh, with the tiniest of gaps between wheels. That is why it is not something to decide to try out for the first time in an important race.

The now four Cervelo girls in the British team, following the addition of Lucy Martin for 2011, had the luxury of another 12 months in the same trade team to hone their lead-out train for their sprinter, knowing that they would all be in the GB team on a sprinter's course at the end of the year. I'm not sure how many times they practised their leadouts over that period; I personally never saw a race where they did it. Certainly when the seven of us assembled in Copenhagen, we never discussed a possible team order of riders, or at what point on the course we might start a train.

In the meeting to discuss tactics on the Wednesday night, the agreed plan was that Lizzie would have the team set her up for the finish and I would be a free agent. On Thursday, the last day of practice on the course, I asked Lizzie if she wanted me to help in a leadout for the sprint. The response was that I could 'tag along' if I wanted. I followed the threesome of Emma, Sharon and Lizzie as they weaved in and out of obstacles and cyclists on their way to the finish line. They did it once. I remembered back to my first World Championship as a junior in Plouay, where a week before the race and at a time when the road was clear, with Dad and Craig acting as leadout riders, I practised sprinting the last 500m on the course. I had been on the verge of a professional career and intended to optimise my preparation as a professional should.

The full team meeting that night again confirmed the plan from Wednesday night. However, on Friday evening, the night before our race, Shane, who had not attended any of the earlier meetings or spoken to me during the week, called us for another impromptu meeting. Here I was told that Lizzie insisted I led her out.

This was quite some change of heart from the 'tag along' attitude of the previous morning, which suggested that the initiative had not come from Lizzie herself. I pointed out the flaw in this plan was that we had never practised doing this, either as a drill or at the end of a race, or even together the day before, and it was doomed to failure. I don't know what the others thought of my criticism, but the outcome was immensely vague. I agreed that I would lead Lizzie out, while the rest of the team would 'look after her'. Apart from that, there was a lot of looking at the floor and ceilings. Again, I reflected back on a previous World Championship, in Madrid in 2005, where I had taken along the video of the 2002 race to show the others how the Italians had worked together. This year we didn't even have that, only a vague aim. There was no detail, such as where to assemble, on the right or left of the bunch, how far from the finish, who would be the sweeper, how many of us would be in the line. What were the others to do? Was it a leadout train of one rider?

The race was an incredibly boring affair. All the main teams were busy closing down attacks during the race to ensure a bunch finish. Clara Hughes of Canada had escaped by herself and was away for a long time, caught only through the efforts of the Dutch with 4km to go. There followed some more individual attacks off the front and crashes near the back of the bunch, as the riders became nervous for the finish. The contenders for the win were all in the first 20 places. I couldn't see Lizzie and it was too late to go back to find her. She needed to be up near the front and there were still her strong trade team-mates all there with nothing else to do and capable of getting her up to the front section of the race.

We swept round the right-hand bend into the finishing straight with 800m to go. Now as a lone sprinter, my aim was to get on someone else's leadout train. I was on Marianne's wheel in the Dutch leadout. The other two teams already prepared were the Germans and Italians. Maybe the Dutch had done too much already, as they had been chasing Clara for a long time. One German sprinted away up the left, with about 500m to go, but too hard for anyone to follow. The Dutch gradually peeled off one by one. The Italians waited until the last 200m when Marianne was left alone, then they accelerated up the right-hand side. They still had two riders left. The result was the same as the previous year: Giorgia Bronzini gold, Marianne silver, but this time Ina-Yoko Teutenberg of Germany was third and I was fourth. Lizzie had come up from a long way back, on her own, and finished seventh, while Emma Johansson was only 14th.

After the race I attended the anti-doping testing and was last of the team to arrive at the hotel, still in my race kit not having showered. As I approached my room, Simon Cope told me Shane had instructed that they were going to have a post-race meeting and it was going to take place in my room, right then. Everyone followed me in. My room-mate Catherine Williamson looked on amazed as the crowd assembled round our beds. Shane's understanding of the race failed to take into account several key elements, but he was in no mood to be corrected as he singled me out as being at fault. As Shane gave us the benefit of his wisdom, none of the Cervelo girls was going to admit that they could have done more to help move Lizzie up to me, while she was not in a mood to accept that she had been in the wrong half of the race at the critical time. With experience she would understand that positioning at this stage of the race is vital and quite difficult as others want to be at the front as well.

All three medallists had team-mates working for them in the last kilometre, and frankly I could only despair. Two years in succession I had been on my own. Each time, specifically on team instruction, I had not a single rider allocated to help me, yet managed two fourth places. I will let others debate what might have happened if I had been supported with just some of the talent that was available to GB at that time. We were almost doomed to fail before we even got to the start line. British Cycling then dismissed Simon Cope. Certainly he was not responsible for the late change of tactical plan, and I'm not too sure whether he can be blamed for four trade team-mates not learning how to conduct a leadout train or move their team sprinter up into the front half of the race.

Maybe with hindsight, the Cervelo girls will look back and recognise that scapegoating me was not the high point of their cycling careers. Sadly, it was not the end of the issue. When Lizzie Armitstead was interviewed by the media later, an issue that was best kept behind closed doors was suddenly a public spat. I was in Perth, staying with Craig, when the story hit the papers, and even though I was on the other side of the world, it didn't lessen the blow. Lizzie's harshest comment was that I was a selfish rider who never did anything for team-mates. It was an unfounded claim, for which Lizzie did apologise when we next met. I have made many mistakes of my own over the years, so I put it down to her inexperience. We both had bigger things to think about, with the Olympics now just a few months away.

CHAPTER TWENTY-TWO
Exposing the Drug Cheats

The only people I can name in this book as being users of Performance Enhancing Drugs (PEDs) are those who have both tested positive and had the decision confirmed by the authorities and any appeal rejected. If I come into my shared room and see a team-mate hooked up to a drip, as I have, I might have a very strong opinion that it is PEDs they are infusing, but if they state that it is just saline solution and they are 'hydrating', and the evidence is disposed of very quickly, it becomes just my word against theirs. I can't man-handle them, complete with drip in arm, down to the local police station.

I shared this experience soon after it occurred with the relevant agency in the UK and was told very clearly that there was nothing they would do with the information. So from that point on, I made it very clear to my managers and team-mates that I would not tolerate any activity like that. Thereafter, I never had another problem like that again.

A good number of commentators were able to analyse my 2013 retirement statement and place some dots between the gaps and then draw conclusions. Where was I invited into the campervan and asked what 'help' I needed? Again, it can be quite easy when there is a situation like that of William

Dazzani and his involvement at Deia–Pragma–Colnago. But that took the full weight of long-term phone taps and other instruments of state vigilance to bring evidence that led to his arrest. It involved multi-agency work over many months to take it that far in line with what Fany Lecourtois and *directeur sportif* Giorgio Zauli were able to tell me months before.

I had my dream ... and that is what it was. Mum and Dad supported me but were always striking a note of caution – plenty could go wrong, just one element of which was finding a mountain that you could only get to the top of by using PEDs. The financial realities of the circuit were evident before I even joined it. I had my top A-level grades and could go to university. 'I will participate in the sport of cycling on my terms' is the attitude I took to dealing with all facets of what I found. While sitting at home on the sofa watching the Sydney road race, knowing I was the best British road racer but blocked by a bureaucracy of uninformed men and a rule that appeared every bit as conveniently as those that outlawed Graeme Obree, it was crystal clear before I even started my professional career that such an attitude would win me few friends. But I wasn't about to trade in my moral code and principles. If it was ever going to happen for me, it was going to happen my way.

Did I really think I could do it clean? For a window into my mindset, I need to describe to you what I was exposed to. In the UK, as most everywhere else, this was a man's sport. No GB girls really went about it properly, training day in day out during their youth. At the age of 13, I was able to make clean sweeps of all the BSCA titles because the other girls didn't train like I did. The level up – British clubwoman – was populated either by late entrants to the sport or by those who continued the quasi social/sporting manner that I encountered in the girls I rode against. Above that were the WCPP women. They might be full-time athletes and be surrounded by all the trappings of being elite riders – but let's go back to that first British Track Championships at Manchester. Femke, Claire, Danielle, Laura and I, along with all the others, put on a proper race. They knew they had to take me on, and now I had been given a showcase, I was not about to give it second best. We schoolgirls ran an identical format race, minutes faster than the senior women. In 1998 and 1999 at those track championships in Manchester, Dad and I watched very carefully. The British senior athletes held absolutely no fears for me. I had six years of dedicated training under my belt as my body formed.

Women's cycling had made its debut at the Olympics in 1984. The circuit was on an upward trajectory, but only in the very recent past had it gone global. Therefore, I thought that the quality of competition would not be truly elite, as there had not been time for it to develop. The top 16 in every Wimbledon Championships have all been training seriously since a very young age. I was bringing that same history of youth development to the sport of cycling at what I hoped was exactly the right time.

Another opinion-forming event was that World Road Race Championship of 2000. Looking back in hindsight, the conclusions I made were wrong. In lap five of nine, Zinaida Stahurskaya broke away from a small bunch, then caught the break. She attacked and then rode the last few laps to the finish on her own. On the day, it appeared too good to be true. That only eight months later she tested positive and was banned for four months left a very clear concept in my mind about who I could trust. Zinaida was using PEDs, but the fact that the chasing group couldn't catch her was testimony that drug abuse was not widespread.

In the summer of 2001, as I shelved plans to go to university and committed to trying out the full-time athlete role, there were other encouraging events. The Italian police raided Marco Pantani's hotel room during the Giro, found syringes and other evidence, and he was removed from the race. Italy's most famous and charismatic rider had been exposed as a common liar. Elsewhere, Dane Bo Hamburger was the first rider to test positive as a result of the brand new EPO test. Needless to say, he squealed that he had never taken anything, the bungling officials didn't handle his B-sample correctly and he was free to run out the rest of his career as a 'clean' athlete. On his retirement, he struck a book deal and cashed in on his 'tell all', admitting he had been using EPO.

Others were caught with this new test. I went to Canada and you will recall Genevieve Jeanson rode away from the bunch and it took a committed chase by four of us, the next four best riders in the race, some 60km to pull her back. That day I didn't doubt that Jeanson's performance was anything other than false, but the fact that like Zinaida she was one, and the rest of us were at another level, was very heartening. I just looked at her and prayed that her day would come. When I saw the little group gather around her later that week and she retired from the race, I was pondering several scenarios. All of this gave me plenty of confidence that the Festina scandal of 1998 had been a watershed. PED abuse was now shifted to centre stage and quality efforts were being made to develop tests, and even if the sporting authorities seemed, at best, inept, at least the civil authorities were taking the matter seriously.

One thing of which I was certain was that I could stand up to any pressures of bullying from team-management or team-mates. British Cycling and the antics of that minority of unprofessional staff had hardened me to what I needed to do. In 2000, I had let Simon Burney laugh at me and tell the mechanic that he should not do as I so politely asked and put my bike back how I wanted it. Now I would tell anyone in the same circumstances exactly what I thought of him and take the bike to another national team and ask them to do it. I was ready to stand my ground with any drugs issues and had mentally steeled myself for that likely encounter.

And let's put this completely in context. There would be a bunch of men working very closely with young women and the men would hold positions of power. Dad and Mum researched the problems and shared with me studies from Sweden and Canada, showing endemic abuse of position by male coaches with female athletes. I didn't think for a moment that such basic motives would recognise international boundaries. PED abuse was just going to be one of several factors I would have to deal with.

Those first few months of 2002 were critical to confirming or destroying my ideas about whether I could be competitive at elite level. As you now know, I won my second race. What I could not know was that preparation through the winter of 2001–02 would only ever be matched by that of 2006-07 in my whole career.

In my first year, I was exposed to pressures by the team. I said 'no', didn't get my wages and didn't last the season. I pressed the UCI, and by early 2004 I'd got my wages and later Dazzani was arrested for supplying PEDs. It would be nice to point out that I had been instrumental in helping expose the drug-pushers at this time, but I wasn't. I trusted in the new tests and the ever-more aggressive actions of the civil authorities. At Deia-Pragma, the fact that the first rider I met, Fany Lecourtois, had been so solid morally, was a great fillip. That Giorgio Zauli had not let us come to him but had actively come seeking us, even after he had left the team, to warn us about Dazzani, was another great boost. There were decent people in women's cycling; around us the war was fully engaged and I thought at the time being won.

And who could I take my experiences to if I did want to get involved? After starting the year with a debilitating battle with my home federation, that only came to an end when they turned up at a race without the right number of riders; we had just a few weeks of truce before the next crisis that was only solved when the email was found stating what they denied they had said. My home federation was not casting itself in a role that trust in them could be countenanced.

I am proud that at the end of 2002, at the start of negotiations with Maurizio Fabretto, I made it very clear that no drips, syringes or any other products were to be kept in the team house in which I would live. It worked, and it is a pleasure to record that Maurizio never put any pressure, overt or subliminal, on me to use PEDs, nor did any other team-mates suggest anything. I was clean – and if you lived in the house with me you had to be clean there as well.

Again, with Rochelle Gilmore and Dutch sisters Chantal and Ghita Beltman I found house-mates who I could trust. In the summer of 2003, UK Sport worked with my solicitor Mike Townley and they recognised the changes we – Mike, Dad and I – wanted within the sport to strengthen its governance; one of the elements was an Athlete Charter to formalise the relationship between national governing bodies and the athletes they were meant to be supporting. The other aspect of change was in relation to PEDs, and the first opportunity for me to properly address the issue was on 29 October 2003.

Michele Verroken at Drug-Free Sport, the forerunner of the UK Anti-Doping Agency (UKADA), had given a presentation and sent out a brief email asking how we were finding the voluntary 'whereabouts' policy. In the USA, they had recently introduced a 'three misses and you get a positive' rule. What did we think? Sara Symington was our cycling representative and responded truthfully, stating that she was not aware of any whereabouts system being run at all by British Cycling and cited athletes who were not present when testers called, which at that time carried no sanction whatsoever.

I wrote back, copying all on the circulation list with three pages of detail, telling them that we had to press for compulsory whereabouts diaries and out-of-competition testing in British Cycling. Reading it now, I can see I also urged that the then exemption for out-of-competition positive for amphetamines be removed, as this was a weakness in the system. I regaled everyone that in anti-doping at one race on the continent, I was shocked to see one rider take in a big file full of medical exemptions. Would she have a 'prescription' for every adverse substance that might show up in her sample? The whole process needed tightening up.

I am proud of several of the things I wrote that day in October:

This is not an issue to sit on our hands and let go by us. It is the biggest issue in our sport. In 1998 at the time of the Festina affair, doping was endemic in cycling ... Either it matters to us whether a set of druggies steal the medals off us at Athens or it does not. Either we are going to do something about it or we are just going to watch.

In this area I think there is zero chance of a lead being shown by the male side of the sport. Just look at the history of most of the *directeur sportifs* ... They are also talking big bucks. For the women at least we do not have the issue of big bucks!! And I honestly think there is a significant number of girls who do not take drugs and want to see those that do driven out of the sport, a far more effective number than in the men's pro peloton.

I spoke to David Brailsford very strongly about this very issue on Monday, urging him to get on the back of the UCI. As you know I am quite prepared to stand on my own at any time, but on an issue as big as this, I suggest it is in all our interests to work together. Is it worth you all emailing David Brailsford and asking him to take up the various issues with the UCI? That will be your decision. My position is clear.

My email was forwarded to Michele Verroken and Miriam Batten, an officer at Drug-Free Sport. She wrote back, and we started a dialogue. I placed myself on the list for voluntary testing, supporting a WADA programme in relation to a test they wanted to develop for Human Growth Hormone, at that time undetectable. WADA hoped to have it ready for Athens. Anything I could do to speed up the process of snaring the criminals.

Dave Brailsford and I swapped a couple of emails on the subject and Dad spoke to him at length. The disappointing news at this time was that while a number of other sports had signed up to the WADA protocol, football and cycling had not. On 20 February, I wrote to Dave asking if he could get British Cycling to press for a change of heart at the UCI. Our representative was Brian Cookson, the BC president. Dad and I wrote reminders about the same thing on 15 March, 28 March, 6 April and 16 May, all to no effective response.

When I spoke out to the press in late May about this, and about some of the competitors I would be lining up against at Athens, it caught the press. At this time Jeanson's Canadian doctor had testified under oath to his professional body that he had prescribed EPO to Jeanson for non-medical purposes, but the cycling authorities had decided, in their infinite wisdom, that such evidence was not a suitable reason for suspending her racing licence, especially with an Olympic road race a few months away. I must have pointed out the ridiculous nature of this stance to a journalist. Next thing I had a BOA press officer ring me up to tell me not to talk about such things, as the authorities were dealing with all of this very effectively and I should not let it worry me.

It was an extraordinary line to take. You try getting on the start line with somebody juiced up with EPO and try to win the one race that is going to make your career. I thought the authorities were doing nothing and would continue to do nothing because they had their heads stuck deep in the ground. We sent the BOA the whole string of correspondence dating back to 20 February, with a polite suggestion that this position was false. Dad wrote to Dave Brailsford again on 15 June and then everything blew up when Dave was taken into custody along with David Millar.

Dave now became more supportive and suggested that my proposal be put to the Board of British Cycling. Cookson replied that if I wished to do something I could do it myself, but that British Cycling were not going to act on my suggestions. Via Dad, I then shared all my experiences of life in the peloton with John Scott, head of Drug-Free Sport, and Liz Nicholl, director for Elite Performance at UK Sport. One of the interactions between Dad and Dave from this time is worth quoting. Dave was always saying the male pro riders returning from the continent did not want to participate in out-of-competition testing in the UK, as they were tested enough already. I had an entirely different view.

*

From Dad to Dave:

Be very proud of what you are doing Dave. Nobody has got near to sorting it out before . . .

Nicole keeps on telling me, 'Dad, you just don't understand their point of view. They do not think like you. They don't view it as cheating, they ignore the health risks, putting them alongside the risk of a crash and if you try and stop them, they will think you are robbing them. They also think that every single other rider in the world is using drugs as well. They cannot contemplate the idea that anyone could ride clean.'

Dave responded:

Despite all the problems of late I do feel that the one good to come out of the Millar affair is that it has given me a window of opportunity to play hardball on this issue and now is the time to act.

. . . I also believe UK Sport will back me . . . I will keep you updated on progress.

Dave received the support from Liz Nicholl and John Scott at UK Sport and out-of-competition testing and haematological screening was introduced for all BC cyclists. I did not introduce it, Dave did; but I am proud of the pressure I brought to the matter.

For the remainder of 2004 and 2005, I stayed with Acca Due O and continued to live with Nonna in a house where I was confident none of the other cyclists were keeping PEDs. The new tests caught out Tyler Hamilton, and on the women's side there was a single positive at Athens, that of a Colombian cyclist who won a bronze on the track, Maria Luisa Calle Williams. She was immediately stripped of her medal. The system seemed to be working.

Later, I had a stand-off with Maurizio before a stage race when he wanted to introduce a new rider. I knew that this rider had an instance where a 'health rest' was imposed on her because her haematocrit was above the 48% threshold allowed for female riders. I was delighted that Maurizio went with my call and this girl did not join us.

In June 2005, Maurizio told me Calle Williams was going to join our ranks. I was astonished, as I thought she would still be serving a two-year ban, but a quick bit of research showed that on 27 April she had beaten Kristin Armstrong to become Pan American Champion. After that in May, she had ridden a round of the road World Cup that I was doing my hardest to try and win. What on earth was going on? Her defence was that the team doctor instructed her to take a medicine for her headache that he did not know contained a banned product, and that she was an innocent caught up in the incompetence of others. With that I can sympathise greatly.

I got on to John Scott in early June to find out what was going on. That she had her licence back and was riding seemed to catch everyone on the hop. John wrote back saying:

. . . we have had extensive dialogue with WADA in putting this response together for you.

Maria Luisa Calle has lodged an appeal to CAS against the IOC decision to withdraw her medal. We understand the case will be dealt with by CAS on August 25, 2005. We are continuing to investigate what the procedure is for the IF (UCI) when an athlete is sanctioned at an Olympic Games as you make the point about her continuing to race.

Over a month later and after another telephone call and another email reminder, John again wrote back, on 13 September:

> ... we are continuing to probe these issues but it has been difficult to get information from the UCI. We clearly have to maintain a good working relationship with them and so I cannot push too hard. I am continuing to pursue them and will get back to you as soon as I have clarification ...

I replied and then John wrote again on 28 September – a lovely response. He was getting nowhere with the Colombian Federation and 'similarly the UCI are being equally uncooperative ...'

The UCI being uncooperative – now who would have thought that? So what was going on? In September or October 2004, the Columbian Cycling Federation assembled a panel to hear Calle Williams's appeal. This panel found in favour of the appeal, and then appealed to have the IOC judgement set aside, so she could have her medal back. This went before the CAS who heard the case in two hearings. The first on 11 March 2005 heard evidence and then, 'before it had completed its award on 15 April 2005, the UCI solicitor, Verbiest, presented opinion from himself dated 14 April and support from an expert witness Dr Saugy dated 16 April [ie. the day after the decision was to be confirmed] that generated a second hearing on 25 August.'

In the meantime, Calle Williams got her licence back in April 2005 and was riding again. With the support of John at Drug-Free Sport and Liz, I continued to badger. I was particularly upset that she was riding the 2005 road World Cup before the CAS had even heard all the evidence, let alone concluded.

So much for WADA protocol. Dad represented me at a meeting with John Scott in London. He took with him this and a number of other issues. Prominent and still burning with me were the number of riders I saw going into anti-doping with files of exemptions from their doctors. Surely some sort of audit could be done; surely these riders couldn't be taking all this medication simultaneously? Dad came back from the meeting in London very despondent. The officials claimed there was nothing they could do on any of the issues. Apparently there were very many, very poorly, athletes competing at elite level. Well, I don't know about any of the others but if I was unwell, I never finished in any of the top positions and always seemed to finish near the back.

Correspondence went back and forth until in early 2006, John was good enough to send me a copy of the report from CAS. After that, once again, if I wanted something changed I could write to WADA myself. I wrote to WADA president Dick Pound. After receiving a prompt acknowledgement, all went quiet. I wrote again and again. Eventually, I sent electronic mail and a 'signed for' written copy asking when my inquiry might receive the answer promised in the acknowledgement. The next day I received a reply from Oliver Niggli, who had not been at the hearing in March 2005 but had represented WADA in August 2005 at the CAS. The Colombian Federation could find Calle Williams innocent and thus had authority to remove any personal sanction. The CAS were responsible for determining whether she was disqualified from the Olympic result. That the two decisions were based on entirely separate evidence sets seemed something he did not want to write to me about. I wrote again on 12 December and eventually received a reply saying that no further correspondence would be engaged in.

I did my best. Was Calle Williams innocent and deserving of her medal? I will let you research more and develop your own opinion. Was this due process effective? I would like to believe that, by being a thorn in their side, I would cause those in authority to think twice when acting in future. As to the biggest question – should home federations be entrusted to determine decisions? – I think the historic evidence is that too often they fail to act as they should. It had taken me until January 2007 to push through the system to a conclusion. Calle Williams would have completed her two-year ban before that! However, as to what mattered to the team and me, Maurizio was again superb. He turned down Calle Williams and I didn't have to ride on the same team as her. Thanks for backing me, Maurizio, we'll do it clean and burn trying.

I was always happy that I could resist temptation myself, and I trusted that small number of team-mates and team helpers who I allowed close around me. If convictions were rare on the men's side, they were even more of a rarity on the women's. Beyond the few who were positive or given 'health rests', the reality was that there were a good number of characters on the women's scene whose behaviour and actions raised suspicions. If I wanted to live a life where I did not come into contact with them, I needed to give up professional cycling.

Mostly the evidence was soft. Someone might take a sudden detour in the team car to pick up a parcel – why did it have to be picked up now? What's in the box? Shoes? Can I have a look at them? No. But of course, this was a large group of women, not all of whom were that interested in winning the race; there were other motives, so counter stories and gossip formed a constant background noise. I learnt to rely only on what I experienced at first hand or second hand from a tiny group of very close friends. Associating and working with the 'suspicious' was a necessary evil I came to terms with very early on.

What to do when there was one of those jaw-dropping moments? I remember once during the drive after a stage when I was in a car with one of the male helpers; I was in great form, but I had just been made to look very ordinary in a hilly stage by the winner and was questioning quite what the nature of her training could be. What was she doing to make her so much better than me?

'It's not the training, it's the preparation,' came the response.

'What do you mean?'

'It's what she uses to prepare for the event.'

'How do you know how she prepares for the event?'

'Well, I have supplied it to her in the past.'

A furious argument broke out. What did this guy think he was doing? But I knew that I could scream all I wanted and he would deny it and possibly smear in some sexual story of how he had rejected the advances of a crazy mad woman. It would go nowhere. At that time there were no hotlines. Later, I informed British Cycling, but I knew there would be nothing they could do about it.

In Andy Walser I found somebody who I trusted implicitly. He shared my views on doping, and in the years I worked with him, he never once gave me a single cause for worry in respect to PED abuse. He had removed himself from a far more lucrative equivalent position on a male professional team to work with riders in an environment where he felt there was less doping. We both knew it was going on, but Andy was as determined as I was to try to carve out what we could from the sport, clean.

Later in our relationship, as my knee became a debilitating factor, Andy introduced me to Fabio Bartalucci, the doctor I would work with for two periods of my career, April 2008 to the end of the year, and 2011 to mid-2012. In all the time I worked with Fabio, I never encountered anything that generated any suspicion. I did know he was a medical doctor and that he had worked with men's teams in the past. He never spoke to me about PEDs, he certainly had a keen doctor's understanding of the operation of the knee in relation to cycling, and most critically was a keen cyclist himself. Why I think he was more effective than anyone else working with me, is that he would accompany me on rides and observe me at first hand. Together, we worked out a system of arrangements of tape to be applied to my knee to support the muscles. In the main, his training advice was always that I was overdoing both the volume and intensity and too often I arrived, ready to go out on a ride together, overtrained.

British Cycling were impressed with his work with me on my knees. I extolled his virtues to them, just as I did in newspaper interviews enquiring how my rehabilitation was progressing. Jonathan Webb is the surgeon that so successfully operated on my knee, but Fabio was the one who ensured I was able to train and race on it without further damage, just at a time when I was thinking of retiring. I was able to tell British Cycling that he never offered me any PEDs and was always very professional, and that his work with me was exemplary.

After I released my retirement statement, Dad was able to direct me to the forum of Cyclingnews.com. The research capacity of some of the posters is to be marvelled at. There I found out that Fabio had been detained at the Giro of 2001 in a sweep that netted a total of 86 riders and support staff, including Max Sciandri. From this, 11 (not including Fabio) were taken to court and six were found guilty and five acquitted. Some observers have made the link: doctor, male team, dope expert.

I would be naive to think that 'not proven' equates to 'innocent', but if, as some would like, all athletes are guilty by association then David Millar's arrest places every single Team GB cyclist of the last 12 years in that same group, because Dave Brailsford was also taken in for questioning with him. If I am discredited because of association, then there is not a single cyclist of the last 40 years who is not similarly tainted. Dazzani I can name, others I cannot because of the libel laws, but rest assured UKADA have their names and a number of those names the forerunner of UKADA had many years ago.

My contemporary comments on David Millar's return to Team GB are known. Not public are my comments I put in writing on 19 July 2004 to Dave Brailsford on learning that Millar might be a rider representative for anti-doping. One of the conditions I proposed to be placed upon him before even contemplating such a position was the return of his 2001 and 2003 medals and acceptance of his lifetime ban from the Olympics. He had his 2003 medal stripped but retains his 2001 medal, and of course he returned to ride at London 2012. By his actions, he does not understand how doping robs others. He cannot possibly represent clean athletes. He might sit on the committee at WADA as rider representative, but certainly he does not represent me. When he can properly suffer for his principles, then he might.

Towards the start of this section, I stated that in hindsight the views I took with me into my first season were wrong. I think they were wrong because I underestimated how hard a minority of my rivals trained. In fact they trained far less than I expected them to. I also underestimated how distorted a view a minority had of the sport. They wanted the glory without the work. Therefore, PED usage was greater than I imagined. After my first year, I made it very clear, at the teams I was at, that I would not countenance any doping practices around me. I thank Maurizio for appeasing me in 2005. In our little house in Switzerland with Univega, again I was content. In 2008 with Halfords, in 2009 with my own Vision 1, and then back with the U23 girls, it was a relief that I had no need to worry about PEDs. With Walter Ricci, I set my stall out very clearly and I did not encounter any doping practices while at the teams he managed in 2011 and 2012.

Is the sport cleaner now? I'm not in a position to answer that. Only the technical experts can advise on how they are countering the threats ahead. But the main factor is that the agencies have a new sense of determination about them now. Just look at how diligently the Italian authorities pursued Alejandro Valverde in the Operation Puerto case. The Italian Olympic Committee (CONI) bided their time and waited until the Tour came to a finish in Italy and Valverde was then within their jurisdiction. I would love to have been there the day they got him, but then there are so many events to choose from: Millar, Jeanson, Lance, Tyler. I must not dwell on the ones that got away, those who I cannot write about in this book. The truth is: there are a lot of names still in the record books that should not be there.

CHAPTER TWENTY-THREE
London 2012

I n the last four years of my career it was difficult to see beyond the rolling series of misfortunes, in some of which my own decisions were the main factor, others chance events, and finally there was that group generated by the inequalities within the sport. There were bright spots that I can now see and am proud of: the belief that I could make a difference with a young team, the determination to persist in the face of opposition from the administration of the sport, and the ability to rise to the occasion of the World Championships. I lamented the results at the time, like those two fourth places in World Championships. The winner in me was never satisfied with anything but the best.

As I began the 2012 season, I wanted to do it one more time, with the London Olympics beckoning. The course couldn't exactly be described as tough and was certainly no spring classic course of successive steep climbs. Nevertheless, it did include two ascents of Box Hill in Surrey, so it did offer possibilities. I wanted to be at my best, so decided to go out to Australia for the winter. I spent four months in Perth, self-funded, staying with Cathie and Mick Beckingham, friends of Craig who I had met two years earlier and who kindly put me up in their spare room. Emma Pooley was also in Perth and also self-funded. I trained with Craig, doing huge rides, believing that sheer hard work would turn me into a winning machine. What was I doing? I should have spent a month with the bike locked in the garage, resting the legs and clearing my mind. Then, once I started to crave the lung-bursting sprints and that exhausted feeling after training rides, I would be ready to begin again.

Instead, I was jaded before I began, carrying over the mental and physical fatigue. With Simon Cope gone and no women's coach in place, the situation was such that Shane Sutton was *de facto* the only person that mattered with respect to performance issues and London. Shane was in Perth with the track squad on their annual warm-weather trip. After numerous calls and texts producing little communication, eventually I went to the track and met him there. When we spoke, he told me that Lizzie Armitstead would have the ability to select the team for the Olympics. The best possible motive someone could possibly interpret from Shane's actions was that perhaps there was misguided good intent, hoping to fire me up to be my old self. I contacted Dave Brailsford and he reassured me that only the selection board had the power to select. However, all of this had an immediate negative impact on my motivation.

The Cipollini-Giordana sponsor and management had separated at the end of 2011 and I decided to stick with team manager Walter Ricci and his new team. I returned to Europe for the start of the season but didn't exactly create a good first impression with my new *directeur sportif*, Fortunato Lacquaniti, Too late, I realised that in my determination to get fit in Australia I had fallen into my old trap of overtraining. My poor form was highlighted by a woeful performance in the first few events of the season, particularly in the Ronde van Drenthe

World Cup, where I struggled to keep up with the main bunch let alone play an active part in the finish.

In the second stage of the Energiewacht Tour of Holland in April, I fared even worse, finishing almost ten minutes behind the leaders and finishing mid-field in other stages. On the last day, I was determined to do something to prove to myself I was not finished. If I couldn't do anything, I needed to give up the London dream. I had to show there was something of the old me left. I was actively looking for an early breakaway, and in the very first move of the day, a group of nine riders formed. We worked well and instead of becoming the 'rabbit' to be caught in the last 5km, we built up enough of a lead to put the peloton off the chase. Achieving a successful lone breakaway on a straight and dead-flat final 4km was something I treasure. There were no corners or hills to use as launch pads, and within the break there were teams with two riders, who could then mark me out. Finishing 20m ahead of a speeding break proved to me I had not lost my guile and sense of timing.

The win gave our team its first victory of the season, but it did not hide my problems, which Fortunato was rightly concerned about. I had promised that I would train hard in the off-season and return to lead the team in the spring classics and win races. But other than my surprise win in Holland, I hadn't even been close to a podium.

I went to Canada in mid-May feeling more content in my form. In the GP Gatineau, I made a number of attacks and led out Rochelle in the sprint. However, it now looked as if the team was having financial problems because, despite promises, there was no mechanic in Gatineau and then no spare bike when, a week later in the last stage of the Exergy Tour in Idaho, I got tangled up in an early crash, breaking my frame, and was forced to retire from the race.

I returned to Lugano and was informed that the Olympic selection had been extended to include races in Spain as well as the Giro del Trentino. In the first Spanish race, Durango, the spokes in my rear wheel broke on the decisive climb and I had to get a wheel from neutral service as my team had no spare wheels. The 'repaired' rear wheel then broke another spoke in the last stage of Emakumeen Bira, and I just scraped a top 20 finish. In Trentino, I finished top 20 on both days, but break-away groups were up the road fighting it out for the win and I was out of the real racing.

When the call came from the newly appointed, part-time British women's manager, Chris Newton, that I was on the GB Olympic team with Lizzie Armitstead, Emma Pooley and Lucy Martin, Chris recognised the tone of my voice.

'You sound surprised.'

'I am,' was all I could muster.

But the euphoria and sense of security of knowing I was going to compete in a home Olympics did not have time to take hold and motivate. Next up was the British Championships. I could find excuses, but the truth was I wasn't good enough, missing the early break of five riders including Lizzie, Emma and Sharon Laws. Sharon had not been selected for the Olympic team, the fourth slot being given to her team-mate Lucy Martin. Sharon escaped from her two trade team-mates in the closing miles of the race to win alone.

I hoped things would improve in the Giro d'Italia the following week, but the overtraining had taken hold and I suffered like a dog. I desperately needed a rest rather than a ten-day Tour, but in a team that was clearly struggling financially and whose managers were taking their frustrations out in a variety of ways, there was no option.

There was a clause within the contracts to fine riders. Normally it was rarely enforced, but here it was for often bizarre reasons. Fortunato went even further, refusing to allow us to have massages between stages, which seemed counter-productive given that we were tired and needed to recover. These issues just compounded the problems, particularly as most of us were owed wages. I had been paid once in six months, but the managers argued it away, insisting that 'Italy was in an economic crisis' and therefore they couldn't pay.

For the Olympic race, I accepted that Lizzie was the team leader with the best chance of winning, because it was clear that no matter what I had hoped to achieve, my form was not good enough. I wanted this one chance to perform well in front of my home crowd, but knew that I was not the rider on whom the team could rely for the gold medal.

In Copenhagen, we had failed because we never developed and practised a plan. This time would be different. The final ascent of Box Hill was so far from the finish that it could never be more than a springboard for an attack, but Emma could be key to deciding how that final ascent would be run off. Emma would put pressure on the ascents of Box Hill, with a view to forcing the field to splinter. Lizzie would be just behind to exploit any moves or counter moves that would follow. I was free to go in an early break. Come the finish, we were all to support placing Lizzie on the front with 200m to go. On the afternoon before the race, we visited the finish and Lizzie spent time discussing with her trade team-mate Lucy how she could be led out. If Lucy wasn't there, I would do the same job.

My feelings were mixed on race day. I still had the heart-thumping desire to give absolutely everything I had and race for the win, but knew I didn't have the physical condition to take the race on and would have to ride carefully rather than aggressively. I desperately wanted the team to perform and to do well in front of the watching nation.

We were met with thunder and lightning as the gun sounded to start the race, a reminder of Beijing. As the race left London at a fairly easy pace, it was fantastic to see and hear the vast cheering crowds despite the rain. In Athens and Beijing, there were sections of road with no spectators at all, but Great Britain was putting on one of the best Olympics of all time and the course was lined with spectators for its whole length. My last four years in the sport featured many painful moments, moments that even now bring great sadness, but just being part of that experience that day was worth staying in the sport for those four years. I could only admire how my country, the country whose jersey I had worn so many times and had tried so hard to do my best for, was all out supporting us. Thank you London, thank you Great Britain. I never had the chance to ride in front of you when I was at my peak, but I always knew you were with me.

As we headed towards Box Hill for the first time, there were a number of crashes due to the wet and narrow roads and the nervousness of the riders in such an event. I knew that I should have been at the front, but lack of strength to overcome delays due to a series of trivial incidents thwarted my intentions. I didn't want to expend too much energy competing on Box Hill, as I needed to preserve my strength for the right moment on the run in to London, or for leading out Lizzie alongside Marianne Vos or Giorgia Bronzini.

Emma Pooley set a fierce pace the first time up Box Hill to reduce the number of riders in the bunch. I slipped back and then regained the leading group as economically as I could, preserving my energy but trying to place myself, ready for the second ascent. Lucy lost contact the first time up Box Hill, so we were now a team of three.

On the second ascent, Russian Olga Zabelinskaya attacked, getting away by herself. Then coming off the hill, Marianne attacked followed by Lizzie and American Shelley Olds. Lizzie had spotted the right move and followed Marianne, and was now faced with the question of how hard to contribute to working in the break once they had caught Olga. Four riders would mean that one would miss out on a medal. Marianne might not be keen to be sprinting against Shelley Olds, as she had been beaten by Shelley in a sprint finish at the Giro d'Italia a few weeks before, so she might prefer that this group would be caught and then try again to obtain a different combination.

I think a number of key rivals around me thought that the break wouldn't be too cohesive and so there was no strong chase. Lizzie was there, so I switched into defending mode, keeping an eye on the chasers leading the bunch and marking Marianne's team-mate, in case the break was caught and the counter attacks started. A few kilometres later, the situation changed when Shelley punctured. With a significant time gap to the remains of the peloton, there were now three riders who all had the greatest incentive to work together to share the medals. All three were experienced and would have a very clear understanding of their relative sprinting abilities, ensuring no surprises at the finish on The Mall.

For all three, there could be no better race situation. The gap increased, the rain bucketed down and it became obvious that my race was now reduced to one of policing the chase and stopping it becoming too effective, not that I was needed in this regard. I was happy to see that in the rain and poor visibility, several key teams did not spot Shelley waiting at the side of the road and so did not understand what a game-changer had occurred. Even when she appeared in their midst and was 'encouraging' her team-mates to start a chase, it was disjointed. There seemed to be mixed motives in the German team and the Italians were not organised, so there was no serious chase that I needed to disrupt.

I was very happy for Lizzie, who got the silver medal behind Marianne. She had put herself in the right place at the right time, and often in a cycle race that is very hard to do. She had learnt from her previous mistakes and rode a very smart race.

I had some lovely times during the Games in London. I felt my capital and the people I had spent so much of my life representing around the world were just brilliant. I was so proud of you all, the games-makers in the public places, the girls and guys behind the counters in the food-hall, so many cheery smiles. All of my great rivals from cycling told me how impressed they were with Britain and the way we put on the Games. My event was early and so I could go and see events and travel around the city. On the underground, people were excited and talking non-stop about it! They certainly spoke to me and so many warmed me with their recollections of my win at Beijing. I had to hold back the tears so many times when people said, 'Yours was the best, it was the one that started it all off.' I don't think it was quite that simple, but certainly each minute in London 2012 was worth all the four years of pain since Beijing. I could now leave my racing bike to gather dust in the garage. To London, and the people who travelled there from all over the country, thank you all for giving me that.

My decision to retire came at a natural checkpoint, first plotted as a teenager when I mapped out what I hoped my future would bring. In the days after winning in Beijing and Varese, I committed myself to the next major challenge. I had given it my best shot in 2012 and now I was ready to confirm that the ride was over.

You have my retirement statement and you now have my autobiography. It has at times been an uncomfortable write, and I'm sure it has often made for an uncomfortable read. I hope I have filled in most of the blanks. Did I have a great time? – heck, yes. Would I have done it differently? – yes. But I wonder if I had done it differently, whether I would cherish the good bits quite like I do. I enjoyed the highs and hated the lows. I'm not rich in terms of money, but I certainly have a bountiful supply of good experiences. I'm not the first woman to battle against a male establishment and come out of it with plenty of scars, cuts and bruises. The men in power don't like it.

Within the picture section you will find a photo of what every mum and dad would want to see for their daughters and sons: the two winners of the Tour de France standing side by side in the Champs Elysées. That was 1984, but now there isn't even a women's Tour – so what went wrong? So much has been lost of the vibrant international scene I so looked forward to joining as a new professional.

The most popular sport on the planet is soccer. During the First World War, with so many men away, a lot of sports opened their doors to women, and football was no different. Women's football took off. By 1917, the best team of the day, Dick Kerr's ladies football team, regularly drew crowds of over 10,000 to watch them play. In 1920, they achieved a sell-out for a match at Goodison Park, home to the Everton men's team, of 53,000, with, reputedly, a further 14,000 turned away. Two weeks later at Old Trafford, home of Manchester United, 36,000 turned out to watch them. The future of women's football was looking bright, but that was all to change.

By December 1921, the men in charge at the FA stated that

any club affiliated to their organisation was expressly forbidden from allowing their grounds to be used for women's matches. So the British women set off for America and Canada in 1922 to tour there. However, as the *Washington Post* reported on 23 September 1922: 'Dick Kerr's team of English women soccer football players arrived today on the steamship *Montclare* en route to the United States where they will play a series of games. The girls will not be allowed to play Canadian soccer teams, under order from the Dominion Football Association which objects to women football players.' The tour in the USA, where they were allowed to play, was a great success, with the team playing against male sides in front of crowds of up to 10,000. One of them met her future husband and returned to live there.

In 1947, the men at the heart of the British sporting establishment showed they had lost none of the meanness of spirit of their predecessors, when the Kent County Football Association suspended a referee because he was working as a manager/trainer with Kent Ladies Football Club. It justified its decision with the comment that 'women's football brings the game into disrepute'. Women's soccer died then and, with it, the aspirations of so many girls.

The misguided men who take these bad decisions will often dress it up with all sorts of pseudo justifications, but it only ever appears that they are clinging to power. I would have been dumb thinking it was going to work any other way throughout my career. The reaction of the men in charge to what I brought to cycling in Britain is most keenly shown by the facts relating to British Cycling's entries at the Junior World Championships. There were always plenty of girls after me they could develop and send to those championships, but for years the management sent nobody. Could it be that the last thing on the planet they needed were more Nicole Cookes? Because of our differences of opinion on so many things, there was never any way they could reliably claim my success as their own. Later, as my star faded, they opened the gates a little to support the new girls following my path, and took the reflection of their success as somehow made by themselves.

In the 2002 Commonwealth Games, out of all the home countries combined, Britain came away with only two cycling gold medals, Chris Hoy's and mine. Dad and I, along with a little band of others, put an immense amount of pressure on British Cycling to change its practices for the better. BC were reluctant to listen, director of the WCPP Peter Keen didn't want to listen; UK Sport were reluctant to take responsibility, but eventually they announced his resignation on the day after a letter posted from Wick arrived at their offices. I feel sure that this change in leadership was the start of a process that has put British cycling at the top of the world, and so see my role in this as one of my greatest achievements.

Women's cycling will not be fixed until those in charge at the UCI and British Cycling treat female competitors and women's race organisers in exactly the same way as they do on the men's side. If, instead of allowing the women's versions of the great classics to be abandoned, the UCI had insisted that its World Cup organisers needed both a men's and a women's event, then the whole cycling scene would be completely different. This lever remains available today, but for that to happen we need leaders with vision. Certainly, a minimum wage is a necessary step before a 'satisfactory' can be contemplated for the report card.

Close to home, the executive management of British Cycling needs to take a very serious look at itself. The fundamental question is why, in 2008 and 2009, post-Beijing, as they drafted the plans for the great success they have achieved with Team Sky, did they consider it acceptable to ignore the British women riders? When organising the London Olympic trial events in 2011, they could not be bothered to put on anything for the defending Olympic champion or Emma Pooley, who was then the current World Time Trial champion. We were ignored. Resources unmatched anywhere else in the world were made available for the men, but virtually nothing for the girls. In the era of the internet and social media, they could hardly ban us from riding like the English FA did with the women footballers, but was what they did so very different?

The wonderful British public, who did such a super job at London 2012, hosting the greatest show on Earth, clearly confirmed, by their support, that they valued their daughters equal to their sons. I am very confident that their opinion will eventually prevail and sweep away the obstacles created.

I will settle for the title some kind commentators placed on me: 'Nicole Cooke – Trail Blazed.' If I ended up taking a lot of knocks, so what? There was no path at all ahead of me as I left home, an 18-year-old, off to ride with team-mates and managers I had never met, in a house, in a town I had never been to. Now it is different, now there is a path, now girls can see a route and a destination. I set out holding tight the dream of a 12-year-old, hoping that if I achieved half of what that little girl wanted, I would be happy. Others will eclipse me with their achievements – that's the way of life. They will dig up my little track and build a motorway along its route. In years to come, no one will remember my path and certainly no one will think about what was there before. But, I have a whole sackful of firsts that people can have only as seconds or thirds. I will share in the conquests of those who follow and think of the wilderness that was in front of me when I started.

I'd like to think that little dreaming 12-year-old would be proud of all I achieved both on and off the bike. Like her, I fell off a few times and took a good few knocks – but each time, I got back on my bike.

Nicole Cooke
May 2014

Acknowledgements

My first thank you is to my competitors and rivals throughout my career. From Jo Lally, aged 11, through to Marianne Vos, who succeeded me as World No.1 and Olympic champion: I couldn't have had the career, the fun and the ups and downs without any of you. Sometimes I won, more often I lost. There is nothing I loved more than a rival who would not give me an inch. I just loved fighting to the bitter end, the victory or even the defeat that took a photo finish to separate us. Those memories are still in full technicolor and supersonic sound in my brain right now. My heart beats faster just thinking about them. Thank you, all of you.

Secondly, I asked a few of the people close to me and who stuck by me every inch of the way, if they wanted a paragraph or a page of thanks. I even showed them what I had written. Every one of them said 'no'; Mum said it made her toes curl and she ripped it up. I have tried not to forget anyone, and if I have, it's not because I don't love you, it's because writing this book has driven me crazy. So in alphabetical order by surname, here they go:

Nonna Marcella Albanese, Peter Baker, Fabio Bartalucci, Marcus Baumann, Cathie & Mick Beckingham, Sue Belcher, Marco Bendinelli, Darryl Benson, Aristide Beretta Piccoli, Dave Bishop, Prue & John Bishop, Charlie Botero, Steve

ACKNOWLEDGEMENTS

Bunce, Leonie Burford, Cardiff Ajax CC, Paola Casanova, Shelly Childs and all at Continental, Colnago family, Matt Cosgrove, Cooke family, Ermanno Comalli, Steve Cottrell, Del DelaRonde, Claire Dixon & family, John Donnelly, Fran Donovan, Tobi Doppler, Ron Dowling, Tony Doyle, Martin Eadon, Anne Ellis, Dan Ellmore, Rhiannon Evans, Maurizio Fabretto, CJ Farquharson, Brendan Gallagher, Lorenza Gentilini, Silke Gersbach, Giancarlo Ghillioni, Mauro Giacomazzi, Tiziana Goffo, Emma Grant (née Rickards), Geoff Greenfield, Wayne Greenhalgh, Primo Grespan, Win Griffiths, Sally Harlin (née Hodge), Imad Harmoush, Rachel Heal, Richard Hendicott, Larry Hickmott, Marcus Höss, Bob Humphrys, Alessandro Ippoliti, Mick Ives, Caroline & Matthew Jackson, Dr Rod Jacques, Louise & Phil Jones, Jon Kilmartin, Haider Knall, Laquaniti family, Fany Lecourtois, Alison Livesey, McClelland family, Gianni Maffei, Daphne Major, Marco Mariotti, Roberto Merlo, Jon Miles, Shirley Myall, Andrea Natali, Phil O'Connor, Richard Owen, Mario Penariol, Dr Steve Peters, Andi Pfister, Arlette Pfister, Pinarello family, Cliff Polton, Chris Price, John Pritchard, Hayden Rees, Millie & Field Rickards, Walter Rixon, Judith & Brian Rourke and all at Brian Rourke Cycles, Courtney Rowe, Celestino Salami, Katherine Selby, Bill Snowdon, Stuart Thom, Gayle Thrush, Davina & Mike Townley, Frances & Keith Townley, Peter Valentine, Andy Walser, Deborah Walsh, Mr Jonathan Webb, Alex Wharton, Debbie Wharton, Derek Williams, Gareth Williams, Helen Williams, Steven Worley-James, Margaret & Gordon Wright, Helen & Stefan Wyman, Marco Wyser, Yerby (mum's) family, Giorgio Zauli, Federico Zecchetto.

Index

(the initials NC in subentries refer to Nicole Cooke)

INDEX

447

INDEX

INDEX

INDEX

INDEX

INDEX

INDEX

INDEX

INDEX

INDEX